D1236448

THE ANNUAL
OF
PSYCHOANALYSIS

THE ANNUAL
OF PSYCHOANALYSIS

A Publication of the
Institute for Psychoanalysis
Chicago

Volume XVII

Published by The Analytic Press, Hillsdale, NJ.

Distributed solely by

Lawrence Erlbaum Associates, Inc., Publishers
365 Broadway
Hillsdale, New Jersey   07642

Library of Congress Catalog Number 72-9'1376
ISBN 0-88163-092-6

Printed in the United States of America
10 9 8 7 6 5 4 3 2 1

With this volume of *The Annual* we change publishers and Dr. George Pollock has stepped down as Chairman of the Editorial Committee. We hope that future volumes will continue the high intellectual caliber of the first seventeen.

Arnold Goldberg

When the first volume of *The Annual of Psychoanalysis* appeared in 1973, it was our hope that the series would become an established source for the latest thinking in psychoanalytic theory, practice, and application. This current volume is the seventeenth — and the last for which I will serve as chairman of the Editorial Committee. *The Annual* has, over the years, included works covering the full range of Freud's scientific humanism. And I am very pleased with what has been accomplished. I wish to take this opportunity to personally thank all of the individuals who submitted their manuscripts for our consideration, those authors who permitted us to publish their writings, the members of the Editorial Committee for their devotion to the reviewing task, and the manuscript editor and managing editor for their assistance in producing the volumes. I also wish to thank International Universities Press, publishers of previous volumes in this series, for their cooperation and flexibility. And I am especially grateful to Fred M. Hellman, whose generosity and whose support in so many ways has made these seventeen volumes possible.

George H. Pollock

CONTENTS

Contributors   xi

I

THEORETICAL STUDIES

An Epistemology of Transference   3
JOHN E. GEDO, M.D.

Toward a Phenomenological and Minimally Theoretical Psychoanalysis   17
EDWIN R. WALLACE, IV, M.D.

II

APPLIED PSYCHOANALYSIS

*The Creative Relationship of Internal and External
Determinants in the Life of an Artist*   73
MAVIS L. WYLIE, PH.D. AND HAROLD W. WYLIE, JR., M.D.

*Charismatic Followership as Illustrated
in George Eliot's Romola*   129
JEROME A. WINER, M.D.

On Migration — Voluntary and Coerced   145
GEORGE H. POLLOCK, M.D., PH.D.

*From Transformed Scream, through Mourning, to the Building of Psychic
Structure: A Critical Review of the Literature on Music and Psychoanalysis*   159
MARTIN L. NASS, PH.D.

III

PSYCHOANALYSIS AND PARENTHOOD

Blaming the Parent: Psychoanalytic Myth and Language   185
F. DIANE BARTH, M.S.W., C.S.W.

Fatherhood and the Preference for a Younger Child   203
HELEN R. BEISER, M.D.

IV

PSYCHOANALYSIS AND GENDER

What Is the Relation Between the Psychoanalytic
Psychology of Women and Psychoanalytic Feminism?   215
NANCY J. CHODOROW, PH.D.
   with discussions by BARBARA S. ROCAH, M.D.
                        BERTRAM J. COHLER, PH.D.

Sexual Doubles and Sexual Masquerades: The Structure of Sex Symbols   263
WENDY DONIGER, PH.D.
   with discussion by HARRY TROSMAN, M.D.

V

PSYCHOANALYSIS AND CHILD DEVELOPMENT

A Prospective Constructionist View of Development   287
E. VIRGINIA DEMOS, ED.D.
   with discussions by MARIAN TOLPIN, M.D.
                        MARJORIE C. BARNETT, M.D.
                        BERTRAM J. COHLER, PH.D.

Index   343

CONTRIBUTORS

Marjorie C. Barnett, M.D.
   Faculty Member, Child and Adolescent Therapy Program, Institute for Psychoanalysis, Chicago.

F. Diane Barth, M.S.W., C.S.W.
   Supervisor and Faculty Member, The Adult Psychoanalytic Institute at the Postgraduate Center for Mental Health, New York, and the National Institute for the Psychotherapies, New York.

Helen R. Beiser, M.D.
   Training and Supervising Analyst (child and adult), Institute for Psychoanalysis, Chicago.

Nancy J. Chodorow, Ph.D.
   Professor of Sociology, University of California, Berkeley; Affiliate, San Francisco Psychoanalytic Institute.

Bertram J. Cohler, Ph.D.
   William Rainey Harper Professor of Social Sciences, The College, and Professor, The Committee on Human Development, and Departments of Psychology, Education, and Psychiatry, University of Chicago.

E. Virginia Demos, Ed.D.
   Director, Program in Counseling and Consulting Psychology, Harvard Graduate School of Education.

Wendy Doniger, Ph.D.
   Mircea Eliade Professor of the History of Religions, University of Chicago.

John E. Gedo, M.D.
   Training and Supervising Analyst, Institute for Psychoanalysis, Chicago.

Martin L. Nass, Ph.D.
   Professor Emeritus, Brooklyn College, City University of New York; Clinical Professor and Supervisor, Postdoctoral Program in Psychotherapy and Psychoanalysis, New York University; Faculty, Training and Supervising Analyst, New York Freudian Society.

George H. Pollock, M.D., Ph.D.
Professor of Psychiatry, Northwestern University School of Medicine and the Graduate School; Training and Supervising Analyst, Institute for Psychoanalysis, Chicago.

Barbara S. Rocah, M.D.
Training and Supervising Analyst, Institute for Psychoanalysis, Chicago.

Marian N. Tolpin, M.D.
Training and Supervising Analyst and Faculty, Child and Adolescent Psychotherapy Program, Institute for Psychoanalysis, Chicago.

Harry Trosman, M.D.
Professor of Psychiatry, University of Chicago; Training and Supervising Analyst, Institute for Psychoanalysis, Chicago.

Edwin R. Wallace, IV, M.D.
Professor and Acting Chairman, Department of Psychiatry and Health Behavior, Medical College of Georgia; Professor of Social Work, Graduate School, University of Georgia, Athens.

Jerome A. Winer, M.D.
Training and Supervising Analyst, Institute for Psychoanalysis, Chicago; Professor of Clinical Psychiatry, College of Medicine, University of Illinois at Chicago.

Harold W. Wylie, Jr., M.D.
Training and Supervising Analyst, Baltimore-Washington Institute for Psychoanalysis; Associate Clinical Professor of Psychiatry, Georgetown University Medical School.

Mavis L. Wylie, Ph.D.
Staff Psychologist, Dominion Hospital, Falls Church, VA; Private practice, Washington, DC.

I

THEORETICAL STUDIES

An Epistemology of Transference

JOHN E. GEDO, M.D. (Chicago)

It was in the concluding chapters of "Studies on Hysteria" (Breuer and Freud, 1895) that Freud first reported his astonishing discovery that neurotic patients, when seen in psychotherapy on a daily regimen, tend to reexperience certain aspects of their past in relation to their physician. Within a few years, Freud (1900) realized that it is the childhood past that clamors for repetition in such a transference. Moreover, he soon concluded (Freud, 1909) that the transference consists in repeating both sides of a childhood conflict — in other words, that resistance phenomena are just as revealing about pathogenesis as are direct expressions of infantile wishes.

In 1914, when he prepared his rebuttals of the criticisms of his theories by skeptics such as Adler and Jung, Freud specified that pure "transference neuroses" can only be expected to develop in the course of analyses with patients whose childhood development had culminated in an "infantile neurosis." Whenever the vicissitudes of early life led to alternative possibilities — the contingencies Freud then conceptualized as an excessive shift in the direction of "narcissism" — he conceded that psychoanalytic treatment could not succeed, precisely because the availability of the analyst would fail to evoke infantile love and hatred and the defenses against them.

As I believe I demonstrated in a recent book on the history of dissidence within psychoanalysis (Gedo, 1986), the most significant clinical controversies since Freud's reformulation of his theories in the early 1920s — the revision necessitated by the realization that his initial

Presented as a Plenary Address at the Eleventh Regional Conference of the Chicago Psychoanalytic Society, March 19, 1988.

hypotheses could not account for many forms of adaptive disorder—revolved around the issue of the appropriate treatment of cases wherein a transference neurosis either did not occur at all or, if it did manifest itself to some degree, did not constitute the most significant determinant of the pathology.

To summarize the history of these still unresolved disputes: A more conservative faction of analysts generally advocates the standardization of psychoanalytic technique, the application of stringent criteria of analyzability in patient selection, and meticulous attention to those ancillary conflicts that tilt the balance in the direction of regression from the vicissitudes of an infantile neurosis toward more archaic adaptive equilibriums. This has been the position of those with more modest therapeutic ambition, such as Freud himself (1937), later Anna Freud (1965), and the school of "ego psychology" (e.g., Hartmann, 1964; Hartmann, Kris, and Loewenstein, 1964). In contrast, those who wished to extend the curative range of psychoanalysis beyond the transference neuroses, such as Ferenczi (1908–1933), Melanie Klein (1984), and both British and American advocates of theories of object relations (e.g., Winnicott, 1931–1956, and 1957–1963; Kohut, 1971, 1977, 1984), took up positions that represent the mirror images of the conservative ones: they broadened the scope of analyzability and permitted themselves greater freedom in altering analytic technique; at the same time, they postulated that structure formation preceding the crystallization of an infantile neurosis could have a decisive influence on pathogenesis—as Kohut (1966) put this, a separate line of development.

Depending on one's adherence to one of these alternative traditions, the clinical experience of an analyst is bound to yield widely disparate observations. Although I have always leaned toward the more radical alternative, for my analytic work has convinced me that Freud's concept of a "pure" transference neurosis is a theoretical fiction that no analysand can ever approach, in my conceptual efforts I have tried to take an ecumenical position. I am convinced that, if we refrain from deliberately tilting the course of an analysis in any specific direction, we can almost invariably elicit phenomena that support the views of both conservatives and radicals.

In response to the traditional elements of psychoanalytic technique, we will evoke some variety of a transference neurosis (see Gedo, 1981a, Epilogue); if we pay close attention to various regression-promoting factors, such a repetition of the infantile neurosis will gradually recur in clearer and clearer form. At the same time, we have the opportunity to observe the emergence of a different set of transference phenomena—a set I prefer to call "archaic transferences" (Gedo, 1977). These are repetitions in the analytic situation of the childhood developments Freud collected under the rubric of "narcissism." Systematic analysis of "narcissistic transferences" became possible as a result of Heinz Kohut's work of the mid-1960s; unfortunately, some of his followers have tended to narrow the focus of their analytic attention to this set of transferences, thereby mirroring the reductionistic error of Freud's clinical theories before 1914. Lest we throw out the baby with the bath water, however, it is important to reiterate that transference neuroses and archaic transferences (the problems of "Guilty Man" and "Tragic Man," respectively [Kohut, 1977]) are generally to be found in almost every analysis; to put this somewhat differently, the analyst may deal with one or the other of these potentialities exclusively, by means of certain technical choices and/or selective attention and inattention (see Gedo, 1980).

My own attempted contribution to clinical theory (Gedo, 1979a, 1981b, 1988) has been to call attention to the repetition in the analytic situation of certain primitive behaviors that do not form part of either an infantile neurosis or an archaic transference. These phenomena correspond to the manifestations of what Freud (1920) called the "repetition compulsion" — automatisms that do not necessarily involve any object relationship and certainly cannot be understood in terms of either the reality or the pleasure principle. These behaviors stem from the persistence of areas of primitive mentation that have never been encoded in symbolic terms. In the majority of instances, such activities are not pathological; they are woven into the fabric of adaptation seamlessly, as building blocks of the person's individuality — basic components of self-organization that guarantee continuity of the subjective sense of self (Stern, 1985).

In accord with the principles of the hierarchical model of mental life I proposed in my collaborative work with Arnold Goldberg (Gedo and Goldberg, 1973), the several categories of repetitive transference experience I have just outlined are universally expectable in any adult capable of functioning outside of a sheltered environment. The emergence of any of these patterns in the analytic situation as a consequence of the purposeful regression set in motion by this form of treatment is largely a matter of the acuity of a trained observer in noting the relevant phenomena. Nonetheless, it should be stated that the relative significance assumed by these alternative modes of functioning at any stage of an analysis is heavily influenced by certain technical choices on the part of the analyst.

In order to illustrate this principle, let me refer to the work of Harold Searles, especially as reported in his most recent book (1986). Searles, whose views seem to be congruent with my own, has found that he evokes what he calls "borderline psychotic transferences" in all of his analytic cases — which include work with literally dozens of colleagues! Because he has found a nonintrusive, expectant, and largely silent approach to be optimal in handling such transference developments, Searles has adopted this technical approach as his standard operating procedure in analysis. Although he does not say so explicitly, I believe it is also true that Searles's ability to evoke the primitive transferences in question is a direct consequence of this chosen technique, which maximizes the analysand's regressive potentials.

Let us contrast the technical choice advocated by Searles with the analytic technique Freud (1909) used in the case of the Rat Man — the treatment he offered as a prototype of his work with the transference neuroses. As the excerpts from his daily notes on this case published in the *Standard Edition* (10:251 ff.) clearly show, Freud established an active and vigorous dialogue with his analysand, whom he dealt with at all times as a rational adult fully capable of joining in the enterprise of examining the material of his associations. I need not go beyond the reminder that when the Rat Man came to his session hungry, Freud felt free to offer him food, to substantiate the point that the treatment situation barely departed from the conventions of ordinary social intercourse. I choose this example from an era before the standardization of analytic technique as a result of insight into the role of character-resistances in obstructing the emergence of regressive material in order to clarify the contrast with the technique of Searles: eighty years ago, Freud's technique merely allowed him to gain a glimpse of the compromise formations that bound derivatives of previously repressed material that threatened to elude the censorship.

If this pair of contrasting technical approaches, separated by three generations of psychoanalytic development, strikes the reader as an artificial dichotomy, let me buttress the point by offering another set of examples from the contemporary psychoanalytic scene. Let us recall the fact that Kohut (1977, 1984) ultimately decided that psychoanalysis cures not so much as a result of insight, promoted through interpretation of unconscious content, as by means of internalizations set in motion by optimally managed frustrations at the hands of an empathic (self)object. Consequently, the school of "self psychology" advocates a treatment technique stressing the empathic acceptance of the subjective point of view of the analysand. Given the consistent application of this approach, it would be difficult to discern any material beyond the analysand's reactions to this nurturant, structure-promoting activity on the part of the therapist. In other words, this technique is only suitable for the evocation of "selfobject transferences"; little wonder that Kohut also concluded that these are the most crucial repetitive phenomena encountered in the analytic setting! Contrast this with the "classical" technique of analytic traditionalists, wedded to the primacy of interpretation (i.e., the elucidation of hitherto unconscious conflicts concerning infantile wishes). How could the consistent application of such a technical prescription eventuate in the emergence of a "selfobject transference"? No wonder traditionalists look upon Kohut's observational data as iatrogenic artifacts! And vice versa: no wonder Kohut arrived at the conclusion that the emergence of infantile sexual wishes in the course of analysis is merely the pathological consequence of a traumatically unempathic treatment method . . .

On this occasion, I do not cite the self-fulfilling nature of the prophecies of both schools of thought in order to call out a plague on both houses (although they probably deserve no less!). I have outlined the circular nature of their clinical theories, treatment techniques, and the resultant observational data in order to underscore an inescapable dilemma that afflicts us all. If, as an ecumenicist, I have hedged my bets by using as complex an analytic technique as I am able to master (see Gedo, 1979a, 1988, Epilogue), thereby keeping open the possibility of eliciting the repetition of modes of functioning characteristic of numerous phases of childhood development, I have merely avoided the grossest kinds of reductionism — it is *not possible* to avoid the distorting consequences on subsequent events of whatever we do in the analytic situation.

Perhaps all that I have said thus far is actually self-evident — an application, after the passage of half a century, of Heisenberg's insight about the epistemological constraints on physical experimentation in the field of psychoanalysis. But if it is granted that we do, indeed, labor within such constraints in making analytic observations, we must also face the inevitable inference that all of our concepts are therefore in need of thorough revision. To be sure, this task has already begun to be carried out in certain quarters: consider only that in 1987 the Chicago Psychoanalytic Society heard Robert Gardner present a challenging paper wherein he tried to illustrate that the context of human attachments unceasingly exerts its distorting influence on our self-inquiry.

Let me put the matter in terms of a chemical analogy: for the past century, we have operated within the assumption that our observational field was like a clean vessel through the use of which we have an opportunity to study the properties of that strange compound, the human mind. If we have recognized that we are, in fact, participant-observers — an insight long proclaimed by the interpersonalists among us — we have likened our role to that of a solvent that does not react with the material that we study. Very recently, we have begun to concede that the minds we observe have powerful effects upon us that cannot be dismissed as mere countertransference complications; but we have thus far failed explicitly to concede that, in fact, some degree of mutual reactivity is inevitable, that we are bound to exert at least as much personal influence on the mind being observed as the observed person exerts upon us. There are no clean vessels in psychoanalysis — our observations are never about the analysand per se; they are at best about the nature of the mutual influence exerted within the analytic dyad. Analytic "neutrality" is not merely an unattainable theoretical fiction: it is also a mischievous notion that leads us into an epistemic never-never land.

In order to avoid misunderstanding, I need to reiterate that I am not simply asserting once again that analytic observation is handicapped by the unavoidable subjectivity of the observer. That is an essential truth about the limits of our reliability, but one for which we are able to arrange scientifically acceptable controls through the use of multiple observers. It must never be forgotten that *all* of our knowledge is "personal knowledge," as Michael Polányi (1974) put it; in other words, psychoanalysis is no different in this regard than other branches of science. I am trying to say that our field *does* differ from all others because our very presence as observers drastically alters the data we are attempting to apprehend, and the person we observe is likely to skew our perceptual capacities.

What are the logical consequences for our views on transference phenomena if we accept that psychoanalytic data gathering is inevitably skewed by the qualities of the observer-subject transaction? Clearly, what requires revision is not the manifest content of what we have observed over the past century in the psychoanalytic situation; rather, we have to abandon the assumption that the behaviors in question are manifestations of the analysand's mental dispositions in pure culture. Instead, we must view them as products of a system of mutual-feedback mechanisms. This means that, if we wish to draw valid conclusions about the "subject" of our observations, we have to assign a certain valence to the input of the observer. For the moment, I do not believe we are adequately prepared to accomplish this task, but it may not be too early to list some of the accumulated clinical experience that has a bearing upon it.

Let me begin by noting the inconsistency of our usual position about the sex of the analyst as a cogent factor in the treatment process. On the one hand, we all seem to believe that the analyst is a screen blank enough to provide any analysand with an adequate surface upon which the gamut of his or her potential transferences may be projected. I certainly know this to be true in my own case. Yet few of us seem to have the courage of our convictions about this matter, for in referring patients to an analyst — particularly when it is a question of a second or third analyst we are called upon to answer! — we tend to give some thought to their special needs for a person of one sex or the other. So the truth seems to fall somewhere in the middle: the analyst's sex does not generally preclude the development of transferences repeating transactions with a person of the other sex, but the actuality of the analyst's person does seem to have a certain weight in evoking those transferences for which he or she is, so to speak, "typecast."

Although very little has been written about the subject, the issue of "typecasting" seems to apply with regard to the analyst's age as well. Shortly before he died, Max Gitelson (personal communication) called for some thoughtful attention to this issue, but I do not believe it has ever been addressed. As I get older, it does seem to me that I find it easier to evoke grandparent transferences than used to be the case; I also have the impression that it has become a rarity for me to be experienced transferentially as a sibling figure. But I can make the same point much more confidently from a slightly different perspective: one can scarcely avoid pouring fuel on the fires of a potential for idealization as one gets older and more prominent as a psychoanalytic author and/or educator. Contrast the actualities confronted by the patients of such a "Guide to the Perplexed" with those presented to the potential analysands of young candidates: how hard those patients must work to create the stuff out of which an idealizing transference is woven!

To turn from these unalterable and obtrusive facts about the analyst's actual person to issues of greater subtlety, I believe the degree to which the participants in the analytic dyad share a single cultural matrix has a tremendous bearing on the ease — or difficulty — of recapturing the analysand's relations with the early childhood milieu. Some years ago, I reviewed my analytic experience in this regard (Gedo, 1979b) and was surprised to discover that I had had startlingly less success with people from certain subcultures than with the rest of my clientele: specifically, I had little luck with analysands of Southern background and with those whose parents were European immigrants of peasant stock. Not only are both of these subcultures relatively unfamiliar to me — I am afraid I may have approached analysands from these backgrounds with certain prejudices the nature of which never became clear to either of us.

The other side of this same coin is represented by the fact that, no matter how carefully we intend to maintain our analytic anonymity, we have no way of concealing what we know, what we believe, who we are. I do not mean that it is obvious to our patients whether we voted for

Harold or Fast Eddie, or neither! — it is much more difficult not to reveal our commitments to high culture or professional football, to free enterprise or current fashion. The very choice of magazines in our waiting rooms reveals important things about us, as do the clothes we wear, the holidays we choose to observe, the furnishings we provide for our office, or the professional books we keep — and do not keep! — on our shelves. Of course, these are only external manifestations of "who we are" — but by that token they are relatively easy to discuss.

More direct evidence about the specifics of our inner world is externalized by means of our language, including its paraverbal aspects. Some years ago, I asserted (Gedo, 1984, chap. 8) that analytic success is contingent on the development of a "shared language" between the participants — a viewpoint I still believe to be valid. However, here I wish to call attention to the other side of the coin — namely, to the fact that however we may try to keep a low linguistic profile, our verbal communications remain as unalterably individual as the "voice" that carries them. Not only are our vocabulary and idioms as personal as our fingerprints; our very syntax, however "correct" it may be, betrays our innermost being through the choices that characterize our rhetoric. Did those of my analysands whose forebears were members of an oppressed peasantry hear the language of their exploiters in my incompletely Americanized *façon de parler?* How many of my readers would succumb to the temptation to ape the aristocrats of a Tolstoy novel by lapsing into French at such a juncture as this? But I can assure you that I came by this affectation honestly — not by reading highbrow literature alone, but by following the manners of my admired grandfathers, including their penchant for such books. I know these ways are no longer acceptable to everyone, but I can no more dispense with them than I can lose my specific accent.

Although most aspects of our language are unalterable, we do, of course, possess some degree of latitude about the manner in which we communicate with our analysands (see Gedo, 1984, chap. 9). The laconic style that gradually gained currency as *the* classical technique of analysis clearly provides less intimacy than many otherwise analyzable patients can bear, and promotes the rapid emergence of negative transferences referable to the earliest phases of development — as the recent exposé of psychoanalysis by a writer whom it literally drove to drink poignantly demonstrated. It is true, of course, that in these matters there do exist circumstances in which less is more — but that self-evident truth does not mean that we may assume that more is necessarily less. In other words, it behooves us to think through at every turn what effects the form as well as the content of our discourse may produce on the analysand.

I am convinced that the nature of the transference (or sequence of transferences) we evoke is strongly influenced not only by the *extent* of our verbal participation in the analytic dialogue—it is also influenced to a similar degree by a number of other choices we make in encoding our messages. As I have emphasized on a number of occasions (Gedo, 1981a, p. 291; 1988, p. 218), one of the most important of these concerns the degree to which we infuse our communications with the affect appropriate to our words. Obviously, this choice is simultaneously contingent on decisions about whether or not to engage in a direct dialogue, as though one were one of the characters on the stage that is the psychoanalytic setting, whether to provide the patient with opportunities to cushion the impact of our message by making clear that our affectivity is under total control, etc. At any rate, the more direct and affect-laden our communications are, the more likely they are to tilt the analytic relationship in the direction of transferences of relatively archaic origin. Interpretations offered in a really dispassionate manner and/or in a formal style, especially if we introduce conceptual issues as we explain ourselves, call upon our patients to exercise secondary-process capacities—even those for abstract thought—only available in midlatency or even later.

At the other end of the spectrum of communicative possibilities, resort to the language of posture and gesture, to wordless vocalizations, such as moans, growls, laughter, grunts of skepticism, astonishment, or contempt, to the whistling or humming of familiar tunes, etc., etc., push the analysand in the direction of earlier modes of relatedness and the transferences attendant thereon. As Fred Levin (1980) has shown, a predominant use of metaphors straddles the gap between the foregoing communicative styles; I would predict that such a compromise between primary- and secondary-process thought may optimally evoke oedipal transferences.

We could elaborate the fascinating technical vistas opened up by these and similar considerations about the rhetorical dimensions of analytic activity; but I may already have given a sufficient number of examples suggesting that the analyst's language plays an important role in determining the development of specific transferences to make it more desirable to move on to more general and fundamental issues. If the actualities of the analyst's age and sex, sociocultural background and language, and a host of less obvious components of identity can skew the nature of the transferences he or she can evoke, not to speak again of the effects of technical choices dictated by theoretical preconceptions, what are the implications of these sobering facts for our views on psychopathology and on the formation of character?

I believe we have consensus about differentiating a psychoanalytic nosology from one based on other-than-analytic premises on the ground that personality assessment should focus on the individual's propensity to form specific transference types. One of the early statements of this viewpoint was Zetzel's (1968) important paper distinguishing those "hysterics" whose symptomatology reflects the conflicts of an infantile neurosis from others, with essentially the same manifest behaviors, whose hysteroid characteristics screen problems of an archaic nature. In his initial statements about what he then called "narcissistic disturbances," Kohut (1971) similarly cautioned against basing personality diagnoses on phenomenology; he insisted that only the unfolding of the transference could reveal whether a person suffered from oedipal or narcissistic pathology. My own recent book on psychopathology (Gedo, 1988) carries this stress even further: I assert that diagnostic predictions cannot reliably be made on the basis of any time-limited sample of behavior and/or extraanalytic observations, not only with regard to oedipal vs. narcissistic problems, but also for the gamut of functional possibilities.

What are the consequences for a nosology tied to the sequential development of transferences in the analytic situation of the conclusion that the specific transferences evoked in psychoanalysis are codetermined by the analyst's technical convictions and his or her actual characteristics as a person and a personality, beyond any issues involving unresolved problems on his or her part (cf. Kantrowitz et al., 1987)? It would seem that such a view compels us to confine our diagnostic schemata to statements about the emergence of a series of transference positions in the context of particular analytic circumstances. To give you only the most obvious of illustrations: if, in an analytic situation conducted in accord with the "classical" technique—i.e., one wherein the analyst's interventions are truly confined to interpreting unconscious material and an attitude of expectant neutrality otherwise prevails—there develops an archaic transference of passionate intensity, with recurrent crises whenever the analysis is interrupted, even briefly, we can only conclude that we have evoked a "borderline psychotic transference," as Searles calls this; it is not legitimate to postulate that such a contingency is a marker of a "borderline syndrome." The same analysand, if met with the active provision of a "holding environment," as Modell (1984) advocates in certain cases, might well respond with the formation of an idealizing transference. And *that* development would not justify making a diagnosis of a narcissistic disturbance. And so forth.

It is precisely considerations of this nature that have led me to conclude that an optimally conducted analysis should permit the analysand to relive as many kinds of transferences referable to all phases of early development as possible. In order to facilitate insight into these dispositions and to permit their gradual resolution by means of interpretation, it is generally convenient if they emerge for analytic processing more or less sequentially, one by one. If the transition from one type of transference to another is to be made feasible, the analyst's contribution to this dyadic shift must be to alter the analytic situation whenever the previously established status quo has outlived its usefulness. One dimension along which such shifts may be made is the hierarchy of therapeutic modalities Goldberg and I (1973) appended to our development model of mental functioning.

As you will recall, I later elaborated this schema, in a book entitled *Beyond Interpretation* (1979a), stressing that analytic technique has always encouraged shifts from interpreting, either to confining our activities to the role of an empathic witness, or to more active measures designed to lend patients psychological expertise. Here I must reiterate that the hierarchical schema we devised almost twenty years ago was deliberately skeletal, that its five-stage rendering of development was arbitrary— intended to encourage hierarchical conceptualization by offering relative simplicity. In other words, the schema is too coarse to differentiate the profusion of transference possibilities from each other; consequently, it also cannot pretend to offer any therapeutic prescription about the analytic posture most appropriate to evoke particular transferences— it merely provides one gross indicator of the directions we may follow in that quest.

Perhaps the time has come to conclude this presentation by returning to our starting point. Psychoanalysis is best characterized as that science of mental life which is built on the observation and understanding of the ever-recurrent cycles of repetition in human behavior. Our standard observational setting is the psychoanalytic situation, and the analysand's repetitive behaviors in that context are called transferences. Because we impose a dyadic transaction on our data gathering, most of the transferences we have the opportunity to observe necessarily reproduce ways of relating to others in the past, particularly in childhood. In order to reenact these old transactions, the analysand needs the compliance of the analyst—if not as an actor in restaging the old script, at least as a willing puppet to whom the necessary roles might be attributed. The ever-shifting consequences of these complex cybernetic mechanisms have generally been mistaken for static internal conditions characteristic of the analysand. Systematic correction of the resultant misconceptions is an enormous task awaiting the next generation of psychoanalysts.

REFERENCES

Breuer, J. & Freud, S. (1895), Studies on hysteria, *Standard Edition,* 2. London: Hogarth, 1955.

Ferenczi, S. (1908–1933), *Bausteine zur Psychoanalyse,* vols. 1 & 2. Leipzig/Vienna/Zurich: Internationaler Psychoanalytischer Verlag, 1927; Vols. 3 & 4. Bern: Hans Huber, 1939.

Freud, A. (1965), *Normality and Pathology in Childhood.* New York: International Universities Press.

Freud, S. (1900), The interpretation of dreams. *Standard Edition,* 4 & 5. London: Hogarth Press, 1953.

_____ (1909), Notes upon a case of obsessional neurosis. *Standard Edition,* 10:153–250. London: Hogarth Press, 1955.

_____ (1914), On narcissism: An introduction. *Standard Edition,* 14:73–102. London: Hogarth Press, 1957.

_____ (1920), Beyond the pleasure principle. *Standard Edition,* 18:3–64. London: Hogarth Press, 1955.

_____ (1937), Analysis terminable and interminable. *Standard Edition,* 23:216–253. London: Hogarth Press, 1964.

Gardner, R. (1987), Some self-analytical reflections on self-analysis. Presented to the Chicago Psychoanalytic Society (October).

Gedo, J. (1977), Notes on the psychoanalytic management of archaic transferences. *J. Amer. Psychoanal. Assn.,* 25:787–804.

_____ (1979a), *Beyond Interpretation.* New York: International Universities Press.

_____ (1979b), A psychoanalyst reports at mid-career. *Amer. J. Psychiat.,* 136:646–649.

_____ (1980), Reflections on some current controversies in psychoanalysis. *J. Amer. Psychoanal. Assn.,* 28:363–383.

_____ (1981a), *Advances in Clinical Psychoanalysis.* New York: International Universities Press.

_____ (1981b), Measure for measure: A response. *Psychoanal. Inquiry,* 1:286–316.

_____ (1984), *Psychoanalysis and Its Discontents.* New York: Guilford.

_____ (1986), *Conceptual Issues in Psychoanalysis.* Hillsdale, NJ: The Analytic Press.

_____ (1988), *The Mind in Disorder.* Hillsdale, NJ: The Analytic Press.

_____ & Goldberg, A. (1973), *Models of the Mind.* Chicago: University of Chicago Press.

Hartmann, H. (1964), *Essays in Ego Psychology.* New York: International Universities Press.

_____ Kris, E. & Loewenstein, R. (1964), *Papers on Psychoanalytic Psychology.* New York: International Universities Press.

Kantrowitz, J., Katz, A., Greenman, D., Humphrey, M., Paolitto, F., Sashin, J. & Solomon, L. (1987), The patient-analyst match and the outcome of psychoanalysis. Presented to the American Psychoanalytic Association (December).

Klein, M. (1984), *The Writings of Melanie Klein,* 4 vols. New York: Free Press.

Kohut, H. (1966), Forms and transformations of narcissism. In: *The Search for the Self,* ed. P. Ornstein. New York: International Universities Press 1978, pp. 427–460.

_____ (1971), *The Analysis of the Self.* New York: International Universities Press.

_____ (1977), *The Restoration of the Self.* New York: International Universities Press.

_____ (1984), *How Does Analysis Cure?* Chicago: University of Chicago Press.

Levin, F. (1980), Metaphor, affect, and arousal: How interpretations might work. *This annual,* 9:231–49. New York: International Universities Press.

Modell, A. (1984), *Psychoanalysis in a New Context.* New York: International Universities Press.

Polanyi, M. (1974), *Scientific Thought and Social Reality.* New York: International Universities Press.

Searles, H. (1986), *My Work with Borderline Patients.* New York: Aronson.

Stern, D. (1985), *The Interpersonal World of the Infant.* New York: Basic Books.

Winnicott, D. (1931–1956), *Collected Papers*. New York: Basic Books, 1958.
——— (1957–1963), *The Maturational Processes and the Facilitating Environment*. New York: International Universities Press, 1965.
Zetzel, E. (1968), The so-called good hysteric. *Internat. J. Psycho-Anal.*, 49:256–260.

Toward a Phenomenological and Minimally Theoretical Psychoanalysis

EDWIN R. WALLACE, IV, M.D. (Augusta, Ga.)

> Science is a house built on piles above a swamp. . . . The piles are driven down from above into the swamp, but not down to any natural or "given" base; and if we stop driving the piles deeper, it is not because we have reached firm ground. We simply stop when we are satisfied that the piles are firm enough to carry the structure, at least for the time being [Popper, 1965, p. 106].

For years clinicians and scholars sensed that something was seriously awry in analytic theory. Those from outside psychoanalysis — especially the phenomenologists and existentialists — were perhaps the first to recognize it (e.g., May, Angel, and Ellenberger's 1958 anthology). Within dynamic psychiatry itself Fairbairn (1952), Sandler and Rosenblatt (1962), Boss (1963), Home (1966), Holt (1972, 1976), the philosopher Ricoeur (1970), Guntrip (1971), G. S. Klein (1976), Gill (1976), Schafer (1976), Kohut (1977, 1984), and Atwood and Stolorow (1984) helped articulate the problem: To wit, psychoanalysis is, above all, a historical and interpretive approach to symbolically mediated human experience and behavior, and yet its allegedly ultimate explanatory framework, metapsychology, is a web of physicalistic ("force," "tension," "structure," "energy," "cathexis") and biologistic terms and concepts.

Preeminent ego psychologists, such as Hartmann (1939, 1964), sought to reduce meaning to its reputed biologic determinants. Explanations invoking intentionality, goal, and purpose were suspect as teleological and hence, in their minds, acausal. Even some of the most noted "object"-relations theorists, while generally closer to phenomenology,

Abbreviated version presented to the Atlanta Psychoanalytic Institute and Society, October, 1988.

17

build scholastic systems of structures within structures and energies behind energies — often with only a wisp of connection to clinico-empirical data.

Variously termed the "psychology versus metapsychology" or "clinical versus natural-science languages" debate, it was vitally present within Freud himself (Ricoeur, 1970; Gill and Holzman, 1976; Wallace, 1985). This essay strives to clarify, codify, and elaborate upon the work of a variety of writers — including this author (Wallace, 1983a–in press b) — rather than itself developing novel ideas. It is presented as a sort of manifesto for a phenomenological and minimally theoretical psychoanalysis, and hence, it is hoped, will be forgiven its length. Following a brief introductory recapitulation of Freud's divided discourse, the essay is presented in outline. Six sections and a number of subsections develop axioms and propositions for a phenomenological, minimally theoretical psychoanalysis.

By "phenomenology" I mean that of which one is *aware* — "experience," the only immediate given in the human universe — as opposed to mentation of which one is momentarily (preconscious) or more enduringly (unconscious) incognizant. Phenomenology hence needs no definition, for it is that with which we are intimately familiar — though we by no means fully know its originating and ongoing causal processes. To attempt to define it would invite conceptions that would themselves demand defining, and so forth and so on ad infinitum. Nor is phenomenology true or false; it simply is — or, better, becomes. Propositions about it are alone true or false (in an open, Popperian, not absolutist, sense).

The phenomenology to which the analyst has access is not of course the analysand's raw experiencing, his or her ever-flowing stream of consciousness. The patient alone momentarily knows — through living — such experiencing. To the clinician it manifests at most nonverbally in its ever-onward course. Otherwise its bygoing currents are redacted and reconstructed by the patient to a clinician clothed in the former's imagoes.

Observable actions ("behaviors") are always accompanied and preceded by motivation and interpretations, though the analysand is by no means fully aware of these antecedents, concomitants, and consequents. Fringe and finger-tip mentation is preconscious; prerepressed and repressed mentation unconscious. From a quasi-nomothetic grasp of human nature, and an idiographic knowledge of the patient's patterns, the analyst can at times infer aspects of mentation and behavior of which the analysand him- or herself is unaware — and then test these inferences in light of the patient's subsequent experience and behavior. This is a theoretical-empirical, mutually interpretive endeavor — the analysand interpreting his or her evanescent stream of consciousness to the analyst (whom the patient is likewise interpreting) and the analyst reflecting, clarifying, and interpreting the patient's interpretations and behaviors back to him or her. Correctly conducted, this process permits mutual correctives and consensual validations–invalidations along the way.

Freud's (1915c) deliberations over the existence-nonexistence of unconscious affects was a quarrel over words, not concepts. As clinical theoretician, not linguistic philosopher, Freud proceeded as if unconscious feelings were a matter of course. He was correct to do so. How else could one build a theorem of unconscious mentation except from paradigms modeled upon consciousness? This is the ur-assumption from which a gradational phenomenological-behavioral approach to unconscious mentation will be derived. Psychoanalysis ever broadens the analyst's and analysand's awareness of their psychically/dyadically determined mentation and behavior—to the end of better perceiving-interpreting the realities of the interaction and of better comprehending the motivational-interpretive-defensive matrices of *both*. In short, even though the objective is the understanding and transformation of the patient's mode of existence, and even though the analyst rarely communicates his or her private experience to the former, if the analysis proceeds properly the latter learns about, and is to some degree changed, him- or herself.

Thus, by a "phenomenological psychoanalysis" I intend one that, methodologically, aims at unfolding the patient's particular experience, behavior, and history and that, theoretically, moves toward explanatory concepts maximally derived from, or relatable to, this experiential, behavioral, and historical data base. This approach is not, I hasten to add, in any way meant to impugn the place of theory or to pretend that we could ever have a purely empirical or atheoretical psychology. Neither does it deny the role of universal lawlike or nomothetic aspects in the causation of human behavior (Wallace, 1985, pp. 29–57).

Nor does it practice Husserl's (1939) "phenomenological reduction"—suspension of belief in a reality existing independently of the agent's sentience—or its "hermeneutic" variants (e.g., Schafer, 1976; Spence, 1982; Geha, 1984). Husserl's "reduction" is not only nonparsimonious and implausible, but a sham—for "belief" in a reality to some degree independent of one's wishes and will, imposing its constraints and compulsions, is evolutionarily built into the human species and organism, else they would not have survived. Husserlians who continue to live and write give the lie to their doctrine at each meal or street crossing. Paradoxically, these solipsists deny, rather than respect, phenomenology: experience itself impels us to believe in the existence of others and objects, though we "know" these existents only as our perception-interpretation of them is codetermined by our mental sets interacting with their actually existing configurations and activities — via, that is, a "perspectival realism" (Wallace, 1988c). Similarly, psychoanalytic hermeneuticians plunge us either into skeptical nihilism or permission to believe whatever we wish, as long as it tells a pretty story and apparently helps someone.

Introduction: Freud's Divided Discourse

BIOGENETIC AND "INSTINCTUAL" CAUSATION

Freud (1905, p. 241) asserted that the order in which the component instincts emerge is biogenetically determined. He explained (1918, p. 85) the Wolf Man's castration anxiety as a recapitulation of the phylogenetically inherited attitude toward the brutal primal father — even though the threats of castration in the patient's boyhood all emanated from women. The repression of sexuality in the latency period was also posited to be biogenetically based (pp. 177–178). Freud (1930) even speculated that crucial characteristics of the superego are ontogenetic recapitulations of phylogeny. The biogenetic current runs strong in his theory of culture and religion (1913, 1938; Wallace, 1982b).

Nevertheless, despite the pervasiveness of the biogenetic strain in aspects of Freud's theorizing, clinically he pays little attention to phylogenetic factors and, where he invokes them, usually brings forth ontogenetic explanations that do not require phylogeny to sustain them. Freud (1918, p. 97) even chided Jung for putting phylogenetic factors ahead of ontogenetic ones.

Holt (1976) has written trenchantly on Freud's instinctual determinism which, like me, he deems distinct from, and in practice subordinate to, Freud's clinical concept of purposeful determinism. "The Project" is Freud's (1895) earliest expression of the determinative primacy of "instincts," more accurately termed "drives" (*Trieben*). The central nervous system is conceptualized as "receiv[ing] stimuli from the somatic element itself — endogenous stimuli — which have equally to be discharged. These have their origin in the cells of the body and give rise to the major needs: hunger, respiration, sexuality". Coitus, for example, is caused by "an endogenous tension . . . noticed when it reaches a certain threshold" (p. 317) Clearly the causal concept in "The Project" is closely associated with that of tension and the "principle of inertia" (i.e., the tendency of neurons to divest themselves of excitation). It is discomfort associated with the sensation of increased tension that motivates the individual to a variety of discharge-oriented maneuvers. The organism's aim to maintain its state of internal excitation at a minimal level would become known as the "constancy" or "pleasure principle."

This model, and the one subsequently developed in "The Interpretation of Dreams," draw heavily upon a stimulus-response, reflex-arc paradigm of causation: "All our psychical activity starts from stimuli (whether internal or external) and ends in innervations" (Freud, 1900, pp. 537–538).

"Three Essays on the Theory of Sexuality" (1905, pp. 215–216), "Two Principles of Mental Functioning" (1911b), and "Instincts and Their Vicissitudes" (1915a, p. 120) continue to propound instinctivist theories of motivation. Instinct theory and emphasis on constitutional factors remained important to the end. In "New Introductory Lectures on Psycho-Analysis" Freud (1933) declared the neuroses "severe, constitutionally fixed illnesses" (pp. 153–154).

Nevertheless, Freud never ignored, in even his most instinctivist and phylogenetic moments, the role of history and environment. For example, in "Three Essays on the Theory of Sexuality" (1905a) he tells us that the recrudescence of sexual activity at the close of the latency period is "determined by internal causes and external contingencies" (p. 190). "Though it was necessary [in the study of the perversions] to place in the foreground the importance of the variations in the original disposition, a cooperative and not an opposing relation was to be assumed as existing between them and the influences of actual life" (p. 231). "The constitutional factor must await experiences before it can make itself felt; the accidental factor must have a constitutional basis in order to come into operation" (p. 239).

This line of thought culminates in the "aetiological equation." Adult neuroses are posited to result from the interaction between a disposition due to the infantile fixation of libido and the accidental traumatic experiences of adulthood. The childhood fixations themselves were determined by the interaction between "sexual constitution" and "infantile experience" (Freud, 1915–1917, p. 362).

The dynamic culturalists would, of course, carry this line of thought much farther, arguing that there is no hard-and-fast line between biological and social dynamisms. Objecting to Freud's tendency to view the environment as important primarily insofar as it stimulated, gratified, or opposed the instinctual drives and their derivatives (considered the prepotent motor of human behavior), they argued that social factors are as determinative of human behavior as biological needs.

PSYCHOLOGICAL CAUSATION

A recent monograph (Wallace, 1985) evidenced that Freud's preponderant (indeed earliest) concept of causation was psychological — the affect-
laden "phantasy," "intention," "wish," or "purposive idea." Such phrases
abound and are the best rebuttal to Schafer's (1976, p. 232; 1978, p. 74)
charge that psychoanalytic causation is a "mechanistic" and "sub-
humanizing" or "dehumanizing" language of "impersonal forces" (see, for
example, Freud, 1887–1902, pp. 204–212; 1898, p. 297; 1899, p. 322;
1900, pp. 530–531; 1901a, p. 240; 1905, pp. 42, 45, 67, 85; 1911a, p. 47;
and 1915–1917, p. 36).

Moreover, Freud's model of causality includes the dimension of
meaningfulness and functionalism. In other words, symptoms persist
because of their function within the individual's intrapsychic economy
and vis-à-vis his environment (see Freud, 1905, pp. 42–44; 1909a, pp.
235–236). In numerous places meaning is declared an essential component of psychical causality.

"The Introductory Lectures" (1915–1917) make it Freud's explicit aim,
in investigating parapraxes, "to leave all physiological or psycho-
physiological factors on one side and devote ourselves to purely psychological investigations into the sense — that is the meaning or purpose — of
parapraxes" (p. 36). Again, the "sense of a psychical process" is defined as
"the intention it serves and its position in a psychical continuity." The
cause of Frau Emmy von N's stammering and clacking — the "conflict
between her intention and the antithetic idea (the counter-will)" — was
also termed the "meaning" of her symptomatology (Breuer and Freud,
1895, pp. 92–93).

In "The Interpretation of Dreams" Freud shifts back and forth between
speaking of the "causes" and the "meaning" of the dream (see also Freud,
1905, p. 15). Dreams were conceptualized both as the effects of
underlying causes — i.e., wishes — and as disguised communications (see
also Freud, 1915–1917, pp. 100–101). To interpret a dream is both to
elucidate its meaning and to assign it a place in a causal nexus: "for
'interpreting' a dream implies assigning a 'meaning' to it — that is by
replacing it by something which fits into the chain of our mental acts as
a link having a validity and importance equal to the rest" (Freud, 1900,
p. 96). Freud (1915–1917) elucidated the "meaning" of the symptom with
reference to "its 'whence' and its 'whither' or 'what for' — that is, the
impressions and experiences from which it arose and the *intentions* which
it serves" (p. 284; my emphasis). "Symptoms have a sense and are related
to the patient's experiences," he continues (p. 257).

In sum, Freud's concept of psychical causality was an assertion that (1)
all observable or (potentially) self-reportable behaviors and experiences

are the result of antecedent mental activities; (2) these activities are purposive strivings; (3) they are meaningful communications; and (4) they serve some function within the individual's mental economy and current interpersonal environment. Throughout his case histories, explanations in terms of intention, purpose, aim, goal, wish, meaning, and function far outnumber those in terms of instincts.

Freud's inability to accept the extent to which his psychological truth had cracked its biophysical mold left him, as Holt (1976) suggests, with two concepts of causation — a mechanistic, biological and a purposive, meaningful one. His metapsychological commitment to biological reductionism had two unfortunate consequences: (1) it committed psychoanalysis to confusion and ambiguity, as Freud (1915a, pp. 121–122; 1915b, pp. 147–152; 1915c, p. 177) was painfully aware, on one of its basic theoretical concepts — "instinct"; (2) it condemned him to mind-body dualism (Freud, 1915–1917, pp. 121–122). Finally, it left him with a core theoretical concept whose reputed referents are not empirically accessible to psychoanalytic technique. "The theory of the instincts is so to say our mythology, instincts are mythical entities, magnificent in their indefiniteness. We are never certain that we are seeing them clearly" (Freud, 1933, p. 95).

Laboring under the necessity for fealty to Brucke's truncated version of materialism, Freud never fully appreciated psychoanalysis for what it is: the science of the psychical emergents of the interactions between two species of matter/energy — the sentient and symbolizing human body and its ambience. The empirical-explanatory domain of psychoanalysis comprises the symbolically mediated and motivated dimensions of human activity. This reflects a theoretical-methodological (i.e., biological-psychological), and not an ontological ("mind"-"body"), split — as explicated in Section I.

Axioms and Basic Propositions

It is by now commonly accepted that psychoanalysis is no monolithic affair. It is composed of a number of (in varying degrees) interlocking and interdependent assumptions, hypotheses, propositions, and methods; moreover, there have been many theoretical and therapeutic innovators working within the "psychodynamic" tradition as broadly defined. Nevertheless, suffice it to say that most dynamic schools of thought agree on the four following core principles: (1) *exceptionless psychical causality* (all psychological events have determinative psychological antecedents); (2) *historical determinism* (the present-day configuration of the personality — including one's conscious and unconscious interpretations of self and world, and one's desires, fears, inhibitions, and observable behavior patterns—is a function of the history of the individual's actual and fantasied interpersonal relations); (3) *unconscious mentation and motivation* shape conscious experience (phenomenology) and behavior; and (4) *conflicting unconscious motives and psychical organizations* play the central etiologic role in character and psychopathology formation.

There is, of course, considerable intertwining among these principles. There are, as well, other key concepts embedded within them. Six axioms and a number of subsidiary propositions will be outlined: (1) a position on the mind-body problem; an analysis of (2) motivation and (3) causation; (4) a consideration of history, transference, phenomenology, and unconsciousness; (5) an examination of the concepts of intrapsychic conflict, signal anxiety, defense, and compromise formation; and (6) an evaluation of aspects of the structural model, object-relations theory, self psychology, and adaptation.

Section I: Monistic Dual-Aspect Interactionism*

This model clears space to consider motivation and meaning without violating either materialism (understood as the axiom that "*but for* matter and energy nothing in the universe would exist") or the thesis of man's psychobiological unity. That "mind" (read "mentation" or "symbolically mediated, motivated activity") cannot exist independently of matter and energy I take as axiomatic; that mind assumes certain properties radically different from other organizations of matter and energy I take as empirical fact. The reconciliation of these two I regard as a mystery upon which I throw no light. But I know no physicist who claims to know, for example, the essence of "gravitation," though he or she does not consider the referent of this concept any less real or causally efficacious for all that. Moreover, interactions among organizations of matter-energy at levels far less complex than the plane of human organism and environment produce novel emergents in no way predictable from a knowledge of the properties of each entity "in isolation."

In dealing with fundamental conceptions scientists and philosophers must accept that they will have their ambiguity in one place or another. In any event, that thinking, feeling, and willing should arise from the human body poses no more—indeed less—problem than if it is credited to a conjectured "soul" or "spirit" whose "properties" are notoriously indeterminate. In short, what we term "mental" is best understood as the imaginal and symbolic *activity* of the intact human organism-in-world.

Adhering to an objectivist or realist epistemology and a correspon-

---

*Wallace, in press b.

dence theory of truth (i.e., that true propositions and theories approximately represent aspects of real organizations with structures and functions whose existence is to some degree independent of the presence of the investigator) (Wallace, in press a), I reject what I view as the most plausible alternative explanations — neutral monism and linguistic dualism. These latter perspectives assert that human reality corresponds to neither biological nor psychological propositions, but is in some sense a "neutral" entity, process, or whatever, about which the "biological" and "psychological" are purely convenient scientific fictions or modes of discourse. I eschew neutral monism-linguistic dualism for yet another realist reason — the wealth upon wealth of clinical and commonsense data making it extraordinarily difficult to espouse theories that disallow interactions between the meaningful and symbolically mediated features of human existence and those understandable in purely physiological or pathophysiological categories. If the "biological" and the "psychological" are simply ways of talking, without factual referents in human existence, then they cannot be said to "determine" anything — except perhaps the theories and methods of their practitioners.

In this section I propose an ontology (i.e., a theory of being or existence) — for I suggest that if we scrutinize any approach to this problem, we shall find an ontology (often several) buried somewhere. Moreover, while such ontologies are presently more or less metaphysical, they are not without definite clinical implications and empirically testable consequences. Hence, it behooves the psychiatrist to do some serious self-reflection and hard-thinking about the ontology embedded in his or her clinical and investigative practice.

At the current level of psychological, biological, and philosophical sophistication any approach to the mind-body problem is scandalous; none avoids logical and empirical pitfalls. What I outline should be construed as an image or primitive model rather than a theory, as a device intended to promote theorizing and data gathering.

I adhere to a jawbreaking, if hardly novel, "monistic multilevel, single-aspect–dual-aspect interactionism" (to be called simply "monistic dual-aspect theory" henceforth): multiple levels of ("horizontally" and "vertically") causally interacting activities from the subatomic through the organ systemic to the interpersonal somehow yield, at the highest level of integration, *one* reality with *two* aspects. Let us call this reality at its highest level of integration and emergence, (i.e., "dual-aspect") "mind" (i.e., the organization of imaginal and symbolically mediated or "meaningful" activity), and accept that it is successive states of mind that we strive to connect causally. Desiring to avoid, as much as possible, Spinoza's ambiguity about the ontological status of "aspect" (see

McIntyre, 1967), let me say that I intend it to refer to something *very real* and not to an operational "scientific fiction"—call it a "face" or "facet" if one prefers.

And what is the nature of these "faces" of mind? They are best *approximated* by our neurobiological and our socioculturally-cognitive psychologically informed psychodynamic propositions and theories, respectively. Beyond this I shirk essentialist questions. We understand enough about neither of the two aspects to answer them: a century's extraordinary advance in neurobiology has driven home how fundamentally little we know about the incredible complexities of brain circuitry and neurotransmitters, much less about their precise correlation with mental states; and our psychosocial theories of humankind, though clarifying and converging in important respects, are still in flux, ferment, and confusion.

Thus, I propose that all activities of the human organism may be divided into *"single-aspect"* and *"dual-aspect"* processes. The latter, as just explicated, are the representational and symbolizing activities of mind— characterized by faces captured by neurophysiologic-anatomic and psychologic theories, respectively. It is essential to appreciate, when considering *dual-aspect activities,* that *neither the physiologic nor the psychologic aspect is considered the cause of the other.* Each is conceptualized as a *different* facet of *one* reality. *Single-aspect processes,* by contrast, are those grasped by physicochemical-physiological explanations—such as digestion, biliary secretion, renal filtration, and so forth—though they themselves may of course be influenced (as later explicated) by dual-aspect processes.

Dual-aspect processes (incipient mind) probably begin at some point in early infancy. The ability to differentiate, integrate, and, eventually, maintain internal representations of human and nonhuman environment progresses through later infancy and early toddlerhood. With the onset of verbalization the capability of engaging in progressively sophisticated symbolically mediated activity begins.

"Mind," the total, more or less enduring organization of dual-aspect activities, is overwhelmingly unconscious, as Freud held. The experience and activity of which we ultimately become conscious is a function of causal interactions among dual-aspect processes *within* mind itself and *between* mind and single-aspect processes. Among the most important of these single-aspect processes are endocrine and brain functions that do not themselves possess a psychologic aspect, though they influence mentation by interacting with its physiologic face.

The events of the outside world are communicated to mind via a multitude of single-aspect processes of the sensory organs, peripheral nerves, and central nervous system. Within mind itself these environmental inputs are first processed unconsciously: they interact with a number of dual-aspect structures and functions such as cognitive-interpretive schemata, conflicting motivational states, defensive maneuvers, memories, and so forth. The eventual contents of consciousness (phenomenology) are derivatives and vectors of these unconscious activities of mind. Hence, *all* perception begins *non*consciously (single-aspect processes) and *un*consciously (dual-aspect processes); it becomes preconscious and conscious only insofar as it is unopposed by unconscious defensive maneuvers and cognitive structures. Perception is shot through with memory, cognitive-affective structure, and psychical conflict.

For any sensation—whether exteroceptive, proprioceptive, or coenesthetic-enteroceptive—to be consciously experienced *it must pass through and impinge upon mind*. Meaning, as explicated elsewhere (Wallace, 1988a), is necessitated in the constitutionally intact, postinfantile human being. It is in this sense that there is no such thing as a purely "physical" or "physiological" experience. We do not experience single-aspect phenomena directly, but only insofar as they are mediated by mind. I thus oppose the James-Lange theory of emotion, whereby we are said to *first* experience a "physiological happening"; and *then only afterward* endow it with meaning through attribution and interpretation.

Rather, I contend that what is consciously experienced is *already* the fruit of the interaction between a single-aspect process (whether it be indigestion or joint pain) and the unconscious dual-aspect processes of mind. This is not to say that we cannot then subsequently laden the experience with additional meaning—certainly we can and do; but it is to assert that the experience is meaningful from the outset. What is actually meant by "physical" or "physiological" experience is the human individual's experience of his or her body. And this is as much the fruit of the history of one's fantasies and interpersonal relations (including especially the attitudes of important others toward one's body and its processes) as of the sensory, proprioceptive, and gnostic functioning of peripheral nerves, thalamus, somesthetic cortex, and association areas. Hence, Freud was quite correct to locate the sense of the body in the mind, or "psychic apparatus" ("id" and "body ego").

In fine, the individual's conscious experience and activity is the effect of unconscious state-of-mind, itself a function of interactions among dual-aspect structures and processes and between dual- and single-aspect activities. If, to use a well-worn analogy, mind is an iceberg then consciousness is its tip. Although a thorough understanding of the patient's conscious experience must precede and inform our psychobiological explanations, a clear distinction must be drawn between the patient's phenomenology and our explanations of it. Phenomenology hints at and points the way toward hypotheses, but never, as some philosophers and psychiatrists would have it, simply explains itself— without reference to nonconscious (single-aspect) and unconscious (dual-aspect) causal processes. For the most part, as Freud maintained, consciousness is a sensory organ—registering nonconsciously-unconsciously determined changes in total state-of-being. Moreover, to remain with the iceberg analogy, its apparent causal efficacy is largely carried by the unconscious processes continually underpinning it.

Nevertheless, by considering conscious experience and activity as the effect of interactions among underlying nonconscious and unconscious processes, I am not necessarily declaring that the sensory activity of consciousness itself exerts no causal influence on subsequent states of mind. Conscious experience, while its potency was vastly overrated by pre-Freudian psychologists, may well causally affect reality—including that reality whence it has arisen. Certainly, if conscious mentation possesses no causal efficacy whatsoever, then it is difficult to understand, by the Darwinian tenets of natural selection and adaptation, how and why it has persisted (Wallace, 1986b).

It may be helpful to depict what is, after all, an image or model in the diagrammatic medium appropriate to it (see Fig. 1). The arrows indicate directions of causality. Unfortunately, this sketch cannot portray the *intersectional* (see Section IIID), as opposed to externalist, nature of the cause-effect relationships; nor can it take account of the invariable nonconscious-unconscious overdetermination both of mind itself and of its derivatives in consciousness. Neither does it do justice to the continual interaction with a physical and symbolic-interpersonal environment. Important aspects of this schema will become increasingly clear in the remaining pages.

Within this framework human intraorganismic and organismic-environmental *interactions* can be characterized as: (1) single-aspect processes with single-aspect processes—e.g., the interaction between the vascular diathesis of diabetes mellitus and renal structure and function, the spinal-reflex arc, and, as Weiner (1977) suggests, certain features of environment-brain and intrabrain-intrabrain interactions that precede or accompany, but do not directly contribute to, state-of-mind; (2) single-aspect–double-aspect—e.g., the interaction between Penfield's (1950) electrical probe and the patient's hitherto unconscious meaningful memory trace, the so-called somatopsychic disorders; (3) double-aspect–single aspect—e.g., the "psychosomatic" or "psychophysiologic" diseases, such as the relationship between historically-situationally determined interpersonal "stress" (itself a genuinely psychobiological concept) and duodenal activity; and (4) double-aspect–double-aspect—e.g., the stimulation of

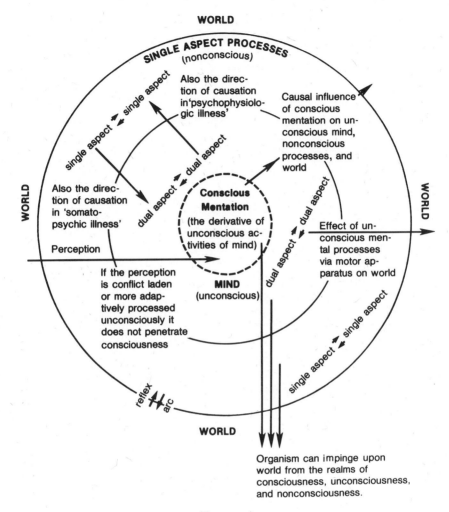

FIGURE 1.

one association by another or of multiple associations by an unconscious complex, the generation of a hysterical paralysis by an unconscious intrapsychic conflict, the relationship between the great Penfield's presence and the neurosurgical patient's symbolizing sentience.

Where it is a case of double-aspect–double-aspect causation, as in that between consecutive unconscious states of mind underpinning two conscious items in a chain of association, there is causal continuity between *both* the psychological and the physiological aspects of each state of mind. Since mind (the organization of dual-aspect activities) is not pronounced immaterial (no essentialist claims are made), and since it is asserted that mind has a physiologic, as well as a psychologic, face, then it neither loses its footing in brain-body as is threatened in Popper and Eccles' (1984) dualist-interactionist model nor becomes a spiritual entity requiring a bridge to materiality as with Descartes.

In instances of double-aspect–single-aspect causation, such as the stressful interpersonal event and the peptic ulcer, the causal efficacy is presumably carried from the *physiologic face* of the stressed state-of-mind to the *physiologic (and only) face* of the duodenal activity. Dual-aspect realities, such as a state of grief, may affect single-aspect realities, such as the immune system, so that yet further single-aspect realities (e.g., an infection) ensue.

Conversely, when processes with a purely physiologic face (say, an infectious disease with pyrexia — possibly the same infection partly caused by the grieving) influence dual-aspect reality, the effect is presumably mediated *from the physiologic (and sole) face* of the infectious process *to the physiologic face* of the dual-aspect state-of-mind. If the altered status of the latter includes, for example, disinhibition of ordinarily repressed derivatives of unconscious structures of meaning and motivation, then one assumes that the pathophysiology of the infection has in some manner impinged upon the physiological face of the activity of repression.

But our hypothetical situation is supremely complicated by the fact that, from the outset, the infection *means* something to the patient — within the context of the history of his or her prior infections and their interpersonal-affective matrices. This meaning itself plays a determining role in the subsequent state of mind and consciousness (whether the infection connotes, unconsciously or consciously, welcome opportunity for dependent succor, a punishment for real or imagined misdeeds, and so forth). In this sense the term "infection" actually subsumes *two* causal realities: on the one hand a purely single-aspect process comprehensible in terms of the pathophysiologies of bacterium and host; on the other hand a dual-aspect, meaningful activity itself contributing to both the subsequent pathophysiologic course of the infection and the subsequent meaningful states-of-mind with their conscious effects. Similar considerations apply to the impact of medication on state of mind and conscious experience.

Hence, the monistic dual-aspect interactionist model allows not only for the generation of meaning (dual-aspect reality) by dual-aspect reality (meaning), but also for *the influence of single-aspect realities on meaningful states of being — via the physiologic face of the dual-aspect reality*. Clinically and commonsensically, it appears indispensable that a model allow for this latter. Consider the effect of strokes and epilepsy on state of mind.

Would anyone, for example, argue that the impact of a gin and tonic on one's state of mind is carried solely by the historically-situationally determined meaning of the cocktail?

Moreover, the model comprehends that *overdetermination* is the rule in explaining human experience and behavior. Multiple lines of single-aspect–single-aspect, single-aspect–dual-aspect, dual-aspect–single aspect, and dual-aspect–dual-aspect determination converge to produce the unconscious state-of-mind and the phenomenology deriving from it. To return to the cocktail, we now appreciate that the experience and behavior during intoxication are even partly shaped by cultural factors (Lithman, 1973).

From our thesis it follows that certain disorders ("medical" and "psychiatric") and states of mind may yield to pharmacologic *or* psychotherapeutic interventions, or to a combination of the two. Consider, in this regard, that both chemical (amytal) and psychotherapeutic (hypnosis) modalities can precipitously influence the activity of repression—the former presumably primarily through its physiologic aspect, and the latter largely through its psychologic (though also its physiologic) face.

Psychiatry seeks to comprehend causally "human states of being as experienced and enacted" in order to influence them through environmental input in the form, most especially, of pharmacologic substances and words. Each of these interventions—and its effects—is no more or less material and "somatic," or meaningful and "psychic," than the other. Words are meaningfully patterned sound waves intercepted and processed by sensory organs, a peripheral nervous system, and, ultimately, those dual-aspect activities known as mind. Medications are physiologically active substances dispensed within the context of the historically-situationally determined meanings of a doctor-patient relationship. Alterations in states of mind effected by either modality include changes in both psychologic and neurophysiologic-anatomic aspects of mentation. In regard to the latter, fascinating studies suggest that actual structural changes in neuronal processes accompany new learning and experience (Reiser, 1984; Kandel, 1978, 1983; Bailey and Chen, 1983).

By way of closing this section, I emphasize that no assumption is being made about the place in organic evolution at which dual-aspect realities arose—whether only at the inception of human symbolic activity (language) or at some much earlier point in mammalian development. Suffice it to say that there is a broad sense in which, for the more intelligent mammals, events appear to take on "meaning"—e.g., a puppy's handling ("history"—and it is history whence meaning arises) affects the mature dog's perception ("interpretation") of a variety of situations.

Animal behavior, as Darwin (1872) appreciated, exhibits similarities to human behavior too striking to dismiss as coincidental. Among these, I would conjecture and exemplify, are: the cross-communicational capacities of man and the "higher" mammals; parallels in emotional expressiveness among them; the often exquisite mutual empathy between master and dog; commonalities in mechanisms of learning and problem-solving; the apparent capability of the more intelligent mammals to hold nonverbal representations in mind (Hall's 1959, pp. 43–44, "infra-symbolic capacity") and to engage in what amount to primitive defensive maneuvers (displacement); apparent "phenomenology"—a dog's shame when scolded or sense of rejection when ignored—presumably akin to the human's; even—in the case of certain chimps—the apparent ability to manipulate symbols; and, above all, universal subjection to the evolutionary constraints and compulsions of natural and sexual selection and the requirements for phylogenetic and ontogenetic adaptation (to which an overly molecular-biological psychiatry is well advised to attend).

In these senses, it may well be appropriate to speak of the "mind" of certain organisms other than man. If so, "mind" would have arisen, like any other living phenomenon in the material-energic universe, through the adaptive advantages conferred upon its possessors. All anthropomorphism aside, I wager, however, that self-reflective consciousness did not arise until late in human biological and cultural evolution (nevertheless, see Goodall, 1971). It may be the most singularly human characteristic of man.

In sum, from this model it follows that psychoanalysis is a science limiting its perspective and explanatory program to the experiential-motivational and psychosocial face of dual-aspect phenomena. Within this empirical domain, and by its concepts and methods, psychoanalysis can say nothing whatsoever about the biological aspects of human mentation and behavior, though it provides invaluable data and hypotheses for rigorous psychological-neurobiological correlational work. Hence, this particular approach to mind-body allows psychoanalysis a degree of autonomy in its proper sphere—symbolically mediated, motivated human experience and activity—without either declaring its subject-matter in any way disembodied and "spiritual" or pretending that its explanations are necessary *and* sufficient.

Section II: Motivation

(A) Behaviors falling into the purview of psychoanalysis as an explanatory and therapeutic enterprise are significantly determined by motives—

i.e., meaningful, affect-laden fantasies; goal-directed strivings; purposive ideas — "wishes" in short. These wishes are not, as Schafer (1976, 1978) charges, hypostasized theoretical constructs. Rather, they are a shorthand notation for the individual's determinative personal activity — "wishing." History suggests that man's current *sense* of his self-determination took millennia to evolve (see Wallace, 1983b, 1985).

(B) Many motives are experienced as possessing both a meaningful and a tensional, energic, or drivelike side — e.g., certain varieties of sexual and aggressive motivation whose satisfaction is often perceived as tension release or discharge. While Holt (1976) brilliantly accents the inadequacies of a purely tension-release concept of human motivation, it is likely that what Ricoeur (1970) applauds as Freud's mixed energic-symbolic discourse is to an extent theoretically-empirically, as well as clinically-phenomenologically, justified. Moreover, *experiences* of pleasurable tension and *observations* of organisms' hunger for environmental stimuli do not necessarily contradict Freud's constancy-pleasure principle — for the latter is posited as the underlying, *non*conscious mechanism of motivation (i.e., its physiologic "face"). This may be psychoanalysis' closest approach to the neurobiological aspects of mentation to which it otherwise lacks access.

(C) Motives are not derivatives of instinctual drives, but result from converging factors comprehensible psychobiologically and socio-culturally. As early as 1939 the social psychologist Bartlett and the psychoanalyst Kardiner underline this. Bartlett (1939) says, "It is not a question of the conflict between biological impulse and social blockage. The driving forces are quite as much social products as the social barriers which block them" (p. 73). As Kardiner (1939) put it, we are not confronted directly by biological forces within the individual, but with "the finished products of the interaction of biological forces and external realities . . . Man is not an animal whose *needs* and behaviors are all phylogenetically fixed . . . Variations in social structure will change some needs, or create new ones" (Kardiner's emphasis). In any event, contemporary biology's concept of instinct is now quite complex and includes attention to environmental factors (see Lifton, 1978).

At the level of psychoanalytic discourse, it is impossible to dissect the factors in human motivation neatly and identify some as purely biological and others as purely social. Human biology interacts with the pressures and opportunities of its environment from the outset. Consequently, the individual's patterns of motivation are as much a function of prior socialization as of biology; the psychoanalyst confronts affect-laden motivating fantasies that are end products of the interaction between the two.

(D) Motives, as M. Klein, Fairbairn, and other object-relations pioneers emphasize, are person-directed from the outset—both toward figures in the current environment and toward historical others whom the former represent in the individual's unconsciousness (see VIB). Hence, raw aggressive, sexual, and other strivings do not lie in wait for any "object" of gratification. Our urgings are people-connected from the outset. "In the individual's mental life someone else is invariably involved, as a model, as an object, as a helper, as an opponent; and so from the very first individual psychology, in this extended but entirely justifiable sense of the words, is at the same time social psychology as well" (Freud, 1921, p. 69).

(E) It is a core assumption of psychoanalysis that all motivation begins unconsciously and may remain so, while still powerfully affecting behavior and experience of which we become conscious. It is not a question of conscious and unconscious motives. It is a matter of whether we ultimately become conscious of our motivation and interpretation, and this, to be elaborated upon, is largely a function of the degree to which they are defended against (see Wallace, 1988b). Again, consciousness is, as Freud held, primarily a sensory organ.

However, this is not, once more, to assert the causal inefficacy of consciousness. Consciousness of motivation can lead, as every analyst knows, to important differences in the manner in which such motives are assessed and whether or not they are acted upon. Motives of which we become conscious and upon which we deliberate may perhaps be termed "reasons" (Wallace, 1986b), a subspecies of causation.

Section III: Causation

(A) This topic is, of course, intimately related to the preceding. Motivation and meaning do not, as most "hermeneuticians" contend, contravene causality. If a motive is understood to begin prior to an observable or self-reportable behavior and to be a necessary condition for that behavior, then the motivational explanation is compatible with causation. Motives are meaningful causes, themselves the effect of the confluence between previously existing psychobiological and environmental factors. Nor does motivation's telic or goal-oriented aspect impugn causality, for the purpose *antedates* the behavior (see Bunge, 1979, on the compatibility in psychology of teleology and causality).

As for "meaning" itself, it bears at least three points of relation to "causation."

(1) Motives, the preeminent determinants of human behavior, as symbolically mediated purposive strivings, are themselves meaningful.

(2) Meaning—understood as the individual's total (conscious, preconscious, unconscious) feeling-toned interpretation of his or her situation—is itself the *effect* of antecedent motivational, defensive, and cognitive structures; it is the necessitated function of the person's historically-constitutionally determined mental set interacting with the current environment. By contrast, the idea that the individual's personal experience and interpretation arise de novo and arbitrarily would represent the height of meaninglessness. The resultant meaning, moreover—i.e., the agent's conscious-unconscious interpretation of the situation—decisively influences his or her action upon it. The phenomenologic method bids us first elucidate the individual's patterns of experience and interpretation *before* attempting to place them in a cause-effect nexus.

(3) Meaning refers to the expressive or communicative aspect of mental activity. Such meaning arises (as stressed below) at the intersection of sender and recipient. "Expression," in this sense, is one aspect of the *effect* of the prior mental cause. Contra Grünbaum (1984), an activity need not be (consciously or unconsciously) intentionally communicative to, in effect, communicate—albeit in a compromised manner.

The free-association method is based on a thoroughly causal conception of the genesis of meaning. It asserts that the patient *cannot* do other than spin out his or her associations as he or she does and that, consequently, these associations are derivatives of an underlying unconscious complex of intentions, fears, and inhibitions. By this way of thinking, meaning and causation are interdependent: compromising causation by removing necessity compromises intelligibility by inserting arbitrariness. If each expression might equally well have been any other, then have we not lost intelligibility along with necessity? The analysand could then avow that his or her parapraxis could just as well not have occurred and that the chain of associations and activities might as well have been otherwise—such that they tell us nothing significant about the individual who produced them (see Wallace, 1986a, 1986b, 1988a, in press a)!

(B) While there are doubtless instances of rather sharp demarcation between causes and effects in human behavior, there are more cases where the Humean, atomizing approach to motivation, so typical in experimental assumptions and models, violates reality. The philosopher Mandelbaum (1977) poses a useful revision of the Humean model: a "state of affairs is viewed not as an isolated event, but as the end point of a process, of which the effect is viewed as its end point or result; the cause of this result is the process itself" (p. 57).

Unless we engage in imaginary cinematographic analysis of an otherwise continuous process, Mandelbaum seems correct that this model of causation corresponds more closely to experience than do Hume's pairings of razor-sharp slices of cause-events and effect-events.

In this sense, "motives" or "intentions" need not be cleanly separated from the observable behaviors we take them to determine. Rather, there is a sense in which the motive does not first arise and *then cease,* and the behavior *begin;* it is often difficult to assert when one becomes the other. It seems more accurate to say that the motive operates throughout, and is expressed in, the observed activity. This continuum is what we call "motivation." It does not violate causality, for the *earlier* part of the series is still the *necessary* condition for the later—hence neither the necessary condition nor temporal criterion for cause-effect relations is abrogated.

(C) As Rapaport (1960) stressed, in human psychology all motives are causes, but not all causes are motives. Not only are the previously mentioned, nonconscious "single-aspect" processes necessary for motivation (which itself always has a neurobiological face), but cognitive structures, such as those elaborated on by Piaget (1929), Chomsky (1968), Lévi-Strauss (1963), and the cognitive psychologists, play a vital role in human mentation as well. Beside these presumably universal, epigenetically developed cognitive structures are the more idiosyncratic (largely unconscious) styles of interpretation constructed through culture and personal historical experience. These interpretive schemata may have motivational or defensive components as well—reflecting the manner in which the individual *wanted* to experience earlier key interactions or reflecting his or her *denial* of what actually transpired. To whatever degree they are determined by actual and psychical reality, such interpretive styles function as filters and templates through and around which the individual experiences and organizes the self-in-world—both the private fantasy realm and that of public interpersonal relations.

They are the more or less idiosyncratic, unconscious "paradigms" or "theories" that govern, in interaction with consensually validatable aspects of the environment, each person's perceptions, longings, fears, and expectations in all situations. The relationship between these (largely historically derived) interpretive structures and motivation is complex: motivation—whether wishful or defensive—both significantly determines, and is determined by, these schemata. Whether such structures may come to persist independently of the motivation and mnemonic representations that spawned them is an interesting question.

Finally, apropos non- or only quasi-motivational species of causality we must consider what William James (1890, pp. 104–127) bluntly termed "habit." It may be, as James suggests, that through sheer inertia repetitive activities can assume an existence and determinative power autonomously of their originating causes. It would be interesting to speculate on the possible overlap between aspects of James's "habit" and of Freud's (1920) "repetition compulsion," allegedly operating "beyond the pleasure principle." Clinically, the founder of American psychobiology, Adolf Meyer (1948), relied heavily on James's concept (i.e., "habit training").

(D) Causation in psychoanalysis, as elsewhere, is neither internalist ("immanent") nor externalist ("transeunt"), but what I (Wallace, 1985) have termed "intersectional." Let me begin explicating this by way of a clinical vignette (p. 194). This could as well be illustrated by a conflictually codetermined perception or action of a therapist himself or herself.

> Mr. D.'s father died on Monday. Two days later he attempted suicide. What do we mean when we say that the former event "precipitated" the latter? Do we mean that it caused it in the way a gamma ray transforms a molecule? Of course not. This causal statement is a short-hand notation omitting reference to a complex array of interacting determinants. A more complete causal explanation would read as follows: Mr. D. had been ignored and intimidated by his well-known and highly successful father throughout childhood. He reacted to this by developing powerful fantasies of murdering and surpassing father. At times he acted so obnoxiously that he actually aggravated father's withdrawal and abusiveness. Eventually, because he feared father's retaliation and the condemnation of his own conscience, he repressed these hostile longings. However, he continued to entertain them unconsciously and substitutively expressed them by entering and rising in the father's profession. When the combination of his own success and father's death fulfilled his unconscious wishes, Mr. D. reacted with an inordinate (unconscious) sense of guilt. In other words, his unconscious conflicts over patricidal aggression (themselves the effect of his *relationship* with father) caused him to unconsciously misinterpret his father's death as a murder and himself as the murderer. He then punished himself as if he had actually committed this crime.

This was but one of many probable motives for his self-destructiveness. My point is that the *cause* of the self-punitive fantasy that itself determined his suicidal behavior lay neither in the external event (the father's death) purely nor in the personality structure of the patient purely. Rather, the precipitating cause lay at the *intersection* of Mr. D.'s historically-constitutionally determined desires, fears, and interpretations with the external event itself. In other cases, such as with "fate neurotics," we deal, not merely with a neurotically determined misinterpretation of "precipitating" events, but with an active, though unconscious, engineering of them.

I believe, moreover, that this concept of causation is implicit in Freud's clinical formulations themselves (see, for example, Freud, 1909b, pp. 198–199, and the Wolf Man case history, brilliantly exemplifying the mutually determinative interaction between the Wolf Man's fantasies and "external" reality); recall also Hartmann's thinking about the "inner world" and the developmental psychology of Erikson (1963), Spitz (1965), and Thomas and Chess (1977). Consider too, in this regard, Freud's (1938, pp. 184–185) concept of infantile trauma, whose etiology is placed at the interface between the external stimulus and the state of the psychic apparatus (i.e., its immaturity).

An intersectional model of causation holds, not merely for situations of psychopathological interaction with one's fellows, but also for perception, interpersonal relations, and human communication in general (including, of course, the psychotherapeutic encounter). This is true whether one engages in the most refined Socratic dialogue or reacts to the crassest insult from another. If, in the case of the former, we adopt a novel position because of the superior logic of our partner, then he or she will be said to have given us "good reason" to do so; the cause lies at the intersection of his or her argument and our understanding. In regard to the latter, we can predict that the insult will cause, among other things, varying across individuals, (conscious or unconscious) anger in the recipient, but the final reaction to this anger—for example, fearful withdrawal, guilt feelings, anxiety, depression, aggressiveness, or self-destructiveness—depends on the history and dynamics of the target.

The intersectional model obtains, as averred, for the transactions between analyst and analysand. Mr. G's (Kohut, 1971, p. 93) precipitate haughty aloofness was caused by the interaction between Kohut's unwontedly unempathic and defensive tone (when announcing his forthcoming absence) and the patient's historically determined narcissistic psychopathology. But the effect of even the most empathic and clinically appropriate intervention (or nonintervention) is a function of its interaction with the personality structure of the patient. It is a truism that the "same" therapeutic comment or maneuver with two different patients may mean two quite different things to each of them—depending on the particular complexes and motivational-perceptual-interpretive sets.

Hence, intersectional causation is not a simple "environmental stimulus-organismic response" model. Even when a person responds to overwhelming environmental stimuli, one can look at the resultant behavior from either side of the interaction. In other words, the "stimulus" is as much a function of the individual's motivational-perceptual-interpretive activity as of the matter and energy in his or her environment. From the outside we "see" an event touching the individual, from the inside his or her mental set impinging upon the event. The person (unlike the molecule bombarded by the gamma ray) grasps the environment with his or her interpretations, desires, and defenses.

This concept of causation is quite compatible with a view of the individual as interpreter and world-maker. It denies neither personal phenomenology nor activity. It is not, as Schafer (1976, 1978) charges, a theorem of causes acting upon the agent from without; it takes account of the impact of the environment while conceiving of activities internal to the individual as the proximate and prepotent causes of his or her behavior (Wallace, 1985, pp. 193–200). It is the intersectional nature of causality that permits unforeseen (though perhaps not, in principle, unforeseeable) possibilities in human lives and that renders false the notion of internally fixed potentials—as best seen in the results of an optimal therapist-patient fit.

The intersectional quality of causation in human behavior does not sequester it from causality in the purely physical and biological realms: the effect, for example, of the addition of one chemical reagent to another depends on the properties of both as they interact with one another. The phenomenological-symbolic aspect of causation in man is what differentiates determinism in the two spheres.

It is plain that an intersectional model of causation (the only universally valid model of causality there could ever be) acknowledges what Atwood and Stolorow (1984) term the "inter-subjectivity" of the analytic enterprise, though these authors themselves deny both causality and all vestiges of a realist epistemology. In fact, the "subjectivities" of analyst and analysand, impinging upon and to some degree transforming one another, are as objectively real as any other feature of the universe. Aspects of the patient's psychical reality may even be inferred through the clinician's countertransference, evoked as it is partly by the patient's activity.

To be more precise, "intersectional causation" bids us grasp "experience" or "phenomenology" as something neither "subjective" or "objective"—nor "intersubjective." Though we may speak clinically of "inner" or "outer," we must understand that all phenomenology, motivation, and apperception-interpretation are functions of a person-in-a-situation. It is in this sense that Sullivan (1950) correctly, if hyperbolically, argued for the "psychological unreality of the concept of the individual." By "objective" we mean potentially or in principal "consensually validatible," by "subjective" the person's world as he or she experiences and interprets it (Wallace, in press a). Neither refers to activity that is totally determined by the individual's mental set or by the environment, but rather by the intersection between both.

Before turning from intersectional causation (which, however, we encounter in altered form in the "history" subsection), let us briefly examine the charges of Masson (1984) and Miller (1986) that psychoanalysis has given short shrift to external causation—especially in overlooking the frequency of intrafamilial child sexual, physical, and emotional abuse and its impact on adult psychopathology. Kohut, with his etiologic emphasis on deficient and distorted parental empathy, moves in a similar externalist direction. Early studies of post-traumatic stress disorder (PTSD) appeared to support the preeminence of purely adult environmental causes.

Such writings bear an important message for psychoanalysis which has, indeed, focused on (especially early) history, psychical reality, fantasy, and intrapsychic facets of causation at the expense of current "outside" reality—see Freud's "Dora" as a case in point. Nevertheless, in line with the principle of intersectional causation, it would be mistaken to act as if we ever confront an either-or. There is *always* a contribution from "inner" historical and constitutional factors in even the most traumatic current or environmental situation—as borne out in the most recent studies of PTSD sufferers. Hence the partial absurdity of the behaviorist "stimulus"-response paradigm and of instruments purporting to quantify "stressors" as if they exist independently of individual mental sets.

It is indeed important theoretically and clinically, moreover, to determine whether (and how frequently, in what manner, etc.) incest, deprivation, or abuse actually occurred. Failing to explore such issues thoroughly would, among other things, leave the patient feeling mistrusted and misunderstood. Nevertheless, the sequelae of an actual seduction will not be worked through unless the psychical reality—the fears, fantasies, feelings, images, and interpretations preceding, during, and following the incest—are worked through as well.

From a related perspective, it is unfortunately true that psychoanalysis, like psychiatry, has by and large failed to embrace sociocultural-economic factors in its theory and therapy. And yet we know of the tremendous impact of religious and cultural symbolism upon pattern of intrapsychic conflict, mode of compromise formation, means of adaptation, and even phenomenology (e.g., of depression). Moreover, it is well documented that rates of marital discord, child abuse, addictions disorders, depression, and suicide increase with economic decline and are profoundly affected by cultural patterns and attitudes (see Kleinman, 1988, for multiple references).

From the other direction, analysis contributes to understanding society and culture by emphasizing the role of institutionalized psychological mechanisms such as defense, compromise formation, and attempts to actively master passively experienced group traumata (see Wallace, 1983b). While important foundations for psychoanalytic–social-science integration have been laid, it remains mostly a task for the future. Nor — ironically, given the care that analysts since Freud devote to the design and decoration of their offices — is there an adequate theory of the impact of physical ambience on mood and state of mind, Searles (1960) being one of the few taking the "nonhuman environment" seriously (a milieu that, however, always carries a personalized and anthropormorphized dimension).

(E) Causation in the psychoanalytic clinical-investigative enterprise is assigned in some cases through inference, and in others through relatively direct observation. The former is the Humean inductive mode, where causality is inferred from repetitive correlations between events such as disrupted love affairs and depressions. The inference to motives and preoccupations from patterns of association is another instance. While this may not lead to conjectures as secure as those in tightly controlled experimental situations, indeed our surest path to veridical knowledge in many spheres — the variables are too rich, multiple, and intertwined to allow atomizing approaches.

Moreover, the behavioral experimentalist pretends, with a simplistic "external" stimulus-"organismic" response model, that intrapsychic motivational-defensive-interpretive factors play no role in shaping the nature and content of the "stimulus" and the "subject's" perception of scientist and situation. This lulls investigators into a certitude about the causes of human *experience* (if attended to at all) and observable behavior that is presently unobtainable. Of course, it may be that this paradigm can be remedied through a combination of sophisticated conceptual analysis and operationalism, semi-quantification of variables (e.g., Dahl's linguistic and Luborsky's thematic analyses), the intelligent application of multivariate statistics, and better experimenter acquaintance with the concerns and methodology of social psychology and dynamic psychiatry.

In many instances, however, we seem to have direct and immediate apprehension of causal relationships. Certainly some of our most prominent contemporary philosophers (e.g., Searle, 1983) believe, contra Hume, that causal relationships — including that when one billiard ball strikes another — are often directly observed rather than merely inferred. For example, a man need not know all the psychobiological processes intervening between seeing a beautiful woman and his subsequent arousal to *know* that he has *experienced* a causal relationship; nor must a prize fighter know the physiology of the solar plexus to be convinced of the determinative role of the fist in his pain. Such appreciations are instantaneous, requiring no inferences from correlations or large-n series. Indeed, immediate apprehensions of certain first-time causal relationships appear evolutionarily built into the animal kingdom. A dog need be hit by a man with a stick only once to apprehend, in its mode, a causal relationship and betray this in subsequent encounters with such humans.

In other cases it may be a combination of direct apprehension and inference. Consider a patient with a history of parental desertion, disinterest from extended family members, many failed relationships in adulthood, and a strong expressed sense of worthlessness and unattractiveness. If the therapist answers the phone in the midst of a session and the patient coughs, shifts nervously, and glances ruefully at the floor, what sensitive observer would not immediately perceive the causal relevance of the clinician's action to the latter's behavior? Do we not know and feel — both from immediate grasp of nonverbal cues, perhaps coupled with more inferential factors such as our own (however attenuated) reaction to the distraction of important others and our instantaneously empathic imagination of the heightened sensitivity to rejection of a patient with such a history — that there is a causal connection between the phone call and the patient's discomfort? If all this is "inference," then it is lightning-fast inference. While it is logically and empirically possible that we are mistaken — perhaps the patient experienced a temporal-lobe seizure resulting from a nonmeaningful neurological causal chain totally independent of the phone call — in the realm of social reality we are unlikely to be amiss. And, in any event, we can gauge our perception-conjecture against the patient's subsequent communication and behavior in the session.

(F) Psychoanalysis holds that by far the majority of imaginally and symbolically mediated behaviors are overdetermined — that is, functions of the vectorlike addition of complementary or conflicting unconscious motives and cognitive-interpretive, "object"-related structures. This is not merely to restate the classical "necessary and sufficient conditions" concept of causality, but it is also more complex. The relationship among the various causes and the resultant human activity (say, a psycho-neurotic symptom) often appears to some degree additive. For example, unconscious intrapsychic conflict, current family relationships, and secondary gain may all contribute to the intensity and persistence of a symptom in such a way that touching only one of the three factors produces no observable or patient-experienceable change.

This is puzzling: it ostensibly violates the logical tenet that if a condition is indeed necessary, then removing it cancels the effect. In other instances, one of multiple etiologic factors may be sufficiently preponderant that removing it alleviates an important aspect of the symptomatic constellation. In still other situations, the intrapsychic, historical, and current interpersonal factors are so intimately interwoven and mutually determinative that to ameliorate one is to ameliorate the other—e.g., when working through the intrapsychic conflicts binding a patient to a pathological family structure (needing and fostering the patient's dependence) enables him or her to leave. Finally, as Freud (1901b, p. 53) and Brenner (1976) point out, the chief motivation of a symptom or character trait may change over time in response to subsequent life events. Originating causes may cease and maintaining ones (such as secondary gain) supervene.

Most often it is probably best to view the multiple factors converging to produce and preserve a symptom or character structure as part of one interrelated causal complex—as, if one will, *the* necessary and sufficient condition itself—which must be dismantled "piece by piece" through an interpretively mediated cognitive-affective process (again, "working through").

(G) As we saw in the Introduction, Freud included "function" in the purview of psychical causality. This does not carry the same difficulties encountered by sociologists and anthropologists who also wish to incorporate notions of function (manifest and latent) into their concepts of societal causality. The argument, for example, that entreaty of the gods is only the manifest function of a particular Hopi religious ritual, while maintenance of social cohesion is the latent and prepotent function, poses apparent problems from the standpoint of causality. No mechanism is provided to turn the alleged latent societal function into an individual motivation (cause). In other words, if increased social cohesion is the effect of such rituals, how does the *group's* "unconscious" (if this is not, in fact, an hypostasis) aim to achieve this become translated into a causal *individual* intention?

Of course, the group behavior—say, a rain dance—need not reflect either an individual or collective desire to subserve cohesion; it would be sufficient that the ritual be a *consequence* of quite different individual and group intents—to placate and move the rain gods. The dance could still confer an adaptational advantage (such as enhanced social cohesion) on groups practicing it. Thereby the consequence, or latent function, would itself come to act as a cause (unbeknown to the dancers) of the fitness and survival of the tribe, and the rain ritual *ipso facto* continue to be enacted.

However, dynamic psychiatry is not faced with even this ostensible problem, for it is concerned with the causation of *individual,* not societal behaviors. In the case of a symptomatic behavior such as, e.g., drug abuse, one may posit that avoiding certain affect-laden fantasies and recollections is both the *function* and the *cause*. However the drug use itself originated — through identification with an addicted parent or whatever — its alleviation of dysphoria and reinforcement of defense would themselves become motivation (i.e., cause) for *subsequent* drug-taking. Hence the aspect of function is fully covered by the concept of psychical causality. Such ideas would, of course, be quite consistent with the emphasis of evolutionary biology on natural selection and adaptation as determinants of behavior.

Nevertheless, in assessing the patient's motivation, we can hardly dispense with its shaping by reactions to, and consequences for, family and social network. Maintenance of a pathologic family equilibrium, as systems theorists and therapists propose, can be both a *consequence* and, through feedback interaction, a *cause* of incipient and maintained individual psychopathology. Conflict, motivation, defense, interpretation, and fantasy all occur and manifest at psychical and interpersonal levels.

For treatment of related items, beyond the scope of this essay — free will and the ethical implications of psychical causality and historical determinism — see Wallace, 1986b and 1986c. In regard to man's apparently perennial need for overarching systems of meaning and purpose in life and his confrontation with "existential" issues, psychoanalysis need not deny them causal force, but only bid us recognize their coloration by unconscious wish, defense, and personal history. Such systems may well reflect what Atwood and Stolorow (1984) call the "ur-motive" — man's need to maintain the organization of his experience. With reference to the preeminent existential issue — death — Becker (1973) and Lifton (1978) are undoubtedly correct that analysts have ignored the possibility that its idea is repressed, and that aspects of man's behavior may be motivated by a desire for actual or symbolic immortality that denies its presence. Recall Freud's negation of any unconscious belief in death, his lifelong preoccupation with death and superstitious death-dates, and his metaphysical tracts on the death instinct (Wallace, 1984).

Section IV: History, Transference, Phenomenology, and Unconsciousness

(A) Historical determinism is the handmaiden of psychic causality. Although the two concepts are not identical, there is a circular relationship between them. By this I mean that the idea of psychical causality is the rationale for taking a history, and yet the operation of psychical causality is best revealed by that history. By "historical determinism" in psychoanalysis I mean that: the present-day configuration of any personality has arisen out of previously existing ones, that any individual's current (conscious and unconscious) interpretations of self-in-world, and present desires, fears, inhibitions, compromises, and behavior patterns are effects of the history of his or her motivated, actual and fantasied interpersonal relations. By "history" is meant the course of interaction between the individual's constitution-personality structure and the environment.

The psychoanalytic theory of psychopathology as a maladaptive way of dealing with unconscious aspects of intrapsychic-interpersonal (each hand-in-hand with the other) conflict is, of course, founded squarely upon the bedrock of historical determinism. Both the conflict, and the maladaptive means of handling it, arise from the interaction between one's biological endowment and nascent personality structure on the one side and the environment on the other.

Symptomatic and characterological modes of coping with conflict are special cases of atavism — the persistence of once adaptive, historically determined modes of interpretation and behavior into the present, where they are no longer necessary and useful. "Our task," as Freud (1915–1917, p. 270) said, "is then simply to discover in respect to a senseless idea and a pointless action, the past situation in which the idea was justified and the action served a purpose." Adult neuroses and character styles are thus conceptualized as consequential to historically conditioned conflicts, behaviors, and misinterpretations of reality.

Curiously, Sir Karl Popper (1965), well-known philosophical opponent and misrepresenter of psychoanalysis, unwittingly endorses an essentially Freudian view of psychopathology and its etiology: "I am inclined to suggest that most neuroses may be due to a partially arrested development of the critical attitude; to an arrested rather than a natural dogmatism; to resistance to demands for the modification and adjustment of certain schematic interpretations and responses" (p. 49)!

There is evidence that, as Freud thought, the nature and timing of early traumata are specifically related to the form of adult psychopathology — e.g., that oral trauma is important in schizophrenia, anal trauma in obsessive-compulsive disorder, and oedipal trauma in hysteria. Nevertheless, psychoanalysts more aptly think in terms of the child's development as a whole, rather than searching for a singular trauma from the oral, anal, or phallic periods that polarized the patient toward psychopathology once and for all. To be sure, the earliest years have determinative import disproportionate to their duration. Nevertheless, the foundation for adult character and psychopathology is laid, not by events in any given period of two or three years, but by the total pattern of experiences in childhood and adolescence (see, e.g., Hartmann and Kris, 1945). In short, it is *the style of interaction* between the child and his parents (and key others) throughout all phases that is determinative. Nor, as Erikson (1963), Levinson (1978), and others remind, does development cease in adulthood.

The aims and methodology of psychoanalytic treatment follow logically from the conception of psychopathology as an atavistic mode of handling unconscious, historically determined intrapsychic conflict connected to the mental representations of persons. These "object" representations are condensations of historical and current others, as codetermined by the patient's motivated and learned expectations-interpretations and the actual behavior of others.

Because of the mutual interpenetration of the patient's and others' representational worlds and behaviors, his or her abortive attempts at adaptation are to a realm that is simultaneously intra- and inter-personal. There is, again, no psychical disequilibrium that does not present interpersonally, and vice versa. Hence the fallacy of sharp separations between psychodynamic and family-social systems theories of psychopathology.

The analyst's neutrality, minimal self-disclosure, and relative verbal inactivity are all designed to permit the maximum possible unfolding of the historical, intrapsychic aspects of the determination of the patient's associations, inhibitions in associating, feelings, fantasies, parapraxes, remembering, forgetting, silences, and reporting. By minimally influencing the analysand's fears and fantasies, the analyst allows him or her not merely to recollect, but also to act out, a truer picture of the past in the present. The patient transfers, in other words, his or her neurosis from past and present outside psychical-interpersonal contexts to the analytic situation.

At best, this approximates a rough-and-ready version of the experimental method—not to be confused with a pseudo-atomizing that obfuscates more than it illumines. Nevertheless, the competent practitioner is cognizant of the perennial impact of analyst and analytic situation, and strives to understand the analysand's interpretation of these as well. Nor does the doctor equate analytic neutrality with an unrelaxed and inhumane brass-monkeyism (Stone, 1961; Gill, 1982): to do so would be both gratuitously depriving, as well as injecting potentially unanalyzable untoward reality determinants into the situation.

The more the analyst is a benign and understanding listener and facilitator, aware of and hence able to introspectively utilize, rather than act out, his or her countertransference, the greater the contrast between the analysand's historically grounded expectations of the clinician and their lack of justification by the analyst's actual behavior. Being struck by this contrast, and in response to the analyst's interventions, the analysand slowly becomes affectively-cognitively aware that he or she is living atavistically, in the "past" not the "present." This living awareness that he or she has been unconsciously imposing historically determined motives and categories of interpretation upon him or herself—that his or her fears and fantasies are more appropriate to a child of 3, 5, or 10 than to an adult of 30, 40, or 50—is the most transformative aspect of psychodynamic treatment.

If the balance of motives within the patient's mind and the neurotically distorted view of self-in-world have truly shifted, then the patient will change as a matter of course, without prodding or exhortation from the therapist. The analysand will change simply because the old, unsatisfactory ways of seeking and avoiding (often simultaneously) gratification are no longer necessary: ancient dangers are no longer there now that he or she is living in a different reality. In other words, since all behaviors (psychopathological ones included) exist for some adaptive advantage (within the context of both "internal" and "external" worlds), when the intrapsychic and current realities to which they are adaptive change, then the behaviors will too.

The clinician encourages the patient to "write" a certain kind of history—not a distant and affectless report, but an "anamnesis," in the sense in which the word connotes a recapturing or reliving of prior experience. Through studying the patient's successive interpretations of personal history, both analyst and analysand arrive at novel perspectives and reinterpretations that themselves influence the subsequent direction of that history: "the way one's past is seen cannot be overestimated as a force in determining the course of future events" (Novey, 1968, p. 149).

(B) The causation in historical determinism is interactive and *mediate* (i.e., intersectional as well). It is the former in that the infant is impinged upon by the behavior of parents who, in every sense of the word, "shape"—especially, as Stern (1985) points out, through their phase-appropriate anticipations and expectations—his nascent humanness and affective-conative-perceptual set; but they mold it in interaction with the baby's idiosyncratic constitutional endowment (accounting, many feel, for as much as 35 percent of personality variance—e.g., activity-passivity, social introversion versus extroversion, etc.).

Furthermore, the infant's innate activity level, emotional expressiveness, and so forth impinge upon the parents and to some extent sculpt their behavior toward, and expectations of, the former—Moss and Robson (1968) noting, in one study, that more than half the observed interactions were initiated by the infant. After the first few months of life, the baby himself is developing, from interaction between his neurobiological maturation and parental behavior, an "inner world" and interpretive style. Henceforth, the parents impinge upon him *through* this psychical world; the infant's personality structure is then determined not by the parents behavior per se, but by the impact of that behavior on his motivational-defensive-interpretive set—and the reverse holds true for the influence of the infant's activity on each parent.

This is what I mean by "mediate" determinism. The infant is not passively and mechanically buffeted about by his "determinants," but reaches out and grasps them with his own mental set. Freud's (1930) assertion that the degree of superego aggressiveness is a function, not merely of parental aggressiveness, but of the child's projected aggression as well, is a case in point; as is Kernberg's (1975) emphasis on the role of the child's affective state in determining how he perceives his parents. And we must not forget the impact of the child's actual aggressiveness on that of the parents.

The concept of identification is another instance of mediate and interactive determinism. The child's identifications are not merely the passive effects of the parental behavior. Identification is the child's activity—motivation and mental set influencing not only with whom he most identifies, but also his *perception* of the object of identification. The child is part of a social structure in which he enacts a crucial role from the outset. Recall the interactional, "goodness of fit" model of Chess and Thomas (1984), and Erikson's quip that babies raise their families.

In short, by historical determinism we do not mean that history somehow sits outside and determines one. We mean, rather, that the individual remains subject to a set of preoccupations, conflicts, and a self-world view formulated through his or her motivated-interpreted interactions with others. History thus lives on insofar as personality structure is its precipitate; it persists in styles of interpretation and coping, as much as in specific conscious and unconscious images, memories, fantasies, and conflicts.

It is the potency of these constitutionally-historically developed mental-motivational sets that accounts, along with the infinite capacity of human beings to perceive and build the interpersonal environments they (all too often neurotically) "need," that accounts for the patterns and continuities in a life cycle. It is the often unpredictable turns of the environmental wheel, linked with a mind moved or prepared by its own desires and capacities, that determine the apparent discontinuities and the possibilities for beneficent or maleficent change.

The idea of intersectional causation—as expressed through a concept of mediate and interactional historical determinism and the prepotency of psychical causality—vitiates the false charge that psychoanalytic treatment is a hunt for victims and victimizers and an instrument for diminishing one's sense of personal causal responsibility for whence one comes and whither one is going. Analytic therapeusis can produce a will that is adaptive and optimally syntonic with the person's deepest strivings and with the needs and requirements of loved ones and an open society. This is all the freedom that one could have or realistically want; and it is not in the least incompatible with a thoroughgoing psychobiological determinism (Wallace, 1986b).

Finally, since all psychical causes and tendencies are equally current, "genetic" and "dynamic" refer not to differing categories of causation, but to approaches, as Hartmann and Kris (1945) understood: "[Dynamic hypotheses] are concerned with the interaction of the conflicts and forces within the individual and with their reaction to the external world, at any given time or during brief time spans; [genetic propositions] describe how any condition under observation has grown out of an individual's past and extended throughout his total life span" (p. 11).

The genetic and dynamic perspectives converge in Freud's (1900) earliest definition of "wish," the primary causal principle of psychoanalysis:

> An essential component of this experience of satisfaction [of the hunger drive, in this instance] is a particular perception (that of nourishment, in our example), the mnemic image of which remains associated thenceforward with the memory trace of the excitation produced by the need. *As a result of the link that has thus been established, next time this need arises a psychical impulse will at once emerge which will seek to re-cathect the mnemic image of the perception itself, that is to say, to re-establish the situation of the original satisfaction.* An impulse of this kind is what we call a wish; the reappearance of the perception is the fulfillment of the wish . . . [pp. 565–566; my italics].

(C) This lack of a hard-and-fast line between "genetic" and "dynamic" is the problem with Gill's (1982) attempt to obviate the differing objections to history of those like Spence (1982) and Grünbaum (1984) by claiming to work largely in the transference with current, dynamic issues. When one turns from elucidating the particular current perceptual distortions, motivations, images, and defenses manifesting in the transference to explaining how it is that these arise, history cannot be dispensed with. Moreover, in an insight therapy, much less analysis, patients invariably talk history at numerous points. When the clinician interprets transference, patients, countless times, ineluctably recall and relate history (see Wallace, 1988c, in press a).

In fine, Gill's attempt, however valiant, requires a pretense that neither analyst nor analysand can maintain. Although it is true that the analytic process transpires totally in the present (when else could it occur?) and although the analyst must sort out—in line with the principle of intersectional causation—his or her own determinative input, it is by interpreting certain of the patient's current perceptions and behaviors as traces of a past reality (i.e., as "transference") that they are appreciated in their full significance. In other words, without a concept of the past, one cannot fully encounter the present (see Wallace, 1985, in press a for an attempt to refute Spence's [1982] and Grünbaum's [1984] critiques of the analytic historical enterprise). It is in this sense that Brenner (1982) is quite correct in eschewing, on theoretical and methodological grounds, the split between "working" or "therapeutic alliance" (Greenson, 1967; Zetzel, 1956) and transference.

In short, while the patient's transference itself is *co*determined by the analyst's presence, in a properly conducted analysis one learns a great deal about how the patient experiences the world and the clinician, as well as about the episodes through which the patient came to fashion his or her particular fabric of desire, defense, and interpretation. *Elucidating the impact of the patient's motivational-interpretative system and "object" representations on how he or she perceives reality and structures experience is undoubtedly the premier contribution of the psychoanalytic method.*

(D) An important aspect of analysis concerns its grasp of the *logic* of human emotional response, interpretation, and inference formation. A certain part of this work might be considered a refinement of age-old wisdom and common sense. Psychoanalysis examines this "logic" as it manifests in virtually universal or lawlike elements of cognitive-emotional response to certain classes of situation (e.g., the six year old's inner response to a parental desertion) and as it presents in the personal patterns and regularities (between situations on the one hand and the individual's feelings, motivations, interpretations, and behaviors on the other) in idiosyncratic life histories.

In this latter sphere Weiss, Sampson, and the Mount Zion Group (1986) have subjected a completely audiotaped analysis to rigorous, predictive tests of analytically based hypotheses about the analysand's process of unconscious inference formation. Their work, as well as that of Luborsky (1976, 1979) and others, when extended to larger series of recorded analyses, promises to extend such insights to the nomothetic level and to refute Grünbaum's (1984) and Eagle's (1984) contention that analytic conjectures are not testable through the clinical situation itself. Moreover, they can confute the facile, reflexive charges of suggestion perennially brought by such critics (see Wallace, in press a). The psychoanalyst studies the interplay between the idiosyncratic and the universal in the human existence before him or her (Wallace, 1985).

Eventually, he or she must arrive at an interpretation—an action, a provisional commitment—communicating this insight in accurate and healing words appropriate to the particular patient.

Let me emphasize—for these "common-sense" factors are invoked in the next subsection as well—that they do not stamp psychoanalysis as a "primitive" or "proto-" science which, if it would develop to a paragon of physical-science perfection, must jettison and surpass them. While psychoanalysis will likely achieve greater precision and clarification in its concepts and theories, and discover additional lawlike aspects of human mentation, motivation, and behavior, its subject matter does not permit its escaping these common-sense features altogether.

This "common sense" helps discern the more idiographic facets in the life before us, as well as the more lawlike human inferences and responses to situations (i.e., the rejected human being feels, at some level, dysphoria and anger; the ignored and perennially criticized child develops a problematic self-image/self-esteem; injuries to self-esteem itself commonly evoke varying combinations of hurt and anger; persons often recapitulate traumatic events in an attempt to actively master them, etc.). If such "common sense" (itself based on varying degrees of lay unconscious, preconscious, and conscious knowledge of human psychobiological regularities) is "surpassed," then both the theory and therapy will suffer irrecoverably. Again, the complex human phenomena which analysis studies cannot be adequately reproduced in the atomizing experimental laboratory (see Wallace, in press b), divorced from the contextual and associational richness of the analytic situation.

Nevertheless, as previously intimated, this does not mean that this impressionistic clinical wisdom or "common" sense should not be increasingly clarified, operationalized, and tested through statistically informed examination of longitudinal videotaped sessions, as well as through more contrived, if sufficiently sophisticated, experimental and epidemiologic studies. The history of science and medicine is replete with the ostensibly most self-evident propositions that later proved inadequate or erroneous.

(e) While relying on crude covering laws or rules of thumb—e.g., about what sorts of histories tend to produce certain characterological and psychopathological constellations and transferences—the analyst is, nonetheless, investigationally, clinically, and morally committed to each individual patient, whose total (verbal, nonverbal, and behavioral) responses over time are the ultimate epistemic ground and arbiter of analytic conjectures and hypotheses. Hence these universalist, lawlike understandings of human behavior are flexible and open; every effort is made to facilitate the patient's elaboration of phenomenology and history, rather than forcing these into reductive Procrustean beds. Those, like Grünbaum (1984), charging suggestion at every turn, simply do not appreciate how most analytic interventions are directed toward the patient's inhibitions about fleshing out experience, biography, and associations (Wallace, 1986a, in press a). Done properly, psychoanalysis is, as Peterfreund (1983) asserts, a process of discovery ("heuristics"), rather than of strapping patients in theoretical straitjackets—preoedipal, oedipal, etc. Psychoanalysts strive for models and metaphors progressively capturing the patient's conscious-preconscious experience; this unlocks doors hitherto barring the analysand's awareness of unconscious motivational-defensive constellations, images, and interpretive structures.

Hence, phenomenology is a means to the end of arriving at genetic-dynamic causal hypotheses. It is not, as some phenomenological psychiatrists naïvely think, that the patient's "shining forth" (Boss's [1963] favorite term) explains itself without the clinician's confrontations of resistance and intervening selecting and organizing principles (Wallace, in press a). One need only consult their case histories—Boss's "Dr. Cobling," for example, ostensibly presented as an atheoretical narrative designed to prove psychodynamics erroneous—to see they are shot through with implicit theoretical presuppositions (many of them Freudian!).

If psychodynamics without phenomenology is sterile and reductive, then phenomenology without psychodynamics is presentistic and chaotic. The key, as Hartmann (1927) grasped in quoting Kronfeld, is maintaining balance: "Phenomenology is a preliminary approach necessary for any psychological theory which seeks to explain phenomena genetically. . . . It is on the one hand the precondition for the formation of the theories, and on the other hand it demands such theories; otherwise it remains essentially incomplete" (p. 376).

The following vignette (Wallace, 1985, pp. 26–28) illustrates how phenomenology and psychodynamics-psychogenetics illumine one another.

Mr. B. spent the first few minutes of the hour talking about wanting to be "fed" by his parents and explaining that this involved everything from being cooked for to being acknowledged (especially by his father) as one who is worthwhile and lovable; he spoke of his sadness, frustration, and anger at the "conditional" nature of such "feeding" that he received.

Thence he spoke of his wife's new evening job and his assuming responsibility for preparing supper and getting his small children bathed and to bed. He merely touched on this, however, and was prepared to move on when I asked him to elaborate "what it was like" with his wife away and his tending the children. Initially Mr. B. mechanically reported his wife's new job and the evening schedule. I had to request that he flesh out these times. There followed a description of coming home and wanting to have a drink and unburden himself to his wife, only to encounter her as she rushed out the door to work. The more concrete he became, the harder he found it to ignore his hurt, frustration, and anger at her not "feeding" him.

Thence he turned to the interaction with his children. He began dinner at 5:00 p.m. and spent a few frustrating minutes consulting recipes and hunting up ingredients and utensils. Mr. B. became tense and irritated when speaking of the need to stop and settle arguments between the children. Then followed the struggle to get them to the table. He spoke of the frustration of cleaning the kitchen afterward and simultaneously answering a battery of childish questions.

He recounted an incident the previous night, when he lost his temper over his son's relentless queries and spoke of his concern over the boy's response: "Daddy, you make me feel dumb alot." The patient then paused and tearily expressed his fear that he does not give his children sufficient affection—"but I feel like I have to overcome a tremendous block in myself to give to them." I responded, "It's hard to give what you yourself were denied [referring to his frequent descriptions of his father's hypercritical and unloving interactions with him]." He nodded, and spoke of his anger and disappointment vis-à-vis father and his desire to do better by his own children. He closed by bemoaning the rigid and mechanical way he puts his children to bed and how he must suppress the strong urge to belt them when they do not fall rapidly asleep.

Without the phenomenology, and prior possession of a history, I could not have delivered my genetic interpretation; without the interpretation the full significance of the phenomenology would have gone begging. There was ample opportunity in subsequent sessions to return both to the paternal themes, and to address the apparent and increasingly emergent maternal ones.

(F) It might seem astonishing to term psychoanalysis a "common-sense psychology," and yet it manifests the best of the empathy and insight that too rarely occur in ordinary human relations. If one exempts certain aspects of metapsychology, the processes about which Freud wrote are not without counterparts in conscious and preconscious experience—e.g., motivation or intentionality, signal anxiety, various species of defensive avoidance, the coloring of present attitudes by prior history, the presence of conflicting motives, ambivalence, the associative character of mental life, and so forth. In short, I argue, with Atwood and Stolorow (1984) and Nissim-Sabat (1986), that psychoanalysis is firmly grounded in phenomenology.

Freud's contribution was articulating clearly the hitherto largely implicit logic of common-sense psychology and declaring that similar processes occur outside awareness. Psychoanalysis asserts a continuum not, as J. O. Wisdom (1984) would have it, a sharp line of demarcation between consciousness and unconsciousness; psychoanalysis is an investigative-therapeutic procedure whereby the patient becomes *conscious*, oftentimes with little or no assistance from the analyst, of motives, meanings, and memories of which the patient was formerly unaware. Hence crucial aspects of the unconscious are no longer the "unknown [*unbewusst.*]" Unconscious mental content is reached only via observable behavior and communicated preconscious and conscious phenomenology, as instanced by the following case (Wallace, in press a):

> Rev. K. spontaneously recounted a recent dream in which he was driven round in a beaten up old pick-up truck by Mr. T., a parishioner by whom he always felt threatened and intimidated. In the dream, by contrast, Mr. T. was showing the patient his farm in a fatherly or grandfatherly way. Indeed, the patient's first two associations were to similar trucks driven by father and grandfather, also farmers. The latter was a gentle man who often took the patient with him, although the patient despised him for his alcoholism, erratic work habits, and "weakness." The father was an intimidating and verbally (at times physically) abusive six-foot-four inch giant.
>
> As Rev. K. was telling me this, he suddenly became aware that he had been responding to the elderly, diminuitive Mr. T. as if he were his father. Mr. T.'s grandfatherly demeanor in the truck suggested to him that a) perhaps grandfather had been more positively important after all, and b) maybe he even wanted such attention from the feared Mr. T. — and, it immediately occurred to him, from his cruel father as well.
>
> This and supervening sessions furnished ample associational, historical, and phenomenological substantiation of the patient's dream interpretation. For example, while hearing a colleague in a postgraduate seminar describe his recent awareness of the importance of his deceased "dead beat" brother and the colleague's realization that he had never mourned his death, Rev. K. broke into tears about his grandfather and became aware of his own guilt-laden missed mourning. He recognized, independently of any prompting from myself, that there were elements of both fear and desire for fatherly attention vis-à-vis me.

Quasi-experimentally, posthypnotic suggestion is the best demonstration that mental content may be unconscious and yet powerfully determine behavior in waking consciousness. Similarly, one of the strongest foundations for the claim of free association to yield retrospective causal information is that the posthypnotic subject, by associating to the unconsciously suggested activity, can often arrive at knowledge of the previously unconscious cause (i.e., the image of the hypnotist's command) (see Wallace, 1986a, in press a).

Finally, at times one should promote the patient's communicating his or her own causal attributions for his or her problems and life patterns. While often pat or intellectualized, such attributions are integral to the patient's life experience and interpretations of it. They not only yield essential information about the analysand's mental processes, but also offer the clinician causally relevant insights as well. By the law of psychical causality such patient explanations, however inadequate or misleading, bear some compromise (defensive-expressive) relation to the unconscious causal complex of the item in question.

Section V: Intrapsychic Conflict, Signal Anxiety, Defense, and Compromise Formation

Here is another eminently useful constellation of concepts replete with phenomenological referents in everyday life. Who has never been aware of opposing feelings or motives toward an individual, and anxiety lest the other discover this? Has any never committed a discomfiting parapraxis suggesting to self and others the presence of hitherto unconscious or preconscious motives contrary to one's conscious intent? Similar activities are said to occur unconsciously — the signal anxiety warning the "I" ("ego") that something conflictual to the demands of reality or conscience threatens to emerge and bring about any of a number of fantasied dangers — loss of love, physical or verbal attack, condemnation by conscience, or diminished self-esteem. In consequence of this discomfort the ego responds defensively (on a continuum from unconsciousness to consciousness).

Where anticipated dangers correspond to actual social reality — in which case we refer to the dysphoria as fear, not anxiety — we can posit good evolutionary-adaptational reasons for defense. All too often the child's human environment provided him with such adaptational incentives. It is, again, the atavistic persistence of these fears and disavowals into adulthood, where they are no longer indicated, that makes them maladaptive or neurotic — though the individual may of course behave so as to evoke the feared responses in those currently around him, such that his defenses retain a skewed adaptive quality after all (the self-fulfilling prophecy).

These avoidances may come to operate with such immediacy and automaticity that they indeed justify the appellation "mechanism":

Brenner (1982) aptly suggests the phenomenology-near inclusion of "signal depression" which, unlike anxiety, is associated with a catastrophe which one unconsciously imagines *has already occurred.* Genuinely repressed material is a "sleeping dog;" if defensive maneuvers are successful, any intruding mentation is thrust back into repressed unconsciousness; if they partly fail we have a symptomatic compromise; if they fail altogether we have a psychosis or impulse-ridden character disorder.

Where "defense" refers to the person's unobservable mental activity, "resistance" denotes the consequences witnessable by the therapist — e.g., an abrupt shift in subject matter, blocking in associations, reaching for a cigarette, and so forth. The "confrontation," clarification, and eventual interpretation of resistance (and transference — itself, broadly speaking, an aspect of resistance) is the hallmark of psychoanalytic exploration and treatment.

This constellation of concepts is bedrock to the clinical analyst, for the bulk of his or her interventions help the patient identify and clarify resistance, its motivation, and the sources of the underlying dysphoria: "I notice every time we get to the topic of father you shift to mother." "You went from A to B to C to Z. What happened then?" "What occurs to you about this silence?" "You seemed hesitant as you commented on my new desk." In essence, the clinician seeks to uncover what, in the patient's mind, would be psychically and interpersonally dangerous about continuing a line of thought or unfolding a fantasy, experience, recollection, or encounter with self and other images.

Only as these *unconscious* anxieties and their wellsprings subside does the patient realize his or her misinterpretations and conflicting motivations, whence they arise, and how they have contributed to maladaptation and distress. Hence, enhanced consciousness of once repressed, and now secondarily defended, psychical content, and of defensively disrupted connections among conscious-preconscious representations, memories, and affects (i.e., "isolation"), is more the *effect* than the *cause* of therapeutic personality change — a point too little appreciated.

The concept of "defense mechanism" well exemplifies a psychoanalytic construct that is commonsensical and experience-near, yet extremely difficult to test in usual, atomizing experimental situations. It is true that experiments, such as those outlined by Kline (1981) and Silverman (1983), support the central defensive concept, repression — but only if one accepts certain key assumptions endorsed by the experimenters. Moreover, the vast bulk of quasi-experimental "tests" have been designed by those too little conversant with the analytic concepts and hypotheses under examination, yielding a mass of literature essentially worthless.

For the most part, the defense hypothesis derives credibility from parsimonious consistency with multiple lines of converging evidence — much as do those of the historian or paleontologist. The accumulation of countless treatment sequences, such as that below, are potentially of as much value as large "n" experiments. I say "potentially" because, in light of suggestion charges, such treatments must be audio- or videotaped. When this is done, analytic postdictive (regarding early constellations of psychical-actual reality inferred from behavioral patterns in recent and current life within and without the sessions) and predictive (concerning configurations of patient interpretation and interpersonal relations likely to arise in the analytic situation based on prior history) hypotheses can be substantiated or undermined through the patient's subsequent activity — giving the lie to Popper's (1965) famous charge of analytic non-falsifiability (Wallace, 1986a, in press a).

Ms. Z. lost her maternally nurturant grandmother and attentive father during her 12th year. There followed a history of neglect and emotional sadism at the hands of mother — in regard to which the patient recollected or expressed little affect other than painful conclusions that she was in some manner responsible for mother's behavior. Ms. Z. developed a one-day amnesia following the first session in which she experienced anger at mother, an affective-cognitive awareness coupled with her immediate recollection of her much earlier and fleeting fear that her own cold had precipitated mother's fatal pneumonia several years before. In the ensuing sessions Ms. Z. gradually remembered the events of the amnesic day (including those of the session). She did so via becoming aware of intense fears that talking about her mother might magically harm her even in death. Through this process she experienced powerful disappointment and anger vis-à-vis the mother, as well as an equally strong sense of guilt in reaction to this [Wallace, unpublished case material].

Only thorough knowledge of the patient's history and treatment context, an empathic grasp of "common-sense" psychology, and understanding of basic psychodynamics render plausible the notion that hitherto unconscious conflicts over rage at mother caused the amnesia. One inexperienced in analytic methodology as actually practiced, or at least with longitudinal videotapes of dynamic psychotherapy, could never appreciate its predictive value — sometimes literally anticipating, on the basis of history, prior sessions, and current context, the next association or recollection of the patient — and the unsuggested evidence motivating and supporting clinical hypotheses. If one will not use the telescope, one can deny both its worth and the craters on the moon. This, I have argued (Wallace, 1986a, in press a), is Grünbaum's key fallacy.

Section VI: Further Clinical and Theoretical Considerations

(A) ID-EGO-SUPEREGO

While there is some factor-analytic support for these organizations of mental functioning (see Kline, 1981), it is difficult to conceive of their rigorous extraclinical test. And yet without the notion that mind is in important respects fragmented, composed of suborganizations of identification, self-and "object" representation, feeling, interpretation, motivation, and activity, the clinician would be hard pressed to explain much that is encountered. And the notion that these organizations of functions engage in intrapsychic relations with one another (and with actual others in the outside world), and overdetermine conscious mental activity and observable behavior is clinically indispensible. Moreover, if one retranslates these terms into Freud's German originals one is left with much more phenomenological ones: "I (*Ich*)," "it (*Es*)," and "Above-I or I-Above (*Uberich*)."

While phenomenology at times suggests man's integration and unity, there are instances when every human experiences discontinuities in memory and will, intrusions of emotion and fantasy, the emergence of that in himself which he would sooner not face, dysphoric memories called up by associative contexts, or enacts behaviors which deeply trouble him but whose mainsprings he cannot discern. Freud aptly opined that his emphasis on man's psychical fragmentation, rather than the psychosexual theory, is the preponent source of antipathy to psychoanalysis. It may even account for the disbelief of many psychiatrists in multiple personality; exaggerated reports of frequency and iatrogenic factors notwithstanding, this syndrome represents the ultimate fragmentation into organized systems of motivation, perception, and action that Freud taught we all are. The proposition that these mental configurations are characterized by particular modes of functioning—e.g., primary and secondary process, pleasure versus reality principle (as illustrated preeminently in the contrast between dreaming and waking life)—is theoretically and clinically invaluable.

(B) LANGUAGE AND "OBJECT"-RELATIONS THEORY

The anthropologists-linguists Sapir and Whorf emphasized the incredible extent to which language shapes our vision of reality; how, e.g., Hopi categories of time and space yield radically non-Western perceptions of the world. Recent feminists alert us to the subtle discriminatory impact of purely masculine pronouns and gender-exclusionary metaphors (e.g., "soft" and "hard" science).

While many consider such points trivial, words indeed influence thinking, interpretation, and action. At best, much of the jargon of ego psychology and "object"-relations theory is bloodless and intellectualized, at worst dehumanizing. "Where is the patient?," one is tempted to ask.

Take "object," the shibboleth of the self-avowedly most humanistic school of psychoanalysis: there are obvious connotations in referring to a human being as an "object"—or declaring, as does Kohut, that all we relate to are "selfobjects." The former is dehumanizing and the latter both dehumanizing and solipsistic. Can one honestly deny that day-to-day usage of such terms affects habits of mind and even action? This is the strongest point behind those, such as Bettelheim (1982), who would recapture Freud's experiential, at times folksy and earthy, concepts, metaphors, and phrases.

Perhaps we can start by replacing "object" with "other." What is the meat of "object"-relations theory anyway? Is it really so abstruse or does it not primarily contend that there is an inner organization of affectively laden self-other images in a constant and mutually determinative relationship with actual others in the milieu—that there is lifelong oscillation between "internalized," "projected," and "reinternalized" images of motivated interpersonal relations in interaction with actual others themselves.

Likewise, it is important to recognize that, as Kernberg (1976) emphasizes, there is a linkage between self- and other-representations such that there is no distortion or affect related to the one that is not reflected in some disturbance and emotional coloring of the other. Limited to this spare formulation, important aspects of "object-relations" propositions are testable phenomenologically-clinically and, after the work of Blatt and associates (1983), perhaps extraclinically as well—e.g., concepts such as: the capacity for "empathy" with one's self-representation and the key role of incorporating the clinician's attitudes in promoting self-esteem; the domination by hostile, punitive, or even sadistic introjects, which must be projected and reacted to if the person will survive; projective identification as a significantly distorting and disruptive mechanism in interpersonal relations; and mental dialogue with the therapist's auditory-visual image as an intermediate role in the patient's "ego building." Of course, when using terms such as "projection" and "introjection," we refer to unconscious-preconscious mental representational activity and its experiential and behavioral manifestations, rather than to entities actually thrown outside or absorbed by the embodied individual him- or herself—a platitude all too often forgotten by hypostasizing clinicians and theoreticians.

The tenor of the patient's mental representation of the clinician, always to an important degree determined by the actual behavior of the analyst him- or herself, is a prime reason that interpretations alone, if not delivered in the appropriate interpersonal-intrapsychic matrix, may produce too much dysphoria for the patient to use them. The need for individualization of the analyst's contribution to this motivational-defensive-interpretive-affective matrix is why analysis cannot be "cookbooked" and interventions disembodied from the person who gives, receives, or evokes them. Failure to recognize and render explicit such factors is doubtless, as Thoma and Kächele (1986) imply, partly responsible for lack of an adequate theory of therapeutic change and for want of links between this and theories of pathogenesis and development.

Moreover, as Lichtenberg (1983) emphasizes, there is a fundamental, non-"instinctually" driven need for actual others in the lives of even the most infantile human beings. The search for "objects" or others does not merely lean upon and derive from hunger, sexuality, aggression, and other largely or partly constitutionally and neuroendocrinologically compelling strivings. This is exemplified in the behavior of a host of organisms other than man—e.g., a dog's desire to be with its master or even friendly strangers, quite independently of its need for a feeding hand. Stern (1985), for his part, casts doubt on theories denying infants primordial, somesthetic, and sensorimotor-based grasps of self and other. In addition, psychoanalytic developmental theory has emphasized separation-individuation at the expense of acknowledging man's embeddedness in, and need for, a world of others (see Schachtel, 1963).

Lastly, there is not, as is so unfortunately often maintained, a fundamental antithesis between the psychical reality orientation of "object"-relations theory, the interpersonal perspective of social psychiatry and the family-systems model, and the temperamental-interactional framework of Chess and Thomas (1984). To be sure, as analysts hold, psychical reality is the proximate governor of human behavior; but psychical reality is itself partly a function, by the principle of intersectional causation, of the behavior of actually existing (or the affectively-laden images of once actually existing) persons in the environment; likewise, the actions of others are to some degree a function of, and reaction to, the motivationally-interpretively driven behavior of the individual. Correlatively, as averred earlier, there is no psychical disturbance that does not manifest interpersonally, and vice versa.

(C) SELF PSYCHOLOGY

Within the last fifteen years a competing conception of mind has emerged within psychoanalysis—the self psychology of Heinz Kohut (1971, 1978, 1984). From a theory initially intended to illuminate the experience and psychical organization of narcissistic and borderline disorders, Kohut moved to universalistic pronouncements on human psychopathology and psychology in general. Kohut averred that self psychology is more experience-near than classical analytic theory, and phenomenological philosophers (e.g., Nissim-Sabat [1986]) agree.

Kohut charges that structural theory lacks a concept of self. Downplaying unconscious intrapsychic conflict, Kohut accents alleged deficiencies in the cohesion, integration, and *sense* of self. These reflect, he believes, actual weakness and fragmentation in self's underlying *structure*. The individual defends or overcompensates for the impotent self-organ with personal grandiosity or connection to idealized sources of power and self-esteem, lest he or she fragment into psychotic pieces.

Injuries to this organization, particularly by the analyst's lapses of empathy, produce narcissistic wounds to which the patient then reacts with rage, shame, depressive affect, grandiosity, or splendid isolation. Primarily through internalizing (i.e., constructing images of) the analyst's esteem and empathy, rather than analytic interpretation, the patient builds a stronger self-structure—as reflected in a more robust, less externally determined self-esteem and heightened creativity. Nevertheless, the analysand is doomed to relate to a quasi-solipsistic world of "selfobjects," though in a less demanding and controlling way than before. If, as originally intended (Kohut, 1971, 1978), Kohut had limited the "selfobject" concept to capturing narcissists' lack of emotional (more than cognitive—i.e., they are not psychotic) appreciation of the selfhood of the other and the extent to which they may never be able to treat others as ends in themselves, then I could have followed him. Instead, however, he (1984) came to propose it as a general theory of human psychical life and "relations."

In any event, Kohut's "self" remains, purposefully it seems, vaguely defined—referring both to one's phenomenology and image of self, as well as to its conjectured underlying determinative structure. In short, the individual's experience and evaluation of selfhood and its potency are not distinguished from the analyst's allegations in regard to the putative self-structure's strength and weakness. By contrast, many highly competent and otherwise well-adapted individuals may suffer from a sense of self-incompetence which their day-to-day relationships, performance, judgment, and reality testing constantly belie. To interpret that his or her very self-fabric is impotent could easily lower the patient's self-esteem, lead him or her to feel attacked, undermined, and generally unempathized with—and perhaps unwittingly induce an analytic self-fulfilling prophecy.

I see little of what Kohut wishes to address that is not already contained in the traditional concepts of "self" as a congeries of often conflicting, emotion-laden imaginal representations and of "ego" as an organization of functions that may become weakened or empowered, as the case may be. Kohut, by contrast, uses "self" to denote what most would call "personality structure," "mind," or "psychic apparatus." Moreover, many have underlined the similarity between his therapeutic approach and that of Carl Rogers, another contemporary Chicago-based theorist.

In short, from an initial (Kohut, 1971) concept fairly close to the ego psychologist's idea of "self" as a representation within the ego, Kohut (1978) moved to a notion of self as an alternative to the tripartite model of mind. To the last he never clarified the relation between self and id-ego-superego, implying that something akin to the complementarity interpretation of the wave-particle theory of light or the Copenhagen formulation of quantum mechanics applies.

While we may deplore such vagueness, Kohut might have argued that he was operating in the spirit of Freud himself, who often used everyday terminology in a deliberately ambiguous or even self-contradictory way, pleading that at certain stages in its theoretical development a discipline is entitled to do so. Indeed, one would prefer honest ambiguity to sham precision—particularly in the domain of shading, overdetermination, and ambiguity where the analyst works.

Still, it is equally misguided to despair of all logical analysis of "self" and "id-ego-supergo." If Kohut's theoretical innovation ultimately proves viable, then it may well be that a substantial degree of theoretical and clinico-empirical integration is possible. An adequate human psychology must address both the unity *and* the fragmentation of the psyche, both developmental deficiency *and* intrapsychic conflict. To appreciate that the center from which we feel, image, fantasize, interpret, will, and act is unconscious is to *enlarge,* not abrogate, a concept of self. And if the overwhelming evidence for the prepotency of unconscious self-determination and the multicenteredness of psychical life is so disconcerting that some must reinvent a pre-Freudian concept of self, then so be it.

Whatever one's evaluation of Kohut as logician and whether his "deficient parental empathy" theory of the childhood genesis of adult pathology is borne out, surely he has performed services for both clinicians and investigators by: emphasizing phenomenology; pointing to aspects of human experience and relationship hitherto largely ignored — e.g., the selfobject as an insufficiently acknowledged other treated as a source of esteem or potency that one cannot supply oneself — as opposed to being appreciated as a center of motivation and feeling in the other's own right; underlining, like Sullivan (1953), the crucial place of self-regard; stressing the role of empathy (i.e., appreciating the patient's experience, including aspects with which the analysand him- or herself is unable to empathize) through the analyst's attempt to imaginatively take the patient's vantage point and to "resonate" with the patient's emotional state; reminding us of the role of values, goals, and achievements in mental health; and pointing to the ambiguity inherent in the analytic situation and the caring and humanistic aspect of the analytic enterprise. Kohut has proferred another working model of mind for us to personally test in our difficult work.

(D) ADAPTATION

There has been a popular misequation of the psychoanalytic concept of "adaptation" with vulgar conformity or political subservience. Close reading of Heinz Hartmann (1964, pp. 59–60) shows that by "adaptation" he meant neither the above, nor simple biological survival or sheer dominance of self-interest and rationality (recall, for example, his applause of Kris's "regression in the service of the ego"). Adaptation, in its psychoanalytic sense, might best be comprehended as creative and productive engagement with reality (akin to Freud's *Arbeiten und Lieben*) — one optimally suitable for the deeply rooted needs, desires, and aims of self and cognizant of beloved and loving others and the human and nonhuman environments. Surely this blunts the edge of Michel Foucault's (1965) charge that psychoanalysis is primarily a secular heir to the power-hungry and conformity-compelling medieval Catholic church, with its confessional and moral theology the ancestor of allegedly "adjustment"-promoting free-association and analytic interpretation.

If one wants to relate psychoanalytic "adaptation" to its neo-Darwinian version — although it is doubtful that the two can be mapped wholly onto one another — Darwin's inclusion of sexual, alongside natural, selection may be a place to start. In fine, I suggest that sexual selection, as an important source of protoaesthetic variety in the animal kingdom, is the *ur*-mechanism of abundant living (arts, religion, and at least one dimension of the cultural and intellectual life in general).

Moreover, the concepts "autoplastic" and "alloplastic" convey that psychoanalytic "adaptation" means not simple "adjustment" to self and world as they actually are, but active attempts at self- and environmental-transformation. Adaptation not only permits creative action and altruism, but in extreme sociopolitical situations imprisonment or the sacrifice of life itself (e.g., Dietrich Bonhoeffer's courageous martyrdom in Nazi Germany and Martin Luther's refusal to recant in the face of Charles V's Catholic tribunal). Even biological evolutionists do not generally mean only "survival of the individual" by "survival of the fittest". And the most committed of them (e.g., Stephen J. Gould) seldom argue that natural selection correctly explains *all* human activity.

(E) WHO IS LACAN?

Beyond the scope and comprehension of this essay and author respectively are the controversial concepts and practices of the late Jacques Lacan (1973). Like many, I find his work meretricious, obscure, and more a mirror than an illuminator of primary-process mentation and psychoeconomics. To call his technique, as recounted by Lacan and others (e.g., Turkle, 1978; Schneiderman, 1980, 1983) investigationally-therapeutically questionable would be an understatement. Nevertheless, his emphasis on unconscious mentation and motivation, sapping of ego psychology's hypertrophic "ego," and introduction of linguistic-structural-cultural perspectives seemingly compatible with psychical causality and historical determinism, are salutary. Moreover, Anglo-American analysts must appreciate that Lacan operates out of a very different intellectual tradition.

The extent to which his ideas are cogent and integratable with "mainstream" analysis is yet to be determined. Smith (1983), Schneiderman (1980, 1983), Ragland-Sullivan (1987), Clément (1983), Turkle (1978), and Benvenuto and Kennedy (1986) offer informed and various interpretations and assessments of Lacan's writings and significance. In any event, we must familiarize ourselves with semiotic perspectives in order to gauge their relevance for theory, investigation, and practice.

Conclusion

Building on the work of Freud and recent theorists, this essay outlined a phenomenological, historical, interpersonal-psychical, and minimally theoretical psychoanalysis. There is nothing novel here; rather, it is a clearinghouse. It has sketched only those core concepts used by clinical and investigative analysts most of the time. Psychoanalysis has much to gain by trimming its theoretical superstructure to its basic clinico-empirical foundations. The case for drive and psychoeconomic theory is hardly open and shut. Semiquantitative tensional, energic, cathetic, and countercathetic constructs, however logically problematic, capture vital aspects of experience and appear theoretically and heuristically indispensable (i.e., the mixed discourse of semantics and energetics). Axioms and theorems pared to a minimum, we can then modify and elaborate them through interaction with clinical-historical-phenomenological, instrumental, longitudinal-observational, epidemiological, and sufficiently sophisticated experimental data. Moreover, we are advised to accept that certain analytic concepts and quasi-explanatory metaphors — such as parts of structural theory — may never be extraclinically supportable or falsifiable, though they are defensible on grounds of clinical and exploratory utility. Finally, we must practice the difficult double bookkeeping that values theorizing and interpretive engagement, without sacrificing the open, critical, and testing intelligence.

R E F E R E N C E S

Atwood, G. & Stolorow, R. (1984), *Structures of Subjectivity: An Essay on Psychoanalytic Phenomenology.* Hillsdale, NJ: The Analytic Press.
Bailey, C. & Chen, M. (1978), The morphological basis of long-term habitation and sensitization in aplysia. *Science,* 22:91–93.
Bartlett, F. (1939), The limitations of Freud. *Sci. & Soc.,* 3:64–105.
Becker, E. (1973), *The Denial of Death.* New York: Free Press.
Benvenuto, B. & Kennedy, R. (1986), *The Works of Lacan: An Introduction.* New York: St. Martins.
Bettelheim, B. (1982), *Freud and Man's Soul.* New York: Borzoi.
Blatt, S. & Lerner, H. (1983), Investigations in the psychoanalytic theory of object relations and object representations. In: *Empirical Studies of Psychoanalytic Theories,* ed. J. Masling. Hillsdale, NJ: The Analytic Press.
Boss, M. (1963), *Psychoanalysis and Daseinsanalysis,* trans. L. Lefebre. New York: Basic Books.
Brenner, C. (1976), *Psychoanalytic Technique and Psychic Conflict.* New York: International Universities Press.
_____ (1982), *The Mind in Conflict.* New York: International Universities Press.
Breuer, J. & Freud, S. (1895), Studies on hysteria. *Standard Edition,* 3. London: Hogarth Press, 1962.
Bunge, M. (197), *Causality and Modern Science.* 3d rev. ed. New York: Dover.
Chess, S. & Thomas, A. (1984), *The Origin and Evolution of Behavioral Disorders.* New York; Brunner/Mazel.
Chomsky, N. (1968), *Language and Mind.* New York: Harcourt, Brace & World.
Clement, C. (1983), *The Lives and Legends of Jacques Lacan,* trans. A. Goldhammer. New York: Columbia University Press.
Darwin, C. (1872), *The Expression of the Emotions in Man and Animals.* London: Murray.
Eagle, M. (1984), *Recent Developments in Psychoanalysis.* New York: McGraw-Hill.
Erikson, E. (1963), *Childhood and Society.* New York: Norton.

Fairbairn, W.R.D. (1952), *An Object Relations Theory of the Personality.* New York: International Universities Press.

Foucault, M. (1965), *Madness and Civilization.* New York: Vintage.

Freud, S. (1887-1902), *The Origins of Psychoanalysis: Letters, Drafts, and Notes to Wilhelm Fleiss,* ed. M. Bonaparte, A. Freud & E. Kris. New York: Basic Books, 1954.

_____ (1892-1893), A case of successful treatment by hypnosis. *Standard Edition,* 1:115-130. London: Hogarth Press, 1966.

_____ (1895), Project for a scientific psychology. *Standard Edition,* 1:295-397. London: Hogarth Press, 1966.

_____ (1896), The aetiology of hysteria. *Standard Edition,* 3:189-224. London: Hogarth Press, 1962.

_____ (1898), The psychical mechanism of forgetfulness. *Standard Edition,* 3:287-300. London: Hogarth Press, 1962.

_____ (1899), Screen memories. *Standard Edition,* 3:301-322. London: Hogarth Press, 1962.

_____ (1900), The interpretation of dreams. *Standard Edition,* 4/5. London: Hogarth Press, 1960.

_____ (1901a), The psychopathogy of everyday life. *Standard Edition,* 6. London: Hogarth Press, 1960.

_____ (1901b), Fragment of an analysis of a case of hysteria. *Standard Edition,* 7:3-124. London: Hogarth Press, 1960.

_____ (1905), Three essays on the theory of sexuality. *Standard Edition,* 7:125-248. London: Hogarth Press, 1953.

_____ (1909a), Analysis of a phobia in a five-year-old boy. *Standard Edition,* 10:3-152. London: Hogarth Press, 1955.

_____ (1909b), Notes upon a case of obsessional neurosis. *Standard Edition,* 10:153- London: Hogarth Press, 1955.

_____ (1909c), Five lectures on psycho-analysis. *Standard Edition,* 11:3-58. London: Hogarth Press, 1957.

_____ (1911a), Psycho-analytic notes on an autobiographical account of a case of paranoia. *Standard Edition,* 12:3-84. London: Hogarth Press, 1958.

_____ (1911b), Formulations on the two principles of mental functioning. *Standard Edition,* 12:213-236. London: Hogarth Press, 1958.

_____ (1913), Totem and taboo. *Standard Edition.* 13:1-164. London: Hogarth Press, 1958.

_____ (1915a), Instincts and their vicissitudes. *Standard Edition,* 14:111-140. London: Hogarth Press, 1957.

_____ (1915b), Repression. *Standard Edition,* 14:141-158. London: Hogarth Press, 1957.

_____ (1915c), The unconscious. *Standard Edition,* 14:159-218. London: Hogarth Press, 1957.

_____ (1915-1917), Introductory lectures on psycho-analysis. *Standard Edition,* 15 & 16. London: Hogarth Press, 1963.

_____ (1917), Mourning and melancholia. *Standard Edition,* 14:243-260. London: Hogarth Press, 1963.

_____ (1918), From the history of an infantile neurosis. *Standard Edition,* 17:3-124. London: Hogarth Press, 1955.

_____ (1920a), Beyond the pleasure principle. *Standard Edition,* 18:3-66. London: Hogarth Press, 1955.

_____ (1920b), The psychogenesis of a case of homosexuality in a woman. *Standard Edition,* 18:146-174. London: Hogarth Press, 1955.

_____ (1921), Group psychology and the analysis of the ego. *Standard Edition,* 18:67-145.

London: Hogarth Press, 1955.
_____ (1930), Civilization and its discontents. *Standard Edition*, 21:59–148. London: Hogarth Press, 1961.
_____ (1933), New introductory lectures on psycho-analysis. *Standard Edition*, 22:3–184. London: Hogarth Press, 1964.
_____ (1938), An outline of psycho-analysis. *Standard Edition*, 23:141–208. London: Hogarth Press, 1964.
Gill, M. (1976), Metapsychology is not psychology. In: *Psychology versus Metapsychology: Psychoanalytic Essays in Memory of George S. Klein [Psychological Issues*, monogr.36], ed. M. Gill & P. Holzman. New York: International Universities Press.
_____ (1982), *The Analysis of Transference*, vol. 1. New York: Internationsl Universities Press.
_____ & Holzman, P. (eds.) (1976), *Psychology versus Metapsychology: Psychoanalytic Essays in Memory of George S. Klein [Psychological Issues*. Monogr. 36], ed. M. Gill & P. Holtzman. New York: International Universities Press.
Goodall, J. (1971), *In the Shadow of Man.* New York: Houghton-Mifflin.
Greenson, R. (1967), *The Technique and Practice of Psychoanalysis.* New York: International University Press.
Grunbaum, A. (1984), A. (1984), *The Foundations of Psychoanlysis: A Philosophocal Critique.* Berkeley: University of California Press.
Guntrip, H. (1971), *Psychoanalytic Theory, Therapy, and the Self.* New York: Basic Books.
Hall, E. T. (1959), *The Silent Language.* New York: Doubleday.
Hartmann, H. (1927), Understanding and explanation. In: *Essays on Ego Psychology.* New York: International Universities Press, 1964.
_____ (1939), *Ego Psychology and the Problem of Adaptation.* New York: International Universities Press.
_____ (1960), *Psychoanalysis and Moral Values.* New York: International Universities Press.
_____ (1964), *Essays on Ego Psychology.* New York: International Universities Press.
_____ & Kris, E. (1945), The genetic approach in psychoanalysis. *The Psychoanalytic Study of the Child*, 1:11–30. New York: International Universities Press.
Holt, R. (1972), Freud's mechanistic and humanistic images of man. *Psychoanal. Contemp. Sci.*, 1:3–24.
_____ (1976), Drive or wish? A reconsideration of the psychoanalytic theory of motivation. In: *Psychology versus Metapsychology: Psychoanalytic Essays in Memory of George S. Klein [Psychological Issues.* monogr. 36], ed. M. Gill & P. Holzman. New York: International Universities Press.
Home, H. (1966), The concept of mind. *Internat. J. Psycho-Anal.*, 47:42–49.
Husserl, E. (1939), *The Crisis of European Sciences and Transcendental Phenomenology.* Evanston, IL: Northwestern University Press.
James, W. (1890), *Principles of Psychology.* 2 vols. New York: Henry Holt.
Kandel, R. (1978), *A Cell Biological Approach to Learning.* Bethesda, MD: Society for Neuroscience.
_____ (1983), From metapychology to molecular biology: Explorations into the nature of anxiety. *Amer. J. Psychiat.*, 140:1277–1295.
Kardiner, A. (1939), *The Individual and His Society.* New York: Columbia University Press.
Kernberg, O. (1975), *Borderline Conditions and Pathological Narcissism.* New York: Aronson.
Klein, G. S. (1976), *Psychoanalytic Theory.* New York: International Universities Press.
Kleinman, A. (1988), *Rethinking Psychiatry: From Cultural Category to Personal Experience.* New York: Basic Books.
Kline, P. (1981), *Fact and Fantasy in Freudian Theory*, rev. ed. London: Methuen.
Kohut, H. (1971), *The Analysis of the Self.* New York: International Universities Press.

—— (1978), *The Restoration of the Self*. New York: International Universities Press.

—— (1984), *How Does Analysis Cure?* Chicago: University of Chicago Press.

Lacan, J. (1973), *The Four Fundamental Concepts of Psychoanalysis,* trans. P. Sheridan. Hammondsworth, Eng.: Penguin, 1977.

Levinson, D. (1978), *Seasons of a Man's Life*. New York: Simon & Schuster.

Lévi-Strauss, C. (1963), *Structural Anthropology,* trans. C. Jacobsen & B. Grundfest. New York: Basic Books.

Lichtenberg, J. D. (1983), *Psychoanalysis and Infant Research*. Hillsdale, NJ: The Analytic Press.

Lifton, R. (1978), *The Broken Connection*. New York: Simon & Schuster.

Lithman, Y (1973), Feeling good and getting smashed. In: *The Pleasures of Anthropology,* ed. M. Freilich. New York: Mentor, 1987.

Luborsky, L. (1976), Measuring a pervasive psychic structure in psychotherapy: The core conflictual relationship theme. In: *Communicative Structures and Psychic Structures,* ed. N. Freedman & S. Grand. New York: Plenum.

—— Bachrach, H., Geraff, H., Pulver, S. & Christoph, P. (1979), Preconditions and consequences of transference interpretations: A clinical quantitative investigation. *J. Nerv. & Ment. Dis.,* 169:391–401.

Mandelbaum, M. (1977), *The Anatomy of Historical Knowledge*. Baltimore, MD: Johns Hopkins University Press.

Masson, J. (1985), *The Assault on Truth*. New York: Penguin.

May, R., Angel, E. & Ellenberger, H. (1958), *Existence*. New York: Basic Books.

Meyer, A. (1948), The psychobiological point of view. In: *The Commonsense Psychiatry of Adolf Meyer,* ed. A. Lieff. New York: McGraw-Hill, pp. 590–606.

Miller, A. (1986), *Thou Shalt Not Be Aware: Society's Betrayal of the Child*. New York: Meridan.

Nissim-Sabat, M. (1986), Psychoanalysis and phenomenology: A new synthesis. *Psychoanal. Rev.,* 73:437–458.

Novey, S. (1968), *The Second Look: The Reconstruction of Personal History in Psychiatry and Psychoanalysis*. Baltimore, MD: Johns Hopkins University Press.

Penfield, W. & Rasmussen, T. (1950), *The Cerebral Cortex in Man*. New York: Macmillan.

Peterfreund, E. (1983), *The Process of Psychoanalytic Therapy: Models and Strategies*. Hillsdale, NJ: The Analytic Press.

Piaget, J. (1929), *The Child's Conception of Physical Causality*. London: Routledge & Kegan Paul.

Popper, K. (1965), *Conjectures and Refutations: The Growth of Scientific Knowledge*. New York: Harper.

—— & Eccles, J. (1984), *The Self and Its Brain*. New York: Springer.

Ragland-Sullivan, E. (1987), *Jacques Lacan and the Philosophy of Psychoanalysis*. Chicago: University of Illinois Press.

Rapaport, D. (1960), On the psychoanalytic theory of motivation. In: *Nebraska Symposium on Motivation,* ed. M. Jones. Omaha: University of Nebraska Press.

Reiser, M. (1984), *Mind, Brain, Body*. New York: Basic Books.

Ricoeur, P. (1970), *Freud and Philosophy*. New Haven, CT: Yale University Press.

Sandler, J. & Rosenblatt, B. (1962), The concepts of the representational world. *The Psychoanalytic Study of the Child,* 17:128–145. New York: international Universities Press.

Schafer, R. (1976), *A New Language for Psychoanalysis*. New Haven: Yale University Press.

—— (1978), *Language and Insight*. New Haven, CT: Yale University Press.

Schneiderman, S. (1980), *Returning to Freud: Clinical Psychoanalysis in the School of Lacan*. New Haven, CT: Yale University Press.

_____ (1983), *Jacques Lacan: The Death of an Intellectual Hero.* New Haven, CT: Yale University Press.

Searle, J. (1983), *Intentionality: An Essay in the Philosophy of Mind.* Cambridge: Cambridge University Press.

Searles, H. (1960, *The Non-Human Environment in Schizophrenia and Human Development.* New York: International Universities Press.

Silverman, L. (1983), The subliminal psychodynamic activation method: Overview and comprehensive listing of studies. In: *Empirical Studies of Psychoanalysis,* vol. 1, ed. J. Masling. Hillsdale, NJ: The Analytic Press.

Smith, J. (ed.) (1983), *Interpreting Lacan: Psychiatry and The Humanities,* vol. 6. New Haven, CT: Yale University Press.

Spence, D. (1982), *Narrative Truth and Historical Truth: Meaning and Interpretation in Psychoanalysis.* New York: Norton.

Spitz, R. (1965), *The First Year of Life.* New York: International Universities Press.

Stern, D. (1985), *The Interpersonal World of the Infant.* New York: Basic Books.

Stone, L. (1961), *The Psychoanalytic Situation.* New York: International Universities Press.

Sullivan, H. S. (1950), The illusion of personal individuality. *Psychiat.,* 13:317–332.

Thoma, H. & Kachele, H. (1987), *Psychoanalytic Practice,* vol. 1. New York: Springer.

Thomas, A. & Chess, S. (1977), *Temperament and Development.* New York: Brunner/Mazel.

Turkle, S. (1978), *Psychoanalytic Politics: Freud's French Revolution.* New York: Basic Books.

Wallace, E. (1983a), *Dynamic Psychiatry in Theory and Practice.* Philadelphia: Lea & Febiger.

_____ (1983b), *Freud and Anthropology.* New York: International Universities Press.

_____ (1985), *Historiography and Causation in Psychoanalysis: An Essay on Psychoanalytic and Historical Epistemology.* Hillsdale, NJ: The Analytic Press.

_____ (1986a), The scientific status of psychoanalysis. *J. Nerv. & Ment. Dis.,* 17:379–386.

_____ (1986b), Determinism, possibility, and ethics. *J. Amer. Psychoanal. Assn.,* 34:933–974.

_____ (1986c), Freud as ethicist. In: *Freud: Appraisals and Reappraisals,* vol. 1, ed. P. Stepansky. Hillsdale, NJ: The Analytic Press.

_____ (1988a), Psychoanalytic causation revisited. *Psychiat. Forum,* 13:1–21.

_____ (1988b), Mind-body: Monistic dual-aspect interactionism. *J. Nerv. & Ment. Dis.,* 176:1–20.

_____ (1988c), What is truth?: Some philosophical, contributions to psychiatric issues. *Amer. J. Psychiat.,* 145:135–146.

_____ (in press a), Pitfalls of a one-sided vision of science: Adolf Grunbaum's foundations of psychoanalysis. *J. Amer. Psychoanal. Assn.*

_____ (in press b), Mind/body and the future of psychiatry. *J. Med. Philos.*

Weiner, H. (1977), *Psychobiology and Human Disease.* New York: Elsevier.

Weiss, J., Sampson, H. & the Mt. Zion Psychotherapy Research Group (1986), *The Psychoanalytic Process: Theory, Clinical Observational, and Empirical Research.* New York: Guilford.

Wisdom, J. O. (1984), What is left of psychoanalytic theory? *Internat. Rev. Psycho-Anal.,* 11:313–325.

Zetzel, E. (1956), Current concepts of transference. *Internat. J. Psycho-Anal.,* 37:369–376.

August 1987

II

APPLIED
PSYCHOANALYSIS

The Creative Relationship of Internal and External Determinants in the Life of an Artist

MAVIS L. WYLIE, Ph.D. (Washington, D.C.) and
HAROLD W. WYLIE, JR., M.D. (Washington, D.C.)

One widely accepted notion among musicians, writers, artists, and others involved with the arts is that psychiatric treatment interferes with creativity and short-circuits, if not permanently interrupts, the artist's connection to the source of his creativity. "Keine angst, keine kunst." No anxiety, no art.

We have become curious about the persistence of this notion, particularly as we have studied the art and writings of the Norwegian artist Edvard Munch (1863–1944). Cherishing the pain of psychic conflict for the inspiration it brought him, Munch wrote, "All art . . . must be brought forward with one's heart's blood" (Munch, *The Violet Book*, p. 29). "Life's anxiety is a necessity. Without anxiety and illness, I would have been like a ship without a rudder" (Schreiner, 1946, p. 21). We believe, however, that after a period of psychiatric treatment, which dramatically alleviated his torment, Munch experienced no reduction in creative power. Nonetheless, dispute continues about the effects of the psychiatric treatment on his art. The debate centers on the marked changes in Munch's work subsequent to an extended period of residential care.

Munch's advocates (Guenther, 1976; Stang, 1979; Eggum, 1982) claim, as did Munch himself, that after treatment the quality of his creativity remained unaffected. His critics (Messer, 1973; Neve, 1974; Schjeldahl, 1974; Werner, 1979; Heller, 1984) suggest that with the cure, Munch lost his artistic vigor. Messer, for example, states that when Munch was cured of "his illness — and of his tensions, paroxyms, hallucinations — he was also cured of his genius" (Messer, in Craft, 1977,

A version of this chapter was presented to the Denver Psychoanalytic Society, April 15, 1988.

73

p. 50). Neve (1974) and Werner (1979) similarly argue that Munch's creative vigor was the victim of psychiatry. It is our contention that the quality of Munch's creativity was not compromised by his hospitalization and that the supposition of dwindled artistry reflects a lack of familiarity with the content and style of his later works, most of which are to be found only in Oslo.

In this paper we will consider particular portions of Munch's history during what we have called the beginning (1880–1889), middle (1889–1908), and late (1908–1944) periods. We have hypothesized that during the eighteen years that constitute the middle period (1889–1908), the period for which Munch is best known, previously repressed drive derivatives found full expression in his imagery. Toward the end of this middle period, however, disruptive factors in his personal world contributed to the failure of his defensive structures, sapped his creative vigor, and contributed to his poor health. It was at this point that psychiatric treatment prevented Munch from sliding toward greater pathology. Munch was dramatically responsive to supportive psychiatric intervention. He altered his artistic focus and intent in a direction he pursued during the rest of his life.

Munch's history suggests that, in some cases, treatment that assists the ego in bolstering its defensive functions may enhance creativity by enabling the artist to distance himself from the anxiety and depressive affects that impinge on his artistic activity and personal life. Kubie's (1958) recommendation that psychoanalysis may be the best guarantee of continued creative activity applies only to those stable individuals demonstrating a reasonable capacity for sustained object relationships and a capacity to contain neurotic conflict. Although many artistically creative people seek therapeutic help in managing their pathological compromise formations (Brenner, 1982) at a point in their lives where they have become unable to prevent an erosion of their creative suppleness, they are frequently not suitable candidates for psychoanalytic treatment, but require a more supportive approach. In this sense, we believe Munch's late period (1908–1944) represents the triumph of just such an effective psychiatric intervention in the life of an artist.

Many diagnostic formulations have been suggested to explain Munch's illness. The repetitive traumatic events of his childhood provide clues for a range of hypotheses that includes insanity (Scharffenberg, 1895), schizophrenia (Steinberg and Weiss, 1954), depression (Digby, 1955), psychosis (Hodin, 1972), narcissistic personality disorder (Wylie and Wylie, 1980), unresolved grief reaction (Rieder, 1982), and borderline personality disorder (Warwick and Warwick, 1984). The focus of this paper, however, is Munch's Promethean resiliency, his capacity for recuperation and continued artistic creativity.

To this end we will examine two specific intervals of creative activity in Munch's life, both of which resulted in significant new directions in his work. Both intervals were marked by the coincidence of great personal upheaval and profound change in Munch's external environment. At each time, these internal (intrapsychic) and external (extrapsychic) determinants were drawn into and became part of the creative process, and the effect of their interaction was integrated into Munch's artistic products.

These two intervals occurred on either side of Munch's middle, or Expressionist, period and, in both cases, predicted the broader dramatic changes that appeared in his work several years later. In this respect, Munch's psychiatric treatment of 1908 was particularly important in helping him to consolidate artistic and recuperative shifts he had initiated five years prior to his hospitalization.

At this point, a brief review of the facts of Munch's history may be helpful. In 1863, Munch was born into a poor but very well-known Norwegian family of the highest social order—a family with many famous national figures among its ancestors. Following Munch's birth (he was the first son, second child), three more siblings came in swift order. His mother, ill with tuberculosis from the time of his birth,[1] died around the time of Munch's fifth birthday. His father a military physician, twenty years older than his wife, was often away from home on professional trips. In his absence, the children were raised by their mother's sister, Aunt Karen, who had come into the home a year before the death of Munch's mother to help run the household. An amateur artist herself, she nurtured Munch's early talent.

As a boy, Munch was sickly and frequently out of school. He was isolated from his peers and had few playmates with the exception of his beloved elder sister, Sophie, who was fifteen months older than he. At thirteen Munch experienced a near mortal encounter with tuberculosis, followed a year later by the unexpected death of Sophie from the same disease. The loss of this dear companion preserved in an unworked-through state the conflicted issues regarding the original maternal loss.

At sixteen Munch began formal training in art while still living at

---

[1]In all probability, Munch's mother died because she drowned from internal pulmonary hemorrhaging (Comstock, personal communication, 1983), rather than expiring because of external hemorrhaging—as previously assumed (Steinberg and Weiss, 1954; Wylie and Wylie, 1980).

home (*Workers at Dusk—1880/1881*), first as a student at the Royal School of Design and later under Christian Krohg (*Self Portrait—1881/1882* [Figure 1]). At twenty-five he won a sizable grant to study abroad and for the next eighteen years lived almost exclusively in France and Germany, unmarried and with no fixed residence. During this time, Munch associated himself primarily with the artists of Berlin, where, known as the "light from the north" (Eggum, personal communication, 1985), he became internationally regarded as one of the fathers of German Expressionism.

In 1908 Munch entered a psychiatric clinic in Copenhagen and was treated for what today we would call alcohol detoxification and rehabilitation. After his discharge, he returned to Norway to live in a very private way while continuing to exhibit extensively throughout the other Scandinavian countries and Europe. In this solitary, eccentric life, Munch remained productive until he died in 1944 at the age of eighty-one, still actively painting.

In examining the oeuvre of any artist, particularly an artist of Munch's stature, one traditionally attempts to conceptualize stylistic and content changes within an overall evolutionary framework. It is surprising therefore to find that the major shifts in Munch's work (early period [1880-1889], middle period [1889-1908], late period, [1908-1944]), do not seem to fall along one clear developmental line despite the fact that there are traceable thematic and iconographic motifs that run throughout the three periods.

For example, the artistic products of Munch's early and late periods bear sufficiently strong similarity to one another that, when viewed next to each other, the late period work can be seen as a natural maturation of the artistic talent evident during his early years. There is a shared commonality of mood and tone, an emphasis on descriptive and formal elements, the absence of psychological ambivalence in the subject, and the tendency of the artist, at both times, to engage the viewer in an unconflicted relationship.

There are also many parallels in the kind of life Munch led during both the early and late periods. For example, at both times Munch regarded his home as a refuge from the world of confusing, extrafamilial relationships. During his student years, the enormous importance of this milieu to Munch can be gauged by the fact that, despite its rigidly conservative, moral, religious orientation, he continued to live with his family until the age of twenty-five and regarded his aunt as the centrally admiring and admired presence in his life—the stable container of his feelings and mood (*Aunt Karen in her Rocking Chair—1884*). Munch's father, a very religious man, who, although described in some biographies of the artist as markedly eccentric, if not fanatically devout, preoccupied, and unavailable, was, in fact, a father who expressed a great deal of care about his son's welfare. He wrote the young Edvard letters of guidance and advice that reveal (*Family Letters*) a kindly and continuing interest in the boy (*Family Scene — 1885*). He was consistently supportive of his son's artistic efforts, albeit he expressed considerable embarrassment at its occasional "immodesty."

In a similar way, Munch maintained a stable, well-defined home (first at Kragero, later at Ekley) throughout the years of the late period; a home in which he felt he could find respite and seclusion from the world. It differed from the home of his childhood in that he was abundantly secure financially, and the core of his emotional support (formerly supplied by aunt and father) was now supplied by the loyalty of his patrons, the adulation of his critics, and above all by the adoration of his countrymen, whose hero Munch had become and who proved in the end to be the most enduring admirers of all.

Nevertheless, as he had done intermittently in the early perod, in the late period Munch also insulated himself from intimacy of any kind. As a student he had often withdrawn temporarily and assumed the role of silent observer; even as a member of the influential avant-garde, he persistently called himself "an outsider," "a Joseph." In the late period after his hospitalization, Munch retired to an extreme degree, avoiding all casual social contact. With ample opportunity to do otherwise, Munch affiliated with no stylistic school, belonged to no artistic coterie, retained few acquaintances (and those relationship that were maintained, he diluted by time and distance), suffered infrequent visits to his home, and preferred for the most part to limit his interactions to correspondence.

In contrast, a look at the turbulent middle period (1889–1908), which was cushioned on either side by these years of relative calm, reveals a life of highly conflicted relationships and pictures characterized by their violent evocation of feeling. One's impression of this work, in terms of style and psychological effect resembling neither the first period nor the last, is that it arrived "full blown" from some unique source. Its extraordinary impetus and thrust are perhaps best appreciated by realizing that, within barely two decades, Expressionism, largely propelled by Munch's work, erupted as the major art movement of its time. Its abrupt disappearance from the artist's oeuvre after 1908, as unexpected as its occurrence had been eighteen years earlier, begs for an answer.

What is especially puzzling is the relative brevity of this middle period, since it is by comparison to the radically different output of those nineteen years that the work of Munch's early period is called "promising" and that of the late period, "lacking." The explanation most often given, that its arrival was due to a burst of creative inspiration prompted by his father's death and its demise to the evaporation of passion following his hospitalization, is untenable. Such reasoning assumes that without psychiatric treatment, Munch would have continued working in the same Expressionist direction. It disregards the likeness between what preceded and what followed the middle period and concludes that because what came afterward "looked" and "felt" different from the Expressionist period (or put another way, was responded to differently by the viewer), the work was not as creative. More to the point, this kind of thinking overlooks the prophetic indications appearing in Munch's work and life well before the start of both the middle (Expressionist) and late periods which anticipated the subsequent major artistic transitions into these periods.

During these two intervals, Munch who was a prolific writer, recorded his thoughts, memories, daydreams, fantasies, and wishes in journals and letters. These permit us to draw inferences regarding the changing quality of Munch's identifications, transferences, and deployment of defenses. The value of considering such inferred unconscious factors when attempting to understand something of Munch's creative processes is suggested by Gray (1973), who pointed to the importance of attending to shifts in the analysand's verbalizations during the analytic hour as a means of gathering clues to underlying drive derivatives against whose expression the ego is defending itself.

We would add to this the ideas of Weissman (1966, 1967), who has argued that, in moments of heightened creative activity, a process of psychological dislocation occurs in which formerly accepted syntheses (of ideas, values, notions being "played with" during the creative process) become disarranged, desynthesized, and their previous organization no longer acceptable. In short, during the creative process, the "known" is released from the way in which it had been previously known, which makes way for a new order or synthesis to be created. As an important aspect of the disestablishment of the old order, previously repressed drive derivatives (wishes, fantasies, images) may emerge into consciousness. These add particular fire and color to the creative turmoil before they are either integrated as part of a new synthesis (and seen as part of the artistic product) or rerepressed. In essence, Weissman suggests that heightened creative activity operates like an earthquake that shifts continental plates, chaotically heaves materials up from deep below the surface, and produces a rearrangement of the topography.

We believe that with Munch one can observe these phenomena at the two times referred to that flanked the beginning and the end of the

Expressionist, or middle, period; times when the tumult of heightened creativity was amplified by unexpected disruptions in his external life circumstances and by the abrupt exacerbation of internal conflicts. This confluence produced the crucible in which his new artistic ideas and directions were formed. We might refer to these new changes (i.e., the alterations in his work and in his life) as examples of new compromise formations. That is, these metamorphoses reflected significant moderations in Munch's defensive structure, allowing him the greatest gratification of wishes with the least amount of depression and anxiety possible.

Between 1885 and 1886, four years prior to the start of the middle period, the first of the two intervals that we will discuss occurred. During this time, Munch produced three pictures of such shocking disquietude that they stand in contrast to all other works he painted during the early period. Today we can see that thematically, psychologically, stylistically, and in terms of content not experienced in Norway before, they predict later Expressionist directions. However, at the time, only his teacher, Christian Krohg, recognized their genius and prospective importance. Other contemporary critics rejected them across the board, although art historians since then have invariably referred to these three paintings as the "early masterpieces."[2] thus confirming the accuracy of Krohg's original assessment.

We think that by examining the circumstances of Munch's internal and external life at this time, we can shed light on factors that contributed to the production of these three works appearing, as they did, unanticipated in the midst other works executed strictly within the confines of current academic traditions (*Self Portrait—1881/1882* [Figure 1], *Morning—1884* [Fig. 2], *Sister Inger, Age 16—1884*).

In the years before the pictures were painted, Munch's delayed adolescent efforts to disengage from his family had become mired in an ambivalence that held him like quicksand. Studying with Christian Krohg, Munch had begun to meet regularly with a small group of student artists to discuss the meaning of art. Notwithstanding that this group has been characterized by Colditz as "Bohemians without eroticism" (Brenna, 1976a, p. 89), because they met in a church basement and eschewed the promiscuous life, their artistic ideas were radical and compelling. Like other radicals all over Europe (Freud in Vienna, Ibsen in Norway, Nietzche in Germany, Strindberg in Sweden), they sought introspectively

---

[2]Today, the most famous of the three pictures, *The Sick Child*, remains intact; the other two, *Puberty* and *The Day After*, were both lost to fire; one burned in a companion's studio, the other in a storehouse. For them, we have only Munch's later copies.

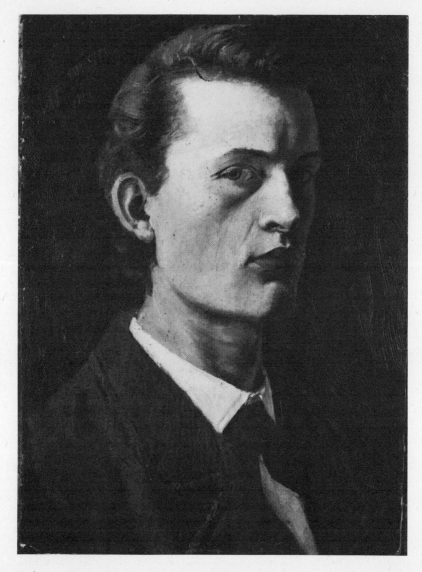

FIGURE 1.   *Self Portrait.* 1881/1882. Oil on plate, 25 × 18.5 cm [courtesy Munch Museum].

to understand meanings hidden beneath surface intentions. Their manifesto stated that to articulate one's suffering is to speak to the suffering of all; to explore the origins of one's emotions is to tap the very sources of one's art. These articles of belief, the antithesis of Munch's Lutheran

FIGURE 2.   *Morning, Girl at Bedside.* 1884. Oil on canvas, 96.5 × 103 cm [courtesy Rasmus Meyers].

family core, stirred his deepest sensibilities, ignited his emotions, excited the ranging of his imagination, and helped put back into gear the stalled process of separating from his family.

For example, Munch would argue late into the night with the Bohemians after first sharing prayers, Bible readings, and the evening meal with the family (and incidentally complying with the family rule of having no house key of his own). In short, although the Bohemians gave full voice to the radical side of Munch's struggles, he could not altogether forgo the nurturant supplies from home. The strength of this ambivalence was such that when his precocious talents were first publicly recognized, at nineteen, in the form of a state grant to study abroad for three weeks, Munch was not able to accept the award. Faced with conflict between going (the first such absence from home) and staying, he succumbed to illness and declined. By the following year, however, Munch had moved sufficiently toward separation to accept the reawarded grant, and at the age of twenty made the brief visit to the art capitals of Antwerp and Paris.

The shy, inhibited young student from bourgeoise Oslo found these cities to be a dizzying Byzantium. It was as if he were caught up in a gigantic carnival of visual and emotional sensations, artistic ideas, creative notions, seductions of free thought on every side, an anything-goes, promiscuous, laissez faire morality that, experienced in the absence of his home's protective girdle, shook him deeply. He came home disoriented both emotionally and artistically.

Directly upon his return, the jarring effects of this trip were intensified and exaggerated by Munch's first passionate infatuation; the object of his adoration was a beautiful married woman, Fru Heiberg, or Milly Thaulow, as she was popularly called among the avant-garde. Munch lamented that when she took his first kiss, he was thereafter unable to be apart from her or to remove her from his mind (Sand and Stabell, 1973). She completely bedeviled him by at once encouraging his attentions and flaunting her other amorous liaisons. He felt helplessly pinioned by her inconsistent, contradictory behaviors. Yet he found her flirtatiousness hypnotic, and he persisted in yearning for her despite the fact that she did not return his adoration and the ambiguity of their relationship affronted his desire for constancy and tenderness in a woman.

Milly Thaulow stirred desires in Munch that had been repressed during a childhood and adolescence in which there had been intense stimulation from living in close company with a houseful of females. However discreet their behavior, he was exposed to scenes that would ignite all measure of castration and voyeuristic concerns for a small boy: bathing and toileting scenes, nudity, menstrual cloths, and the sequelae of three sibling births. This stimulation had been held in check by a rigid denial of all sensuality, denial reinforced by the unconscious aggression associated with the loss and sense of abandonment caused by the deaths of his mother and beloved sister.

Munch's unsuccessful efforts to master the original traumas, as well as his unresolved oedipal issues, compelled him toward a painful repetition of these experiences; first with Milly, later with other women. It was surely more than coincidence that not only was Munch's first love considered by him to have looked, as had his mother, "especially beautiful in black," but she was also married to a military doctor, as his mother had been. The cruel and painful affects associated with Munch's current wounds pooled with the affects and memories of ancient traumas and were together caught up and combined with the creative processes producing the experimental works of 1885/1886.

The three early masterpieces suggest as much. In the *The Sick Child—1885/1886* (Fig. 3), for example, Munch had, by repeatedly scarifying the canvas surface with a palette knife, scraping off, relayering, scraping, and painting again, invented an entirely new style. He also presented Oslo with a picture unexpectedly startling in its sense of conflicted loneliness and its portrayal of the sick child's frailty, generating in the viewer a staggering sense of impotence that extends well beyond the simple elicitation of sympathy.

While such an image was not later unfamiliar to the Expressionist genre, nothing like it existed in 1886. For example, Munch's teacher,

FIGURE 3. *The Sick Child.* 1885/1886. Oil on canvas, 119.5 × 118.5 cm [courtesy National Gallery, Oslo].

Krohg, who had also painted a *Sick Child—1880/1881* (Fig. 4), presents a picture intended to evoke sympathy for its tubercular subject. By contrast, Munch's *Sick Child—1885/1886* forces the viewer to experience his own sense of aloneness in the child's isolation, and in the woman's hand that reaches out to clasp the child's but that (as if she had withdrawn it) remains unable to make contact (as if she were lost to her own sadness).

Both *Puberty—1885/1886* (Fig. 5) and *The Day After—1886* (Fig. 6) obtain their innovative power from the same capacity to render the viewer momentarily helpless by engaging the viewer's inner life with that of the artist/subject. Here the artist stirs in the viewer a sense of resignation before the immutability of the young girl's dysphoric sense of isolation in *Puberty—1885/1886* and the prostitute's depressive languor in *The Day After—1886*.

In the case of *Puberty—1885/1886,* traditionally said to depict a young girl's anxiety over her emerging sexuality, Munch has rendered the subject as if she were a dream figure. He shows us not only the girl, but also memories of ourselves awakening to the dangers of sexual intimacy. In the light of the anxious circumstances of Munch's own anxious initiation into love at this time and of his struggles to establish his masculine self-representation, the subject's gender becomes inconsequential, its ambiguity essential.

In *The Day After—1886,* the layered quality of a dream is again evident, and through the image of the young prostitute, the viewer experiences the sense of being shut out, rejected by the fickle contradiction of her weary invitational pose and her depressive unavailability. It is evident that Munch's enamored feelings for Milly Thaulow surely supplied the model for the beautiful young woman, just as the lassitude weighing her down fully suggests Munch's image of himself.

Despite the barrage of adverse criticism that threatened to swamp the reception of these three works at their first public exhibition in 1886, Munch's teacher, Christian Krohg, (as noted) lauded their innovative significance, hailed his student as "Norway's newest star," and rained praises on him. Given such admiring support from one of the most important artists in Norway and surely the most important influence on the young artist at that time, why did Munch then abandon this new experimental style almost immediately after the exhibition and return to painting in the same naturalistic vein as before their execution (*Inger on the Beach—1889*)?

One could argue that the unexpected "early masterpieces" were the products of an unfinished creative process, the completion of which would have to wait four more years. But this is not sufficient to explain

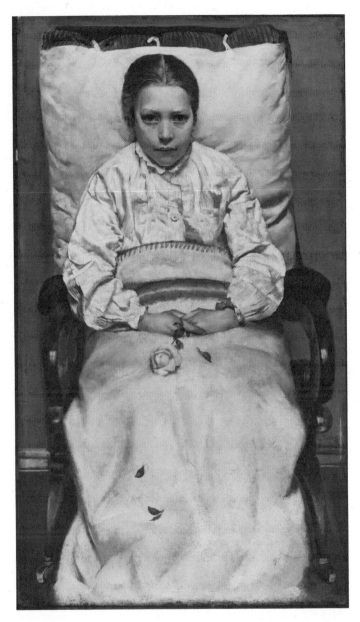

FIGURE 4.   *The Sick Girl,* by Christian Krohg. 1880/1881. Oil on canvas. [courtesy National Gallery, Oslo].

FIGURE 5.   *Puberty*. 1885/1886. Oil on canvas. 150 × 111 cm [courtesy Munch Museum].

FIGURE 6. *The Day After.* 1886. Oil on canvas, 150 × 111 cm [courtesy National Gallery, Oslo].

why, in effect, the blinds were drawn down so quickly and the shutters were closed tight on Munch's introspective innovations.

At this point it is useful to understand that, during this interval of intense creative embroilment, as Munch was coincidentally trying to negotiate his tortuous relationship with Milly Thaulow, attempting to integrate the pervasively dislocating and unsettling effects of his European trip, struggling to articulate in paint visions not yet clearly perceived, he came under the influence of the leading figure of the avant-garde, Hans Jaeger. An explosive, charismatic man, the most infamous Oslo Bohemian of the day, captain of the reknowned Christiania Boheme (at that time Oslo was still named "Christiania"), Hans Jaeger was like the Pied Piper leading Munch to explore the darker recesses of the soul and at the same time inviting his thinking and imagination to soar. The effect of all this on Munch seems to have been to allow previously repressed images, ideas, and feelings about death, separation, and loss to surface and enter his creative reservoir in the three paintings produced that year.

Jaeger, at thirty-two years, was an engaging, energetic, eccentric, iconoclastic figure. His magnetism bound together a widely diverse, egocentric, exhibitonistic, alienated, idiosyncratic, sometimes brilliant group of writers. Jaeger's novels were inflamatory, biting, seditious, and above all sexual. His first novel, confiscated the day after its publication because of its wild heresies and unheard-of perversions, was said to be "unscrupulously taking advantage of young people" (Brenna, 1976a, p. 98). The novel was a cornucopia of unrestrained, primitive, polymorphously perverse sexual fantasies. It is no small wonder that Munch wrote of it, "Never has a book made such an impression on me!" (Brenna, 1976a, p. 92). Alongside his Bible and a volume of Dostoevsky, Munch kept a copy of Jaeger's autobiographical novel, *From the Christiania Boheme,* in a prominent place on the shelf.

In contrast to Jaeger's flamboyancy, Munch perceived himself as awkward, unawakened, chaste. Bear in mind that he had come to his adolescence six or seven years earlier, a sickly overprotected youth, with little exposure to schoolmates who might have helped him ventilate the hothouse of his family relationships. He had passed through adolescence without mitigating the passion of these familial bonds or tempering a conscience so restrictive that his imagination was blind to the natural domains of adolescent curiosity. The crust of strict morality reinforced a repression of his adolescent sexuality.

Almost fifty years later, at the age of seventy, Munch offered a glimpse of the rigidity of that adolescent state in a recollection of the potent anxiety he had experienced when a serving girl living in the

Munch household became pregnant (Prestoe, 1946). At seventeen, the young Edvard had worried guiltily that perhaps he, by daydreaming of her so often, had impregnated the girl. From the vantage of old age, Munch marveled in a humorous and self-deprecating way how an adolescent might have been so naïve as to suppose his thoughts could impregnate the girl. Whereas one appreciates the young Munch's inability to differentiate the wish from the act, one also recognizes the old Munch's continued need to deny and isolate affect from content.

One appreciates, then, the enormity of Jaeger's impact on Munch, still very much an adolescent at the age of twenty-one, an impact encountered first through Jaeger's writings. These works seemed to have given Munch breathing room for his instinctual wishes by describing what a contemporary, Knut Hamsun (1890), called, "the sudden unnatural glimpse of inaccessible realms."

Upon meeting Jaeger in person, Munch found him to be as brilliant, incisive, and magnetic as his books. "His eyes shone. . . . He looked at me" (Brenna, 1976a, p. 10). As for Jaeger, he had been delighted to include in his group this "young and talented descendent of the best of the official families. . . . fetchingly good looking, but imbued with a sickliness which could be interpreted as a result of the establishment's destructive forces" (Brenna, 1976a, p 4). Within Jaeger's aura, Munch became like a soldier in battle whose bond with his officer allows him to perform deeds otherwise unthinkable. Munch's appropriation of the adored leader's permissive superego permitted him to contemplate what had previously been utterly forbidden, thereby allowing, as we have noted, earlier repudiated and forgotten images to enter the creative reservoir and to surface in his work.

At the same time, the quasi-insulting tone of Jaeger's attention to Munch (the compliments peppered with derision that permitted the worshipful young art student to admire Jaeger while maintaining his ardor and idealism at a safe distance) facilitated Munch's identificatory process with his mentor/aggressor as part of his continuing effort to separate from his family. We have speculated that long before becoming involved with Jaeger, Munch's very early wish for the preoedipal love of his father and his later oedipal struggles to cap the erotic wishes stimulated by a female-dominated household had led him to incorporate his father's restrictive superego as part of his own developing ego ideal, transforming it into a still more punitive conscience. Munch then directed this agency toward the repression of both the oedipally dangerous infantile sexual fantasies and much of the subsequent aggression associated with his mother's abandonment of him. The successful containment of these drive derivatives had powerfully inhibited Munch's emotional growth, a developmental arrest particularly felt during his adolescence.

With his attention drawn naturally to matters outside the family through association with Jaeger and the lingering aftereffects of his three-week sojourn in Paris, Munch began to regard his home life as claustrophobic. The more Munch saw of Jaeger, the more strongly the normal developmental push to disengage from incestuous objects became allied to this identification with a new ego ideal. The aggression that he formerly directed almost entirely toward himself (in the form of the stringent inhibition of his development), Munch now directed outward, most particularly toward his father. He not only thereby achieved some distance from the family, in an age-appropriate fashion, but also defended himself against his unconscious deep libidinal attachment to his father. The partial displacement of that attachment to Jaeger was a pattern Munch employed repeatedly throughout his adult life in the serial relationships formed with various strong charismatic male figures.

Within the home, Munch took to arguing vituperatively with his father. He increasingly chafed at this parent's controlling religiosity, which was intended, of course, to reinforce the very repressions being loosened. In view of Jaeger's nine commandments against "Christianity, Justice and Morality" (of which the following are typical), Dr Munch's objections to Jaeger are not surprising.

> Thou shalt write thine own life.
> Thou shalt sever thy family roots.
> Thou canst not treat thy family harshly enough.
> Thou shalt take thine own life [Stang, 1979, p 52].

Over his father's wishes, Munch more and more frequently substituted Bohemian gatherings at the cafe for attendance at church (Stang, 1979). He adopted Jaeger's proclivity for written self-examination. Since in the opinion of the Bohemians, writing had more to do with free expression of thought and the ranging of imagination than with requirements of literary style, Munch took this as license to explore the archives of his own traumatic childhood. And, like his model, he wrote voluminously, keeping extensive journals.

In the fall of 1886, as a measure of his attachment to Jaeger, Munch had attended the opening of Oslo's important annual art exhibition with him. As we have pointed out, this was the exhibition at which the three early masterpieces, the seminal works of the artist's later Expressionistic period, had their first public baptism. The significance of Munch's behavior in arriving with Jaeger at this particular "Autumn Show," as it was called, cannot be overestimated. That the artist had eschewed the company of his old teacher, and had come instead with his new mentor, was extraordinary given the longevity and strength of Krohg's influence on Munch, for up to this point, not only had Krohg's work provided the general model, but it had often determined the content, mood, and style of his student's work as well.

But it appears that, for Munch, the closeness in their work bore too many resemblances to the similarities of their lives. Krohg, like Munch, had lost his mother in childhood and a sister in adolescence. He, too, had been raised by a maiden aunt. Although Krohg had become a controversial figure in Oslo society because of his outspoken social views, he remained nevertheless, like Munch, a member of a highly respected family within that same Oslo society. However, as Munch experienced increasing restiveness in his father's company, he began to experience the relationship with his teacher in a similarly claustrophobic manner. The gradual detachment from Krohg, as from his own family, appeared inevitable as Munch's relationship with Jaeger grew stronger.

Ironically, the day after the exhibition, Jaeger wrote a review in the local newspaper first damning Munch with faint praise, complaining that the works were not "complete" (*Aftenposten,* October, 20, 1886), then admiring him with trenchant reservations ("What Munch presented. . . . is something that cannot be learned. What he has *not* accomplished is at least that which can be learned.") Of *The Sick Child—1885/1886* Jaeger wrote, "There is genius in the unfinished work. . . . but it doesn't achieve form truly enough." And finally, joining with the other critics in deriding Munch's "crudeness," he asserted, "The paint has run down the poor failed picture. . . . Munch, Munch, no more pictures like that!" Munch nevertheless persisted undeterred in his idealization of the man.

His response to Jaeger's critical arrows appears to have been to ally himself more firmly than ever with Jaeger. He turned his back on Christian Krohg's praise and mentorship (Krohg having showered Munch with superlatives), took Jaeger's advice, discarded the new experimental style Krohg had so admired, presented his teacher with *The Sick Child—1885/1886* at the close of the Autumn Show and took up painting again in the naturalistic romantic vein. Not, however, before painting one other picture for Jaeger.

The "other" picture (one that had "no paint falling down") was a sensual half-nude. *Hulda—1886,* which is now lost, was given to Jaeger to accompany him on a sixty-day jail sentence for indecency and blashemy. Jaeger's comments about *Hulda—1886* (the model for the later masterpiece, *Madonna—1894/1895,* [Fig. 7]) were once again blunt, critical, and

FIGURE 7.   *Madonna*. 1894–1895. Oil on canvas, 91 × 71 cm [courtesy National Gallery, Oslo].

only passingly complimentary. "No, she is unfinished. Munch never finishes anything. The throat and breast are fresh surely enough, but further down there is nothing" (Brenna, 1976a, p. 6).

After *Hulda,* Munch worked like a dervish for the next three years to learn "what he did not know." In Jaeger's image, he obsessively explored memories, feelings, thoughts associated with his traumatic past in writing; seeking in the roots of his emotions, the source of his art.

At the end of three years, by the age of twenty-five, Munch had produced a Herculean number of works, 110 in all. It was enough for the first one-man show ever arranged for a Norwegian artist (Dittmann, 1982, p. 39) (*Inger in the Sunshine — 1888, Military Band on Karl Johann Street — 1889,* [Fig. 8]).

This time the critics, far from dismissing Munch, were pleased to see traditional subjects so well rendered. The harshest critic of two and a half years before, Andreas Aubert, now acknowledged Munch as an artist of "promise" (*Dagbladet,* May 19, 1889). As a result, Munch gained suffi-

FIGURE 8.   *Military Band on Karl Johann Street.* 1884. Oil on canvas, 102 × 142 cm [courtesy Kunsthaus, Zurich].

cient support from those influential within academic circles to secure a substantial state grant for an extended period of study abroad.

In October 1889 — his head ringing with praise, ears full of Jaeger's radical notions (including Jaeger's recommendation that Munch should consider killing his father), supremely confident as a painter, seen as a promising traditionalist, essentially free of Milly Thaulow — Munch sailed for France with his father's blessing to study with Leon Bonnat.

Scarcely a month later, his father was dead of a stroke. It was shocking news, and, unlike the death of his mother, totally unexpected. His mother's death had been traumatic, in part because of the prolonged state of helplessness which a diagnosis of tuberculosis in the mid-1800s imposed upon a family, particularly on a young boy. The timing of his father's death, on the other hand, coinciding as it did with Munch's recent artistic triumph and recent demonstrations of late-adolescent rebellion, not only exaggerated all aspects of his oedipal guilt, but also overwhelmed him with grief. Munch had lost not only a father, but also the object of his powerful preoedipal paternal attachments, and the object of those maternal attachments he had displaced to his father upon his mother's death. At the same time, his father's death reawakened the unresolved sense of abandonment and grief over the death of mother and sister — a case of "old ghosts tasting fresh blood."

Munch responded to the stress in several ways. His constitutional vulnerability to pulmonary illness depressively worsened. Unable to contain his many conflicted feelings within a personality structure acutely dependent on narcissistic nourishment for stability and overly susceptible to its deprivation, he contracted bronchial pneumonia. In a brief period of hospitalization that followed, Munch reenacted the pattern that had characterized his childhood. He became ill, withdrew, was hospitalized and nursed back to health over the next several months, all the while still painting.

However, it is far more significant that powerful and marked as these tendencies of Munch's were toward somatic compliance, they diminish dramatically in stature when compared with the storm of activity that followed this illness. Out of that subsequent creative turmoil (which, in fact, represented a resumption and continuation of the extraordinary momentum first apparent in the three masterpieces of 1885/1886), there emerged a complete transformation of Munch's artistic intentions. As he plunged back into his work, he produced in this period of extended, driving creativity, a style and content that represented a brilliant artistic turning of passive into active. He also unconsciously, ingeniously, and persistently avoided the working-through process associated with mourning; for the intensity of the energy and focus given to midwifing this revolution effectively blocked Munch's need to confront his grief and protected him from an unmanageable sense of isolation upon his father's death.

(Ironically, it is compelling to realize that as Munch's revolution "fathered" modern German Expressionism, Munch, with an intransigence and adamance that lasted his entire lifetime, refused to accept the Norwegian tradition that he, as the eldest son, should, upon his father's death, assume his father's place.)

Inextricably joined to the radical artistic innovations that Munch had conceived of (and intimately associated with their effective implementation) were the equally dramatic realignments that Munch affected in his psychological priorities. First, by projecting responsibility for his father's death onto Jaeger and the Bohemians, he alleviated the surface aspects of his own guilt *(Munch's Father Crucified—1890)*. With Jaeger as his whipping boy (whom Munch pilloried for being "hard and irresponsible . . . my father's greatest sorrow" [*The Violet Book*]), the artist felt free to eulogize his once irascible parent as having been "soft as wax and with a great heart" (*Old Man Praying—1902*). This reparative idealization appeared to restore some balance to Munch's narcissistically depleted psyche.

Next, as rapidly as Munch had once accepted Jaeger's 1886 critical disparagement of *The Sick Child—1885/1886, Puberty—1885/1886,* and *The Day After—1886* (so instrumental in his decision to quit this direction), he now aggressively reclaimed its ownership. By incorporating elements of his current French studies with this experimental initiative, Munch was able to create a form and style flexible enough to accommodate his radical new intentions.

Concurrently, Munch defined a new purpose for his art. Articulating what was later known as "the St. Cloud manifesto," Munch announced that henceforth he would produce pictures only of "people who live, love and suffer" (Bang, 1963, p. 87); that "I will no longer produce pictures of women knitting. I will move the viewer."

This aggressive articulation set out verbally what the experimental pictures of 1885/1886 had stated visually: namely, that Munch intended to move the viewer and stir in him the same painful, resonant memories, feelings, fantasies of abandonment as his parents had stirred in him by dying. In this sense, he substituted the viewer for his parents as the objects in whom he would mobilize fear and anxiety. Rather than relinquish his lost objects through an adaptive process of mourning, Munch maintained his attachments to them intact and transformed his ambivalent feelings into the content, technique, and impact of his art.

For the next nineteen years Munch did just that. He essentially cathected his own artistic activity, substituting the creation of artistic products for the finding of satisfactory new objects and the establishment of viable relationships in his personal life. Those relationships that Munch did initiate failed almost without exception. Yet his incapacity to engage in a reciprocal loving relationship (explored elsewhere, Wylie and Wylie, 1980) did not inhibit Munch from expressing in potent artistic images the very conflicts that maimed his personal life.

Paradoxically, Munch drew heavily on the damned Jaeger's iconography to do this. However, far from simply appropriating Jaeger's metaphors to costume his own set of personal conflicts, Munch infused the Bohemian's jaded verbal images with the universal affects of his own traumatic past. He transformed what from Jaeger's pen had been essentially abreactive, quasi-pornographic theatricality into art. At the same time, by mapping his sublimatory route along the path first explored by this rebellious iconoclast so hated by his father, Munch permitted himself a measure of unconscious retaliation toward his father for his abandonment.

What kept Munch's use of Jaeger's imagery from being merely sensational, what truly elevated Munch's themes above the merely personal is that the viewer, who indeed feels assaulted by these pictures, also has the feeling of being understood. It is this "I have felt that way myself" sense that was uniquely Munch's contribution.

Four images recast from Jaeger demonstrate the point and illustrate those psychological factors we suspect lay within Munch that pressed him first to select and then to externalize through these themes, his own specific internal issues. This does not, of course, alter the fact that one could also accurately interpret Munch's choice of image within the context of historical artistic literary social influences (such as the iconoclasm of the times, the avant-garde's flirtation with themes of the unconscious and the psyche, and so on).

1. *The Scream — 1893* (Fig. 9): Together with its variations (*Evening on Karl Johan Street — 1893/1894, Anxiety — 1894*), *The Scream* owes much of its inheritance to a novel by Jaeger, *Prison and Despair,* part of a trilogy written in the popular autobiographical genre common among the Bohemians. The language of Munch's notes for the picture (on the back of the canvas) so closely resembles that of Jaeger's novel that we believe his book to have been the most direct influence on Munch despite the fact that "the cry through nature" was an avant-garde metaphor prevalent throughout northern Europe and familiar to all Bohemians. Of note is how Munch's image has vastly empowered the concept of mood projected onto the environment by evoking in the viewer a remembrance of the emotions that produce so fearsome a mood; terrors of abandonment, loneliness, desolation, annihilation.

FIGURE 9.   *The Scream.* 1893. Oil. casein, and pastel on cardboard, 91 × 74 cm [courtesy National Gallery, Oslo].

A lithograph, finished eight years later, called *Dead Mother and Child—1901* (Fig. 10), although similar to *The Scream,* demonstrates more clearly how Munch transformed his symbolic debt. One sees in the child's frantic gesture of hands to head that Munch has joined *The Scream's* signatory pose with his own despairing childhood memory. Going one step further, as the viewer studies the child's reaction to his mother's corpse, he finds himself not so much moved to sympathy as disturbed by an intrusive ambivalence toward the child, and, more disturbingly, toward himself. Even as the viewer identifies with the child's sorrow and bewilderment, he identifies with and is repelled by this small creature's strange appearance, which is, Munch shows us, how the abandoned one, child or adult, suffers the bitter assault of his own recognition that he is ultimately abandonable.

The state of utter isolation in the presence of death was repeated many times in a related group of pictures, in which Munch portrayed it as a self-imposed condition (*The Chamber of Death—1892* [Fig. 11], *Study for the Death Chamber—1892, Death in the Sick Room—1893, The Death Chamber—1896, At the Death Bed—1896*). These works are peopled by figures locked within themselves and rigidly constricted by their own private emotions. They seem to touch, but in fact make no contact (their backs so often

FIGURE 10. *Dead Mother and Child.* 1901. Etching with aquatint and drypoint [courtesy Munch Museum].

FIGURE 11.   *The Chamber of Death.* 1892. Oil on canvas, 89 × 66 cm
[courtesy National Gallery, Oslo].

turned to the viewer), unable to share their feelings, recalling the adult in
Munch's *Sick Child* whose hand hovers over, yet never touches the child's.

2. *The Vampire—1893* (Fig. 12): In another novel that Jaeger wrote five
years before the picture's execution (while Munch was still living in
Oslo), he had envisioned a double suicide with his lover Oda (whose
husband, Christian Krohg, was Munch's first art teacher). Jaeger
described, in a virtual blueprint for the picture, the scene of dying with
his head buried in Oda's lap, face pressed against her warm belly and
breasts. Munch took Jaeger's image of this relationship and drew from it,
the ambivalent conflict that feeds its depressive core, the attraction to and
fear of merger with another. That is, the wished-for seductive embrace of
fusion that is twinned to a terror of death by engulfment.

3. *Jealousy—1896* (Fig. 13): While it is obvious that Jaeger hardly

FIGURE 12.   *The Vampire.* 1893. Oil on canvas, 91 × 109 cm [courtesy Munch Museum].

invented the idea of inconstancy of the loved one (a perspective bitterly shared by most of the avant-garde), it was on Jaeger's description of the painful sequelae of love among the Bohemians (particularly *Sick Love*), that Munch had cut his first Expressionist "teeth" back in Oslo. In the many revisualizations that Munch made of this theme, one sees the cumulative legacy of the conflicts associated with the childhood losses of mother and sister. Although as we have noted, while the sequelae of these unresolved conficts continued to cripple Munch's personal relationships, his graphic portrayal of the same conflicts remained uninhibited. They fully depict his unremitting attraction to women, which was always paired in his mind with his agitated preoccupation about and expectation of their unfaithfulness.

4. *The Dance of Life—1899/1900* (Fig. 14): The central image here is based on Munch's first meeting with Jaeger at a masquerade ball in 1886. Munch had come dressed as a monk and Jaeger, pouncing upon the

FIGURE 13. *Jealously.* 1896. Oil on canvas, 67 × 100 cm [courtesy Rasmus Meyers].

similarity of the name "Munch" to "munk" (Norwegian for "monk"), used the pun to burlesque Munch's reserved manner among the promiscuous Bohemians. Over the years of their association, Jaeger spun out his jest with endless teasing at Munch's expense. In this picture, by expanding Jaeger's quip into a metaphor of larger dimensions, one suggesting the painful conflicted isolation underlying his sexual inhibition, Munch rescued the priestly image from the stereotyping that Jaeger's narrower Bohemian frame of reference had given it.

This sense of conflicted sexuality is suggested in many of Munch's portrayals of women during this middle period. On the one hand, it is suggested by the ambivalent mood and gesture that he has given his female subjects and/or by his androgenous rendering of them, and on the other hand, it seems confirmed by the viewer's mixed emotional reaction to these women, a mixed reaction that Munch orchestrates by extinguishing the observer's sexual fantasies, even as he arouses them. For example, looking at *The Voice—1893* (Fig. 15), the viewer is immediately drawn to the girl by the ingenuous, invitational way she has leaned her face and shoulders forward. In the same moment, the viewer is simultaneously thrust away from her, "put off" by the rigid manner in which she holds

FIGURE 14.   *The Dance of Life.* 1899/1900. Oil on canvas, 126 × 191 cm [courtesy National Gallery, Oslo].

her arms behind her back—with implications of an overly chaste restraint.

In another instance, *Death of Marat—1907* (Fig. 16), the androgeny of the woman is evident not so much because she lacks hips or an indication of a bosom, but because her face, throat, and breasts are flat and sexless. By contrast, in *Madonna—1894* (Fig. 7), the viewer is quickly attracted by the artist's implication of the subject's voluptuousness, only to be frustrated on inspection because, as Jaeger commented about his original version of the picture (*Hulda—1886*), one finds "nothing below the waist" (Jaeger, in Brenna, 1976b, p. 189). No curved hip, no belly, instead a lower torso so unsensual and unfemalelike that it is difficult to excuse it as "unfinished" or "sketched." Although there are some (Heller, 1978; Messer, 1973) who have called *Madonna* a picture of a woman at the height of sexual ecstasy, such interpretations seem to overlook the fact that, to paraphrase Jaeger again, the artist has deliberately truncated her sexuality below the waist. More significant than these differences among critics, however, is the fact that *Madonna* remains one of Munch's best-known and best-liked works. This speaks, we think, as much to the psychological resonance that the artist's ambivalence finds in the viewer,

FIGURE 15.   *The Voice*. 1893. Oil on canvas, 87.6 × 107 cm [courtesy Boston Museum of Fine Arts].

as to the viewer's appreciation of the finesse and skill of Munch's line and color.

As he worked on these images, Munch referred to them and their variations, as well as a number of others not discussed above, as components of a single opus called *The Frieze of Life*. Together they constitute a visual catalogue of affects, ideas, and sensations generated by the ambivalence conflicts with which Munch struggled in his personal relationships during this period.

Half a decade into the middle period, the expansive potentials suggested by graphic reproduction captured Munch's attention. Over the following five years he became absorbed in learning the various techniques of the unfamiliar media of drypoint, woodcut, etching, mezzoprint, each of which requires the artist to attack the surface with knife, stylus, or acid. The possibilities of multiple reproduction of a single image dovetailed with Munch's wish to expand the range of his influence, striking, so to speak, as many viewers as possible with a single blow (remember that for Munch one of his intentions was to "move" the

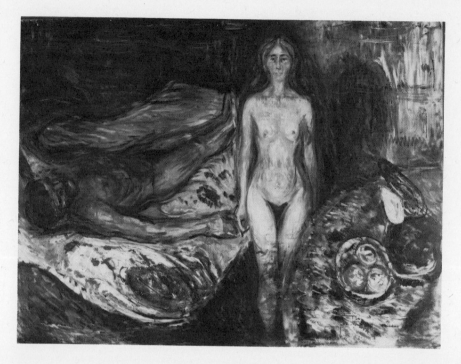

FIGURE 16. *The Death of Marat.* 1907. Oil on canvas, 150 × 199.5 cm
[courtesy Munch Museum].

viewer). They also allowed him to experiment with and, by the end of the
century, fully master permutations of color and line in a manner that
yielded maximum return for a minimum of wasted effort (*Vampire —
1894, Scream — 1895, The Lonely Ones — 1895, Death Chamber — 1896, Women
on the Beach — 1898, The Lonely Ones — 1899*).

Throughout these years of innovation and development of his Expressionistic style, one cannot overestimate the support that the sustained
intactness of his defenses gave to Munch's creative activity. Of these
defenses — repression, isolation, reaction formation, identification with
the aggressor — the last appears to have been the lynchpin. In his role as
l'enfant terrible, the artist who painted the unthinkable, the bête noir of
the critics, Munch was able with impunity to shock, assault, and destroy
rigid ideas of what was and was not artistically acceptable. As the role
gained Munch recognition and a certain amount of notoriety, it also
provided restorative sustenance for his narcissistically vulnerable personality.

For nearly a decade, between 1889 and 1899, Munch's work earned him a chronically indignant public and continuing castigation by critics. In addition to notoriety, the chastisement that he earned provided some relief from such guilt as attended Munch's unconscious identification with Jaeger. In this way his role as beleagured artist fit neatly with his conscience's need to see himself punished both for his father's death and for his unconscious identification with his father's nemesis.

By the turn of the century, however, as critical outrage shifted to critical interest, the efficacy of this defense came heavily under seige. He was no longer considered either the Peck's bad boy of painting, or the artistic underdog. So he began to substitute public misbehavior, disordered drinking, chronic problems with indebtedness (despite the fact that he was no longer poor) to gain attention. By these unruly behaviors he invited ad hominem the censure previously reserved for his "unforgivable" works.

Munch was not unconflicted about his intemperate behaviors, however. Yet he persisted in them. Even as he decried the harried pace of his life, expressed discontent with his transient living style, deplored the frustration and hopelessness of his personal relationships, and acknowledged as early as 1900 that alcohol was sure to poison him, Munch continued to conduct himself, despite rapidly accelerating critical approval and particularly when drunk, in an excessive and bellicose manner.

Concurrently, Munch grew restive and dissatisfied with certain aspects of his own work. Having superbly mastered the technique of graphic reproduction by the end of the 1890s, he now expressed concern that perhaps his art was not, in his words, "progressing" (Munch, *Diary Notes*). When his critics called for more of the same, Munch remarked angrily that they wanted him to walk backward "like the crawfish." He complained that his art was in danger of becoming mannered in content.

Here the puzzle that presents itself is, if indeed Munch felt he was not progressing creatively, why was he apparently unable to find within himself resources for creative renewal as when he extended his artistic options by learning graphic reproduction. Now, although Munch was self-critical and disapproving, his efforts lacked the gathered, focused thrust of earlier innovative shifts in artistic orientation.

Part of the explanation for this depressive plateau lies in the adverse joining of internal and external pressures at this crucial time. These pressures interacted in a circular fashion to inhibit Munch temporarily from the further growth of his creative activity. They not only delayed the emergence of the new ideas, but also weakened his network of defenses and contributed to the destabilization of his health.

We have pointed out that when Munch's work failed to provoke the expected antagonistic responses (thus suddenly depriving him of his power to offend, and of the cachet of negative "nourishment" that enhanced his sense of importance and helped him maintain psychological balance), his key defense, identification with the aggressor, began to falter. Aggression, no longer adequately bound, assumed the form of an anxious depression and turned, like the scorpion's self-stinging tail, back upon Munch as the object of its discharge. To mute this growing depression, Munch relied more and more heavily on alcohol. Only partially successful as an anesthetic, the alcohol succeeded in blunting Munch's creative acuity and increased his depressive outlook. The combination of a curtailed efficacy of creative effort and augmented depression left the artist exposed to his own sense of depletion and vulnerable to still further erosion of defenses.

In 1902, the painful rupture of a lengthy and difficult relationship with a beautiful, wealthy, possessive, and willful young woman from Oslo added a critical quantum of stress to the artist's overburdened ego. Unstable and frustrating though his peripatetic affair with Tulla Larson was, she had utterly preoccupied him for three years (*The Sin — 1901*). Yet his fear of the entanglements of marriage (despite his mesmerized attraction for her) was characteristic of Munch's emotional paralysis and his inability to engage in a reciprocal relationship. Munch's alcohol abuse, obsessive rumination, and rowdy behavior did not dull the mortification or temper the fury caused by her sadistic rejection of him — something which he repeatedly illustrated (*Death of Marat — 1907*). To frighten him, Tulla had feigned suicide, and Munch, in a rage over this fraud, had accidentally shot himself through the ring finger of his left hand.

At about the time that this cruel affair was terminating, Munch, made distraught by Tulla, disquieted by the praise (not the objections) of his former critics, drinking ever more heavily, met a man who, like Jaeger thirteen years before, became pivotal in the artist's life and work. If Jaeger had been the iconoclast who radicalized Munch, Dr. Max Linde (who soon became Munch's most important patron) was the first to assist him in regaining stability and to offer encouragement for substantially altering the orientation of his work. The course of Munch's relationship with this man (which lasted thirty-eight years, from the time of their first meeting in 1902 to Linde's death in 1940) reveals the way in which the pathologically regressive currents in the artist's internal life contended with the powerful and persistent forces in his creative life driving him toward continued productivity.

Dr. Max Linde was a foremost collector of Rodin (Epstein, 1983) who had, by the time he met Munch, already published a book about the artist, thus establishing, in Munch's mind, his specialness to Linde and Linde's to him. (It is of note that seventeen years before, Jaeger in a similar manner had also become first known to Munch through his writings.) The eventual closeness between Munch and Dr. Linde laid the groundwork for the later therapeutic relationship between Munch and his psychiatrist during his hospitalization of 1908.

In addition to being an owner, lover, and scholar of art, Linde lived and practiced opthalmology in the German city of Lubeck. He was a husband and father who maintained a tender interest in his children, an enduring devotion to his wife. By consistently retaining a strong measure of formality and distance in his connections with Munch, Linde appears to have helped contain the growth of the deadly, magnetic conflicts which had in the past contaminated all Munch's close relationships with both women and men. Whereas those earlier associations had foundered on the artist's stormy efforts at intimacy and his inability to manage the intensity of his dependency wishes, Linde maintained sufficient professional distance for Munch to tolerate his patron's interest, responsiveness, and direction with greater equanimity than he had been able to maintain in any relationship before. Certainly, Linde's attentiveness was conducted with infinitely more care than that of any female with whom Munch had been involved and certainly more than his history of relationships with men would indicate.

Heretofore, Munch's relationships with men had, with few exceptions, been intense and chaotic. Before Linde, there had been Hans Jaeger, the playwright Strindberg, the poet and medical student Stanislaus Przybyzewski, his first teacher Christian Krohg, all of whom were characteristically rebellious (if not always anarchistic), gifted, often brilliant, charismatic figures, noted neither for their compassion nor for their nurturant qualities. The history of Munch's involvement with each followed a similar course: overidealization, disappointment (as Munch found each to be inadequate and untrustworthy), followed by termination of the relationship (which, if not directly precipitated by Munch, almost always was certainly provoked by him), and then a lingering quasi-affectionate attachment to the memory of the individual. The latter was limited strictly to post hoc ruminations during which Munch would refer nostalgically and regretfully to these once-important characters.

In contrast, Munch's relationship with Linde gradually metamorphosed from a traditional patron/artist alliance, conducted primarily by mail, into a different kind of dyad. Linde came more and more to serve the artist in a kindly, supportive role: as financial counselor, worrier over Munch's poor health and alcohol dependence, critic, and adviser. And, as noted above, by importantly not forswearing the structured orientation of their relationship (though in a number of respects, he [Linde] had adopted many of the same platonic, caretaker roles Munch had sought to cultivate in Tulla Larson), Linde maintained the essential interpersonal distance in the relationship without which Munch could not have managed his dependent longings.

Without question it was important to Munch that, from the start of their relationship, Linde allied himself with the artist's ardent wish to restore his health and sense of well-being. Linde unequivocally and uncritically supported each of Munch's endeavors to control his "growing nervous disorder" and to curtail his worsening dependence on alcohol (Lindtke, 1974). Between 1902 and 1908, these attempts were many, inconsistent, diverse, and scattered. Nevertheless, Linde wrote Munch solicitous, supportive letters of kindly advice concerning his health, what food he should eat, the amount of milk he should drink, where and how he should live, much as Munch's father had done when Munch was a child. Linde wrote: "Drink a lot of milk, no alcohol. . . . The more quietly you live, the better" (Lindtke, 1974, July 22, 1905); "It makes me feel happier than anything to hear that you can work. . . . Peace and solitude and keeping away from the alcohol devils are like the elixir of life for your nerves. The big city is too much for you" (September 23, 1905); "Berlin is a dangerous place" (April 16, 1906).

By 1905, Munch was told that he showed signs of peripheral neuropathy and that alcohol would eventually kill him. The news frightened him badly, and, in hopes of curing himself, he took a number of lengthy vacations in the country and by the sea, each time abandoning Berlin and Paris completely. To Linde he wrote of the yearning he felt for the therapy of being by himself with nature. Excerpts from his letters, when compared with those above from Linde, reveal the concordance and compatibility of a relationship focused on Munch's health, work, and well-being. "If I could remain here (in the country) for a year alone, I could begin a new life" (June 2, 1905); "The cities make me quite kaput" (June 17, 1905); "Summer and peace away from my countrymen will restore me" (June 6, 1906).

The complicated interplay of Linde's varying artistic, pragmatic, empathic functions and the breadth and range of Linde's influence on Munch are suggested by the following example. In 1905, Linde commissioned Munch to paint a series of pictures for his children's new nursery. In outlining his wishes, Linde stated that " 'It would be best to choose something with a landscape, as landscapes are neutral and will also be understood by the children' " (Stang, 1979, p. 247). Although Linde refused purchase of the project when it was completed because it was not sufficiently "neutral" for his children's larger room, he soon afterward purchased another picture in its place (*Summer Night—1903*). While Munch's disappointment over Linde's rejection of the nursery murals did not appear to damage their relationship, it is of note that Munch's health began to deteriorate from this point on.

However, what is of greater significance is that Munch had in fact been more responsive to Linde's intructions vis-à-vis the nursery painting than might initially appear. At his patron's request, he had produced a work far milder (albeit not adequately so) than those characteristic of him during this period. Of still greater significance are the indications that Linde's advice to Munch that he should paint subjects neither "sensual nor frightening" seems to have partnered with Munch's own strong sub rosa interests in exploring precisely that. It was to this bond that Munch was clearly sentient two years later when, over the brief summer months of 1907 and 1908, his work moved in a direction that did not so much hark back, as take off from and expand upon this recommendation.

During the two summers of 1907 and 1908, Munch vacationed in the small town of Warnemunde on the Baltic coast. There he produced a series of pictures entirely different from his customary middle-period style. These were of male figures which, though nude, were distinctly "nonerotic" and not "frightening" (*Self Portrait on the Beach—1907, Men Bathing—1907* [Fig. 17]). They were nudes conveying a nobility, heroism, and virility, a nonsensual idealization of the human figure that had not appeared, to speak of, in Munch's work since 1889 before his father's death when Munch was still a pupil of Leon Bonnat.[3] Although the many portraits that Munch had been commissioned to paint during the middle period can, for the most part, be said each to depict the "fine figure of a man," none is truly heroic, none idealized (*Consul Christian Sandberg—1901, The Frenchman—1901, Gustav Schiefler—1905*). The summer figures of 1907 and 1908, however, were both idealized and heroic, and, we think, represented Munch's wishes for grandeur, optimism, vitality, and benign importance.

In the fall of both 1907 and 1908, however, Munch returned to drinking, occasional fighting as he had before, and painting (again, reworking such images as *Death of Marat—1905/1907* [Fig. 16]). His summer experiments were put aside, echoing, it would seem, the history of the first experimental efforts of 1885/1886. Like that earlier, anticipatory surfacing of change, which was later picked up by Munch in a more amplified and developed fashion, the essence of the Warnemunde

---

[3]Exceptions were the times that Munch painted and sketched children at various times throughout the middle period.

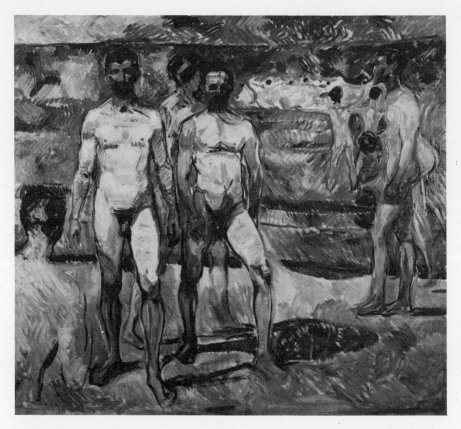

FIGURE 17.   *Men Bathing.* 1907. Oil on canvas, 206 × 227 cm [courtesy Munch Museum].

figures would also be picked up in an expanded form by Munch after his hospitalization.

Before that, however, Munch was hospitalized by his friend, the poet Emanuel Goldstein, at the private clinic of Dr. Daniel Jacobson in Copenhagen after a protracted binge in the fall of 1908. There, Munch was treated for an acute toxic psychosis precipitated by alcohol. Although the artist recovered from this critically ill state within two weeks, he remained at the clinic for nearly eight months more, on the advice of his psychiatrist.

It is universally agreed that following his hospitalization Munch's life and work altered dramatically. Thereafter, he lived a relatively abstemious existence, enjoyed good health (for the first time in his life), and produced art that was no longer intended like an arrow to pierce the viewer's soul. For the most part, critics and art historians have regarded these changes as the treatment's doing, so to speak. But the fact is that neither Jacobson nor the clinic "caused" the changes. Together they facilitated and consolidated processes Munch himself had begun half a decade earlier. What becomes grist for speculation is why and how these factors (Jacobson and the clinic), in concert, proved such uniquely effective psychological and artistic catalysts at this point in Munch's life.

Foremost among these factors is that Munch came to the hospital convinced he was dying. Second, it is particularly germaine that Munch was met and cared for by a physician who matched all the criteria of the artist's idealized parent: stern, authoritarian, respectful, deeply admiring of the artist, at once solicitous, distant, protective, and demanding. Jacobson was the doctor/parent Linde could only approximate.

Third, the combination of the crisis that precipitated Munch's hospitalization, his misperception that he was dying, and Dr. Jacobson's expression of absolute confidence that he could cure the artist offered Munch a dramatic revision of nearly identical traumatic events that had occurred long before at the beginning of his adolescence.

At thirteen, Munch had been terrified by a frightening episode of hemoptysis associated with his tuberculosis. He believed, as had his father, that he was moribund and that Dr. Munch was helpless to stop young Edvard's hemorrhaging. His father was incapable of comforting the boy, could only admonish his son to pray as he would soon be joining his mother in heaven. The cure, he said, lay not with man but with God. Although the young Munch survived, similar circumstances tragically repeated themselves ten months later, when Munch's beloved fifteen-year-old sister, Sophie, died suddenly from the ravages of the same disease. Dr. Munch was as unable to save her as he had been unable to save Edvard's mother eight years before.

It is not surprising, then, that in the Copenhagen of 1908 Dr. Jacobson's sure promise of health offered so compelling a contrast to the perceived limitations and failure of the artist's father that Munch at once became a candidate for what William James called a "conversion" (James, 1902, p. 163), or, perhaps more accurately, a candidate for reconversion. Over the next eight months at the clinic, Munch engaged in a reclamation of his adolescent ideals of temperance, uprightness, and asceticism through the person of Jacobson.

To find confirmation of Jacobson's impact on Munch, we need look no further than the idealized portrait Munch painted of this "savior" while at the clinic (*Dr Daniel Jacobson — 1908/1909* [Fig. 18]). It recapitulates the dyad of the admiring and the deeply admired — the caring parent,

FIGURE 18.   *Portrait of Dr. Daniel Jacobson.* 1908/1909. Oil on canvas, 204 × 112 cm [courtesy Munch Museum].

attendant to the needs of a special, precocious, talented, desperately ill child. Believing he would be restored to health following the advice of his psychiatrist, Munch adhered strictly to Jacobson's recommendations. He immediately (1) stopped drinking, (2) returned to work, (3) remained within the protected environment of the clinic.

Jacobson's unequivocal position — that if the artist wished to survive he would have to submit to deliberate physical and social isolation — substantively supported the direction of Munch's own efforts by siding with the mainstream of his conscious intent (Gillman, 1979). Jacobson's vigorous advocacy of this turn-of-the-century equivalent of the "self-insulating sanctuary" (Bush, in Niederland, 1976, p. 194) actualized the artist's longtime, but heretofore unsuccessful, effort to avoid the specific psychosocial stressors that had unmercifully exacerbated his anxiety. This makes it very understandable why Munch so readily accepted Jacobson's treatment recommendations. From the time of his childhood throughout his student, Bohemian, and German years, Munch had intermittently used isolated withdrawal to escape the turmoil of his life in the reparative hope of finding health and peace of mind.

By extending Munch's inpatient status at the hospital, Jacobson effected an environmental manipulation that created a structured, protected, and nurturant "work" milieu for the artist (Wylie and Wylie, 1980). In this sense, Jacobson acted as Munch's Thor (Roark, personal communication, 1987), protecting him against invasion by the trolls (i.e., drinking friends, bedeviling females, and his own attendant conflicts), so that he could arrange a manageable resolution of these conflicts. And indeed, while following Jacobson's orders to become directly, actively, and productively engaged (drawing, painting, photographing, writing, sketching animals at the zoo), Munch consolidated a major revision in the direction of his work and his life, which, like the shifting of the continental plates, again involved a fundamental upheaval of the artistic topography and psychological priorities.

Upon the completion of his illustrated prose-poem, *Alpha and Omega,* in 1908 (of which Eggum [1982] wrote, "Consciously or not, *Alpha and Omega* concludes Munch's intense concern with the struggle between the sexes . . . " [p. 41]), Munch embarked on what we have called the late period, a period characterized as much by the absence of the disquieting images of the middle period as by the presence of the buoyant motifs anticipated in the Warnemunde figures.

Without doubt the parallel creative processes (one artistic, the other psychological) that Munch engaged in directly after his perceived deathlike encounter with alcohol were extraordinarily like those with which Munch had been deeply involved just after his father's death. In that brief St. Cloud interval, as he was recuperating from pneumonia early in 1890, Munch effected a reordering of psychological and artistic priorities and introduced the middle period. In Copenhagen in 1908, the structured, caretaking milieu of the clinic provided a similar opportunity for the consolidation of artistic elements, the reconstitution of defenses temporarily lost during his decompensation, and a reassessment of life goals. By removing the seductions of alcohol and, as importantly, by allowing Munch to divest himself completely of the frustrating personal entanglements that had stirred his anxiety and depressive affects to so menacing a level, the way was cleared for a return into Munch's imagery of the libidinal drive derivatives of his maternal cathexis. These had been largely repressed during the middle period.

By maintaining a sanctuary of virtual isolation for himself after leaving the hospital (uninterrupted except for his trips to the Continent for exhibitions, the occasional company of visitors, and the intermittent care of housekeepers), and by avoiding insoluble conflicts with his environment, Munch was able to keep the utility of these newly reminted defenses intact. This guaranteed the fresh direction of his artistic activity.

Early in the student years (1880–1889), Munch's defensive structure had been powerfully buttressed by a rigid family structure. In particular, the defense of repression had importantly supported his efforts to contain disturbing drive derivatives. Although as we have noted, Munch eventually found the repressive demands of his family too claustrophobic, at that time, the very tightness of the family structure, by attending so gratifyingly to the arrested dependent/developmental needs of the admired exceptional eldest son, allowed Munch to idealize unambivalently the important objects in his life.

In the late period, support for repression of the negative side of Munch's unresolved ambivalence came not from family, but from the nearly impregnable, self-imposed isolation which he had selected for himself. On top of this, significant reinforcement came from a new and unexpected source, one that amply nourished his need for admiration and attention. Munch's relationship to the public and his critics underwent further stunning revisions as he suddenly became the hero of Norway. In December 1908, barely two months after his admission to the clinic, the Norwegian government dubbed Munch a Knight of St. Olaf and recognized him as one of the great artists of Norway. This established the artist among the heroes of his country, firmly within the honored tradition of his own family. As Dittman (1982) wrote, "Born into one of the most distinguished families of his nation, [Munch] counted among [his] early ancestors great landowners, high-ranking military officers, parish ministers of legendary standing, bishops, and in more recent times, Norway's first important portrait painter Jacob Munch, the nation's foremost historian Peter Andreas Munch, and Andreas a poet and dramatist whose works had inspired Ibsen" (p. 15).

When the National Gallery of Oslo hung five of Munch's major works as part of its permanent collection, the purchase gave Munch the enormous satisfaction of receiving yet another long-overdue honor. Four months later (March 15, 1909) his friend Jappe Nielson wrote to him, describing a third unprecedented achievement: a one-man show of Munch's work in Oslo greeted with such a massive popular acclaim that "the place [was] black with people!" (Bang, 1963, p. 59).

The continued outpouring of public respect and appreciation (in concert with Munch's isolation) provided an uncomplicated avenue of libidinal gratification which, for the rest of his life, he drew upon as the wellspring of his creative activity. Directly upon leaving the hospital, supported by Dr. Jacobson's affirmation and his country's adulation, Munch began work upon designs for the heroic university murals depicting the mythical origins of Norway. In this way, Munch realigned himself with his early ideals of childhood and adolescence and set for himself the goal of winning permanent acknowledgment as Norway's foremost artist.

Munch's new relationship with the public involved a fundamental revision of his perception of the viewer. Whereas during the middle period Munch had made his public the recipient of aggressive drive derivatives (doing to the viewer what he felt had been done to himself), Munch now bathed the viewer in the warmth of the idealizations of which Munch was currently (from his public) and historically (from mother/father/aunt) the recipient. In short, he made the viewer the object of the positive side of his infantile attachments.

So long as Munch kept this mirroring viewer at a distance, impersonal and unscrutinized, he experienced its admiration without the threat of disenchantment, demand, or the conflict of personal entanglement. As a result, throughout the late period, Munch's sense of reward remained untarnished, his sense of satisfaction essentially untainted. In this sense, Kris's (1955) observation that "The choice of sublimation is most successful when this activity at the same time represents a bond with the love object" (p. 40) applies equally as well to Munch's late as to his early period.

Not for a moment, however, is this to suggest that on an individual basis Munch was capable (any more than he had been in the middle period) of reciprocating the viewer's unstinting admiration with similar personal grace. Respect, fame, good health, and the divestiture of unpleasant personal ensnarements had not made Munch any more sanguine. On the contrary, despite being described as a man of occasional great charm (Gierloff, 1946), it appears that Munch far more commonly took a perverse pleasure in speaking sardonically about the very public whose attention he claimed to abhor, but without whose interest he would have perished. While barely concealing his pride in his new celebrity status, he depicted individuals as burdensome, interfering, and time-consuming. In 1910 he wrote to Jappe Nielson, "The telephone's been busy all morning because of these highly unpleasant people who want to force my pictures from me with the help of Mammon" (Bang, 1963, pp. 85–86).

In reality, the pain of the critics' original rejection of him during the middle years was never fully out of mind during the late years. As one of his more knowledgeable acquaintances put it in his recollection of Munch, "All the admiration of later years soothed the wounds, but never healed them and they kept breaking open" (Schreiner, 1946, p. 26). Munch seems to have kept his outsized sense of injury under control, however, on the one hand by registering his many thoughts on the subject in his correspondence with family members and old friends, and in his diaries, and on the other hand by referring to it often enough to his occasional visitors. He could be eloquent, "A young German once said they [the Germans] wished to carry me on their shields. . . . The Norwegians squeezed [me] between their shields" (Schreiner, 1946, p. 27), or rancorous, "Do not step on my spiritual corns — then you know the poison fangs will come out" (p. 13).

Unlike those with whom Munch had futilely attempted relationships in the middle period, the individuals who knew him and had contact with him during this late period appear to have been uniformly tolerant of his complaints, undemanding in their expectations. Those who weren't, were not asked back (or, like Munch's neighbors, were left to deal with his unpredictable, fitful, eccentric nature as best they could). Acquaintances invited to return, like his personal physician, Schreiner, riding out periodically from Oslo simply to visit with the artist, seem to have been fascinated and a little in awe of Munch. They were careful to learn to read the artist accurately, observant of when to speak, when not to ask too much about his work. In brief, they remembered to be cautious and follow Munch's often erratic, always egocentric lead. Their record of conversations with the artist make it clear how closely their accepting, undemanding, admiring stance resembled the soothing, patient, responsive nature of the "absorbent" good-enough maternal object.

Given the worried, frequently bitter nature of his ruminations, the general optimism of Munch's works throughout the late period may appear almost paradoxical. Nevertheless, the comprehensive, long-lasting, and all-pervading changes that characterize the content and orientation of the late period are also an accurate reflection of substantive and fundamental intrapsychic shifts which Munch negotiated at Jacobson's clinic. A full measure of this can be quintessentially observed in Munch's altered handling of the female form.

Although from the beginning of his artistic life Munch had regularly produced prints, sketches, paintings of nude females that were full and sensual ([*Reclining Nude — 1896* [charcoal], *Seated Model — 1906* [charcoal, pencil, watercolor), *Standing Nude — 1900* [tempera, colored chalk, charcoal]), the fact that during the middle period he far more often chose the equivocal androgenous nude female form (*Jealousy — 1896* [Fig. 13], *Madonna — 1894* [Fig. 7], *The Three Stages of Woman — 1894*) suggests that he unconsciously found it a more precise expression of his conflicted feelings at that time. However, after 1908, once he was encastled within his protected environment, liaisons and distressful companions dispensed with, his aggressive cathexes to women repressed, Munch proceeded to portray the female form qua female — not female qua harpy or vampire.

As a result, the nudes of Munch's late period are not only clearly womanly, they appear consistently and voluptuously available. They invariably invite the eye's caress. In *Female Nude, Anna — 1920* (Fig. 19), *Standing Nude — 1920,* and *Kneeling Female Nude Crying — 1919* (Fig. 20), for example, one repeatedly marvels at the smooth and luminous quality of the model's skin, its luster reminiscent of Renoir's captivating nudes. Their likeness derives less, we think, from similarity in painting style than from the obvious delight both artists took in looking at and admiring, activities they invite the viewer to share.

His visual pleasures notwithstanding, Munch remained true to the abstinent end of his creative bargain, and throughout the thirty-six years of the late period avoided the toxic effects of any lingering affair or passionate infatuation with housekeeper and/or model. Of his changed perception of his relationship to women Munch wrote:

Women I will let remain in heaven as the old Italian artists [did] — The thorns of the roses are too nasty — I am beginning to feel the enjoyment of women as flowers — [But] smell the flowers aroma and admire the beautiful petals without leafing through them, then. . . .one won't be disappointed [Bang, 1963, p. 34].

Coincident with his having assumed a state of emotional celibacy, Munch's center-stage interest in the psychological mood of the subject sharply diminished. Nineteen years before, in 1889, Munch had announced that his goal was to "illustrate mankind's joys and sorrows [seen]

FIGURE 19.   *Female Nude, Anna.* 1920. Oil on canvas, 59″ × 41 3/4″ [courtesy Sarah Campbell Blaffer Foundation].

FIGURE 20. *Kneeling Female Nude, Crying.* Oil on canvas, 39 1/2″ × 47 1/4″ [courtesy Sarah Campbell Blaffer Foundation].

at close quarters" (Langaard and Revold, 1961, p. 84), "Just as Leonardo da Vinci studied human anatomy and dissected corpses, so I try to dissect souls" (Stang, 1979, p. 111). Now in the late period, he stated he would present the powerful forces of the elements, and portray man apart from himself, as part of nature. He thereby exchanged the close inspection of his soul and the scrutiny of personal agony to embrace an idealized view of nature of which man is only one aspect.

This is articulated as directly and clearly in Munch's splendid mural, *The Sun—1909/1914* (Fig. 21), as in any other single piece. Of this work, part of the great university-murals, much has been written. Suffice to note that its explosion of color and its optimistic aura leave the viewer glowing with pleasure and energy, and comprise as surprising a change from the middle period as *The Sick Child—1885/1886* did from its predecessors in the early period.

The majority of works of the late period generate a similar energetic

FIGURE 21.   *The Sun.* 1912. Oil on canvas, 163 × 205.5 cm [courtesy Munch Museum].

responsiveness in the viewer, evoking a very different quality of tension than do the works of the middle period. The passion with which Munch had before so persistently rendered conflicted issues he now directed with equal energy and conviction to questions of form, color, and composition. As a result, the viewer who looks at the works of the late period finds himself caught up by the visual excitement of the artist, his unconflicted response consonant with the artist's intense interest in the compelling dynamics of color, form, and composition.

This is a very different perspective from that of the viewer of middle period works who repeatedly recognizes hidden and disturbing aspects of himself in his identification with the artist's (and subject's) feelings. Yet the viewer experiences the sense, even as he sees these externalized conflicts "painted with the artist's own heart-blood" (Munch, in Eggum, 1984, p. 9), that he has been empathically understood.

It is this difference in viewer response that has been interpreted by some later critics as evidence of the passion "lost" in the course of Munch's hospitalization. Yet Munch's writings make it clear that, despite changes of direction and manner in which he wished to stir the viewer, he continued to regard moving the viewer as the primary function of his art. In 1925 he wrote,

> "By painting the colors and lines and shapes I had seen in moments of emotion . . . I tried once again as on a gramaphone to re-awaken the vibrant emotions [in the viewer] [Langaard and Revold, 1961, p. 85].

In this sense it seems he perspicaciously anticipated Ernst Kris (1953) who wrote three decades later:

> The reaction of the public repeats in reversed order and in infinite variations some of the processes which the artist experienced . . . they are all changes involving movement of the audience from passivity to activity. . . . [so] in the end, the audience may experience some of the excitement and some of the release of tension which arises when barriers separating unconscious from preconscious or conscious are loosened [p. 486].

Munch's ability to stimulate such activity without recourse to his Expressionistic iconography speaks to the astonishing flexibility and power of his work after the hospitalization. A brief consideration of Munch's handling of color in this late period provides some insight regarding his altered psychological perspective, as well as some appreciation of the way in which Munch generated excitement in the viewer.

During the middle years Munch had characteristically externalized in his pictures the affects that he could not satisfactorily organize within himself or manage in his interpersonal relationships. By turning passive into active, he had been able, with a high degree of efficacy, to mobilize those same out-of-control affects in his viewers. Over and beyond executing this through his remarkable expressionistic vocabulary, Munch had underwritten the impact of these images principally through a brilliant strategy of color and line. In *Dance of Life—1899/1900* (Fig. 14) for example, Munch focused the viewer's attention on the psychological alienation of his dancers by isolating each of the figures within a single strong color, then segregating each unto itself with a distinct black outline. As a result, Munch forces both a visual and an affectual identification with the quarantined state of each figure.

Munch's emphasis on the contrast, rather than on the resonance, of his colors was singularly congruent with his tendency during the middle period to perceive relationships as either all good or all bad, and to alternate, rather than to integrate, such perceptions. His unceasing struggle with such differing emotions found its analogue in this strong proclivity for colors whose values did not so much interact as strike their lightnesses and darknesses against each other. There are, of course, exceptions to Munch's preference for this; the portraits of children, *Summer in the Park—1903/1904* (part of the *Linde Frieze*), *Summer Night—1903*, and others. However, by comparison, even the briefest survey of the late period landscapes informs one of the altered importance Munch now gave to colors which can speak to one another across an entire canvas (Vogt, personal communication, 1986) (*Bathing Man—1918* [Fig. 22], *Man in a Cabbage Field—1916* [Fig. 23], *Waves Beating Against the Rocks—1916*, *Starry Night—1923/1924*, *Galloping Horse—1910*, *Winter in Kragero—1912*, *The Wave—1921* [Fig. 24].

As Munch turned his attention from the issues and dilemmas within his own internal landscape (i.e., within the subject) to pictorial questions of color and form, he took his viewers with him. That is, from the beginning of the late period he "stood together with the viewer outside the picture's frame" (Rasmussen, personal communication, 1986) to look at and react to surface events of the canvas with an emotional distance that did not exist (for either artist or viewer) in the middle period. This was a perspective Munch maintained for the rest of his life.

FIGURE 22.   *Bathing Man*. 1918. Oil on canvas. 138 × 199.5 cm [courtesy Munch Museum].

FIGURE 23. *The Man in the Cabbage Field.* 1916. Oil on canvas, 136 × 181 cm [courtesy National Gallery, Oslo].

If one takes color as a reliable litmus of affect, one can see that, concurrently with his ensured isolation and the restoration of his defenses, Munch altered the spectrum of his palette. From 1909 onward, he lightened, brightened, mixed, and blended his colors, creating virtual tapestries of hue. He repeatedly directed the viewer's attention to consider color as color in its own right, rather than to regard it as the handmaiden of form and line (the ancillary uses to which Munch had previously assigned it). Even as he continued to guard vigilantly against any kind of personal emotional involvement, Munch explored the delicate nuances and interactive subtleties of color patterns. As he did so, he ignored the notion of precisely defined boundaries with which he had once maintained the isolation of his subjects. Instead he became concerned with integrating figures intimately with their environments (*Bathing Man — 1918* [Fig. 22]). During the first two decades after he had left the hospital (1908–1928) Munch was particularly interested in how these color patterns might be played contrapuntally across the spatial and

FIGURE 24.   *The Wave.* 1921. Oil on canvas, 100 × 120 cm [courtesy Munch Museum].

figural relationships already established in a picture (*Man in a Cabbage Field—1916* [Fig. 23]). The result was a knitting of background to foreground as he led the viewer's eye a merry kinetic chase across the picture's surface.

The enduring nature of the intrapsychic shifts, which we hypothesized underlay Munch's transition into, and sustained his creativity during the late period, can be assessed by considering a picture that Munch completed close to the end of his life. Painted two years before his death, *Between the Clock and the Bed—1942* (Fig. 25) is his last full self-portrait. At seventy-nine, his creative vitality undiminished, Munch was still capable of impelling his viewer to be intrigued as he was intrigued, to see as he saw, to respond to what he thought important, and to be outraged by what outraged him—namely, the paradox with which age had confronted him, a puzzle that Munch considered not so much cruel, as unfathomable.

FIGURE 25. *Between Clock and Bed. Self Portrait.* Oil on canvas, 149.5 ×
120.5 cm [courtesy Munch Museum].

Showing us the contrast and ironic contradiction of his body's physical
frailty (which we see in the stooped posture of this elderly fellow who we
know is Munch) against the unattenuated vigor and skill of his artist's
observant eye (seen in the inventiveness and wit with which he has

repeatedly visualized the paradox for us), Munch tells us again and again
that age is a puzzle whose *only* solution is absolutely unacceptable to him.
He emphasizes this by defiantly spreading the liveliest pattern and
brightest colors across the soon-to-be deathbed, playing with repetitions
of the diamond shape of his own skeletal face in the counterpane (not
unmindful that it is his Expressionist legacy of pictures which he echoes
in this scene), and by robbing the clock (that inescapable timekeeper,
painted ironically in the identical colors with which he has painted
himself) of hands and face. Not without formidable brilliance he then
merges past remembrances and present essentials to a single plane by
flattening the perspective. In the end he has dealt unambivalently with
the depressive interference of age, while losing nothing to that depressive
reality. He has painted nothing timidly, left nothing visually ill-
conceived. Above all, he has gripped the viewer with his vision. Our eye
has been excited by his. In the end Munch himself might have written
Dylan Thomas's lines:

> Do not go gentle into that dark night
> Old age should burn and rave at close of day;
> Rage, rage against the dying of the light.

Conclusion

Creativity is not a psychoanalytic concept. Defined by Hagglund (1978)
as the act of bringing into being that which has not existed before, its
re-creative and reparative characteristics may or may not serve a
defensive function. During periods of heightened creative activity when,
as Weissman (1966, 1967) has written, the ego's dissociative function is
particularly operative, an artist may effectively have access to drive
derivatives activated by the derepression of old conflicted material. The
opportunity is then available for a fresh integration of old and new issues
within the artistic product. To us, such appears to have been the case with
Edvard Munch. His work after the death of his father in 1889 reflected
an altered level of creativity that was respondent to, and incorporative of,
the effects of that loss as well as to current external factors. This brought
to maturation earlier creative precursors which had been temporarily
abandoned. Similarly, after 1908 there was an acceleration in creativity
that was respondent to and incorporative of intrapsychic shifts consolidated during the eight-month period of hospitalization. This helped bring
to maturation innovations that had surfaced long before but had not
earlier been fully realized.

If, however, as in the case of Munch, the ego capacity to manage these
drive energies is overwhelmed, creative activity may be severely jeopar-
dized and come to a halt. Jacques (1965) makes this point cogently,

citing many examples of highly creative individuals ravaged by unregulated conflicted drive energies who die prematurely. This appears to have been the direction Munch was headed during the five or six years prior to his hospitalization, despite his efforts to the contrary. For Munch, as perhaps for those individuals of whom Jacques writes, psychiatric treatment was crucial in assisting him in the reerection of former defenses in order to preserve the ego's capacity for creativity. Had Munch not stumbled upon the most fortunate treatment situation of Dr. Jacobson's clinic, which helped him first reestablish and then reinforce his basic characterological defenses by drawing upon efforts already initiated by him to regain his health and redirect his creative focus, not only would the products of the later artistic activity have been lost, but Munch himself would also, in our judgment, surely have perished.

In Munch's instance, psychiatric treatment facilitated a major shift in his goals, not by assisting him in integrating polar elements of his ambivalence conficts, but by supporting that which could contain the conflicts. It helped him restore a system of defenses — with repression as its core — that depended on physical and emotional isolation to safeguard his ego against overtaxation from the drives. In this instance, a provisional period of inpatient treatment, environmental manipulation, and a dramatic alteration in lifestyle proved remarkably successful.

REFERENCES

Bang, H. E. (ed.), (1963), *Edvard Munch's Krisear.* Oslo: Gyldendal Norsk Forlag.
Brenna, A. (1976a), Hans Jaeger and Edvard Munch, the friendship. *Norfisk Tidskrift,* 52:89–115.
_____ (1976b), Hans Jaeger and Edvard Munch, painting and literature. *Nordisk Tidskrift,* 52:188–215.
Brenner, C. (1982), *The Mind in Conflict.* New York: International Universities Press.
Clark, K. (1973), *Edvard Munch, 1863–1944.* The Arts Council of Great Britain. Exhibition Catalog.
Craft, R. (1977), Edvard Munch: Self portraitist (Notes from a diary). *New York Review of Books,* January 20.
Dedichen, J. (1981), *Tulla Larsen og Edvard Munch.* Oslo: Dreyers.
Digby, G. W. (1955), *Meaning and Symbols in Three Modern Artists.* London: Faber & Faber.
Dittman, R. (1982), *Eros and Psyche: Strindberg and Munch in the 1980's.* Ann Arbor: University of Michigan Press.
Eggum, A. (1982), *Edvard Munch Expressionist Paintings 1900–1940.* Madison: Elvehjem Museum of Art, University of Wisconsin-Madison.
Epstein, S. G. (1983), *The Prints of Edvard Munch: Mirror of His Life.* Oberlin: Allen Memorial Art Museum.
Family Letters. Oslo: Munch Museum Arcives.
Gierloff, C. (1946), In: *Vennene Forteller* (Friends Narrative. Oslo: Dreyers.
Gillman, R. (1979), Brief psychotherapy. Address to the Maryland Psychiatric Society. January.

Gray, P. (1973), Psychoanalytic technique and the ego's capacity for viewing intrapsychic activity. *J. Amer. Psychoanal. Assn.,* 21:474–494.

Guenther, P. W. (1976), *Edward Munch: An Exhibition.* Houston: Sarah Campbell Blaffer Gallery.

Hagglund, T-B. (1978), *Dying: A Psychoanalytic Study with Special Reference to Individual Creativity and Defensive Organization.* New York: International Universities Press,

Hamsun, K. (1890), *Samtiden.* Munch Museum Archives.

Heller, R. (1978), Love as a series of paintings. In: *Edvard Munch, Symbols and Images* (Catalogue), Washington, DC: National Gallery of Art, pp. 87–111.

_____ (1984), *Munch, His Life and Work.* Chicago: University of Chicago Press.

Jacques, E. (1965), Death and the mid-life crisis. *Internat. J. Psycho-Anal.,* 46:502–514.

Jaeger, H. (1893), *Syk Kyaeeerlighet* (Sick Love). Paris: Lorient.

_____ (1902a), *Bekjennelseeer* (Confessions). Paris: Lorient.

_____ (1902b), *Faensel of Fortvilese* (Prison and Despair). Paris: Lorient.

James, W. (1902), *Varieties of Religious Experience.* New York: Modern Library.

Kris, E. (1953), Psychoanalysis and the study of creative imagination. In: *Selected Papers of Ernst Kris.* New Haven: Yale University Press, 1975.

_____ (1955), Neutralization and sublimation: Observations on young children. *The Psychoanalytic Study of the Child,* Vol. X.

:   –   New York: International Universities Press.

Kubie, L. (1958), *Neurotic Distortions of the Creative Process.* New York: Noonday Press.

Langaard, J. H. & Revold, R. (1961), *A Year by Year Record of Edvard Munch's Life: A Handbook.* Oslo: Forlangt, Asheborg &. Co.

Lindtke, G. (ed.) (1974). *Max Linde/Edvard Munch,* Lubeck: Amt fur Kulture, Vol. VII.

Messer, T. M. (1973), *Edvard Munch,* New York: Henry N. Abrams.

Munch, E. Diary notes. Unpublished manuscript.

_____ The violet book. Unpublished manuscript.

Neve, C. (1974), Echoes of Edvard Munch's scream. *Country Life,* 3998:302–303.

Niederland, W. (1976), Psychoanalytic approaches to artistic creativity. *Psychoanal. Quart.,* 45:185–212.

Prestoe, B. (1946), *Edvard Munch, Menn esket og Kunstneren.* Oslo: Gyldendal Norsk Forlag.

Sand, B. & Stabell, D. (trans.) (1973), *Edvard Munch: Tegninger, Skisser og Studieser.* Oslo: Oslo Kommunes Kunstsamlinger Katalog A-3. (From Epstein Library, Washington, DC)

Schjeldahl, P. (1974), Munch: The missing master. *Art in Amer.,* 3:80–105.

Schreiner, K. E. (1946), In: *Vennene Fortelleeeer* (Friends' Narrative). Oslo: Dreyers.

Stang, R. (1979), *Edvard Munch, the Man and His Art.* trans. G. Culverwell. New York: Abbeville Press.

Steinberg, S. & Weiss, J. (1954), The art of Edvard Munch and its function in his mental life. *Psychoanal. Quart.,* 23:409–423.

Weissman, P. (1966), Psychological concomitants of ego functioning in creativity. *Internat. J. Psycho-Anal.,* 49:464–478.

_____ (1967), Theoretical considerations of ego regression and ego functions in creativity. *Psychoanal. Quart.,* 36:37–50.

Wylie, H. & Wylie, M. (1980), Edvard Munch. *Amer. Imago,* 37:413–443.

Charismatic Followership as Illustrated in George Eliot's Romola

JEROME A. WINER, M.D. (Chicago)

This paper will use the charismatic relationship between the fictional character, Romola, and the historical figure, Girolamo Savonarola, as he appears in George Eliot's 1863 novel, *Romola*,[1] to illustrate and enlarge upon previous theoretical understandings of charismatic followership (Winer, Jobe, and Ferrono, 1985). The current work is not an attempt to illuminate the entire novel by means of the application of psychoanalytic principles. Nor is it an attempt to link events in the novel with elements of the actual life of George Eliot (Mary Ann Evans, 1819–1880). It is, rather, an explication of the appeal, power, and influence that Savonarola had on Romola. The novel will be summarized, with the five times Savonarola and Romola are in each other's presence given the lion's share of attention.

The novel is set in Florence and opens in 1492, shortly after the death of Lorenzo the Magnificent, the Medici ruler. Portents denote that the time is out of joint—lights shoot in the sky, thunderclaps are heard in the clear night, cows and women bear stillborn. Lorenzo's waxen image in the Church of the Annunziata falls at the time of his death. Savonarola, Dominican prior of San Marco, has been preaching that, because of its sinfulness, the divine purging of Florence is imminent. He claims that visions have revealed him to be God's prophet. A handsome, twenty-three-year-old, shipwrecked Greek, Tito Melema, appears in Florence. He is penniless but for some jewels saved in the disaster that separated him from the father who had adopted him as an urchin of seven.

---

[1] All references are to Eliot (1863).

Charming and clever, the young scholar establishes himself in Florence by selling the jewels that could have served as a means of searching for and ransoming his father. He arranges an introduction to the blind, aged scholar, Bardo Bardi, and his beautiful eighteen-year-old daughter, Romola. Motherless, (George Eliot does not tell us for how long) Romola had devoted herself exclusively to assisting her father in his compulsive studies of ancient Greek and Roman literature, none of which has led to any critical product. Selfish and vain, Bardi has essentially imprisoned the devoted but ambivalent Romola in his library, utilizing the meager resources of a prominent but impoverished Florentine family to purchase more and more antiquities and books. Among many other things, his study contains a headless statue with an uplifted arm wielding a bladeless sword and a headless feminine torso. Several years earlier, Romola's already grown brother, Dino, had left his father's side to enter the Dominican Order. This had infuriated the old man because it deprived him of the collaborator he believed essential for the gathering together of the many threads that his research had laboriously disentangled. In fact, the task had always been impossible, the work meaningless. Romola dutifully reads to him, writes for him, and waits on him.

Bardi is unwilling to release Romola to marriage and, in essence, to womanhood, for she has been an ersatz son to him. In one of the few references to her mother, Bardi says to Romola, "And thou hast a man's nobility of soul: thou hast never fretted me with thy petty desires as thy mother did. It is true, I have been careful to keep thee aloof from the debasing influence of thy own sex, with their sparrow-like frivolity and their enslaving superstition, . . ." (p. 100). He goes on to misquote Plautus to say, " 'No woman is really good, though one may be worse than another' " (editor's translation, note 26, p. 699). Further evidence that Romola has been masculinized, despite her feminine beauty, can be found in the unpublished epigraph that George Eliot selected for the chapter in which Romola is introduced.

> She was most courteous, she was gentle,
> Honest, wise, chaste and modest.
> Like a man, she always kept promises,
>   [p 685]

Soon Tito has become Bardi's collaborator and Romola's beloved. It seems Romola will be released to enjoy the fullest affirmation of womanhood. Romola's brother returns to Florence deathly ill with the message for Tito that his father, Baldesarre, is alive and being held for ransom. Tito keeps the news secret and elects to do nothing.

Savonarola is introduced through a conversation on the street among Florentine citizens. One holds that he is but a loud, barking hound prone to railing prophecies; another, that he rails not against any man but against vice. We meet Monna Brigida, Romola's obese, fifty-ish widowed cousin, the nearest woman she has to a mother. She is upset by Savonarola's attack on false long hair and the jewels she and other widows find fashionable. Romola visits her dying brother who is lodging at San Marco with Savonarola, and we and Romola encounter the prior for the first time. Romola is at her brother's deathbed. Dino, her brother, holds a crucifix, and a crucified form rises high and pale on the frescoed wall. Romola's first emotion, after recognizing the brother she had last seen in childhood, is repulsion for "the dastardly undutifulness which had left her father desolate . . ." (p. 209) *and* her in his place. Expecting penitence for the long years of desertion of their father, Romola is indignant to learn that instead Dino is totally unrepentant. Instead, he offers her a vision admonishing her not to marry. Savonarola enters, calls Romola his daughter, warns her that death is near, and asks that she kneel. His first words to Romola—who has been brought up to disregard church authority entirely, in favor of the classics—are: ". . . bend thy pride before it is bent for thee by a yoke of iron." Romola fixes first on his voice with its tone "not that of imperious command, but of quiet self-possession and assurance of the right, blended with benignity," then on his hands ". . . very beautiful and almost of transparent delicacy," then on his eyes ". . . seeming, like the hands, to tell of acute sensitiveness" (p. 213). Savonarola, it seems to me, has the hands and eyes of a woman mixed with the obvious male countenance partially hidden beneath a cowl! Like a woman, Savonarola nurses Romola's brother, Dino, touching his lips with a wet sponge. Slowly, Romola falls to her knees—". . . in the renunciation of her proud erectness, her mental attitude seemed changed, and she found herself in a new state of passiveness" (p. 214). Romola is subservient to the Dominican against her father's anti-Christian teaching. She is now passive to Savonarola rather than to her father, to Savonarola, the androgynous nurse of the physically and spiritually sick. Savonarola gives her Dino's crucifix to take away as he dies.

Dino's death has enormous effect on Romola. "It seemed to her as if this first vision of death must alter the daylight for her for evermore" (p. 217). Later, she places the crucifix next to her portrait of her mother, one of the few and brief references to the mother in the entire novel.

Romola and Tito marry, but Tito sinks deeper and deeper into self-serving evil. After he abandons her father, Romola must again serve as her father's amanuensis until his death some months later. Through clever machinations, Tito rises in the city's political hierarchy. When his own adoptive father, Baldesarre, reaches Florence as a prisoner, Tito pretends not to know him, claiming him to be a madman.

With her father dead and Tito proving to be controlling and unloving, Romola encounters Savonarola for the second time. He is preaching to the spellbound multitude in the Church of San Marco and George Eliot describes him as awe inspiring. In a Florence full of lasciviousness, lying, treachery, and a corrupt church side by side with the patronage of polite learning and the fine arts, Savonarola preaches that a scourge is at hand. His own burning indignation at the sight of wrong is coupled with "an ardent, power-loving soul, believing in great ends, and longing to achieve those ends by the execution of its own strong will . . ." (p. 272). Much like an Old Testament prophet, he foretells the imminent doom of the wicked Florentines. From an incisive tone of condemning authority, the preacher's voice melts to entreaty: " 'Listen, O people, over whom my heart yearns, as the heart of a mother over the children she has travailed for!' " (p. 293). With outstretched arms, he then offers to be crucified so that iniquity may not prosper. As he sobs and falls to his knees, even those in the assemblage who are not in sympathy with him are carried along by the great wave of feeling. Romola's presence in the church is only her second exposure to Savonarola, and she is not moved until he volunteers to be crucified. Then she sobs.

Tito sells the beloved library that old Bardi had planned to give to the city as his one lasting accomplishment. Romola realizes Tito has exploited and forsaken her and that she is in a loveless and hopeless marriage. Romola decides to flee Tito and Florence, noting that "There seemed to be something more than madness in the supreme fellowship with suffering" of those who sink "in ecstasy before the agonies of martyrdom" (p. 396). Disguised in religious garb, she is intercepted by Savonarola. In this third meeting, he tells her to return and claims that he does so under divine command. Angered at first, she is overcome by his facial expression which conveys "interest in her and care for her apart from any personal feeling. . ." (p. 429). For the first time, Romola calls him "my father." He again points to the crucifix, "Conform your life to that image, my daughter; make your sorrow an offering:" (p. 433). "Bear the anguish and the smart. The iron is sharp—I know, I know—it rends the tender flesh" (p. 436). "Romola felt herself surrounded and possessed by the glow of his passionate faith. The chill doubts all melted away; she was subdued by the sense of something unspeakably great to which she was being called by a strong being who roused a new strength within herself" (p. 436). His message is that she take the way of the cross—to die daily by the crucifixion of selfish will, to bear the pain of the sharp iron, to serve the unfortunate citizenry, to endure a hopeless marriage.

Romola is aware of a new fellowship with suffering and once again falls to her knees in submission to Savonarola. "By the one act of renouncing her resolve to quit her husband, her will seemed so utterly bruised that she felt the need of direction even in small things" (p. 437). The charismatic bond is firmly established. Savonarola has but to order and Romola will obey.

Romola enters into a saintly, self-denying life of service to the poor and sick, a life of sadness but of active love. Tito is committed to intrigue and treachery at the highest levels of Florentine government. He had also been secretly keeping a mistress and had sired two children. The lives of Tito and Romola barely touch. "Savonarola was something like a rope suspended securely by her path, making her step elastic while she grasped it; if it were suddenly removed, no firmness of the ground she trod could save her from staggering, or perhaps from falling" (p. 465). Romola moves habitually among scenes of suffering. Her affinity for sadness makes her "unjust toward merriment" (p. 502). Often seen as a madonna, it is in fact Savonarola upon whom her behavior is patterned.

Then, the disillusionment. Romola learns that, for political reasons, Savonarola has countenanced a prophetess. The prophetess had claimed that Christ had appeared to her to command that Romola's godfather, an important Florentine political figure, be thrown from a palace window. Her beloved godfather is arrested and condemned to death. In their fourth meeting, Romola pleads with Savonarola to use his influence on her godfather's behalf, only to be told, " 'I meddle not with the functions of the State, my daughter' " (p. 572). Savonarola, however, had spoken out in behalf of one of the other political prisoners, one who had personally supported him. Romola confronts Savonarola with the claim that his furthering of God's kingdom is actually limited to what strengthens Savonarola's own party. Savonarola replies, " 'The cause of my party *is* the cause of God's kingdom.' 'I do not believe it!' said Romola, her whole frame shaken with passionate repugnance" (p. 578). In Savonarola's words, Romola hears only egoism. George Eliot comments explicitly that a position such as Savonarola's is needed to engender all energetic belief, that more tender feeling is skeptical toward the larger aims which give rise to religion.

Romola's kindly godfather is executed. "Romola had lost her trust in Savonarola, had lost that fervour of admiration which had made her unmindful of his aberrations. . . . she saw all the repulsive and inconsistent details in his teaching with a painful lucidity . . . that his striving after the renovation of the Church and the world was a striving . . . that had come to mean practically the measures that would strengthen his own position in Florence" (p. 588). George Eliot, speaking to the reader, says that anyone who has ever lost "faith in a fellow man whom he has profoundly loved and reverenced," loses not only faith in God, but the dignity of self, "and all the finer impulses of the soul are dulled" (p. 588). In essence, she describes the depression that follows massive and abrupt disillusionment. Wishing that death would come to her passively, Romola allows herself to drift away in a small boat. She awakens in a plague-ridden village. Her recovery comes through risking her life by arduously nursing the sick, a parallel to Savonarola's nursing her dying brother early in the novel. She also demonstrates his ability to command in getting the villagers to assist her, despite their terror of the plague. She, like Savonarola, is experienced by the passive villagers as sent from God to rescue those who are about to perish.

Meanwhile, in Florence, increasingly doubted, Savonarola is challenged by an opposing monk to prove himself to be God's prophet by walking through fire. When the pyre is prepared, Savonarola stalls via ritualistic argument, then offers a surrogate. Although rain intervenes to end the test, Savonarola's influence is clearly over. The next day, mobs are in the streets, San Marco is stormed, Savonarola is taken prisoner. In the tumult, Baldesarre finally catches up with a nearly drowned Tito and strangles him. Savonarola is put to torture and retracts prophetic claims. Romola condemns her past self as "rash, arrogant, always dissatisfied that others were not good enough" . . . (p. 651). Then the self-reproach lifts. She experiences a sense of debt to Savonarola for his inspiration and she decides to return to Florence. Once she is there, after learning that her husband is dead and gathering in his children and mistress, she spends long periods of meditation dispassionately weighing Savonarola's attributes. She finds in the documents of his confession, a man who had indeed sought his own glory but "sought it by labouring for the very highest end — the moral welfare of men — " (p. 664). She sees in him a "blending of ambition with belief in the supremacy of goodness. . . . It was the habit of Savonarola's mind to conceive great things, and to feel that he was the man to do them" (p. 644). Romola's thoughts are of his anguish that must have followed the confession, of the "depth of sorrow which can only be known to the soul that has loved and sought the most perfect thing, and beholds itself fallen" (p. 665). No longer his follower, no longer disillusioned either, she is her own woman — compassionate and empathic.

Romola, hoping that at the last moment Savonarola will retract his confession, goes to his execution. But he does not. In the Epilogue, set some eleven years later, we find Romola living with Tito's children and their peasant mother. She speaks of Savonarola as one who had the greatness that "belongs to a life spent in struggling against powerful wrong, and in trying to raise men to the highest deeds they are capable of" (p. 675). The novel closes with Romola saying, " 'There are many good people who did not love Fra Girolamo. Perhaps I should never have learned to love him if he had not helped me when I was in great need' " (p. 676).

Modern studies of charisma speak chiefly of the charismatic relationship, not of charisma as inherent in a given individual (Balter, 1986; Post, 1986; Tucker, 1968; Willner, 1984). In an earlier work (Winer, Jobe, and Ferrono, 1985), a psychoanalytic formulation was offered to explain the susceptibility of well-developed personalities to the influence of charismatic leadership. Such followers might be described as functioning in the neurotic rather than in the borderline or psychotic areas at the time of their involvement with the charismatic leader. Briefly recapitulated, the formulation is this: The charismatic leader must have an uncommon supply of physical energy, a gift for dramatization, an indefatigable capacity to kindle hope, and adroit skill at obtaining and handling power. But his specifically charismatic appeal lies in the leader's communication of an unconscious fantasy wherein he has reversed the situation of his own passively endured helplessness into one of activity vis-à-vis a passive other. He shares this fantasy via his mission or message much as primal fantasy can be elaborated in a poem or play, sufficiently disguised to avoid blatant presentation, yet discernible enough to resonate with the unconscious of another person, the reader or playgoer (Freud, 1908). Hamlet's oedipal wishes for Gertrude, unconsciously resonating with those of the playgoer, are the best-known example (Freud, 1900; Jones, 1949). In my model of the charismatic relationships, a current crisis of induced passivity in the potential follower activates his or her matching unconscious fantasy of traumatic passivity at the hands of an active other and the wish to identify with the active other to avoid painful affect. The charismatic leader serves as the identificatory object for the wished-for reversal. The follower's unconscious recognition of the matching patterns gives rise to the willingness to attribute special powers to the leader and the substitution of hope for despair.

To restate my formulation in other words, an acute personal crisis causes the reenactment of a repressed trauma (real or fantasied) in which the subject endures a specific passive position vis-à-vis an active other. The affect of depression accompanies the sense that something bad has already happened (Brenner, 1974), in contrast to anxiety, in which something bad is impending. The charismatic leader's message or mission presents a similar unconscious fantasy in two stages—the first in which he was similarly passive, the second in which he has achieved activity. He serves as an identificatory model for the reversal of the enforced passivity to willed activity. His message or mission communicates the unconscious internalized object relationship in a disguised yet unconsciously discernible fashion. In fact, the messages of most charismatic leaders are so overdetermined and richly ambiguous that they carry more than one such unconscious fantasy. The unconscious fantasy or internalized object relationship does not necessarily reflect actual past object relationships. Rather, as expressed by Kernberg (1987), internalized object relations "reflect a combination of realistic and fantasied—and often highly distorted—internalizations of such past object relations and defenses against them under the effects of activation and projection of instinctual drive derivatives" (p. 201).

In Romola's case, an acute personal crisis—the death of her brother, Dino—causes her to feel permanently and helplessly entrapped in the role of daughter/son to her feminized father. Her forced participation in the shared fantasy enslavement began in childhood, with her mother's early death followed by Dino's departure and her already aged father losing his sight and his only son. The ground had been prepared long before by her father's intolerance of women. He could love Romola only for male qualities. The headless female torso suggests the dissociation of Romola's physical femininity from her enforced life of the mind. Old enough to be her grandfather, Bardi as castrated is suggested by his blindness and the headless statue holding a bladeless sword. There is an overt reference to Oedipus and Antigone when the painter, Piero di Cosimo, asks Bardi to sit for his painting of Oedipus and calls Romola, "Madonna Antigone." Like Antigone's, Romola's Oedipal victory has yielded poor spoils. On a preoedipal level, Bardi in advanced age has made a ministering mother out of a daughter, much as King Lear hoped to do and as the blind Oedipus did for twenty years (between *Oedipus Rex* and *Oedipus at Colonus*). Romola marries Tito with the hope that he will replace her as her father's coadjutor and free her. The realization that her husband is a self-serving political and personal manipulator, rather than a loving male who will affirm her as a woman and truly take Dino's place, intensifies Romola's crisis.

Stage One of Charismatic Followership: Self-Initiated Repetition of Passivity

Savonarola first presents his message to Romola as he nurses Dino on his deathbed. Dino's impending death and her rage at him threaten Romola's ego integrity. Her rage at his final lack of regret threatens the values and defenses that have organized her existence. Yet she kneels, despite a lifetime aversion to Christian teaching and monks. Why? Romola repeats her submission to the castrated (celibate) father because this time *she can choose* to do so. It is an act of her own volition. George Klein's (1976) principle of self-initiated active reversal of passive experience speaks to the motive to reexperience impositions in order to make them self-syntonic. "A relationship is re-experienced so that, in relation to the self, it is changed from an imposed experience to one that, even if painful, is self-generated; it is made part of 'my' experience" (p. 262). Klein goes on to claim that "reversal behaviors concern experiences that threaten self-continuity" (p. 265). McDougall (1985) also sees, in the compulsion to repeat, the desperate need to maintain the feeling of ego identity at any cost and the need to cling to ways of maintaining libidinal and narcissistic homeostasis. Gedo (1979) defines the self-organization as the cohesive hierarchy of personal aims, the "relatively permanent structuring of goals and values into potentials for action" (p. 178). The compulsion to repeat despite unpleasure is understood by Gedo as manifestation of an overriding need to restore self-cohesion, no matter what the cost. It is my contention that *self-initiated repetition is the first of three steps in the reversal of enforced passivity (with respect to an internal object) to a specific willed activity.* In this first step, the charismatic leader is the external transference figure who represents the active controller of the internal unconscious object relationship. A friar who voluntarily gave up his male sexual prerogative becomes the feminized dominator, akin to Romola's aged, blind father. The mother is involved in the internal object relationship only in that she has abandoned Romola to the castrated feminized father who uses her as his phallus and his preoedipal mother.

Stage Two: The Alternation and/or Merger of Self and Object Representations

When Savonarola gives Dino's crucifix to Romola, which she keeps, he is inviting her to use him as he has used his own charismatic, identificatory object, Jesus, the androgynous, dutiful child who submits to a sadistic father. But Jesus also became one with that father (Dundes, 1981). The crucifix signifies, then, the second step toward reversal (after the first step—the self-initiated repetition of passivity), the alternation and/or merger of self and object representations. Alternation or merger of passive self with active object is a midway step between reversal of passive self to active self. Savonarola makes the offer to be crucified in the same sermon in which he begins in a voice threatening consuming fire and pestilence. From an incisive tone of *paternal* authority, his voice melts as he literally claims to be a *mother* anguishing over her children, the people of Florence. After saying, "my heart yearns, as the heart of a mother over the children she has travailed for!" (p. 293), Savonarola places himself in the role of the female turtle (dove) of the Song of Songs: "for your sakes I would willingly live as a turtle in the depths of the forest, singing low to my Beloved, who is mine and I am *his*" (p. 293; my emphasis). Sounding much like a masochistic woman about to submit to intercourse, he says, " 'O Lord, thou knowest I am willing—I am ready. Take me, stretch me on thy cross . . ." (p. 293). Romola, seeing Savonarola for only the second time, is unmoved until he invokes this martyrdom. Then she sobs: "she felt herself penetrated with a new sensation—a strange sympathy with something apart from all the definable interest of her life. It was not altogether unlike the thrill which had accompanied certain rare heroic touches in history and poetry"[2] (p. 312).

After demonstrating the self-initiated repetition of passivity, Savonarola has gone on to the second-stage alternation and/or merger of self and object. Side by side, Savonarola is male and female, active and passive, and in the offer to be crucified, he merges both. Edelheit (1974) relates crucifixion fantasies to the primal scene and believes that primal-scene representations have a characteristic potential for double identification (with both copulating parents) which may be simultaneous or alternating. He coins the term *primal-scene schema* to encompass such independent polarities as active-passive, victim-aggressor, sadist-masochist, viewer-exhibitor, and such alternations as eating and being eaten. Patients who have crucifixion fantasies identify at times with Jesus as victim; at other times, with the active, sadistic aggressors. The crucifixion as a public spectacle also suggests the child's visual horror and stimulation at the primal scene. Following Edelheit's (1974) *primal-scene schema,* Savonarola's offer to be crucified presents the model for alternation and/or merger of the active-passive, victim-aggressor, sadist-masochist relationship to Romola. He is both God's chosen, active agent and His willing victim. If Romola can be like Savonarola, she is no longer only the passive, acted-upon self. It is the Lord who will stretch the passive Savonarola on the cross; it is Savonarola who actively threatens destruction to the sinner; and it is the active aggressor with whom Romola can now identify as well.

---

[2]George Eliot is unknowingly citing the very mechanism I am espousing—that hidden in Savonarola's sermon is the unconscious fantasy that feels new to Romola but moves her so because of its familiarity (Freud, 1908). That Romola is in the midst of a huge sobbing crowd listening to Savonarola in San Marco should not be forgotten as a catalyst in the effect he has on her (Freud, 1921).

The third meeting between Savonarola and Romola occurs when she attempts to flee Tito and Florence. The attempt at flight is an active effort that is new for Romola. For the first time, Romola calls Savonarola "my father." He points to Dino's crucifix hanging on a cord around Romola's neck. " 'Conform your life to that image, my daughter; make your sorrow an offering' " (p. 433). Again, there is a call to identify with Jesus and more implicitly with his persecutor, his own father. He demands that she return to die daily by the (self-) crucifixion of her selfish will (i.e., that she be both active persecutor and passive victim). This turning of her newly acquired sadistic activity *toward herself* makes her feel the need for his direction in everything. She has repeated the situation with her father of total enslavement to his will but with "a new presentiment of the strength there might be in submission . . ." (p. 430). I believe that strength to lie in the merger of self-representation with the active aggressor-father object representation (Savonarola railing at sin, Roman executioners, God sacrificing his son) provides Romola with behavior unavailable to her before. The passive-submissive self-representation is, at times, side by side; at times, it is merged with the active-inflictor self, just as described in Edelheit's primal-scene schema. When it is merged, Romola turns aggression against herself, i.e., in self-"crucifixion of her selfish will." When passivity and submission are side by side, Romola performs self-effacing service to the unfortunate while being "unjust toward merriment" and indignant about oppression.

Savonarola has become the rope suspended securely by her path without which she would struggle and fall. The object relationship with Savonarola has not been converted into structure, however. In Schafer's (1968) terms, Savonarola remains an introject, "an inner presence with which one feels in a continuous or intermittent dynamic relationship" (p. 72)—a felt presence by which patients feel attached or gratified and to whom they are passive. Romola is in the position of most neurotic charismatic followers, dependent for the maintenance of belief on the internal object relationship with the charismatic leader, a relationship that functions at the level of alternation and/or merger with the active introjected object. It is only when Romola rejects Savonarola that she becomes identified with him which is the third stage in the reversal of enforced passivity to willed activity—true identification with the lost charismatic leader which leads to a change in psychic structure.

Modes of Internalization and Their Application to the Charismatic Relationship

Meissner (1981) has proposed a classification for modes of internalization that seems most applicable to the charismatic relationship. To Meissner, *incorporation* is the most primitive taking in of the object, leading to a complete merger with the self-organization. In adult life, such a process usually connotes psychosis. It is the psychotic and borderline or severe narcissistic characters who relate to the charismatic leader in this way. Many cult members operate at the level of incorporation of the leader. *Introjection* is a less primitive mode of internalization, having the motive of preserving union or the motive of defense. What is internalized in introjection, in Meissner's view, is a transitional object relationship. Meissner believes that introjects may be internalized to different degrees. As well as Schafer's "felt presence," Meissner claims some introjects are, in fact, taken into the subject's unconscious and often lose their independent quality, becoming merged with the subject's sense of self. Meissner also finds reversibility in the introjective configuration with respect to self-and-other experience. This process is akin to what I believe happens in the second stage of charismatic followership of the neurotic type. The charismatic leader is introjected, but his loss in the external world is not prerequisite, as is the case with more traditional uses of the term introject. A fluidity of attributes between self and object representation persists. It is the charismatic leader's later loss through disillusionment that converts introjection to identification or alternatively to renewed depression based on a sense of renewed passivity with continued charismatic susceptibility.

To Meissner, the end products of identification, in contrast to introjection, are specific structural modifications within the ego system. They are not capable of separation from the core (Loewald, 1962). Identification depersonalizes the internal object relationship, and the product is resistant to regression and possesses a high degree of autonomy. "Identification is a process of structure formation in the internal world of the psychic apparatus and not merely one of cognitive modification of the inner representational world" (Sandler and Rosenblatt, 1962). Identification operates in relative autonomy from instinctual pressures but rather arises from "specifically non-instinctual and relatively conflict-free tendencies of the ego toward self-integration and meaningful object relatedness" (p. 62). Identification modifies not only the self-schema but also the ego and the internal world itself. It is this level of development that Romola achieves.

Stage Three: Resolution of the Charismatic Followership—From Introjection to Identification

Romola goes beyond charismatic followership to independence and some character change after her disillusionment with Savonarola. Romola's disillusionment is based on the realization of Savonarola's narcissism ("egoism") and grandiosity. When Savonarola says, "The cause of my party *is* the cause of God's kingdom," Romola experiences a break in the charismatic bond. In my opinion, the idealization characteristic of the charismatic bond requires the charismatic leader to perpetuate the illusion wherein he is object-related to the follower. Should he appear totally narcissistic (my cause is God's cause, my motives are patently self-serving), he must manifest supernatural powers on the spot or lose his followers. We can speculate that if Savonarola's statement had been accompanied by a flash of lightning or a finger of fire writing on the wall, Romola's disillusionment would have turned to awe. But, in fact, Romola realizes that Savonarola is not what he presents himself to be but is mindful chiefly of himself. His relationships with people are based largely on the psychological functions those people can perform for him (Kohut, 1971). His need for "mirroring" by the follower can no longer be reciprocated by the provision of an idealizable imago for the "ideal-hungry" follower (Kohut, 1984).

A further refinement of the necessary object relatedness of the charismatic figure is repeated demonstration of activity in a crisis. To do nothing in the face of Romola's godfather's death sentence when Romola begs for his help—to say, "I meddle not with the functions of the State, my daughter, . . ." (p. 572)—is to remain passive when activity is mandatory.

Disillusionment with a charismatic leader is, then, the loss of an introject who has served as a transitional object to the self—with resultant depression. That object had offered the real or illusory opportunity to reverse a traumatic state of passivity by merger and assumption of the property of activity. Unlike most disillusioned charismatic followers, Romola's depression is short lived, however. After placing herself on the waters to drift off to death passively, only to survive, she rapidly becomes the active, self-effacing nurse and nurturer. At this point, she continues her life identified with the active role Savonarola could not live up to, but not as his follower. Her motives are self-initiated, coming from a self-representation that has identified with Savonarola's motives rather than being in an inner relationship to him. Savonarola's loss as an introject leads to enduring changes not only in Romola's self-representation but also in her (external) relationship with him. She is dispassionate, admiring of his strengths, tolerant of his weakness. Their relationship is no longer a charismatic one, without need of fantasized involvement with the introject. Partial ego identification has occurred.

Although a contributor to mankind's betterment, Romola remains unmarried and childless in the epilogue. Yet, in the epilogue, while

Tessa, the mother of Tito's children, and Monna Brigida grow fatter and sleep away their days, it is Romola who now actively controls Tito's son, Lillo, who is memorizing from Petrarch. Tessa has surrendered him to Romola. Romola is teaching him to be a scholar and makes explicit reference to her own father. Romola is the ersatz father of the household. She, through her relationship with Savonarola, has achieved the active role, teaching, counseling, and controlling the obedient son. No longer related to Savonarola as an introject, Savonarola has become part of her value and motivational system, an enduring aspect of the inner core of her ego.

Summary

The charismatic relationship between Savonarola and George Eliot's fictional character, Romola, is used here to illustrate elements of a psychoanalytic theory of charismatic followership. Charismatic susceptibility occurs when the follower undergoes an acute personal crisis that activates an unconscious fantasy of enforced passivity with respect to an active other. The charismatic leader presents himself through his mission or message as an identificatory object for the reversal to activity of enforced passivity in the object relationship. Leader and follower share the same unconscious fantasy. The follower passes through a stage of self-initiated repetition of passivity, followed by a stage of alternation and/or merger of self and object representations. If disillusionment occurs, either recurrent depression or identification with the lost charismatic leader ensues. Types of charismatic followership are characterized by the mode of internalization involved.

REFERENCES

Balter, L. (1986), Religion, the state and the socialization of children. In: *Psychoanalysis the Science of Mental Conflict*, ed. A. D. Richards & M. S. Willick. Hillsdale, NJ: The Analytic Press, pp. 393–418.

Brenner, C. (1974), Depression, anxiety, and affect theory. *Internat. J. Psycho-Anal.*, 55:25–32.

Dundes, A. (1981), The hero pattern and the life of Jesus. *The Psychoanalytic Study of Society*, 9:49–83. New York: International Universities Press.

Edelheit, H. (1974), Crucifixion fantasies and their relationship to the primal scene. *Internat. J. Psycho-Anal.*, 55:193–199.

Eliot, G. (1863), *Romola*, ed. A. Sanders. New York: Penguin Books, 1980.

Freud, S. (1900), The interpretation of dreams. *Standard Edition*, 4 & 5. London: Hogarth Press, 1953.

———— (1908), Creative writers and daydreaming. *Standard Edition*, 9:141–153. London: Hogarth Press, 1959.

———— (1921), Group psychology and the analysis of the ego. *Standard Edition*, 18:67–143.

London: Hogarth Press, 1955.

Gedo, J. E. (1979), *Beyond Interpretation: Toward a Revised Theory for Psychoanalysis*. New York: International Universities Press.

Jones, E. (1949), *Hamlet and Oedipus*. New York: Norton.

Kernberg, O. F. (1987), An ego psychology-object relations theory approach to the transference. *Psychoanal. Quart.,* 56:197–221.

Klein, G. S. (1976), The principle of self-initiated active reversal of passive experience. In: *Psychoanalytic Theory: An Exploration of Essentials*, ed. M. M. Gill & L. Goldberger. New York: International Universities Press, pp. 259–279.

Kohut, H. (1971), *The Analysis of the Self*. New York: International Universities Press.

———— (1984), *How Does Analysis Cure?* ed. A. Goldberg & P. E. Stepansky. Chicago, IL: University of Chicago Press.

Loewald, H. W. (1962), Internalization, separation, mourning and the superego. *Psychoanal Quart.,* 31:483–504

McDougall, J. (1985), *Theaters of the Mind*. New York: Basic Books.

Meissner, W. W. (1981), *Internalization in Psychoanalysis [Psychological Issues*, Monogr. 50]. New York: International Universities Press.

Ogden, T. H. (1983), The concept of internal object relations. *Internat. J. Psycho-Anal.,* 64:227–241.

Post, J. M. (1986), Narcissism and the charismatic leader-follower relationship. *Pol. Psychol.,* 7:675–688.

Sandler, J. & Rosenblatt, B. (1962), The concept of the representational world. *The Psychoanalytic Study of the Child,* 17:128–145. New Haven, CT: Yale University Press.

Schafer, R. (1968), *Aspects of Internalization*. New York: International Universities Press.

Tucker, R. C. (1968), The theory of charismatic leadership. *Daedalus,* 97:731–756.

Willner, A. R. (1984), *The Spellbinders*. New Haven, CT: Yale University Press.

Winer, J. A., Jobe, T. & Ferrono, C. (1985), Toward a psychoanalytic theory of the charismatic relationship. *This Annual,* 12/13:155–175. New York: International Universities Press.

August 1987

ON MIGRATION—VOLUNTARY AND COERCED

GEORGE H. POLLOCK, M.D., Ph.D. (Chicago)

I

From his earliest beginnings man was a wanderer—whether his wanderings were biologically based (our simian ancestors probably moved from place to place in search of food and shelter) or psychologically based (displaying an insatiable curiosity to explore new terrain or discover new and different environments). As a wanderer, man left what he had and moved on. As psychological and social development unfolded, as our life span increased, we came to realize that perhaps inside all of us was a push for separation and individuation as a means of defining our selves, our being. This urge was most notably seen as children gradually left mother and began new relationships in new settings and later, in adolescence, when they had the biological and social need to move away from the family of origin, establish new intimate ties to others, and so become persons in their own right and ultimately establish new family units. This is the evolution and psychological basis of leaving the familiar and starting something new. Yet within all of us internal and external ties to our past and to our earlier reality still remain. But what about the feelings that come from this leave taking—be it self-motivated or, in increasing numbers, necessitated by social and political upheavals that mandate migration, sometimes as a means of survival? We cannot, we should not, we must not disavow our heritage lest we lose more than we gain. New amalgams of old and new enrich us all.

An earlier version of this paper was presented at the Third International Symposium of the American Society of Hispanic Psychiatrists, Merida, Yucatan, on March 17, 1986.

The mind evolved as a means of adapting to present and future and giving us some control, through memory, planning, thinking, feeling, responding, communicating. The phylogenetic development of mind allowed man to become master of his environment and to some extent of his destiny. Nonetheless, normative and catastrophic events evoke reactions and changes that require adaptive processes to restore equilibrium. One of these adaptive processes, which I have been studying, is the mourning-liberation process. It is my thesis that this process, which has concomitant biological changes, especially in the immune system, is involved in the migration-adaptation process. In fact, it is my belief that the total mourning-liberation process is involved in *all* situations of change and transition.

A colleague recently moved to another city, distant from his prior residence and place of work. The new post was an advancement and one he had sought, although it meant leaving one of the major cities in the United States for a smaller metropolis. His wife described to me the painful adaptation required in the change. She felt lost. The familiar geographic landmarks were absent; the familiar shops and service personnel were gone; places where she and her family had had many experiences (positive and negative) were memory traces not reinforced by reality visits. All of these were gone, and now she and her family experienced the losses, even though they had very much sought the change and the new challenges. I asked about her adaptation to the transitions, and she very perceptively replied that being freed somewhat of what no longer was gave her the impetus to set up new networks, find new facilities, and not expect that identical replacements would be found for what no longer existed.

The stress and resulting strain of elective leaving resulted in responses very similar to what I have described as the mourning-liberation process—a normal, necessary, universal, transformational process that permits us to adapt to change (which is loss), loss of meaningful figures, loss of home, loss of resources, loss of physical and emotional-mental health, loss of memory—in other words, varied kinds of losses. The process may go on without the individual being aware of it and might conclude with new resolves, new "energy investments," and new relationships. Where there is loss of memory, as can be seen in the early stages of Alzheimer's disease, one works with the depression, the anxiety, the rage, the hopelessness, but at times one leaves the denial mechanisms in place. When the loss is due to the death of a significant individual—e.g., parent, spouse, child, sibling, friend—the bereavement process follows a course that in many instances can result in positive outcomes. When the loss, especially in children, is due to recriminative divorces, abandonments, or deaths of significant others at critical developmental periods, the effects on later personality structure can be severe and lifelong.

In my research I have found and suggested that the more general mourning-liberation process has a line of development, beginning very early in life and becoming a critical part of the aging process. I believe aging and development are synonymous. If one cannot successfully mourn past states of the self, then one cannot accept the ongoing aging process as a natural event. The leaf in spring is a bud, in summer it is rich and full with its greenery and verdant appearance, in the fall it turns to other beautiful hues, yellow, red, and brown, and in the winter it trembles in the wind for its days are numbered and it will soon fall off, enrich the earth that nourishes the tree, so that new leaves will come into being, each to repeat the pattern.

But to return to my research on the mourning-liberation process: the normal outcome results in life continuing with new networks and new investments. When a serious traumatic loss occurs in childhood or adolescence, the mourning-liberation process is interfered with in its development, and either it stops, producing an arrest, or if it is of lesser severity, a fixation occurs. If the latter occurs, future life events and tragedies return the individual to the earlier fixation point, and less developed or deviated mourning responses emerge, e.g., anniversary reactions, psychosomatic symptoms. The fourth possible outcome is that of pathological mourning or melancholia. In these instances we see gross manifestations of psychological and mental disorder, e.g., psychotic depressive symptomatology, suicides, homicides, severe alcohol and drug abuse. These somewhat abbreviated descriptive comments outline the focus of my research for over three decades.

In this paper I briefly turn to a newer application of my clinical-theoretical scheme. We have in our time witnessed forced emigration, exile, abandonment by one's mother- or fatherland, incarceration, and death under horrendous conditions. These realities are not new to man, although their scope and brutality cause us to wonder if indeed we have not witnessed a new low in human degradation. People in the past were banished—a form of abandonment with the intent that one became more and more distant, similar to the dead, as one got further and further away. People being tortured to confess, to convert, to bear false witness against friend or relative—these are all too familiar to us because of recent historical tragedies.

When one is forced to leave one's land or home it is a loss and a severance. As a result ethnic and national identities may become reactively intensified. Coming to a new land involves, for many, learning a new language, hearing different songs and news reports, having to participate in or watch new sports (e.g., soccer versus football), getting used to new foods, learning new customs, becoming immersed in new historical and cultural heroes (e.g., George Washington or Simon Bolivar), learning new forms of government, new mores, new folkways, etc. The pain of the severance and loss of security of what one identifies with the homeland is compounded by the fears of the strangers. Depressions occur, and groups, even though they tend to form in the new land in order to retain some of the old and protect against the fears of the new, can develop internal splits and conflicts of loyalty. I recall a political refugee from a South American country telling me how much he missed his beautiful homeland, even with its tyrannies and risks. He dreamed in Spanish, even though he had been in the United States for some time and was a successful professional. He applied for United States citizenship, and not long before it was formally to be conferred upon him he went into a fit of despair. "It is the final break with my motherland." He knew that if he returned as long as the existing political group was in power he was in great danger of either death or permanent incarceration under most unpleasant conditions, and yet loss evoked mourning. We talked about his complex feelings and reality. He is now comfortable with his "new land" and, even though politically life now has changed, he no longer has a wish to return there.

Over the years I have had contact with individuals who had to flee from the Nazis, from Franco's Spain, from Eastern Europe, Greece, the Soviet Union, Cuba, Latin America, and Vietnam, and even though these individuals came from different countries, there was a similarity in their ambivalent responses to having to leave. They fortunately did have the opportunity to leave, although there was no alternative. The European refugees had no choice, and unfortunately many perished under horrendous conditions because they could not escape. Those who did were seen as aliens, and they felt alienated, dehumanized, homeless, abandoned by land, nation, and their gods. Many years ago, a colleague, Percival Bailey, the eminent neurologist and neurosurgeon, told me about the plight of the Armenians. Close to one million were lost and many others had to leave to escape destruction. Involuntary migration, most recently from Vietnam, Cambodia, and Laos, presents unique problems, e.g., anxiety, rage, depression, basic issues of survival. Voluntary migration, though less involved with threat to life, does involve issues of acculturation, earning a living, finding basic housing, in addition to the leaving and loss of what was left behind.

Loss of security in the hopes of gaining greater security involves giving up in hope of future gains. Voluntary migration is not exile, but is it not still isolation even if the entire family migrates at the same time? The family support system can act as a transitional "blanket" from the old to the new land, but there still can be emotional sequelae, especially in the older adults who cannot adapt as easily to the "new life." They feel estranged and at times even in exile, in contrast to the younger members of the family, who adapt more easily. Stein (1985) has suggested that "culture shock" refers to the rekindling of unresolved losses, and can lead to denial of the losses through setting up structures that do not allow for mourning to take place. I would modify this to note that shock is the first phase of the mourning-liberation process. If one denies the loss, one denies the shock phase and the mourning process is stopped cold. Internally one can know that the loss has occurred but externally one acts as if it has not taken place. If the shock experience occurs one can then go on to the next phase of the mourning-liberation process (Pollock, 1961, 1962, 1966, 1968, 1970, 1971a, 1971b, 1971c, 1972a, 1972b, 1973, 1975a, 1975b, 1975c, 1976, 1977a, 1977b, 1978a, 1978b, 1981a, 1981b, 1982, 1983, 1984, 1985a, 1985b).

Cohen (1987), focusing on the migration and acculturation to American society of Hispanic populations, has described the coping and adaptive issues involved in these changes. Her model is linked to stress-stressor reactions and studies of biopsychosocial and cultural systems. Parenthetically, I would also add the developmental system, since changes over the life course seem to play a pivotal role in such adaptations to change.

Not only, however, do these responses occur following sudden, unexpected, massive disruptions, but one can also observe them in normal life transitions, e.g., adolescence, mid-life events, aging in the later years. Although migration and acculturation have unique and distinct features, there seems to be universal reactions to all changes.

Separation in and of itself is not the same as loss and need not have a negative connotation. We separate and individuate throughout our life course. If we did not we would remain fixed or arrested in our development. When one individuates and separates, a normal mourning-liberation process occurs, and this is part of development. Garza-Guerrero (1974) has written about culture shock and its relationship to mourning and identity. The Pierses (1982) also addressed this issue in a more recently published paper that reflects their earlier experiences on being "newcomers" to the United States. They point out that the United States is "a nation of uprooted people, or of children and grandchildren of people uprooted under duress. . . . There were Africans, dragged away and sold into slavery; there were such diverse, hungry or oppressed, or persecuted groups as the Irish, the Norwegians, the Jews, various Slavic groups, various people from the Middle East, from Middle

America and South America, from the Caribbean, from East Asia" (p. 369).

Aside from "culture shock," it is my contention that each individual must go through an individual internal mourning-liberation process so that there can finally be a sense of belonging to the new without giving up all ties to one's heritage that are valuable, needed, and should be transmitted. This mourning-liberation process facilitates the processes of healing the losses and allows for acculturation, identification, and successful adaptation.

In a recent symposium on stress-strain in refugees, Nancy Henkin of Temple University identified a triple jeopardy of older adult refugees in the United States. Henkin said, "They are old, they are in the minority and they can't communicate" (cited in Eastman, 1988, p. 4). There is culture shock, financial insecurity, language barriers, emotional isolation, and intrafamilial generational conflict. If they are physically ill, if they have not been able to mourn the loss of their homeland, if they cannot invest in the new land, they are at great risk. They wish to keep ties with their land of origin and its customs and traditions, but this may not be possible. These people, not only the elderly but the young and the nonelderly adult groups, need assistance and care, be it medical, psychiatric and psychological, legal, nutritional, linguistic, educational. As more and more people come to our communities, we should plan for assisting these individuals and families who need help.

In a pioneering study of psychoanalysis in the Third Reich, Spiegel, Chrzanowski, and Feiner (1975) note that "Freud felt that as exemplar of psychoanalysis it was his duty to remain to the last possible moment [in Austria], that 'he could not leave his native land; it would be like a soldier deserting his post' " (p. 481). Freud had earlier written to Ferenczi that he did not wish to leave his possessions, his comforts, and his treatments for his cancer. He wrote, "In my opinion, flight would only be justified by direct danger to life" (cited on p. 481). But Freud left and faced the dilemma of choosing the few who could accompany him to safety, recognizing that those who stayed behind would perish. Even though he was not young, Freud's dying soon after arriving in England leaves some questions unanswered. Was his death perhaps related to his inability to mourn for all who were lost? Perhaps he had guilt about the choices he had to make — Sigmund's Choice — a diabolic scheme of the Nazis.

A more current study of migration is that of the Grinbergs (1984), who also emphasized the mourning reactions "for objects left behind and for the lost parts of the self" (p. 13). In this significant report, the authors distinguish between leaving and arriving; both events are traumatic, but I believe need not be pathogenic unless there is a predisposing propensity or vulnerability before the exit and entrance experiences take place. Certain losses in infancy, childhood, or adolescence — e.g., loss of a parent — deform the subsequent personality with serious consequences. But not all who experience such losses have resulting psychopathology. We also know that the adult's loss of a child can have serious and ongoing effects on his or her subsequent mental life. Thus, in addition to the developmental, the prior predisposing vulnerability, one must consider the issues of loss of hope, planning for the future, motivations and psychic resiliency, and support systems. The Grinbergs very perceptively describe the steps in what they call the migratory process. From my point of view these are very similar if not identical to those in the mourning-liberation process.

II

Man probably wandered from Africa to Europe and Asia. From Asia man probably came to the Western hemisphere by one or two routes, e.g., across the Bering Straits and then southward and/or from Polynesia to South America. There is evidence that the Norsemen explored the eastern part of North America. But man, the discoverer, the explorer, the investigator, searched not only geographic terrains, including the North and South Poles, the moon, and the planetary system, but also newer areas of thought and artistic worlds. These could be viewed from the broad perspective of self-generated migrations. When one left one's land of origin in order to earn a better living, to have greater freedom of opportunity, or to deal with one's religion, this, too, was a voluntary migration. Despite the voluntary aspect of this venturing, there still were and are elements of mourning, loss, nostalgia, memories, and feelings of the past that were positive as well as negative. Such "migrants" speak of their homeland, their "mother-land," their "father-land," but no references are made to a "sister-land" or "brother-land." Fellow inhabitants (in the broad sense) may be called "brothers" or "sisters," but this sibling label does not extend to the land, which is seen as parental. The "homeless" have no "home-land," and we are familiar with this plight.

In contrast to voluntary migration, we find the "forced migration" in which one has to leave in order to protect oneself and one's family from destruction, torture, or incarceration. The reactions may include nostalgia, mourning, longing, but also rage, depression, and a feeling of being abandoned by one's "homeland" and also of abandoning what is familiar and loved. Such depressive responses are similar to variants of abnormal mourning reactions. What awaits one is the new terrain, the fear of the unknown, and even fear of death—especially as it reverberates with the fear of the strange and the stranger. But the mourning-liberation process does unfold, acculturation can occur, and adaptations take place. In the instance of soldiers conscripted for war, we find a variant of the "forced-migration" phenomenon, and here again the pain of loss, the fear of the unknown and death, the necessity to kill or be killed—all contribute to the pathology we see on the battlefront and now in the post-traumatic stress disorders which I believe have elements of unresolved or abnormal mourning patterns. We have seen this in survivors of the Vietnam War and especially in those soldiers who now show serious "post-traumatic stress disorders" and have high suicide rates.

III

Ticho (1971) and Garza-Guerrero (1974) wrote on culture shock and its relationship to the mourning process, vicissitudes of identity, and transference and countertransference reactions. Garza-Guerrero focused on two fundamental elements of culture shock: "the mourning related to the loss of a culture and the vicissitudes of identity in face of the threat of a new culture" (p. 409). I would broaden Garza-Guerrero's definition of culture shock to include, basically, the loss of one's "home base," be it the abandoned or abandoning culture, family, friends, language, music, food, and culturally determined values, customs, and attitudes, or one's base of knowledge, one's profession, one's outlook on life—in other words, the loss of anything that has been meaningful and has been given up or that one has been forced to give up. The connection with loss of trust, confidence, and self-esteem, particularly in the vulnerable, is obvious. The shock is the initial phase of this loss reaction, and the adaptive acculturating outcomes are aspects of what I feel are the consequence of the successful mourning-liberation process. This "shock" phase is seen, for example, when divorce is announced to children, when a sudden death occurs, when one loses a position or job. Garza-Guerrero's divisions into the phases of culture shock are quite useful and applicable to the larger loss-reactive process. The "new identity" that is his endpoint of the culture-shock crises is comparable to what I call the resolution of the mourning-process, with the liberation of investments in the past for use in creative and productive relationships.

However, in my comparison of adults who have lost one or both parents in childhood or adolescence, who have lost one or more siblings in childhood or adolescence, who have lost a spouse, or who have lost a child, I have observed that it is in the last instance that the mourning process is never fully completed—"One cannot mourn for one's future (the child), when that future is dead" (personal communication from an older adult woman whose son died in infancy and who never could complete her mourning for him). In ongoing studies comparing loss through death with loss through divorce or as a result of abandonment (Pollock, 1985b, 1986), significant differences seem to be emerging, and these can be applied to the voluntary and involuntary migration situation. In children, the use of a "transitional object" helps diminish the threat that results from loss, abandonment, or break in contact. We see these losses in young children, in adults who are threatened, in psychiatric patients who fear abandonment, or in children who fear the dark. "I am cut off from the familiar; what I see and recognize, and am left with my inner fears and fantasies that threaten me" (personal communication). And so groups cluster in the new environment—they speak their "mother tongue," they eat their original "mother foods," they listen to their "mother lullabies" (music), they read their original-language books and papers, they join religious communities that are similar to those they left, and the uprooted seek to keep their roots, which help in their internal mourning process, their transition, and the facilitation of acculturation, if not in themselves then in their children and grandchildren.

Let me close with a few comments on nostalgia, an affect-fantasy state related to the theme of this paper.

IV

Martin (1954) has noted that homesickness has been a dominant theme in the Bible, in Homer's works, in Caesar's writings. He relates homesickness to nostalgia and points out that the term "nostalgia" is derived "from the Greek *nostos*, a return home, and *algos*, meaning pining," giving us the literal meaning of "pining to return home" (p. 93). Sterba (1940), much earlier, related homesickness to the longing for the mother's breast. Freedman (1956) calls our attention to the feelings of nostalgia seen in college students, military personnel, writers, and musical composers.[1] The relationship to preoedipal gratification seems clear, be it with the mother, father, or family.

Although nostalgic tendencies have been associated with an inability to mourn (Kleiner, 1970), I find this may not be so in every instance. In fact, at times, the nostalgic recall is an end-product—a memory trace that is the successful outcome of a mourning-liberation process. When

---

[1]See Miller's (1956) study of Marcel Proust, and Feder's (1982) account of the nostalgia of Charles Ives.

nostalgia becomes a predominant preoccupation, it can be a symptom of pathological mourning — melancholia — and can, if severe enough, lead to suicide. Rosen (1975) has described such instances. Werman (1977) distinguishes nostalgia from homesickness and from fantasy. He describes nostalgia as "an affective-cognitive experience, usually involving memories of places of one's past" (p. 397). He suggests notalgia may be a substitute for mourning and a screen affect.

Winnicott (1974) has noted that nostalgia "relates to the precarious hold that a person may have on the inner representation of a lost object" (p. 27). I do not feel the previous feature is as significant in nostalgia as the indication that there has not been a completed mourning-liberation process for what is "lost" and the nostalgic mood or feeling is indicative of this psychic state. Nostalgia may be an aspect of the mourning-liberation process and hence can be seen in all reactions to losses and changes. It may also serve as a transitory attempt to recapture an aspect of the past in affect and fantasy and thus be temporarily reunited with it. But the feelings and fantasies dissolve and reality takes over. One may see this in viewing family photographs and home movies, visiting sites associated with pleasant memories of the past, or in seeing patients who have similar connections. I have also encountered nostalgic feelings connected with certain smells, sounds, songs, holidays, and other evocative symbols of the past that may still in very transitory fashion elicit feelings of sadness and of pleasure. It is a return to a land that is no more, that may have never been as ideal as it is thought and felt to have been, but that symbolically one still wishes to be with on special occasions.

Ignatieff (1987) has addressed some of the issues of forced migration resulting from the Russian Revolution. He tells the story of his family and their survival attempts to flee from the destructiveness of the Red and White confrontations, the political and economic upheavals, the highly disrupted social and cultural patterns, and the threat to life. The family saga spans four generations and can be appreciated from many points of view. Natural disasters, disease epidemics, wars — civil and external — all seem to follow a similar pattern in the emotional reactions of the survivors.

What Ignatieff catches is the personal human tragedy following these massive disruptions of life, the attempts to cope with them and some of the after-reactions. The abandonment and the enforced isolation of the victims comes through vividly in his chronicle. The "orphans in time" are labeled as outsiders — they are to be viewed with suspicion. They have few friends and supporters and are at serious risk because they have few or no protectors. In this century we have seen many who were sent to concentration camps, who were uprooted because of war, who were expatriated, exiled, and who were torn from their roots. This is the plight of man in other centuries as well. The wish to return to a semblance of normal life, to have the opportunity to mourn and then start life anew, to find an environment where one can belong, be secure, feel accepted and esteemed, find a "home"—all are the goals for having a new sanctuary.

"Homeless" is a term in common usage these days—this terrible situation, which we now appreciate more than ever, involves the loss of home. As Ignatieff (1987) writes, "Belonging now is retrospective rather than actual, remembered rather than experienced, imagined rather than felt" (p. 1). The traumas, however, must be adjusted to, adopted, and encompassed, if we are to reconstitute ourselves and our life. Connections with the past have to be appreciated but recognized as now broken. The photographs in our mind are also reflections of the past—attempts to live in prior time. Yet one must adjust to present reality, reestablish a continuity between internal past and present, pass on our experiences to the present and future generations; and when the mourning process is finished—as far as it can be—the liberation and creativity that can emerge does emerge, under some of the impacts of loss, dispossession, and forced migration.

The relation between loss and creative imagination has been an area of my clinical research for many years. But the healing of the hurt of loss is not easily accomplished—mourning is only one part of the healing process. The fracture resulting from the trauma requires resumption of life.

Ignatieff notes that looking at photographs of ourselves can reawaken a sense of loss "because they work against the integrative functions of forgetting. Photographs are the freeze frames that remind us how discontinuous our lives actually are. It is in a tight weave of forgetting and selective remembering that a continuous self is knitted together" (p. 6).

However, reminders of the past do not always result in a new integration of self. Healing is a process. At times, old fragments appear—washed up on the shore of today but coming from the depths of time. They, too, have to be dealt with, worked out, and appropriately seen as the past. A past is not forgotten, but it no longer holds the pain or impairs the ability to go forth. The release from the past taps into new energies and inch by inch abilities are reclaimed, paths are pursued that seemingly never were known previously, and "past becomes . . . less a fate and ever more a narrative of self-invention" (Ignatieff, 1987, p. 8).

The mourning process heals the wounds of loss, but what is gained can be invaluable—life goes on and can have new rewards and new fulfillments.

REFERENCES

Cohen, R. E. (1987), Stressors: Migration and acculturation to American society. In: *Health and Behavior: Research Agenda for Hispanics.* Chicago: Simon Bolivar Hispanic-American Psychiatric Research and Training Program of the University of Illinois, pp. 59–71.

Eastman, P. (1988), American dream can become a nightmare when older refugees lose their roots. *AARP News Bulletin,* 29/8:4.

Feder, S. (1982), The nostalgia of Charles Ives: An essay in affects and music. *This Annual,* 10:301–332. New York: International Universities Press.

Freedman, A. (1956), The feeling of nostalgia and its relationship to phobia. *Bull. Phila. Assn. Psychoanal.,* 6:84–92.

Garza-Guerrero, A. C. (1974), Culture shock: Its mourning and the vicissitudes of identity. *J. Amer. Psychoanal. Assn.,* 22:408–429.

Grinberg, L. and Grinberg, R. (1984), A psychoanalytic study of migration: Its normal and pathological aspects. *J. Amer. Psychoanal. Assn.,* 32:13–38.

Ignatieff, M. (1988), *The Russian Album: A Family Saga of Revolution, Civil War, and Exile.* New York: Penguin Books, 1988.

Kleiner, J. (1970), On nostalgia. *Bull. Phila. Assn. Psychoanal.,* 20:11–30.

Martin, A. R. (1954), Nostalgia. *Amer. J. Psychoanal.,* 14:93–104.

Miller, M. L. (1956), *Nostalgia: A Psychoanalytic Study of Marcel Proust.* Boston: Houghton Mifflin.

Piers, G. and Piers, M. (1982), On becoming a newcomer. *This Annual,* 10:369–378. New York: International Universities Press.

Pollock, G. H. (1981), Mourning and adaptation. *Internat. J. Psycho-Anal.,* 41:341–361.

_____ (1962), Childhood parent and sibling loss in adult patients: A comparative study. *Archiv. Gen. Psychiat.,* 7:295–305.

_____ (1966), Mourning and childhood loss: Their possible significance in the Josef Breuer-Bertha Pappenheim relationship. *Bull. Assn. Psychoanal. Med.,* 5:51–54.

_____ (1968), The possible significance of childhood object loss in the Josef Breuer-Bertha Pappenheim (Anna O.)-Sigmund Freud relationship. *J. Amer. Psychoanal. Assn.,* 16:711–739.

_____ (1970), Anniversary reactions, trauma and mourning. *Psychoanal. Quart.,* 39:347–371.

_____ (1971a), On time and anniversaries. In: *The Unconscious Today,* ed. M. Kanzer. New York: International Universities Press, pp. 233–257.

_____ (1971b), Temporal anniversary manifestations: Hour, day, holiday. *Psychoanal. Quart.,* 40:123–131.

_____ (1971c), On time, death and immortality. *Psychoanal. Quart.,* 40:435–446.

_____ (1972a), On mourning and anniversaries: The relationship of culturally constituted defensive systems to intra-psychic adaptive processes. *Israel Annals Psychiat. and Related Disciplines,* 10:9–40.

_____ (1972b), Bertha Pappenheim's pathological mourning: Possible effects of childhood sibling loss. *J. Amer. Psychoanal. Assn.*, 20:476–493.

_____ (1973), Bertha Pappenheim: Addenda to her case history. *J. Amer. Psychoanal. Assn.*, 21:328–332.

_____ (1975a), On mourning, immortality and utopia. *J. Amer. Psychoanal. Assn.*, 23:334–362.

_____ (1975b), On anniversary suicide and mourning. In: *Depression and the Human Existence*, ed. T. Benedek & E. J. Anthony. Boston: Little, Brown, pp. 369–393.

_____ (1975c), Mourning and memoralization through music. *This Annual*, 3:423–435. New York: International Universities Press.

_____ (1976), Manifestations of abnormal mourning: Homicide and suicide following the death of another. *This Annual*, 4:225–249. New York: International Universities Press.

_____ (1977a), Mourning: Psychoanalytic theory. In: *International Encyclopedia of Psychiatry, Psychology, Psychoanalysis and Neurology*, ed. B. B. Wolman. New York: Aesculapius, 7:368–371.

_____ (1977b), The mourning process and creative organizational change. *J. Amer. Psychoanal. Assn.*, 25:3–34.

_____ (1978a), On siblings, childhood sibling loss, and creativity. *The Annual of Psychoanalysis*, 6:443–481. New York: International Universities Press.

_____ (1978b), Process and affect: Mourning and grief. *Internat. J. Psycho-Anal.*, 59:255–276.

_____ (1981a), Aging or aged: Development or pathology. In: *The Course of Life: Psychoanalytic Contributions Toward Understanding Personality Development*, ed. S. I. Greenspan & G. H. Pollock. Washington, DC.: U.S. Gov. Printing Office, 3:549–585.

_____ (1981b), Reminiscences and insight. *The Psychoanalytic Study of the Child*, 36:279–287. New Haven: Yale University Press.

_____ (1982), The mourning-liberation process and creativity: The case of Käthe Kollwitz. *This Annual*, 10:333–354. New York: International Universities Press.

_____ (1983), The mourning-liberation process and creativity: The case of Käthe Kollwitz. In: *Art Therapy: Still Growing*, ed. A. Di Maria et al., pp. 9–17.

_____ (1984), Anna O.: Insight, hindsight, and foresight. In: *Anna O.: Fourteen Contemporary Reinterpretations*, ed. M. Rosenbaum & M. Muroff. New York: Free Press, pp. 26–33.

_____ (1985a), Mourning mothers, depressed grandmothers, guilty siblings, and identifying survivors. In: *Parental Influences: In Health and Disease*, ed. E. J. Anthony & G. H. Pollock. Boston: Little, Brown, pp. 235–257.

_____ (1985b), Abandoning parents and abusing caretakers. In: *Parental Influences: In Health and Disease*, ed. E. J. Anthony & G. H. Pollock. Boston: Little, Brown, pp. 349–400.

_____ (1986), Abandonment. In: *The Reconstruction of Trauma: Its Significance in Clinical Work*, ed. A. Rothstein. Madison, CT: International Universities Press, pp. 105–120.

Rosen, G. (1975), Nostalgia: A "forgotten" psychological disorder. *Psycholog. Med.*, 5:340–354.

Spiegel, R., Chrzanowski, G. and Feiner, A. H. (1975), On psychoanalysis in the Third Reich. *Contemp. Psychoanal.*, 11:477–509.

Stein, H. F. (1985), "Culture shock" and the inability to mourn. *The Psychoanalytic Study of Society*, 11:157–172. Hillsdale, NJ: The Analytic Press.

Sterba, E. (1940), Homesickness and the mother's breast. *Psychiat. Quart.,* 14:701–707.
Ticho, G. R. (1971), Cultural aspects of transference and countertransference. *Bull. Menninger Clin.,* 85:313–334.
Werman, D. S. (1977), Normal and pathological nostalgia. *J. Amer. Psychoanal. Assn.,* 25:387–398.
Winnicott, D. W. (1974), *Playing and Reality.* New York: Penguin.

October, 1988

From Transformed Scream, through Mourning, to the Building of Psychic Structure: A Critical Review of the Literature on Music and Psychoanalysis

MARTIN L. NASS, Ph.D. (New York)

One of the most common methodological errors made in applied psychoanalysis is the evaluation of an aesthetic work on the basis of its dynamic meaning in the history of the artist, rather than through criteria that concern themselves with the aesthetic value of the work itself.[1] Aesthetic judgments are reduced to an understanding of the motivation of the individual involved and the work that has been produced is evaluated in these terms. This kind of error, commonly made by dynamic psychology and by psychoanalysis in attempts to arrive at motivational understandings of their subjects on or off the couch bypasses the entire issue of aesthetic or cultural value. Thus a requiem or a piece of sculpture may be "explained" solely in terms of the composer's working through of the loss of a parent. Problems in methodology in applied psychoanalysis are very frequently organized around issues of this nature, and applied psychoanalysis has been subject to proper criticism in this regard. While this problem has been spoken about and referred to in some instances (e.g., Gedo, 1972), there is a body of literature in which this approach continues to exist (e.g., Eissler, 1967), although in more subtle forms.

---

[1]A version of this error is commonly referred to by philosophers as the "genetic fallacy" in which the fact that something current is shown to be related to an earlier version results in its devaluation (see Flew, 1979).

The problem has been one which has been clearly identified over the years. As early as 1942, Susanne Langer stated:

> For the Freudian interpretation, no matter how far it be carried, never offers even the rudest criterion of *artistic* excellence. It may explain why a poem was written, why it is popular . . . But *it makes no distinction between good and bad art* [p. 177; Langer's emphasis].

While I do not believe that psychoanalysis should attempt to be a discipline of aesthetic criticism, it should avoid reductionistic moves toward explanations of creative activity strictly on the basis of conflict and understandings of works of art strictly on the basis of a narrow view of the artist's motivation. With few exceptions (Coltrera, 1965; Feder, 1981a, b; Gedo, 1983; Martin, 1966; Nass, 1971, 1975; Rose, 1980; Rothenberg, 1979; Weissman, 1967), psychoanalytic thought has persisted in its hold on the view of conflict as a sufficient explanation of artistic productions and as a means used by the creative artist to deal with conflict. While this may be partially correct, it is used as a basis of explanation of the meaning of the complete picture rather than as a single aspect of a complex network of factors. The reductionism that analysis has been properly accused of in arriving at formulas to explain patient behavior applies even more strongly to attempts to understand the work of the creative artist. While I do not believe that psychoanalysis should "lay down its arms" before the problem of the creative artist (Freud, 1928, p. 177), many do not demonstrate adequate care and caution in this area, resting content with the belief that the understanding of the individual's conflict explains his work. But the complexity of the creative act cannot be explained on the basis of conflict; nor, since the creative act deals with nonverbal and preverbal phenomena, can approaches that do not examine early developmental issues provide a comprehensive avenue of study. And yet, there surely are valid approaches to the understanding of creative people and the creative process.

I

It has been possible in recent years to arrive at an understanding of the creative act in terms of a multidetermined activity that functions as growth and structure building with the artistic productions arising out of the autonomous structure of the individual, rather than being rooted in his or her psychopathology. One of the factors that seems to me to help produce the confusion between the two is the creative person's greater accessibility to body processes and body rhythms and his capacity to use developmentally earlier modes to reorganize experience. The lower threshold for stimulation and the resulting hypersensitivity of the gifted often result in a narrowing of object distance and an increased narcissistic vulnerability that foster self-esteem problems organized around their talent.[2] To a simple conflict model this appears as a psychopathological motivation for the creative act. One needs to examine the alternative view that both the capacity to reorganize experience, be it motoric, visual, or auditory, and the vulnerability to strong conflict stem from a common set of factors that involve the individual's capacity to be in touch with early experiences, with all that this implies. The talented individual in addition has the autonomous ego gifts that enable him to use this pool of experience to reorganize a view of the world and present it to others, and his talent can function independent of the conflict.

Reports of creative artists have shown that many are able to continue to be creative in the face of massive trauma including periods of psychosis. A recent biography of the writer James Agee (Bergreen, 1984) indicates that during severe alcoholic episodes and periods of lack of personal hygiene that warranted his exclusion from the motion-picture-studio dining room, he continued to write productively to the great surprise of many. Similar experiences of creating under periods of intense disorganization have been reported in the cases of Robert Schumann and Vincent van Gogh, among many others. To view the issue primarily in terms of a normality-pathology dimension misses the mark. I feel that Greenacre's (1957) view helps to explain some of the special developmental issues in the creative. She sees the creative act in certain individuals as serving the function of moving them toward a sense of body closure that has not been achieved for constitutional or developmental reasons, largely related to the heightened sensitivity and body awareness of the gifted; in such instances, the form of the creative act (not solely its content) operates in the service of structure building. Thus the artist who says he *has* to produce and is thus driven is not only communicating a work but is also involved in a quest for narcissistic closure, according to Greenacre. This sense begins early in his development, is elaborated through successive stages, and may have its oedipal version in variants of the family romance. According to Greenacre, it begins in a greater sensory awareness (probably physiologically based), a predisposition to a wide and deeper range of empathy, and a sensorimotor system that has the potential for a wide range of development and a wealth of symbolization.

---

[2]See also Lowenfeld (1941), who states with regard to creative individuals, "experiences which are little different from the experiences of other people, take on a traumatic character and are fitted into the patient's traumatic pattern" (p. 121).

The creative act serves a variety of intrapsychic functions as well as interactive ones, and though it may become involved with conflict (Hartmann, 1939) it does not strictly arise from conflicted behavior. The pattern of sensorimotor organization of the gifted, to my mind, is what we start with, and this then unfolds and interacts with life circumstances. It is not that the talent develops as a reaction to environmental pressures. To state it differently, I see the function of the creative act in some artists as serving to keep them in equilibrium, but I do not see this at all as the cause of their creative capacities. Ego psychology has provided us with a methodology previously unavailable in which the creative individual's talent can be seen as related to autonomous areas of functioning, and the act of creation need not be conceptualized as regressive. Some of the work of David Rapaport (1960) and George Klein (1959) makes it possible to relate the activities to shifts relating to varying levels of cognitive organization, and to activities related to the building and rebuilding of nonconflictual psychic structure. That creators can continue to create in the face of massive psychic disturbance, including psychoses, I feel lends support to this view.

While there are individual meanings to the act of creation in the individual which may dynamically relate to the creation of a child, to the incorporation of the paternal phallus, or to a means of dealing with issues of castration anxiety, the dimensions of ego functioning and the *function* of the creative act in the psychic economy need renewed attention by psychoanalysts to make our understanding of the creative process more complete.

II

The relationship between the artist and the work produced presents a number of unique issues. I will deal first with the difficulty many creative people have in completing a work, separating from it, and "owning" it. This act taps all levels of conflict, ranging from showing unacceptable body contents, to oedipal reenactments in the presentation of love gifts, through dread of surpassing the father and consequent castration anxiety (Arlow, 1984; Kris, 1952) All of these may be played out simultaneously and may involve preoedipal as well as oedipal issues.

Once material has been presented to the public it is no longer under the artist's control, and all levels of separation anxiety are brought into play, relating to the acceptability of the production and the wish to work on it further. At times artists are able to play this out, witness Brahms's reworking of the Piano Trio op. 8 late in his life, and the not uncommon reports of artists slipping into galleries to continue work on a painting that is already on exhibit. The work for them has special meaning, often involving history or conflict, but not necessarily so. Some works reflect a continuation of a childhood experience, where early perceptions and experiences are reworked into the artist's production such as Henry Moore's description of his work on his statue called *Seated Woman* evoking memories of massaging his mother's back (James, 1966). For some, developmental changes are reflected in their productions, such as the several madonnas sculpted by Michelangelo over the course of his many productive years and recently discussed by Liebert (1983) in a work that has generated some criticism (Gedo, 1984) regarding issues of interpretation and the meaning of a work to the artist.

To me, these developmental changes represent the expression of universal issues from an artist's adolescence (his first madonna at age sixteen) to the piece he was working on at the time of his death (the Rondanini Pietà) reflecting a quest for close union with another. Some disagreement concerning which of the figures the artist identified with was expressed by Liebert and Gedo. These appear to me to be unanswerable issues and fall beyond the major consideration of the meaning of a work of art to the artist. I wonder if such material would emerge with accuracy were an artist to be on the couch during the process of working on a piece. Certainly, there is a greater possibility of obtaining these kinds of data in a psychoanalysis than in a retrospective report on the artist's history.

One of the difficulties in working in the area of applied psychoanalysis is the tendency to equate the retrospective gathering of data in a scholarly investigation with the constructions and interpretations one arrives at in the consulting room. There are a myriad of variables which can be reorganized in a wide variety of ways, many of which are plausible and "make sense," and others which come to a different conclusion, but can also be convincing. When we work with clinical data, the medium of the transference helps to sharpen the material, and the analyst has a personal, tested, and convincing apparatus through which to process the information. To attempt to assess specific identifications of an artist's work, even in an ongoing psychoanalysis, is a formidable task—to do so without the medium of the transference must be seen as speculative, and I see greater rewards in understanding the meaning of an artist's work by dealing more with the formal aspects of it.

This is not to say that individual works or aspects of works do not have special meanings. I have spoken with composers who have related the content of compositions to specific experiences of childhood (Nass, 1984). There are also extensive descriptive explanations that some composers have given regarding discursive meanings of their pieces, such as Beethoven's notes for his Eighth Symphony and, at a more personal level, Smetana's (undated) autobiographical reflections on his First String Quartet. However, in an understanding of the creative process and in the psychology of the creative artist, issues of form, structure building, and development are crucial and are often lost to speculations regarding the meaning of a given work. This is particularly true in moving from the nondiscursive to the discursive realm. Some of the recent work of Feder which deals with Mahler (Feder, 1978, 1980b, 1981b) and with Ives (Feder, 1980a, 1981a, 1982, 1984) attempts to form generalizations about the creative process through the interpretations of specific works of these composers and thus to employ a more "clinical" methodology. Such approaches can help to provide a bridge between content and structural methodologies but focus more on the area of biographical studies in which the life of the artist and the relationship of his music to his life are of paramount importance.

I feel that we are indeed in the realm of speculation when we attempt to assess correctly the dynamic meaning of an artistic work. I would even state that the meanings an artist may attribute to the piece can mask other levels that may be more accurate. Although an artist may describe a subjective state experienced while working on something, when there is a shift to the nonverbal, nondiscursive dimension that meaning is no longer the same because there are no point-for-point connections among these modes of expression. Translations of them are approximations, just as words are approximations of feeling states, and for many composers notations are inaccurate portrayals of the sounds they wish to present. It seems to me that our attempts to understand the relationship between an artist and a work of art may often be reductionistic ways to deal with our own feelings regarding the uncertain. Imparting other levels of meaning to them can be ways of reducing the anxiety of not knowing.[3] By maintaining more of a focus on structure and less on content I feel that we can learn a great deal more than we know about the creative process. This problem in music is further complicated by the fact that it is a nonverbal medium and that the earliest developmental roots are being tapped (Nass, 1984). Even in discussing the development of language, Lewis (1977) speculates that the mother's spoken words are initially experienced by the infant as tones and rhythms. A similar point is also made by Loewald (1978) who says:

---

[3]In a letter to P. A. Martin, Conrad Aiken expresses his disturbance over people reading dynamic meanings into his work in a manner that has little to do with his intent (Martin, 1966).

The mother's flow of words does not convey meaning to or symbolize "things" for the infant—"meaning" as something differentiated from "fact"—but the sounds, tone of voice, and rhythm of speech are fused within the apprehended global event. One might say that, while the mother utters words, the infant does not perceive words but is bathed in sound, rhythm, etc. as accentuating ingredients of a uniform experience [p. 187]

Thus, when we use words to describe musical processes and sounds, we are shifting from a basically nondiscursive form to a discursive one (Langer, 1942) with all of the difficulties inherent in such a shift. It seems to me that this is one of the basic reasons why so little work has been done in music and psychoanalysis and why most of the work that has been done has not followed the basic methodology of a modern ego-psychology approach. Style and formalistic issues have not been stressed, and most of the work has focused on issues of content.

III

With this introduction as background, a more specific consideration of the papers dealing with issues of music and its relationship with psychoanalysis will be undertaken. These can be organized in three broad areas: (1) those that deal with the biography of the composer and attempt to understand the composition through events in his life; (2) those that present psychoanalytic studies of musicians and composers; (3) those that attempt a metapsychological approach to understanding the psychological meaning of music.

PAPERS DEALING WITH BIOGRAPHICAL INFORMATION

Several psychoanalytic authors have concentrated on a biographical perspective of the composer they study in an attempt to relate their understanding of the music to events in the composer's life. Among these are Feder (1978, 1980a, 1980b. 1981a, 1981b, 1982, 1984); MacAlpine and Hunter (1952); Pollock (1975b); Schwartz (1965); and the Sterbas (1954).

Feder discusses the content of a great deal of the music of Gustav Mahler in terms of Mahler's lifelong preoccupation with death and abandonment. He relates these issues to Mahler's constant exposure to death from the beginning of his life, having been born soon after the death of a sibling and having experienced over many years the deaths of siblings, the deaths of his parents when he was in his twenties, and the death of his own daughter when she was a child. Feder (1981b) concludes that "The deaths of children and of youths is the theme which permeates the literary and musical aspect of Mahler's *oeuvre* from first to last" (p. 280). This point is also made by Mooney (1968) in discussing Mahler's work and by Pollock (1974, 1975b). The latter makes it clear (and this issue will be elaborated in detail later in this essay) that musical creativity is not dependent upon object loss, but that given such loss, the direction of musical creativity and creativity in general will be influenced by the intrapsychic processes of mourning and memorialization (Pollock, 1974, 1975b, p. 494). He elaborates this point through detailed documentation of Gustav Mahler's multiple experiences involving death.

This issue is also reflected in a different way in Schwartz's (1965) paper on Rossini in which he reports that Rossini's creative output took a radical drop during the last thirty-nine years of his life. Schwartz attributes this to the death of Rossini's mother and to his subsequent depression. Feder (1980a) also understands Ives's lack of musical productivity during the last thirty years of his life to be connected with his having reached the age at which his own father died (age forty-nine) and to an incomplete mourning process. Issues of depression are further reflected in Esman's (1951) study of Mozart, in which he relates the composer's intense periods of work to the working out of depressions. Similarly, Cambor, Lisowitz, and Miller (1962) studied some thirty creative jazz musicians, who, while technically not composers, are involved in composition through their improvisations. They found that virtually all of their subjects suffered from profound depressions and that music was used as a way of expressing feelings and of relating to others in a way in which they were otherwise unable to do. As mentioned above, Pollock (1974; 1975b) considers one aspect of the creative act as a way of dealing with loss.

In his work on Charles Ives, Feder (1980a, 1981a, 1982, 1984) continues in his quest for the contextual and biographical meaning of a composer's work. He relates the specific meanings of a piece by Ives entitled "Decoration Day" to a multidetermined series of memories and events in the composer's life and in his relationship with his father who was a band leader during the Civil War and who died when the composer was twenty.

While such studies, including the one by Editha and Richard Sterba on Beethoven (1954), are contributions to psychoanalytic studies of composers, by and large they do not address the fundamental issue of the meaning of music per se in the broadest sense or in the developmental context of the creative process. Issues of auditory style (Nass, 1971) and of the use of auditory imagery as a way of responding to the world as a formal attribute of life are barely touched on. The notable exception is

Feder (1981b) who in a concluding statement says that musical composition may be related to conflict at times, but describes a function that he
calls a "conceptualizing function" through which the composer thinks

> in tonal, formal, temporal, and essentially, non-representational
> terms. As such it is a unique mode of thinking, but, like the common
> varieties of cognition, a kind that the composer may employ in his
> coming to terms with the world. . . . I speak here not of the verbal
> aspects of music . . . but the purely musical aspect . . . It is a way of
> thinking, hence of coming to terms with the inner and outer world,
> which includes aggression, trauma and loss [p. 282]

It is this approach to understanding the creative function which has
been most neglected in psychoanalytic writings on the creative process
wherein most investigators have placed their emphasis upon studies of
content, meaning, and pathography to the exclusion of a broader
understanding of the meaning and development of the creative act in the
overall psychology of the artist. Issues of sensory style, sensory preference, and the composer's focus on the world of sound (Sessions, 1970)
seem to me to present avenues toward a broader and deeper understanding of the creative process than do works of a strictly pathographic
nature.

There is, of course, a valued place for biographical studies of
musicians and composers. Rather than emphasizing pathography, such
studies would throw greater light on the creative process if their focus
were on the growth of the individual through his work and the way in
which the creative act was used in the service of growth and development.
Feder's (1980a, 1981a, 1982, 1984) studies of Charles Ives move in that
direction. One can also approach Michelangelo's several Pietàs over the
course of his long life from that perspective (see Liebert, 1983), or
Eugene O'Neill's treatment of similar familial themes over the course of
his writing career. Such approaches would place studies of creativity in
general and musical productivity in particular in the context of the
creative individual's overall functioning.

STUDIES DEALING WITH THE PSYCHOANALYTIC
TREATMENT OF MUSICIANS AND COMPOSERS

There are several studies that report on the psychoanalytic treatment of
musicians and/or composers, the earliest being that of Freud's brief
treatment of Bruno Walter (Sterba, 1951; Pollock, 1975a). The treatment
itself consisted of only five or six sessions, following the first of which
Freud advised Walter to visit Sicily to deal with the severe pain in his

conducting arm which interfered with both his conducting and his ability to perform as a pianist. When this prescription was not effective in dealing with the symptom, Freud advised him to continue to conduct and said that Freud himself would take the responsibility for any consequences resulting. Sterba (1951), who interviewed Walter, was told by the latter that the treatment consisted mainly of advice giving in which Freud encouraged him to overcome his neurosis by conscious effort.

Ramana's (1952) report of the case of a musician he treated in India who was a paranoid schizophrenic is of interest in a different connection. Here, too, the treatment was not "classical" in nature. Rather, much of the contact between analyst and patient was through home visits. For this patient music was a "protective field which nobody else could invade" (p. 233). Despite the patient's illness, his functioning as a musician was not severely impaired. As indicated earlier, creative functions have been known to persist despite severe psychopathology, and this case appears to illustrate this point quite well.

Safirstein (1962) reports on the treatment of a thirty-four-year-old woman who was a professional cellist and who suffered from stage fright. Some of the issues around her problem were understood in terms of her fear of competition and the conclusion that "Playing an instrument proficiently was felt as an acutely experienced threat to her basic dependency needs." (p. 39). This paper, however, does not address the fundamental developmental issues of the meaning of music in the psychic economy of this woman, nor does it deal with these issues from other than a descriptive point of view. A similar criticism can be raised with respect to Racker's (1953) paper in which he reports on the treatment of a musician whose singing helped to defend against "paranoid anxiety."

Oremland's (1975) paper on the analysis of a twenty-year-old trombonist is an attempt to deal with these issues, but this study, too, has several areas of question. His patient's father had been treated by Oremland some five years before he began to treat the son, which inevitably had to create some complications in the treatment. In addition, the paper focuses on the conflictual meaning of the patient's talent and does not address the issue of the role of his talent in his overall psychic economy. Oremland discusses the changing meaning of the instrument in the patient's life, from transitional object to a detachable penis. The patient's work at composing music was understood to be his manner of responding to loss and differentiating from his mother. To its credit, the paper is an attempt to assess the meaning of music to a given individual on a deeper level and to relate it to his dynamic functioning.

The studies by Klyman (1980) and by Wittenberg (1980) also present case reports in which music and musical material play a role in the analysis of their patients. In the former case, a good deal of the patient's material was organized through his identification with operatic characters. This also served as a resistance to "plain talking." Wittenberg's patient, who was a performing musician, began to compose music during his analysis. The author feels that the musical material followed the form of dream productions and was inversely related to them. Both the dreams and the musical compositions were treated as key themes in the analysis. Again, both of these studies do not address the structural issues of the creative process.

Martin's (1966) study, while dealing with an operatic plot, does not really deal with music per se. He uses the Marschallin theme from Strauss's *Der Rosenkavalier* as a jumping-off point to develop a category of conflict in which an older woman loves young boys. He feels that it is a common constellation in which the woman identifies with the boy and plays out a homosexual wish, thus dealing with her bisexual identification and desire to have her mother in intercourse.

In a unique clinical study, Bornstein (1977) deals with the psychoanalytic treatment of a congenitally blind musician. His paper attempts to understand the meaning of his patient's talent from several perspectives. Most pertinent in the understanding of the patient's need to play and to practice for many hours is the view of his playing as providing sensory nutriment (Rapaport, 1960) for this sensorily deprived man. Bornstein also addresses the issue of the effects of an individual's talent upon his overall development and psychic structure and also considers the drive-organized meaning of the instrument. While the paper places a strong emphasis on the problems of the blind and makes a contribution to the literature on special issues of the blind, it is the only clinical study encountered which raises many of the questions that I feel are crucial in studies of the gifted and of the role of an individual's talent in his development.

In general, the literature dealing with the psychoanalytic treatment of musicians and composers is rather sparse in nature and, with one notable exception, focuses on issues of conflict, largely ignoring the role of talent in the functioning of the patient. How an individual's talent serves him and what adaptive use he makes of his cognitive gifts are not issues that are considered in most of the studies reviewed. Rather, their focus is on conflict and psychopathology.

STUDIES USING A METAPSYCHOLOGICAL
APPROACH TO MUSIC

There has been a large body of literature relating music and psychoanalysis since the 1920s. The structure of the majority of these papers has followed the basic approaches in psychoanalytic writing at each particular time. Where drive interpretations of psychological processes were paramount in the understanding of psychoanalytic phenomena, these papers dealt mainly with id interpretations of music and of the creative process (see Nass, 1971). There has been very little work which has attempted to deal with the creative act as an autonomous structure that has a positive role in the psychic economy of the artist, the work of Greenacre (1957) and Coltrera (1965) being notable exceptions. It seems that many writers in this area applied their methodology in situations where their knowledge of music was most limited. I am in agreement with Feder (1982) when he discusses the fact that there is an assumption "bordering on the arrogant that psychoanalysis may be usefully 'applied' regardless of the analyst's competence in another field" (p. 305). This is an area in which psychoanalysis has been roundly criticized and justifiably so.

Noy has surveyed the literature dealing with psychoanalysis and music and published his findings in a series of five articles (Noy, 1966, 1967a, b, c, d). His approach, while valuable and comprehensive, is primarily in the nature of a compendium and does not address a particular point of view. It has importance as a documentation of the work done to that time.

As cited above, there is still an active controversy in the literature regarding the creative act and conflict. Some writers, e.g., Feder (1978, 1980a), Mooney (1968), and Pollock (1975b), have interpreted the work of some composers as their ways of dealing with loss and mourning and working through old memories. Segal (1952) also believes that in order to produce the artist needs to experience mourning fully and must have a greater capacity for tolerating anxiety and depression than does the neurotic. However, Pollock (1975b) maintains that loss is not a precondition for creative work, but when present may partially determine the shape of the work. Greenacre (1957) also holds that there is no intrinsic connection between talent and neurosis but that the creative act comes about as a result of particular developmental issues which relate to the early physiological hypersensitivities and intense empathic abilities of the gifted. Her work places the psychology of the gifted within a normal developmental framework.

The works of Eissler (1967), Michel (1960), and Montani (1945) relate the creative act to an expression of conflict and an attempt to deal with conflict. This is also the position of Lee (1947, 1949), who maintains that the creative act is related to the activation of destructive rage.

The created work is something made to bridge the way back to mental health from the despondency into which the artist's destructive rage has plunged him . . . The artist creates in answer to an urgent unconscious need to relieve his suffering by extricating himself from a mobile depression brought on by the expression of unreasonable destructive rage [Lee, 1947, p. 283].

Here, too, is a point of view in which the creative act is seen as the working out of psychic conflict and which ignores the role of creativity in the overall character of the individual (Rosen, 1964). This is also the position taken by Racker (1951, 1953, 1965) who holds that music represents an attempt to annul the separation from the mother, to defend oneself against the bad objects and recover the good ones. The fact that creativity and conflict have been so central to psychoanalytic thought over the years can also be noted in Kris's (1955) statement that "In every process of creation the gradual emergence from conflict plays a part" (p. 32). It is interesting to note in this connection that Freud (1930) pointed the way toward the need to understand aspects of creativity other than their conflictual side when he said, "A satisfaction of this kind, such as the artist's joy in creating, in giving his phantasies body . . . has a special quality which we shall one day be able to characterize in meta-psychological terms" (p. 79). This, incidentally, appears to be a change in the position taken two years earlier in the Dostoyevsky paper (Freud, 1928) holding that psychoanalysis must lay down its arms "before the problem of the creative artist" (p. 177).

Turning to the specific studies of music, one finds in the earlier writings (as well as in many of the relatively recent ones) the strict application of unconscious conflict to the understanding of the musical process. The literature is replete with such statements as "All music represents the deeper sources of unconscious thinking because it is untrammeled by the limitations of language, as in poetry, or by visual imagery, as in painting" (van der Chijs, 1923, p. 379); "The libido concerned in [music] has yet not reached the object-level of development" (Pfeifer, 1923, p. 381); "In music, the pleasure principle replaces the reality principle because music is non-verbalized, it effects the emotions only" (Coriat, 1945, pp. 414–415), and Pfeifer's (1922) attribution of musical sound to the establishment of genital sexuality and to the building up of sexual tensions prior to copulation. Montani (1945) explains the tension created by a diminished third in music to the number "3," symbolizing the phallus (since the diminished third is weaker, it evokes castration anxiety), while Racker (1951) relates the musical tone to a transformed scream. While one can understand these positions in relation to their role in the history of psychoanalysis, they have basically taken the perspective that an analyst can know all on the basis of his methodology and have resulted in psychoanalysis going in over its head (or one could say ears) in attempting to explain some most complex issues. Such theories also equate primary-process thinking with primitive thinking and implicitly place value judgements on nonverbal symbolization being less developed than verbal thinking. This point of view implies that man's greatest creative achievements in the arts (painting, sculpture, music) are less well developed because they do not deal with words. This is a common methodological error which holds the position that "later is better" and that because a function appears on the scene at a later point in development, it is a higher-order function. Brenner (1968) also makes this point, although he seems to consider it more from the side of pathology, when he states that later-appearing functions do not necessarily replace earlier ones.

The works of Kohut (1957) and Kohut and Levarie (1950) are mainly in the same vein, although there is a move in the 1957 paper to apply a structural point of view to the musical processes. Basically, these writers consider music as a means of dealing with tension and anxiety and of mastering the chaotic world of sound, a position also taken by Miller (1967). In his 1957 paper, Kohut follows the classical metapsychological approach in attempting to understand the musical function from id, ego, and superego perspectives and to analyze its function from its relationship to the primary and secondary processes. He explores the id functions from the point of view of primitive rhythmical roots evolving from early experiences of rocking and moving toward adult sexual rhythm. The ego functions involve mastery of early threatening sounds (see also Kohut and Levarie, 1950) in which the ego playfully repeats the original traumatic threat and enjoys it, while the superego functions are said to involve the recognition of and obedience to rules. The tune is viewed as a secondary-process function of music which may cover the basic rhythm, a primary-process layer. Issues of ego mastery over tension-producing stimuli are also considered in the papers written by Berezin (1958) and by Bychowski (1951) who held that "artistic activity is an expression of the power of the ego to bind energy released from the unconscious" (p. 601).

A similar approach to the understanding of the musical process is taken by Michel (1965) in his book on the Freudian approach to music. Michel outlines a psychosexual understanding of music giving oral, anal, and phallic interpretations to the musical function. The oral experience relates to experiences of rhythmic rocking, sucking, and the recapitulation of early body experiences, the anal to experiences of anal flatulent sounds, and the phallic to the qualities of repetition.

As can be noted, the reductionistic quality of these papers is most striking. Their focus is largely on conflict and the nature of conflict. They do not consider the nature and the development of talent, cognitive and sensory styles, or the creative individual's capacity to call forth and utilize early modes of experience and use them in the service of creativity. The formulation of the creative act as regressive (Kris, 1953) has been open to criticism (Coltrera, 1965; Feder, 1982; Nass, 1971; Rothenberg, 1979; Schachtel, 1959; Weissman, 1967), since the creator's ability to contact ambiguous affective and cognitive states, maintain contact with early body and self-states, and continue to use them involves a greater degree of ego strength and higher levels of functioning than are implied by the formulation of a regressive process.

Several interesting approaches to the understanding of music from a developmental perspective have been presented by writers who are not psychoanalysts, but whose methodologies are in accord with a metapsychological point of view. Noteworthy among them is the work of the philosopher Susanne Langer (1942, 1953, 1967), whose work I have considered elsewhere (Nass, 1971). Her work on the nondiscursive quality of music and its ability to render experiences and projections that cannot be presented discursively highlights the very nature of musical expression. To her, this is the very purpose of artistic construction (Langer, 1953). She holds that music can be true to the life of feeling in a way language cannot and can express ambivalent forms simultaneously (Langer, 1942). Langer's (1967) view of artistic conception is that it is not a transitional phase of mental evolution "but a final symbolic form making revelation of truths about actual life" (p. 81). Although not dealing within a psychoanalytic framework or with psychoanalytic terminology, Langer's position is clearly one in which the creative act is not an expression of conflict.

Cooke (1959) also sees music as a language of the emotions. His position is that the intentionality of the composer is experienced by the listener who taps the feelings the composer expresses in writing the particular piece. The composer Roger Sessions (1950) has also taken a similar view, holding that the performer and the listener will reexperience the steps taken by the composer in his original experience of composition. Sessions (1941) feels that one's primary musical responses to music derive from the earliest body rhythms dating to the beginnings of life. That music taps early developmental roots is also considered by Ehrenzweig (1965), Hindemith (1952), McDonald (1970), Nass (1971, 1975, 1984), Niederland (1958), and Sterba (1946, 1965).

A study of Sabbeth (1979) applies a technical musicological approach (Schenker's analysis) to Freud's theory of jokes and finds that both deal with issues of familiarity and repetition, are nonverbal, and deal with structures beneath the surface as well as relating to thinking developed in early childhood. While this is a rather imaginative and unique approach to some relationships between music and psychoanalysis, it does not deal with the basic issues discussed herein, although it deals with some fundamental formal similarities between the two phenomena.

It seems to me that one of the methodological problems frequently encountered in studies of music arises from attempts to render their structures discursively meaningful. Often attempts to give them discursive meaning (e.g., in Noy's [1968] description of a fugue's attractiveness relating to a mother following a toddler) shift the focus away from the music and result in the loss of its intrinsic meaning. There is an attempt to give it particular symbolic value. Such a more formalized approach was attempted in two studies by Knobloch and associates (1964, 1968). They had fifty-nine people listen to fragments of musical compositions ranging from baroque to modern and had them rate the pieces on scales that rated "interpersonal" qualities of the music, to test the hypothesis that the composer attempts to satisfy certain interpersonal needs which are also present in the listener. Their findings did not support their original contention, and they concluded that neither composer nor listener was clearly aware of these "interpersonal" tendencies.

Such approaches, which attempt to find specific "meanings" in musical works, seem to me to miss an essential issue in the area of musical signification and do not address more basic, fundamental factors which are developmental in nature. In fact, the musicologist Leonard Meyer (1956, 1967), in presenting the basic positions on signification in music, is most critical of the "referential" position which seeks external reference points to the understanding of music. The other two positions he cites are the "formal," which attempts to deal with the architectural structure of the music, and the "kinetic-syntactic," which states that the cardinal aspects of music are functional. It is this latter position which is represented by the work of Langer and which Meyer states is the most crucial one to musicologists. This, most interestingly, is the one that relates most closely to a developmental point of view and the one that can move toward an understanding of the creative process from a fresher perspective.

IV: Future Directions

As can be gleaned from the above review and commentary, the status of psychoanalytic writings that deal with music, with few exceptions, presents a rather confused picture. Methodologies often reflect a näive approach to the field and the creative act in general, and musical composition in particular is seen as a means of expressing and attempting to deal with conflict. The perspective of a modern ego-psychology approach which views the creative act as an autonomous function that can be used independently of and in spite of severe conflict is largely ignored. Some of the recent works of Gedo (1983) and of Rose (1980) move in that direction. A developmental perspective can account for structures that arise out of conflict, as in the cases of early exposure to and sensitivity to sound (Niederland, 1958), or in Greenacre's (1957, 1958a, 1958b, 1963) work on the developmental issues in creativity, where familial circumstances interact with the child's unusual sensitivities to foster the development of his talent. McDonald's (1970) work on music as a developmental process is a step in this direction. It seems to me that the data for investigation of the creative process need to be obtained from the creators themselves, whether through their writings, through psychoanalytic investigations, or through intensive interviews dealing with their experience during the creative act. Rothenberg's (1979) work is an example of this approach. Many works have appeared in which composers and musical artists have been most revealing of their inspirational and creative processes, among them those by Amram (1968), Copland (1952), Cott (1974), Hanson (1942) Hindemith (1952), Horowitz (1982), Sessions (1941, 1950, 1970), and Stravinsky (1947).

My study of composers (Nass, 1984) attempts to apply a developmental perspective to the process of inspiration by relating some of the descriptive accounts given by composers to a framework that draws from the works of Greenacre (1957), Mahler (1968), Piaget (1954), Schilder (1950, 1964), Spitz (1963, 1965), and Winnicott (1953, 1967). My contention is that musicians have dealt with separation issues in a unique way, organizing a part of them around experiences dealing with sound or experiences that in some way have been integrated into a musical matrix. Thus some developmental tasks, e.g., the development and maintenance of object constancy, may be handled by the musically gifted child by incorporating them into his special auditory sensitivity and extending them through experiences involving sound. These early forms of expression are retained and are given musical shape. The musician's capacity to retain them and have access to inner workings also leaves him more subject to narcissistic onslaughts and to self-esteem fluctuations. It seems to me that such capacities to retain earlier modes which are nonverbal and preverbal can in no way be said to be less developed than are verbal modes of expression and creating even though they originally stem from earlier developmental periods of the individual's life. I would view them as more of a sign of ego strength than of weakness, as the following statement implies:

In this cultural realm [music] the reasonable and sensible ego suffers irretrievable defeat, for the effect of music is to penetrate to layers of such archaic intimacy that any attempt to translate it into a rational syntax is bound to fail [Eissler, 1967, p. 35].

While Eissler is on one level agreeing with Langer and the other writers who argue against a translation of music into discursive, linguistic terms, the implication in this statement, which is typical of many writings on music in the psychoanalytic literature, is that the more "mature" means of viewing artistic creations is to translate them into rational, verbal terms. This again implicitly equates the continuation of developmentally earlier modes of functioning with psychopathology.

The methodological problems in studies of music and psychoanalysis can therefore be viewed as the methodological problems of applied psychoanalysis in general. They involve the difficulty in understanding the creative act as an autonomous structure which has early developmental roots and which may come under the influence of psychic conflict and may involve early unconscious fantasies (Arlow, 1984), but which is something autonomously driven in the creator and can operate under the most dire circumstances (witness Messaien's compositions in a concentration camp). The creative artist must have the capacity to face intense levels of anxiety which stem from every developmental level and to face them continuously. He must be able to deal with the unknown and unfamiliar and be open to new material. I have understood this capacity of the artist to be open to new material and to reexperience early modes of thought as his capacity to reexperience early separation trauma (Nass, 1984). It involves the ability of the gifted individual to remain open to these nonverbal experiences involving body states and body awareness and to use them in the service of his art. Greenacre (1958b) considers this capacity for enclosure to be related to constitutional and developmental issues of the gifted. Further, artists will frequently experience depression, in some cases of a profound nature, upon completing a work and here, too, all levels of separation anxiety, including castration anxiety are played out.

This capacity to tolerate unclosure and to live with it as a part of one's functioning is a necessary condition to creative activity. It involves the capacity to wait, to discard quick, glib answers to problems, to deal with not knowing for long periods of time rather than supplying a ready answer as a means of obtaining completion. It applies to the work of the analyst (which can be seen in this context as creative activity) as well as to the work of the artist. As suggested in my paper on composers (Nass, 1984) it differentiates the more gifted artist who is able to look at and work with the pathbreaking alternative solutions to problems from the more routine one. It requires the ability to deal with intense feelings of anxiety during the process of looking inwardly, a requirement not unlike some intense periods of analysis.

The issue that I am addressing was beautifully put by the physicist Richard Feynman (1983) in a television interview:

> You see, one thing is, I can live with doubt and uncertainty and not knowing. I think it's much more interesting to live not knowing than to have answers which may be wrong. . . . I don't have to know an answer. I don't feel frightened by not knowing things, by being lost in a mysterious universe without having any purpose, which is the way it really is, so far as I can tell possibly. It doesn't frighten me [p. 16].

To my way of thinking, studies of the creative process which make use of this type of material through interviews with gifted people will increase our understanding of this complex process.

Summary

This paper considers the common methodological errors encountered in the literature that deals with the creative process. These are: (1) a variation of the "genetic fallacy" in which a developmentally later achievement is faulted because it appears earlier in the history of the individual; (2) the evaluation of aesthetic works on the basis of the artist's motivation; and (3) a view of the creative process as conflict-dominant. The relationship between the artist and his work is also considered, and the completion of this work is treated from the viewpoints of varying levels of separation issues.

The literature that deals with psychoanalysis and music is reviewed and is organized according to those papers that attempt to understand musical compositions through the events in the lives of composers, those that deal with the psychoanalytic treatment of composers and musicians, and those that attempt a metapsychological approach to understanding the psychological meaning of music.

Finally, some suggestions are made for the direction of future work in this area. These include the need to view the creative act as an autonomous function, the need for a developmental perspective in studies in this area, and the need for a greater degree of direct investigation of the experiences of the creative individuals themselves.

R E F E R E N C E S

Amram, D. (1968), *Vibrations: The Adventures and Musical Times of David Amram.* New York: Viking.

Arlow, J. A. (1984), Disturbances in the sense of time. With special references to the experiences of timelessness. *Psychoanal. Quart.,* 53:13–37.

Berezin, M. A. (1958), Some observations on art (music) and its relation to ego mastery. *Bull. Phila. Assn. Psychoanal.,* 8:49–65.

Bergreen, L. (1984), *James Agee: A Life.* New York: Dutton.

Bornstein, M. (1977), Analysis of a congenitally blind musician. *Psychoanal. Quart.,* 46:23–37.

Brenner, C. (1968), Archaic features of ego functioning. *Internat. J. Psycho-Anal.,* 49:426–429.

Bychowski, G. (1951), Metapsychology of artistic creation. *Psychoanal. Quart.,* 20:592–602.

Cambor, G. C., Lisowitz, G. M., & Miller, M. D. (1962), Creative jazz musicians: A clinical study. *Psychiat.,* 25:1–15.

Coltrera, J. T. (1965), On the creation of beauty and thought: The unique as vicissitude. *J. Amer. Psychoanal. Assn.,* 13:634–703.

Cooke, D. (1959), *The Language of Music.* London: Oxford University Press.

Copland, A. (1952), *Music and Imagination.* New York: Mentor.

Coriat, I. H. (1945), Some aspects of a psychoanalytic interpretation of music. *Psychoanal. Rev.,* 32:408–418.

Cott, J. (1974), *Stockhausen: Conversations with the Composer.* London: Pan Books.

Ehrenzweig, A. (1965), *The Psychoanalysis of Artistic Vision and Hearing.* New York: Braziller.

Eissler, K. (1967), Psychopathology and creativity. *Amer. Imago,* 24:35–81.

Esman, A. H. (1951), Mozart: A study in genius. *Psychoanal. Quart.,* 20:603–612.

Farnsworth, P. R. (1961), Musicality and abnormality. *Conf. Psychiat. Basel,* 4:158–164.

Feder, S. (1978), Gustav Mahler, dying. *Internat. Rev. Psycho-Anal.,* 5:125–148.

_____ (1980a), Decoration Day: A boyhood memory of Charles Ives. *Musical Quart.,* 46:232–261.

_____ (1980b), Gustav Mahler um mitternacht. *Internat. Rev. Psycho-Anal.,* 7:11–26.

_____ (1981a), Charles and George Ives: The veneration of boyhood. *This Annual,* 9:265–316. New York: International Universities Press.

_____ (1981b), Gustav Mahler: The music of fratricide. *Internat. Rev. Psycho-Anal.,* 8:257–284.

_____ (1982), The nostalgia of Charles Ives: An essay in affects and music. *This Annual,* 10:301–332. New York: International Universities Press.

_____ (1984), Charles Ives and the unanswered question. *The Psychoanalytic Study of Society,* 10:321–351. Hillsdale, NJ: The Analytic Press.

Feynman, R. (1983), The pleasure of finding things out. *Nova,* #002 (WBGH transcript).

Flew, A. (1979), *A Dictionary of Philosophy.* New York: St. Martin's Press.

Freud, S. (1928), Dostoevsky and parricide. *Standard Edition,* 21:175–194. London: Hogarth Press, 1961.

_____ (1930), Civilization and its discontents. *Standard Edition,* 21:57–145. London: Hogarth Press, 1961.

Gedo, J. (1972), On the methodology of psychoanalytic biography. *J. Amer. Psychoanal. Assn.,* 20:638–649.

_____ (1983), *Portraits of the Artist.* New York: Guilford Press.

_____ (1984), Mourning, perversion, and apotheosis. In: *Psychoanalytic Perspectives on Art,* Vol. 1, ed. M. Gedo. Hillsdale, NJ: The Analytic Press, pp. 269–301.

Greenacre, P. (1957), The childhood of the artist: Libidinal phase development and giftedness. *The Psychoanalytic Study of the Child,* 12:47–72. New York: International Universities Press.

_____ (1958a), The family romance of the artist. *The Psychoanalytic Study of the Child,* 13:9-36. New Haven: Yale University Press.

_____ (1958b), The relation of the imposter to the artist. *The Psychoanalytic Study of the Child,* 13:521-540. New Haven: Yale University Press.

_____ (1963), *The Quest for the Father: A Study of the Darwin-Butler Controversy as a Contribution to the Understanding of the Creative Individual.* New York: International Universities Press.

Hanson, H. (1942), A musician's point of view toward emotional expression. *Amer. J. Psychiat.,* 99: 317-325.

Hartmann, H. (1939), *Ego Psychology and the Problem of Adaptation.* New York: International Universities Press, 1958.

Hindemith, P. (1952), *A Composer's World.* Cambridge: Harvard University Press.

Horowitz, J. (1982), *Conversations with Arrau.* New York: Knopf.

James, P. (ed.) (1966), *Henry Moore on Sculpture.* New York: Viking Press.

Klein, G. S. (1959), Consciousness in psychoanalytic theory: Some implications for current research in perception. *J. Amer. Psychoanal. Assn.,* 7:5-34.

Klyman, C. M. (1980), An operatic accompaniment to an analysis. *Internat. Rev. Psycho-Anal.,* 7:89-100.

Knobloch, F., Juna, J., Junova, H. & Koutsky, Z. (1968), On an interpersonal hypothesis in the semiotic of music. *Kybernetika cislo 4 rocnik,* 364-381.

_____ , Postolka, M., & Srnec, J. (1964), Musical experience as interpersonal process. *Psychiat.,* 27:259-265.

Kohut, H. (1957), Observations on the psychological functions of music. *J. Amer. Psychoanal. Assn.,* 5:389-407.

_____ & Levarie, S. (1950), On the enjoyment of listening to music. *Psychoanal. Quart.,* 19:64-87.

Kris, E. (1952), *Psychoanalytic Explorations in Art.* New York: International Universities Press.

_____ (1955), Neutralization and sublimation. *The Psychoanalytic Study of the Child,* 10:30-46. New Haven: Yale University Press.

Langer, S. K. (1942), *Philosophy in a New Key.* New York: Mentor Books, 1951.

_____ (1953), *Feeling and Form.* New York: Scribner's.

_____ (1967), *Mind: An Essay on Human Feelings.* Baltimore: Johns Hopkins University Press.

Lee, H. B. (1947), On the esthetic states of the mind. *Psychiat.,* 10:281-306.

_____ (1949), The creative imagination. *Psychoanal. Quart,* 18:351-360.

Lewis, M. (1977), Language, cognitive development and personality. *J. Amer. Acad. Child Psychiat.,* 16:646-666.

Liebert, R. S. (1983), *Michelangelo.* New Haven: Yale University Press.

Loewald, H. (1978), Primary process, secondary process, and language. In: *Papers on Psychoanalysis.* New Haven: Yale University Press, 1980, pp. 178-206.

Lowenfeld, H. (1941), Psychic trauma and productive experience in the artist. *Psychoanal. Quart.,* 10:116-129.

MacAlpine, I. & Hunter, R. A. (1952), Rossini: Piano pieces for the primal scene. *Amer. Imago,* 9:213-219.

Mahler, M. (1968), *On Human Symbiosis and the Vicissitudes of Individuation.* New York: International Universities Press.

Martin, P. A. (1966), A psychoanalytic study of the *Marschallin* theme from *Der Rosenkavalier. J. Amer. Psychoanal. Assn.,* 14:760-774.

McDonald, M. (1970), Transitional tunes and musical development. *The Psychoanalytic Study of the Child,* 25:503-520. New York: International Universities Press.

Meyer, L. (1956), *Emotion and Meaning in Music.* Chicago: University of Chicago Press.
_____ (1967), *Music, the Arts and Ideas.* Chicago: University of Chicago Press.
Michel, A. (1965), *L'ecole Freudienne devant la Musique.* Paris: Les Editions du Scorpion.
Miller, M. D. (1967), Music and tension. *Psychoanal. Rev.,* 54:141–156.
Montani, A. (1945), Psychoanalysis of music. *Psychoanal. Rev.,* 32:225–227.
Mooney. W. E. (1971), Gustav Mahler: A note on life and death in music. *Psychoanal. Quart.,* 37:80–102..
Nass, M. L. (1971), Some considerations of a psychoanalytic interpretation of music. *Psychoanal. Quart.,* 40:303–316.
_____ (1975), On hearing and inspiration in the composition of music. *Psychoanal. Quart.,* 44:431–449.
_____ (1984), The development of creative imagination in composers. *Internat. Rev. Psycho-Anal.,* 11:481–491.
Niederland, W. G. (1958), Early auditory experiences, beating fantasies, and primal scene. *The Psychoanalytic Study of the Child,* 13:471–504. New York: International Universities Press.
Noy, P. (1966), The psychoanalytic meaning of music. 1. *J. Music therapy,* 3:126–134.
_____ (1967), The psychodynamic meaning, 2, 3, 4, 5. *J. Music Therapy,* 4:7–23, 45–51, 81–94, 117–125.
_____ (1968), The development of musical ability. *The Psychoanalytic Study of the Child,* 23:332–347. New York: International Universities Press.
Oremland, J. D. (1975), An unexpected result of the analysis of a talented musician. *The Psychoanalytic Study of the Child,* 30:375–400. New Haven: Yale Universities Press.
Pfeifer, S. (1922), Problems of the psychology of music in the light of psychoanalysis. *Internat. J. Psycho-Anal.,* 3:127–130.
_____ (1923), Problems of music and psychology. *Internat. J. Psycho-Anal.,* 4:380–381.
Piaget, J. (1954), *The Construction of Reality in the Child.* New York: Basic Books.
Pollock, G. H. (1974), Mourning through music: Gustav Mahler. In: *The Mourning Liberation Process in Health and Disease.* New York: International Universities Press.
_____ (1975a), On Freud's psychotherapy of Bruno Walter. *This Annual,* 3:287–3295. New York: International Universities Press.
_____ (1975b), Mourning and memorialization through music. *This Annual,* 3:423–436. New York: International Universities Press.
Racker, H. (1951), Contributions to psychoanalysis of music. *Amer. Imago,* 8:129–163.
_____ (1953), On music. In: *The Yearbook of Psychoanalysis,* ed. S. Lorand, 9:328–347.
_____ (1965), Psychoanalytic considerations on music and musicians. *Psychoanal. Rev.* 52:405–424.
Rose, G. J. (1980), *The Power of Form.* New York: international Universities Press.
Ramana, C. V. (1952), Observations on the analysis of a musician. *Samiska,* 6:229–242.
Rapaport, D. (1960), On the psychoanalytic theory of motivation. In: *The Collected Papers of David Rapaport,* ed. M. M. Gill. New York: Basic Books, pp. 853–915.
Rosen, V, H. (1964), Some effects of artistic talent on character style. *Psychoanal. Quart.,* 33:1–24.
Rothenberg, A. (1979), *The Emerging Goddess.* Chicago: University of Chicago Press.
Sabbeth, D. (1979), Freud's theory of jokes and the linear-analytic approach. *Internat. Rev. Psycho-Anal.,* 6:231–237.
Safirstein, S. L. (1962), Stage fright in a musician: A fragment of an analysis. *J. Amer. Psychoanal. Assn.,* 22:15–42.
Schachtel, E. (1959), *Metamorphosis: On the Development of Affect, Perception, Attention and Memory.* New York: Basic Books.

Schilder, P. (1950), *The Image and Appearance of the Human Body.* New York: International Universities Press.
———— (1964), *Contributions to Developmental Neuropsychology.* New York: International Universities Press.
Schwartz, D. W. (1965), Rossini: A psychological approach to the "Great Renunciation." *J. Amer. Psychoanal. Assn.,* 13:551–569.
Segal, H. (1952), A psychoanalytical approach to aesthetics. *Internat. J. Psycho-Anal.,* 33:196–207.
Sessions, R. (1941), The composer and his message. In: *The Intent of the Artist,* ed. A. Centeno. Princeton: Princeton University Press, pp. 101–134.
———— (1950), *The Musical Experience of Composer, Performer, Listener.* Princeton: Princeton University Press.
———— (1970), *Questions about Music.* Cambridge: Harvard University Press.
Smetana, B. (n.d.), *Letters and Reminiscences,* ed. F. Bartos. Prague: Artia, 1955.
Spitz, R. (1963), Life and the dialogue. In: *Counterpoint, Libidinal Object and Subject: A Tribute to Rene A. Spitz on His 75th Birthday,* ed. H. S. Gaskill. New York: International Universities Press, pp. 154–176.
———— (1965), The evolution of the dialogue. In: *Drives, Affects, Behavior.* Vol. 2: *Essays in Memory of Marie Bonaparte,* ed. M. Schur. New York: International Universities Press, pp. 170–190.
Sterba, E. & Sterba, R. (1954), *Beethoven and His Nephew.* New York: Pantheon.
Sterba, R. (1946), Toward the problem of the musical process. *Psychoanal. Rev.,* 33:37–43.
———— (1951), A case of brief psychotherapy by Sigmund Freud. *Psychoanal. Rev.,* 38:75–80.
———— (1965), Psychoanalysis and music. *Amer. Imago,* 20:96–111.
Stravinsky, I. (1947), *Poetics of Music in the Form of Six Easy Lessons.* New York: Vintage.
van der Chijs. A. (1923), An attempt to apply objective psychoanalysis to musical composition. *Internat. J. Psycho-Anal.,* 4:379–380.
Weissman, P. (1967), Theoretical considerations of ego regression and ego functions in creativity. *Psychoanal. Quart.,* 36:37–50.
Winnicott, D. (1953), Transitional objects and transitional phenomena. *Internat. J. Psycho-Anal.,* 34:89–97.
———— (1967), The location of cultural experience. *Internat. J. Psycho-Anal.,* 48:368–372.
Wittenberg, R. (1967), Aspects of the creative process in music: A case report. *J. Amer. Psychoanal. Assn.,* 28:439–460.

June 1987

III

PSYCHOANALYSIS AND PARENTHOOD

Blaming the Parent: Psychoanalytic Myth and Language

F. DIANE BARTH, M.S.W., C.S.W. (New York)

Some years ago, when I was working in a residential treatment center for severely disturbed children, I came to know a young girl who both infuriated and amused the staff with her standard response to criticism. Each time someone chastised her for behavior that was inappropriate but, they believed, within her control, she would whine, "I can't help it. It's the way my mother made me." In her therapy sessions as well, this girl was unable to take responsibility for anything she did or even thought. If not her mother, then other people or her hallucinations were responsible for all her actions. While she used the phrase so often that it became a way of making the staff laugh just when they were most irritated with her, it also encapsulated one of her basic difficulties in life. She had no sense of personal agency, no sense of her own power to have an impact on her environment, so that her primary sense of self was, at best, one of helpless victim. Simultaneously, at the very same moment that she felt exploited by others, she was also exploiting them so that they responded with feelings of helplessness and hostility toward her, thereby perpetuating her experience of others as hostile and potentially dangerous.

Psychoanalysts have long regarded the sense of personal agency as an important component of mental health (see, for example, Schafer's [1983] discussion of the subject). Based on his study of infants, Stern (1985) concludes that a sense of self as agent is a vital component of the developing sense of self and a necessary aspect of healthy interaction with others.

Stolorow (1986) agrees with Stern and further points out that not only is the ". . . experience of personal agency . . . a basic constituent of a firmly consolidated self organization, [but it also] is a primary focus of psychoanalytic investigation for many patients" (pp. 391–392).

The girl described above was psychotic and perhaps more seriously disturbed than many people who are seen in psychoanalysis and/or psychoanalytically oriented psychotherapy. Yet, like her, analysts and analysands alike frequently engage in "parent-blaming," often unwittingly perpetuating feelings of helplessness and lack of personal agency which may be a central force in the individual's need for therapy in the first place.

Psychoanalytic tradition is based on a belief that behavior, feelings, and thoughts have meaning that may be unrecognized or incomprehensible to the analysand and may appear maladaptive in the world in which he or she lives. Few analysts would suggest that blaming the parent for the child's psychopathology fits into this tradition. Yet, more and more it seems to be a danger to which analysts and analysands are equally vulnerable.

I am reminded of this phenomenon at the beginning of each year when I commence supervision of candidates in analytic training. Too frequently to ignore, candidates seem to see psychodynamics in terms such as, "The patient is repeating a pattern of interaction which occurred with his or her mother (or father)." When I ask what purpose the repetition serves for the patient, many candidates (no matter what their year of training) are taken by surprise. After thinking for a few minutes, some explain it as part of the repetition compulsion, or as a need for the familiar, or, on occasion, as an attempt to master a painful experience (similar to G. Klein's [1976] active reversal of passive position). Even these more dynamic explanations tend to be based on a belief that analysands are caught in a pattern of repeating early experiences for purposes of mastery or defense, and that such behavior is necessary because of the damage caused by failures in the parents' ability to provide what the child needed.

Most analysts would refute the idea that an analysand's problems can be explained simply by his or her parents' psychopathology. To a greater or lesser extent, most analysts seem to agree that psychodynamics evolve from an intricate interplay between actual experience and the meaning such experience has for the individual. In other words, both the child and the environment bring something to the child's experience and to the adult who the child becomes. Yet the language of psychoanalysis often appears to imply a belief that someone — either the analysand, in classical drive-conflict theory, or the parent(s), in many contemporary theories — is *at fault* in the development of the individual's dynamics. As Schafer (1976) has pointed out, this language often interferes with the psychoanalytic work by promoting an attitude of passivity on the part of the analysand. And this attitude, exhibited by students, analysands, and analysts themselves, can result in a superficial understanding of psychodynamics which can easily be interpreted as "parent-blaming."

The problem seems to affect analysts (not just analysts-in-training) with a wide variety of theoretical orientations, even though the concept of the child as a passive victim of parental behavior is both contrary to findings of the current infant research (see for example Beebe and Lachmann [1987] and Stern [1985]), and also promotes the very opposite of a sense of self as agent — "without which there can be paralysis, the sense of non-ownership of self-action, the experience of loss of control to external agents" (Stern, p. 7).

In this paper I will explore some of the ways in which parent-blaming is promoted (quite often unwittingly and probably unwillingly) in contemporary psychoanalytic theory and language. I will examine some of the implications of such blaming for the analytic process and outcome, and I will posit some hypotheses about possible reasons why both analysts and analysands might engage in parent-blaming.

To understand the concept of parent-blaming, it is important to recall the history of the development of psychoanalytic theory. Parent-blaming is actually one end of a continuum with intrapsychic factors at one end and environmental ones at the other. The question of the relative importance of intrapsychic conflict versus external influence in the formation of human psychodynamics has been an issue since almost the beginning of psychoanalysis. Freud (1918) struggled with this conflict throughout his writings, vacillating between what he called "the old trauma theory of the neuroses" (p. 5) and a theory in which inner conflict (rather than actual experience) was seen as the core of the neuroses (see also Spence, 1982, pp. 117–120). In the end, Freud decided that it was the *meaning* of the experience that was significant, not whether or not it could be proven as historical fact.

Much criticism of Freud and his followers resulted from his focus on structural, drive-related conflict without adequate recognition of the impact of actual interaction with important people on the development of the human psyche. (See, for example, Glenn's [1980] discussion of Dora.)

As a result, psychoanalysts began to move away from a meta-psychology of drive-structure conflict and toward one that integrated drive theory with or abandoned it for theories of ego psychology, object relations, interpersonal relations, and the development of the self. This extremely important evolution of psychoanalytic thinking has tremendously expanded the scope and impact of psychoanalytic work. But it has also brought with it the new danger of focusing on interactional

or environmental influences to the exclusion of intrapsychic dynamics —
that is, from a theory that blamed the child for his or her neurosis to
theories that blame the parents.

Greenberg and Mitchell (1983) have addressed some of the problems
inherent in parent-blaming. Noting the swing in Freud's theory from a
perspective in which "adult seductions of innocent children were seen as
the sole causative agents of psychopathology" to one which focused ". . .
instead on what he argued were biologically based drive impulses and
fantasies generated from within the child's own psyche," they suggest that
"Fairbairn's work constitutes a return of the dialectical pendulum on this
issue." But, they point out, "In . . . placing the blame for all difficulties
in living on parental psychopathology, he [Fairbairn] overlooks such
important issues as: the insatiable and sometimes incompatible features
of infantile needs; temperamental differences among infants and between infants and their particular caretakers; and distortions and misun-
derstandings of experience resulting from primitive perceptual and
cognitive capacities" (p. 181).

Fairbairn *did* note that an internalized parent is *not* necessarily an
accurate representation of the actual parent. About one patient, for
example, he wrote, "While his actual father remained alive, the sinister
influence of the bad father-figure whom he had internalized in his
childhood was evidently corrected by some redeeming features in the real
person: but after his father's death he was left at the mercy of the
internalized bad father . . ." (1986, p. 115). Yet his work does appear to
present psychopathology as the result of parental failure, and not of an
interplay between actual experience and the meaning given to the
experience by the individual.

Fairbairn, of course, is not alone in placing the blame for an
individual's psychopathology on parental pathology and thereby failing to
focus adequately on understanding intrapsychic factors in the development of human psychological difficulties. Similar statements could be
made about other members of the British object-relations school, as well
as about Sullivan and Kohut and some of their followers. Although
Stolorow (1986), for example, insists that the selfobject is an intrapsychic
experience, Kohut (1971) did not always seem to be so clear, often taking
at face value a patient's experience of ". . . traumatic stimulations and
frustrations from the side of . . . severely pathological parents" (pp.
261–262).

In his last book, Kohut (1984) seems to have modified this view
somewhat, but in his earlier work and in the work of some of his
followers, the patient's perceptions of the parent are taken as fact (see, for
example, Kohut's [1979] description of Mr. Z's parents), and descriptions

of the parents' empathic failures are seen as objective depictions of events that *caused* the analysand's psychic difficulties. Defending Kohut from just such accusations, Basch (1986) writes, "Kohut makes it clear that he is not engaging here, as he has at times been accused of doing, in 'parent-blaming.' What he is interested in is understanding, and helping the patient to understand, the reasons for the idiosyncratic course of that patient's self development. To blame parents, like blaming 'instincts,' for what happens to a patient's psychological development is reductionistic and not explanatory" (p. 407).

Most analysts would agree that understanding the analysand's experience is a crucial aspect of analytic work. (Just *how* they understand this experience differs significantly depending upon theoretical and personal beliefs about human nature.) I agree with Basch that Kohut was trying to understand the meaning of the experience from the analysand's perspective, and not specifically to blame the parents, but this point is often blurred by his apparent willingness to accept the analysand's perspective as fact.

Winnicott (1956), too, was probably not purposely engaging in parent-blaming when he wrote ". . . we may gain much by taking the mother's position into account. There is such a thing as an environment that is not good enough, and which distorts infant development, just as there can be a good-enough environment, one that enables the infant to reach, at each stage, the appropriate innate satisfactions and anxieties and conflicts" (p. 300). In fact, he made it clear that he did not think that parent-blaming was useful. He wrote, "the patient is not helped if the analyst says: 'Your mother was not good enough . . . your father really seduced you . . . your aunt dropped you' . . ." (1969, p. 711). Yet he went on to state that "mothers who are not distorted by ill-health or by present-day environmental stress do tend on the whole to know what their infants need accurately enough, and, further, they like to provide what is needed" (p. 715). And again, "in fact, success in infant care depends on the fact of [the mother's] devotion, not on cleverness or intellectual enlightenment" (1951, p. 238). Although this is not parent-blaming per se, a reasonable inference is that Winnicott believed that a "healthy" mother will automatically (and gladly) meet all of her child's needs, and that the adult with emotional difficulties had a mother who did not do so.

Today, for many analysts and analysands, "good-enough mothering" requires "perfect attunement," and parental pride has become "narcissistic investment" and "self-interest" on the part of parents. The concepts of "good" and "bad" internalized objects have been interpreted by many to mean "good" and "bad" parents, all of which leads inevitably to parent-blaming. Defensive blaming, splitting, helplessness, and feelings of victimization are only a few of the attitudes promoted by the contemporary use of this language.

Perhaps it is not particularly surprising that the language of both object relations and self psychology leaves much room for parent-blaming, since both were developed in response to "instinct-blaming" (and inherently "patient-blaming") theory. Yet, as neither theory embraces interactional issues to the total exclusion of the concept of intrapsychic meaning or conflict, one must suppose that it is the language, and not the theories themselves, which is at fault.

Nearly fifteen years ago Schafer (1976) admonished psychoanalysts to examine psychoanalytic language for undesirable messages that we unwittingly communicate through it. It is time for those of us who teach, supervise, and practice psychoanalysis to do the housekeeping necessary to make sure that our language conveys what we want to convey to our students, analysands, and colleagues. Language is one of the most important tools of our trade, and we should be sure that it is as clear of undesired consequences as possible.

Part of the problem may be that, as psychoanalysts have moved away from the drive-structure-conflict theory of human dynamics, we have had some difficulty developing an alternative theory of and language for intrapsychic conflict. It is almost as if, if conflict is not defined in terms of Freud's drive-structure theory, it cannot be defined intrapsychically. Yet there are discussions of nondrive or structure-related intrapsychic conflict in the literature. Balint (1968) and A. Ornstein (1974), for example, have both described intrapsychic conflict between the wish for closeness and the fear of disappointment or hurt. Balint's conflict, which he calls the fear of the new beginning, takes place in the "two-person field" but has intrapsychic components, and Ornstein's also has both interpersonal and intrapsychic components. Lachmann (1986), Stolorow and Lachmann (1984/1985), and Stolorow (1985) are among other analysts who have also described intrapsychic conflict from a nondrive perspective.

The fantasy, held by some analysts as well as analysands, that a perfect parent is humanly possible, has many components. A brief example will illustrate the way such a fantasy, expressed in terms of anger at parental failure, incorporated many aspects of an individual's dynamics, which were not fully integrated into his conscious self experience (see G. Klein's [1976] discussion of split-off self-schema). In the course of his analysis, the analysand more completely integrated conflicting self schemas, became less critical of himself, and no longer needed to hold on to the fantasy that anyone—his parents, his analyst, or himself—was or could be perfect. His fantasy of his own potential perfection and his demand that others meet his needs perfectly gradually gave way to an awareness that to be human is to be imperfect, and to be "good enough" *is* good enough.

Mr. X. was in his early forties, a therapist himself, who had analytic training and had previously been in a "classical" analysis. He felt that some unanalyzed issues arose around the birth of his first son. He sought me out for analysis after hearing me speak about envy. He believed, he said, "You understand something about envy which will help you to understand me."

In an early session he told me that he could have been brilliant if only his parents had been better parents. He had completed his previous analysis with a pride in being "in touch" with his anger at parents whom he saw as deficient and inadequate, but not hostile or purposefully hurtful. But the intensity of his anger and his anxiety about his son's future relationship with him seemed to indicate that he had not completely worked through some of the issues that accompanied his experience of his parents' failures.

As we explored the meaning of this anger, we learned that it had several components. It seemed to provide a protection against the narcissistic injury this man felt at his parents' inability to meet his needs. No matter how he interpreted their behavior, it seemed an injury to his self esteem. If they purposely witheld from him, it meant that they felt that he did not deserve to have the help, support, and love he longed for. And if they were *incapable* of giving these things to him, this also reflected poorly upon him, as the progeny of such feeble and inadequate people. The anger was a defense against feelings of pain, loss, sorrow, sadness, and other less acceptable, less "masculine" feelings — such as neediness — and it was also a strengthening feeling for him, giving him a feeling of power and pride, a feeling of being "a strong man." It represented an identification with his previous psychoanalyst, as well, whom Mr. X saw as approving of open expression of anger. (Whether this was an actual attribute of the analyst or part of Mr. X's preexisting conceptualization of psychoanalysis was not clear, but the meaning for Mr. X had to do with a need to feel that his analyst was proud of him in order to feel proud of himself.) At the same time, Mr. X felt resentful that the analyst's pride in him was "narcissistic" pride. "He feels like he's been successful with me. It means he's a good analyst. He doesn't really care what it means about me." This resentment seemed to be closely related to anger at his parents for their narcissistic investment in him — e.g., their pride in him was only related to their need to feel like they were good parents, capable of producing an intelligent, successful heir.

The anger also represented Mr. X's constant, desperate hope that somewhere, somehow, there was a "perfect parent" who could give him the things that his parents had not been able to give him—essentially, the good feelings about himself which he needed in order to feel proud of himself and complete within himself (his words). As one might imagine, this dynamic surfaced in the transference. Mr. X. repeatedly berated me for "not making me as smart as you." He believed that I was brilliant, and he envied me and simultaneously hated me for withholding knowledge that he believed I could transmit to him.

His anger contained components of Kohut's (1971) idealizing transference and M. Klein's (1957) "poisonous" envy. It was apparent that he *needed* to see me as brilliant in order to feel safe with me and to feel good about being in analysis with me. At the same time, his envy of me interfered with his ability to take in what he could get from me.

Obviously, there were other components to both his anger and his idealization, but for the purposes of this paper, I will only discuss one more of them. Kohut (1977, 1984) believed that aggression was a result of narcissistic injury or empathic failure by a significant other (a selfobject, in his terminology). He called such aggression a "disintegration product"—that is, a product of the loss of self-esteem and self-organization caused by such failures. Some of his followers, including Basch (1986), Lachmann (1986), Stolorow and Lachmann (1984/1985), and Stolorow (1986), have suggested that anger can have intrapsychic meaning as well. For them, the work of the analyst is to help the patient to understand as much of the meaning of the anger as possible.

As I have suggested, Mr. X's anger, which he proudly displayed from the very beginning of his work with me, served several purposes and had several meanings. As we explored some of these meanings in the analytic work (often in the transference), his perceptions of himself and of his parents became more complex, more three-dimensional, and eventually more realistic. This is not to suggest that we ignored or belittled the ways in which his parents did seem to have failed him, not only during his childhood, but even now, in his adulthood, when he still longed for certain kinds of interactions with them which, given their personalities, seemed impossible. But as Mr. X began to understand some of the meanings of his anger and an underlying fantasy that his personal worth was dependent on his parents' ability or desire to give him the responses he so desperately wanted, he began to find other ways of feeling better about himself, and his anger began to diminish.

Thus, to make conscious his anger at his parents, who indeed did not always meet all of his needs (what parents ever do?) had been an important process for him—but it was not enough. This much interpersonal, object-relations, and self-psychological theories have told us. But neither recognizing the underlying, unmet needs nor meeting them could eliminate his frustration or his sense of inadequacy. It was my assessment that his anger was a defense against and a reaction to narcissistic injury, but that it was also related to fantasies of his own potential perfection and that of his parents and parent substitutes (e.g., his analysts). His anger and the precipitants of the anger had personal, subjective meaning for Mr. X, meaning that often centered on both grandiose fantasies and also the wish that no one else should have anything he did not have—or, that he should have anything which anyone else had.

Mr. X had gradually to experience the complexity of his own feelings, as well as of himself in interaction with his parents. He had to understand his parents' behavior from the perspective of an adult—not arbitrarily, but gradually, often as a result of understanding his own adult needs and behavior and the connections between the two.

In order to be comfortable with his own abilities as a parent, Mr. X had to learn to accept his parents' imperfections. This aspect of the work is described by Kohut (1971, 1984) as "optimal disillusionment" and by Winnicott (1948) as the working through of depressive anxiety. As Mr. X came to accept his parents' imperfections (and mine, and those of his previous analyst) he began to accept (without criticism) his own imperfections, as well as those of his child. He made two comments during this part of his analysis which I think are poignant examples of this process (which I believe occurs more or less simultaneously, rather than linearly. That is, the ability to tolerate the imperfections of the important objects in one's life simultaneously strengthens and results from a strengthened sense of self).

In one session, Mr. X was angrily berating his parents for their narcissistic investment in his schoolwork. "They didn't really care that I got good grades for me. All they cared about was that they could be proud. It was a reflection of them, not of me."

He paused for a moment, then continued in a more reflective, slightly puzzled tone. "You know," he said, "I wonder what I would be saying now if they hadn't been proud of my schoolwork. I mean, I guess as a parent I can see that it's hard to completely separate your own needs from your child's. I'm proud of my son's accomplishments. I like it that he's already starting to say words. And part of that's because it makes me feel like a good man and a good father to have a son who's smart. But part of it has to do with him. I mean, I'm just proud of him. He knows it, too. He gets such a kick out of it when he says something, then he looks at me and his grin gets bigger! And I get a kick out of it, too. Is there such a thing as healthy narcissistic investment?"

And at another point, he began to complain about the imperfections "in the world. I mean, look at all the unhappiness. Look at all the lousy parents. Sullivan had the right idea. We ought to get out and train everybody who wants to be a parent. It ought to be like giving people driver's licenses. Nobody can have a kid till they pass the test."

I commented, "Nobody should have a kid unless they can be a perfect parent."

He lay in silence for a moment, then replied slowly, "When you put it like that, it sounds completely unrealistic. I mean, what's perfect, anyway? Who's to say that what one person does is perfect, or what another person does is? If you think like that, Hitler makes sense. Which is completely crazy. Are you asking me if I can live with my own imperfections? And my son's?" Long pause. "And my parents'?"

To reduce all of an analysand's difficulties to a reaction to poor or deficient parenting is, as Basch (1986) has said, every bit as reductionistic as to reduce all difficulties to conflict over drives. It means to ignore the psychoanalytic tradition ". . . that our thoughts and feelings about the important objects in our lives, our behavior towards them and our expectations from them are extremely complex" (Sandler and Sandler [1978], p. 272). It does not take into account the analytic tradition of multiple function (Waelder, 1939) originally utilized in terms of drive-derivatives, but now traditionally applied to most psychodynamics. And it does not take into account the importance of neutrality in the analytic process.

Schafer (1983) suggests not only that the activity of blaming parents is the antithesis of analytic neutrality, but that it can also interfere with part of the analytic work:

> Owing to his or her recognition that over the course of an analysis the analysand will present highly selective and changing pictures of other people, the neutral analyst remains nonjudgmental about these others . . . It is particularly important to maintain this neutrality in relation to parental figures and spouses, for to some extent the analysand is identified with them and is vulnerable to the same value judgments that may be passed on them. Also, the analysand may be referring to other people in order to represent indirectly . . . some disturbing feature of his or her own self. For this reason, too, the analyst must take care to regard these others neutrally" [p. 6].

This is not to say that the analyst should not confirm or validate analysands' feelings at appropriate times, but, that if the analyst can maintain analytic curiosity (or neutrality), he or she and the analysand together will learn what such material means *to the analysand*.

Like Freud's metapsychology of drive-structure conflict, parent blaming of the sort found in Fairbairn and Kohut may be the result of an attempt to make the complex material of human dynamics comprehensible to the human mind. Spence (1982) reminds us that analysts are faced with complicated and confusing material, out of which we are expected to make sense for ourselves and for our analysands. In order to do so, we must screen out material, find themes, look for some kind of closure. Theory helps us to do this. Yet it is important that we remember that theory also tends to reduce complexity. Somehow as psychoanalysts we need to find a way of incorporating human complexity into the theory that informs our analytic work, even while we utilize theory to help make the dense and often disconnected material supplied by our analysands comprehensible to ourselves and to them.

One of the confusing dynamics of human experience is the concept of individual history. Like the history of a civilization, the history of an individual may be described in a number of different, and often equally accurate (or inaccurate), ways. Schafer (1983) and Spence (1982) have both pointed out the shifting nature of historical "truth," which changes over the course of an individual's analysis, as well as over the course of a life. Stern (1985) suggests that memory is not an accurate representation of any single experience, but is, instead, an average of several experiences. Kohut (1971) forecast some of this thinking when he wrote that a single incident in childhood, no matter how traumatic, is less influential in forming psychopathology than is a general atmosphere and ongoing experience of relating and being related to.

If this is true, then memories of childhood experiences will have various components that can be understood from the perspectives of both the child who experienced it and the adult who is still reacting to it. Anger at a parent, for example, would then be understood in the context of what the adult remembers that the parent "actually" did, how the child explained the parent's behavior, what the adult's memory of it means, and how the adult now explains the experience and used it in contemporary interactions.

In line with Stern's theory that certain issues are primary throughout an individual's life, not simply during a certain developmental phase, memories can be understood not simply as screens for unacceptable feelings, nor as factual representations of all experiences, but as constituted of many components, including complex constellations of feelings, some of which may have been split off, disavowed, denied, and/or repressed at various times, and which, during the course of the analysis, must be integrated into the individual's sense of self and other.

Analysts, looking with adult analysands at their childhood memories, sometimes forget that the adult is often still understanding (or misunderstanding) childhood experiences from the stance of the child's perspective. The child understands, or gives "meaning" to experiences on the basis of the child's cognitive and perceptual abilities. During the course of analysis, the meaning of such experiences is reexamined and understood from the perspective of the adult. This includes both an attempt to *reconstruct* a version of "historical truth," and also an attempt to *construct* a history that incorporates the impact of the experience and its meaning from the perspective of the child who lived through it and also from the perspective of the adult who reexamines it at different points in his or her analysis (Schafer, 1983).

Basch (1980) has presented a lovely example of this kind of reevaluation. To summarize briefly, he described a young woman who came into therapy with a characterological defense against her unconscious expectation that all important others would be like her father—critical and unsupportive of her attempts to develop her own capacities. In the course of the therapy, not only was the defense analyzed and the unconscious expectation brought into conscious awareness, but, as the woman's trust grew and the analysis progressed, the original meaning attributed to the father's behavior by the little girl was reexamined on the basis of the adult woman's new understanding of herself and human nature. Her father's criticism was seen as *his* attempt to protect his daughter from the kind of disappointments that he experienced in his life—his own defensive maneuver, enacted with her, to avoid painful and self-esteem-damaging disappointments and failures.

The new interpretation did not take away from the fact that the father's characterological defensive behavior had an important, negative impact on the child, but it did allow the daughter to deal with her father in a new and more satisfying manner. Not surprisingly from a systems perspective, the change in the woman's perceptions and her concomitant behavior had repercussions in her father's behavior toward her. Basch (1980) writes,

> Eventually, through her recognition of her father as primarily frightened rather than angry, she was able to take a different attitude toward him as well as toward herself. Regretfully, and with some temporary depression, she gave up the childhood hope that she would somehow win her father's approval and through him finally become satisfied with herself . . . Once the patient freed her father from the implied demand that he make her feel whole—a task he had not been able to accomplish for himself—his attitude toward her changed markedly. As is often the case, when adolescents and young adults with the benefits of insight won in therapy cease to demand what the parents cannot give psychologically, the relationship improves and is placed on a different footing [pp. 82–83].

Before concluding this paper, I would like to make it very clear that I am not advocating a return to a theory that places the blame for a person's problems exclusively on that person's fantasy life. In fact, I believe that "blaming," whether the target is parents or instincts or something else, is antithetical to the psychoanalytic process. Psychoanalysis is based on an attempt to understand the meaning of behavior, including feelings and the defenses against those feelings which often motivate behavior. It is difficult, if not impossible, to understand something of which one is critical, since inherent in the criticism is the attitude that one should change that attribute. And if one is under pressure to change something, one has difficulty understanding the purpose it serves or the meaning it has.

There are unquestionably times when the analytic work includes uncovering repressed memories of and feelings about parental behavior, and there is no question in my mind that parental behavior can and does have an impact on the child's development. Yet the adult analysand cannot be understood simply on the basis of childhood experiences. Even the abused child, whose parent has caused unquestionable physical and emotional damage, cannot be understood simply in light of the fact that he or she was abused. The child, in most cases, attempts to make sense out of and give meaning to the parent's behavior, based on the child's own personality, dynamics, and cognitive capacities. Understanding the meaning that the child gave to the experiences is a crucial aspect of the analytic work.

Citing recent infant research, Lachmann (1986, 1986/1987) has suggested that both intrapsychic (one person) and interpersonal (two person) experiences develop concurrently and in interaction with each other. Both sources of experience need to be recognized in the analytic situation. Beebe and Lachmann (1987) and Stern (1985) concur that neither the one-person nor the two-person field predominates in human experience, but that, to expand on Stern's phrase, even the subjective sense of self is experienced in an interpersonal context, and the other is experienced in the context of the self. Lachmann (personal communication) has suggested that Winnicott's discussion of the capacity to be alone in the presence of another can be understood as addressing the interrelationship of a one-person and two-person perspective. That is, although experiences may arise in the context of a relationship with another, the individual takes these experiences and elaborates upon them on the basis of his or her own subjective experiences. These personal elaborations are as important as the interpersonal experience. One does not have primacy over the other. The analyst's job is to help the individual to understand both aspects of the subjective experience.

Stern (1985), like Schafer and Spence, questions the adult's ability to capture the "actual" reality of childhood experiences. He suggests that most analysts utilize developmental theory metaphorically (an assumption about which it would be interesting to gather actual data from practicing analysts), and recommends using the historical reconstructions of analysis as a "narrative point of origin" or "key metaphor" for the individual's psychodynamics. He writes:

The fact is that most experienced clinicians keep their developmental theories well in the background during active practice. They search with the patient through his or her remembered history to find the potent life-experience that provides the key therapeutic metaphor for understanding and changing the patient's life. This experience can be called the narrative point of origin of the pathology, regardless of when it occurred in actual developmental time. Once the metaphor has been found, the therapy proceeds forward and backward in time from that point of origin . . . There is widespread recognition that the developmental theories, when applied to a patient, do not deliver *any reliable actual point of origin* for the traditional clinical-developmental issues. Such actual points of origin of pathology apply only to theoeretical infants, who do not exist [pp. 257–258; emphasis added).

And he continues: "The genesis of psychological problems may, but does not have to, have a developmental history that reaches back to infancy. Development of senses of the self is going on all the time, at all levels of 'primitiveness' " (p. 260). Development is not a succession of events left behind in history. It is a continuing process, constantly updated.

Stern suggests that what is most important for understanding the adult analysand is the way that current adult self experience can be explicated by specific memories and the metaphors for the self experience that such memories contain. Along with Schafer and Spence, he does not disregard the significance of the past, but he does suggest that current memories of the past are influenced by current experience. In other words, as Schafer (1983) has told us, the past is constantly being constructed and reconstructed in the course of the psychoanalytic work.

Psychoanalysts are fortunate to have a number of theories upon which to draw when trying to find the "key therapeutic metaphor" for a specific analysand. As Gedo and Goldberg (1973), Pine (1985), and Wallerstein (1983), among others, have suggested, different theories are useful for explaining different patients, or even for explaining the different dynamics of a single patient at different times in the course of the analysis.

In the same way, different theories help to explain why different people react to similar childhood experiences in different ways—or, even when the manifest psychopathology is similar, help to explain each specific individual as different from, as well as similar to, others with similar experiences. For one example, let us return briefly to the adult who was physically abused as a child. Many adults who were abused become masochistic and/or sadistic in response to their experiences. Yet the inner meaning of and the explanations for the masochistic or sadistic behavior will differ from individual to individual and need to be understood on the basis of the specific subjective meaning of the experiences for the individual. One abused child may become a masochistic adult, for example, in an attempt to avoid conscious awareness of intolerable feelings of anger and resentment toward the parent (Riviere, 1936) and/or to protect the parent from the child's aggression and the child from the results of that aggression (Kernberg, 1975). Another might develop masochistic characteristics in what G. Klein (1976) calls an "active reversal of a passive position," that is, an attempt to master the experience through repeating it. A child might become sadistic, an abusive parent himself or herself, in an identification with the aggressor, or, again, in an attempt to reverse a passively experienced trauma. The child might marry an abusive individual for masochistic reasons, or to "contain" his or her split-off aggression (Agazarian, 1986).

Almost all of these children will have developed fantasies to explain the parents' behavior and perhaps, as Bloch (1978) suggests, to avoid conscious awareness of the parent's murderous intent. These are only a few possible ways in which different people may deal with similar childhood experiences. There are still other ways to explain the large variety of dynamics which we see in adults who were physically abused as children, but the point should be clear. Parental behavior has an unquestionable impact on a child's (and later, adult's) psychodynamics, but to paraphrase Winnicott, it is not enough to say, "You are this way because you were abused," or "because your mother or father drank."

Parent-blaming is an attitude rather than a theory. Perhaps related to the *analyst's* unresolved fantasy of the perfect parent, it involves taking the patient's reports at face value without understanding the subjective *meaning* that the experiences had for the child. It interferes with rather than enhances the ability to understand the analysand—the basic analytic work. By placing the focus on what has been *done* to the individual, and not on what the experiences and memories of the experiences mean and how they contribute to the individual's current organization of self and interpersonal world, both analyst and analysand lose the opportunity to understand something important about the person who is doing the remembering. Given the reality that human perfection does not exist, analytic theory needs to take into account the possibility that "good enough" parenting is indeed good enough, and psychoanalysts need to beware of language and theory implying that only perfect is good enough.

REFERENCES

Agazarian, Y. M. (in press), The difficult patient, the difficult group. *Group: J. of the E. Group Psychother. Soc.* New York: Human Sciences Press.

Balint, M. (1968), *The Basic Fault.* New York: Brunner/Mazel.

Basch, M. F. (1980), *Doing Psychotherapy.* New York: Basic Books.

_____ (1986), How does analysis cure? An appreciation. *Psychoanal. Inquiry,* 6:403–428.

Beebe, B. & Lachmann, F. (1987), Mother-infant mutual influence and precursors of psychic structure. In: *Frontiers in Self Psychology: Progress in Self Psychology, Vol. 3.* Hillsdale, NJ: The Analytic Press, pp. 3–25.

Bloch, D. (1978), *So the Witch Won't Eat Me.* Boston: Houghton Mifflin.

Fairbairn, W.R.D. (1986a), The repression and the return of bad objects (with special reference to the "war neuroses"). In: *Essential Papers on Object Relations,* ed. P. Buckley. New York: New York University Press, pp. 102–126.

_____ (1986b), A revised psychopathology of the psychoses and psychoneuroses. In: *Essential Papers on Object Relations,* ed. P. Buckley. New York: New York University Press, pp. 71–101.

Freud, S. (1918), From the history of an infantile neurosis. *Standard Edition,* 17:3–124. London: Hogarth Press, 1955.

Gedo, J. & Goldberg, A. (1973), *Models of the Mind: A Psychoanalytic Theory.* Chicago: University of Chicago Press.

Glenn, J. (1980), Freud's adolescent patients: Katharina, Dora and "homosexual woman." In: *Freud and His Patients,* ed. M. Kanzer & J. Glenn. New York: Aronson, pp. 23–47.

Greenberg, J. & Mitchell, S. (1983), *Object Relations in Psychoanalytic Theory.* Cambridge, MA.: Harvard University Press.

Kernberg, O. (1975), *Borderline Conditions and Pathological Narcissism.* New York: Aronson.

Klein, G. (1976), *Psychoanalytic Theory.* New York: International Universities Press.

Klein, M. (1957), Envy and gratitude. In: *Envy and Gratitude and Other Works 1946–1963.* New York: Free Press, 1975.

Kohut, H. (1971), *The Analysis of the Self.* New York: International Universities Press.

_____ (1977), *The Restoration of the Self.* New York: International Universities Press.

_____ (1979), The two analyses of Mr. Z. *Internat. J. Psycho-Anal.,* 60:3–27.

Lachmann, F. M. (1986), Interpretation of psychic conflict and adversarial relationships: A self-psychological perspective. *Psychoanal. Psychol.,* 3:341–355.

Ornstein, A. (1974), The dread to repeat and the new beginning. *This Annual,* 2:231–246. New York: International Universities Press.

Pine, F. (1985), *Developmental Theory and Clinical Process.* New Haven: Yale University Press.

Riviere, J. (1936), A contribution to the analysis of the negative therapeutic reaction. In: *The Evolution of Psychoanalytic Technique,* ed. M. Bergmann & F. Hartman. New York: Basic Books, pp. 414–429.

Sandler, J. S. & Sandler, A.-M. (1978), On the development of object relationships and affects. *Internat. J. Psycho-Anal.,* 59:285–296.

Schafer, R. (1976), *A New Language for Psychoanalysis.* New Haven: Yale University Press.

_____ (1983), *The Analytic Attitude.* New York: Basic Books.

Spence, D. (1982), *Narrative Truth and Historical Truth: Meaning and Interpretation in Psychoanalysis.* New York: Norton.

Stern, D. N. (1985), *The Interpersonal World of the Infant.* New York: Basic Books.

Stolorow, R. (1985), Toward a pure psychology of inner conflict. In: *Progress in Self Psychology,* ed. A. Goldberg. New York: Guilford Press, 1: 194–220.

_____ (1986), Critical reflections on the theory of self psychology: An inside view.

Psychoanal. Inquiry, 6:387–402.

———— & Lachmann, F. (1980), *Psychoanalysis of Development Arrests: Theory and Treatment.* New York: International Universities Press.

———— & Lachmann, F. (1984/1985), Transference: The future of an illusion. *This Annual,* 12/13:19–37. New York: International Universities Press.

Waelder, R,. (1936), The principle of multiple function. *Psychoanal. Quart.,* 5:45–62.

Wallerstein, R. (1983), Self psychology and "classical" psychoanalytical" psychology: The nature of their relationship. In: *The Future of Psychoanalysis,* ed. A. Goldberg.

Winnicott, D. (1948), Reparation and respect of mother's organized defense against depression. In: *Through Paediatrics to Psychoanalysis.* New York: Basic Books, 1975, pp. 91–97.

———— (1951), Transitional objects and transitionsl phenomenon. In: *Through Paediatrics to Psychoanalysis.* New York: Basic Books, 1975, pp. 229–242.

———— (1956), Primary maternal preoccupation. In: *Through Paediatrics to Psychoanalysis.* New York: Basic Books, 1975, pp. 300–305.

———— (1969), The theory of the parent-infant relationship. *Internat. J. Psycho-Anal.,* 50:711–717.

November 1987

Fatherhood and the Preference for a Younger Child

HELEN R. BEISER, M.D. (Chicago)

Freud's (1900) use of the myth of Oedipus was an important contribution to understanding the negative aspects of the relationship of a boy or man to his father. It is quite possible that the shock with which people first greeted the universality of this mythical relationship had less to do with the incest with the mother than with the fact that there was no evidence of any positive aspects of the relationship of father and son.

Kohut (1982) tried to use the Greek story of Odysseus refusing to kill his infant son to avoid going off to the Trojan war as another facet of father-son relationships, but this reading has not had the impact of the Oedipus myth. Although Freud wrote a book about Moses, showing his familiarity with the Scriptures, it seems surprising that he did not use scriptural references to father-son relationships rather than Greek literature. As far as I can determine, he never mentioned the story of Abraham and Isaac (Genesis 22:1–18) in which Abraham was about to kill his son deliberately. The dynamic complexities seem much greater than in the story of Oedipus. Laius exposed the infant out of fear for his own life, whereas Abraham was acting under the direction of God. Laius had no real emotional tie to Oedipus, whereas Abraham had long awaited the coming of Isaac, and had a strong positive tie to him. The revenge of the son and the incestuous relationship with the mother are lacking in the Abraham and Isaac story, known in the Jewish literature as the Akedah. Another difference is that God changes his mind and has Abraham substitute a goat for the child, allowing him to be raised by his loving parents, whereas the exposed Oedipus is rescued and raised by foster parents. To me, the Abraham story shows to a much greater extent the

203

ambivalence in the father-son relationship, rather than just fear and revenge.

It also seems strange that in the rather long and detailed discussion of sacrifice in Freud's Totem and Taboo (1913), the killing of the father, or the totemic symbol of the father, is considered, but no reference is made to the sacrifice of sons by fathers.

Infanticide

To those who read the story for the first time, it comes as a shock that Abraham would so willingly agree to sacrifice his first legitimate son, even if directed to do so by God. To understand this, it is helpful to realize the extent to which infanticide, or the religious sacrifice of the firstborn son, was practiced in the Middle East (Frazer, 1927). Most people find it hard to believe that infanticide was a common practice, but I have seen the crematoria of Lebanon and the cemetery of the firstborn in Carthage with my own eyes. Infanticide has been widely practiced for a variety of reasons, such as gender control (the killing of girls), population control against starvation, or religious ritual to appease the gods. The latter usually involves the firstborn child or son. Such sacrifice may even include grown sons. In the Second Book of Kings, the king of Moab (3:27) sacrifices his first son in order to defeat Israel in battle. Ahaz (16:3) and Manasseh (21:6) also sacrifice their first sons. Wellisch (1954) has given vivid descriptions of varieties of infanticide in many cultures, including the Greek. He also states that the killing could be softened in a variety of ways. Exposure, as with Oedipus, gave the child a chance of rescue by sympathetic strangers, and animal substitution, as with Isaac, spared the child completely. There may be a strong biological urge for males to kill infants, as so many male mammals of various species tend to kill all infants left untended, including their own.

Kaplan (1986) used the Akedah and the Oedipus myth to compare Greek and Jewish family life. I am not sure this is valid, but I agree that the Akedah demonstrates a higher moral solution to father-son ambivalence. Wellisch also feels this, and it is true that throughout the Scriptures, the practice of human sacrifice is criticized severely (Deuteronomy 12:31, Micah 6:6–8), along with other religious practices of the peoples among whom the Hebrews found themselves living. It is doubtful if such prohibitions would have been necessary unless there was a strong pull toward infanticide, and this may explain why Abraham was so willing to follow God's direction.

In the Scriptures, the struggles against infanticide are many and varied. Even before the Akedah, God makes a covenant with Abraham, requiring that all of his people of the male gender must be circumcised (Genesis 17:10–14). This token is to be offered rather than the life of the boy. The firstborn may also be offered to the service of God in the form of the priesthood. It is stated that the Levites were to be substituted for the firstborn in the sacrificial offerings (Numbers 3:44–51). Aaron (Exodus 28:1), Samson (Judges 13:16), and Samuel (1 Samuel:27–28) are examples. Their lives must be devoted to the service of God, and when celibacy is also required, the sacrifice is even greater. Perhaps God's requirements for the sacrifice of the firstborn are most clearly stated in his words to Moses (Exodus 13:11–16) in which he reminds him that he slew the firstborn of the Egyptians, and the firstborn of the Hebrews must be redeemed, apparently by massive offerings of firstborn animals. Today, I have been informed, infants are still redeemed, but with an offering of money. The regulations in Exodus (29) and Leviticus (1–7) regarding animal sacrifice are rather overwhelming. It is clearly stated that God demands the "first fruits," whether animal or vegetable (Exodus 23:19), and sometimes this is stated as "the one who opens the womb" (Exodus 34:19, 20). Certainly there is considerable ambivalence in God's inordinate requirement for sacrifice and his constant reassurance of favor and love.

The Second or Younger Son

There is another possible substitution in the Bible for the sacrifice of the first son, and that is the preference for the second or later son. I noticed this theme while reading the Bible in its entirety over a period of three years. In my reading group were two men who were first sons who became absolutely incensed after reading the story of Cain and Abel (Genesis 4:3–5). It was clear that God's preference for Abel's offering was without rational basis. He simply passed up the offering of Cain in favor of that of Abel. However, he understood Cain's jealousy, as he allowed him to live after finding out about his murder of Abel, evidence perhaps of God's own jealousy. Stimulated by this observation, I kept notes on other sibling relationships throughout the scriptures. It is truly remarkable how many younger children surpassed the eldest, which, in this context, can be taken as given preference by God.

Abraham must have been a younger son, as he and his nephew Lot were of the same generation (Genesis 12:4–6, 13:5–12). Scholars have some evidence that Sarah, his wife, was a younger daughter. Because Sarah was infertile for so long, Abraham's first son, Ishmael, was by a concubine (Genesis 16:11–15, 21:5–12); the preferred son, Isaac (Genesis

17:18-21) was Abraham's second, although Sarah's first. Isaac's wife, Rebekah (Genesis 24:29, 42-46), was the younger sister of Laban, a rather unsavory character. Perhaps the most notable instance of displacement was the trickery of Jacob, who, with the help of his mother Rebekah, took the birthright from Esau (Genesis 25:23-34, 27:15-40). Although he preferred Laban's younger daughter, Rachel (Genesis 29:30), he was tricked by Laban into marrying the elder, Leah, first, a just punishment. Jacob had many sons by his two wives, but his favorite was Joseph (Genesis 37:3-4), his first son by Rachel. Their youngest son, Benjamin, did not achieve prominence, perhaps because his mother died during his birth (Genesis 36:16-19). However, his tribe produced many prominent people, including King Saul (1 Samuel 9:21) and the Apostle Paul (Romans 11:1). A little-known story involves the twins of Tamar, the children of Judah by his daughter-in-law (Genesis 38:27-30). When the hand of the first twin emerged, the midwife tied a red string around it. However, the second child pushed his way out first, a very concrete example of displacement. Later, Judah, who was the youngest of Jacob's sons by Leah, took charge when the brothers negotiated with Joseph in Egypt (Genesis 43:8-9, 44:18-34). Near the end of Genesis Jacob blesses Joseph's younger son, Ephraim, in spite of Joseph pointing out the error (Genesis 48:14-20).

In the rest of the Old Testament it is to be noted that Moses was the youngest and was set over his brother Aaron (Exodus 4:10-16). Gideon (Judges 6:15-16) is described as "the least in his family," and in the story of Ruth, Boaz was the second man to claim her after her husband died, the first having refused (Ruth 5:5-6). David was the youngest son (1 Samuel 16:11-13), surpassing not only his own brothers, but also the firstborn of his sponsor, King Saul (1 Samuel 1:17-27). Jonathan was killed at an early age, and David succeeded Saul as king. David married Saul's second daughter (1 Samuel 18:18-20), but his sons from that marriage did not succeed him, and fought among themselves. The firstborn son of David's illicit relationship with Bathsheba died in infancy (2 Samuel 12:18-24), which is seen as punishment for his sin. Solomon, who became king over his many older half-brothers, was a younger son of David and Bathsheba (1 Kings 1:1-53).

In the New Testament, sibling position is rarely mentioned. In the geneology of Jesus as given by Matthew (1:1-7), it is interesting that in the first fourteen generations, not only Abraham, Isaac, and Jacob are listed, but also Judah, Perez (the second twin of Tamar by Judah), Boaz, a son by Ruth, and David and Solomon, a remarkable list of favorite younger sons. Jesus, of course, was firstborn and, although attaining remarkable prominence, was also sacrificed. This will be discussed later.

His brother James, who was probably the second son as he is always listed first among Jesus' brothers (Matthew 13:55), attained prominence as head of the Christian group in Jerusalem after Jesus' death (Acts 1:14, Galatians 2:9). In choosing disciples, Jesus took two sets of brothers (Matthew 4:18–21), but it is not clear which are the older. If Andrew was the older, his brother, Simon Peter, certainly attained greater prominence. Similarly, if James was older than John, it was the younger John who was designated by Jesus to take care of his mother after the Crucifixion (John 19:26–27) and is probably the one referred to as "the beloved disciple" (John 13:23).

That the preference for the younger son was still expectable can be demonstrated by one of Jesus' best-known parables, the Prodigal Son (Luke 15:15–32). Here the older son is obviously superior in character to the younger. The older complains, but does not kill the younger, as in the story of Cain and Abel. In a more controversial instance of the use of the preference for the younger child, Paul justifies the preference of God for the new religion of Jesus over the older religion of Judaism (Romans 9:1–13). One of the biggest struggles for the new Jewish Christians was the split over accepting Gentiles into the group without circumcision (Acts 15:1–11). It was very difficult to feel that the new converts were really serious in their relationship to God without being willing to make this sacrifice. I imagine that the Moslems, as the youngest of the three religions that worship the same God, also feel preferred, although they take as their patriarch, Ishmael, the first but illegitimate son of Abraham (Genesis 16:11–15, 21:9–14). The willingness of Moslem soldiers to die in religious wars may mean that they obtain a special relationship to God, or Allah, by becoming sacrifices. It is of interest that Freud occupied a position similar to that of Joseph, the first of his mother but not of his father.

Laws of Primogeniture

Considering the mass of evidence just cited, it is interesting that there is a general expectation that the first son is preferred, and that he is the designated heir of the father. The law is clearly stated in Deuteronomy (21:15–17), as well as in the civil laws of most countries to the present day. The paradox between the law and the scriptural preference has been noted by Biblical scholars (Jacobs, 1894; Goldin, 1979). Jacobs notes that the youngest-son preference may be related to the custom of "borough English," which in rural England had the youngest son inherit the father's flocks because the older ones had already established their own property.

This does not seem to explain the father's emotional preference for younger children. It may be that the laws of primogeniture have been necessary to protect the oldest from the emotional preference. Deuteronomy even states that the son of a favorite wife, such as Joseph, should not be given preference over the oldest son, and that the first son of an unfavored wife should inherit double.

Fatherhood

To understand the problems of fatherhood better, I would like to go back to the story of Abraham. We learn little about his relationship to his biological father from the Scriptures (Genesis 11:26-32), but after his death, he had a long and strong relationship to his God (Genesis 12-17). If we look at this as a symbolic father-son relationship, we are struck by God the father's strange behavior. He separates Abraham from his country of origin, gives him and his wife new names and identities, and promises that his seed will so multiply that he will be the father of a great people. Then he denies him children until he is very old, and gives him his first son by a concubine. When he finally has the son who should carry out the promise, he orders Abraham to kill the boy in a religious ritual, but then saves him. Abraham obeys without question, and Isaac submits without question. It is as if Isaac really belongs not to Abraham, but to God—in other words, to Abraham's father. This makes God out to be a very ambivalent father. Abraham's willingness to kill his beloved son at the behest of God the father indicates that Abraham is a better son than he is a father. Isaac is also a remarkably obedient son. This is certainly different from the situation in the Oedipus myth, although even there, it is unclear what Oedipus's attitude might have been if he had known that Laius was his father. Even if he had, there was no emotional tie between them. From the Abraham story it seems probable that most men are burdened with both positions: the fearful, jealous father, and the loving, obedient son. Moving from the position of son to father may require the resolution of ambivalent feelings that pose considerable stress. Even the ideal figure of God suffers from jealousy. In the Old Testament it is clearly stated, "I am a jealous God" (Deuteronomy 5:9-10), as well as a loving one. Apparently this jealousy can be mitigated by sacrifice, usually the best and first fruits produced by his sons, or by some substitute or symbol of that. His omnipotent powers require that this jealousy be respected and propitiated, even if the man must give up his firstborn son.

In the New Testament, God shows his sympathy for the load he has put on mankind by giving up his own son for sacrifice, for those who believe that Jesus of Nazareth was the son of God. Theologically, this is supposed to relieve men from the necessity of making concrete sacrifices; Jesus is frequently referred to as the Lamb of God (John 1:29, 49), indicating that he is to be the substitute sacrifice that will satisfy God's jealousy. It is stated that God sent his son to be sacrificed out of love for the world (John 3:16). Although there is Old Testament evidence that God was no longer demanding sacrifices (Micah 6:6–8), there is indication in the New Testament (Matthew 2:12) that sacrifices were still part of the temple ritual, as pigeons were sold for that purpose, and Jesus drove the money changers out of the temple. Paradoxically, Paul asks Christians to present their bodies as sacrifice (Romans 12:1), and Dietrich Bonhoeffer also asked for literal sacrifice as an indication of true faith, and followed this prescription himself (1937).

Psychology of Fatherhood

If one shifts from the theological to the internal psychological problems of achieving fatherhood, the process of changing from the position of son to father during the wife's first pregnancy and delivery is experienced as a threat to the creator of the man who is now becoming a creator in his own right. This is no longer the child of the oedipal period who is taking the father's place in fantasy and coveting the mother. This is a full-grown man, now with his own woman, taking his expected position in the world of adults. It is only the unconscious remnants of the early fantasy which make him uneasy, and in many cases, the remaining jealousy of the grandfather who, like God, both wants to see his seed prosper and envies the new creator, even though he created him. Jacob, after being reunited with his favorite, Joseph, claimed his sons as his own (Genesis 48:5–6). When the grandfather has been a particularly strong man, it seems as if the first grandson belongs as much as or more to him than to the father. In devout Catholic families, this first child may be dedicated to God in the service of the church. When there are particularly strong reasons for a father to feel that the first child is not really his, he can feel more at liberty to love a second or later child. The first child serves a function for the family, for society, and for the identity formation of the parent.

Of course, the feeling that the first child is not really his and the tendency to love a later child are not universal. A man who has either not had any conflict in relation to his father, or else has fully resolved it, may feel free to love his first child with little ambivalence. If he himself is a first child, he may feel a much greater identification with a first son than with any later child, although this love may be of a narcissistic nature. On the other hand, if he is a first son and had a sibling of whom he was very jealous, he might identify his first child with that sibling, and see his wife more as a mother who is depriving him of her exclusive love, than as a mate who is providing him with an heir. If he himself received little love and nurture, he may be incapable of loving *any* child. Sometimes, for a highly narcissistic male, it is easier to love a little girl, who will not be a rival, as the first child. This seems to be true in adoptions, when a sterile man has suffered a narcissisic blow. Sometimes, with the best of fathers, the first child is harder to love. Statistically, there is a greater frequency of birth trauma with resulting neurological defect in first children. As a woman remarked to me once, "When making pancakes, you throw the first one out, as it only prepares the pan."

Clinical Examples

Although analysts have dealt with many complex problems of parenthood, the specific one of a man feeling that his first son should be in some way sacrificed to his father has not been addressed. Jessner, Weigert, and Foy (1970), describing a study of college students whose wives were pregnant for the first time, saw a number of different attitudes, although all the women found a need to identify with their fathers. Benedek (1970) described a narcissistic need to parent a child of the same sex. On the other hand, she felt that the attribute of "fatherliness" was produced through identification with a nurturing mother. There is a difference in the development of the man's identity as a father, and his ability to love and nurture a child. Much of the recent literature (Cath, Gurwitt, and Ross, (1982) stresses the ability of men to be nurturing. My point is that this may be easier in relation to younger children because of the peculiar meaning that the first child, especially a son, has in regard to giving the father an identity as father. This has meaning in relation to the actual grandfather, to society, and even to God. I doubt if a child who is the product of casual sex has the same meaning.

The best way to study the development of the identity of father would be in the psychoanalysis of a man during the first pregnancy of his wife, and the delivery of a son. I could not find such an analysis in the literature, nor have I had such a case myself. An early supervised analytic case of mine became the father of his second daughter during the analysis. I learned quite a bit from him about how he perceived himself as the father of this child, but I was surprised, on reviewing my notes, at how little I knew about his relationship to his father. He was a first child, and saw his sister as the preferred one. His rivalry with her was expressed by his getting his wife pregnant immediately after he learned that his sister was pregnant. That he was also rivalrous with his wife was expressed by his constant talk of wanting a very special television set, which he bought in the week following his wife's delivery. He could laugh when I pointed out that he had delivered his own "baby." The reaction formation to his hostile rivalry with his sister and wife was expressed in an inordinate emotional concern for any news item about the death or injury to a small girl. On the other hand, although expressing a wish for a son, he seemed appropriately fond of his daughters. He also realized that he had equaled his father in the number of children produced, and contemplated with a mixture of amusement and dread that his wife, one of five children, might want to compete with her mother. I can only speculate on other aspects of his relationship with his father, who had suffered a severe business failure when the patient was eight. His educational achievements were greater, but he had not done as well professionally as he had hoped to. He was very ambitious, but severe obsessive-compulsive symptoms kept him sharpening pencils for hours, delaying his work. He felt inferior, but also misunderstood and put down by male authority figures. His anger was rigidly controlled by compulsive symptoms, which had precipitated his need for treatment. As the first son, I doubt that he was unambivalently loved by his father. He probably felt that his hostile competition had caused the father's failure, with resultant guilt. Analysis allowed him to work with greater comfort, and at a more realistic level.

Gurwitt (1982) describes in considerable detail the analysis of a man whose wife became pregnant with their first child during the end stages of his treatment. He described working with the patient's envy of the woman's creativity, seeing his coming child as a displacing sibling, and the arousal of his passive homosexual longings in relation to his preoedipal father. His identification with his nurturant mother supported this kind of relationship. In summary, Gurwitt (1982) states, "For this son to become a father like his father, yet not just like him: to become a procreator with a woman who was now linked to his mother, was heavy work" (p. 285). The final step, however, was missing, as his wife delivered a girl, not a boy.

Summary

The myth of Oedipus and the biblical story of Abraham offering his son Isaac for sacrifice have been examined as to their relevance to the problem of becoming a father. In biblical times ritual infanticide, and even the sacrifice of an adult son to propitiate the gods, suggests that

God, or the father's father, demands an indication that the first child belongs to the previous generation. The Judeo-Christian religions have struggled against this sacrifice in a number of ways, one of the more interesting being the paradox of the laws of primogeniture favoring the firstborn, while simultaneously preferring the second or younger child. The process of changing position from son to father, especially for the first son, is beset by problems of envy toward the child and the woman's creativity, and by ambivalence toward the father who seems to be displaced. The grandfather, even the figure of God in the Old Testament, is seen as jealous and requiring propitiation. This may result in a lesser ability to love that first child, especially a son, as compared with later children. It is hoped that analysts will deepen knowledge of this problem by analyzing men during the pregnancy of their wives with the first son.

REFERENCES

Benedek, T. (1970), Fatherhood and providing. In: *Parenthood,* ed. E J. Anthony & T. Benedek. Boston: Little, Brown, pp. 167–183.

Bonhoeffer, D. (1937), *The Cost of Discipleship.* New York: Macmillan, 1963.

Cath, S. H., Gurwitt, A. R., & Ross, J. M. (eds.) (1982), *Father and Child.* Boston: Little, Brown.

Frazer, J. G. (1927), *The Golden Bough.* New York: Macmillan.

Freud, S. (1900), The interpretation of dreams. *Standard Edition,* 4. London: Hogarth Press, 1953.

———— (1913), Totem and taboo. *Standard Edition,* 13:1–162. London: Hogarth Press, 1955.

Goldin, J. (1977), The youngest son, or where does Genesis 38 belong? *J. Bib. Lit.,* 96:26–44.

Gurwitt, A. R. (1982), Aspects of prospective fatherhood. In: *Father and Child,* ed. S. H. Cath, A. Gurwitt, & J. M. Ross. Boston: Little, Brown, pp. 275–299.

Jacobs, J. (1894), Junior-right in Genesis. In: *Studies in Biblical Archeology.* New York: Macmillan, pp. 44–63.

Jessner, L., Weigert, E., & Foy, J. L. (1970), The development of parental attitudes during pregnancy. In: *Parenthood,* ed. E. J. Anthony & T. Benedek. Boston: Little Brown, pp. 230–239.

Kaplan, K. J. (1986), Interpersonal arrangements in Greek and Hebrew families: A biblical view of the father-son relationship. Presented at the Institute for Psychoanalysis, Chicago, February 19.

Kohut, H. (1982), Introspection, empathy, and the semi-circle of mental health. *Internat. J. Psycho-Anal.,* 63:395–407.

Wellisch, E. (1954), *Isaac and Oedipus.* London: Routledge and Kegan Paul.

IV

PSYCHOANALYSIS AND GENDER

What Is the Relation Between the Psychoanalytic Psychology of Women and Psychoanalytic Feminism?

NANCY J. CHODOROW, Ph.D. (Berkeley, Calif.)
with discussions by
BARBARA S. ROCAH, M.D. (Chicago)
and BERTRAM J. COHLER, Ph.D. (Chicago)

This paper is about communication, or the lack of it, among people who write and think about psychoanalysis and women.[1] On one side, among psychoanalysts debate about women and femininity has become a topic of burgeoning interest in recent years. On the other side, psychoanalytic feminists—academic literary critics, philosophers, social scientists, feminist epistemologists—engage in a distinctly different set of discourses, about different questions.

My labels here do not do justice to the complexities of these protagonists' identities. Some who have contributed prominently to the psychoanalytic literature about women and femininity would, if asked, label themselves as feminist—as critical of and wishing to change the gendered and sexual status quo. Similarly, some whom I consider to have contributed primarily to psychoanalytic feminism are practicing analysts or therapists. In the ambiguous middle, a few feminist psychoanalysts— practicing analysts who identify themselves explicitly as feminists—

[1] I am grateful for comments from Elizabeth Abel, Daniel Greenson, Lisby Mayer, Barrie Thorne, and Abby Wolfson. A version of this paper was presented at the conference on Contemporary Women and Psychoanalysis: Critical Questions Reconsidered, Institute for Psychoanalysis, Chicago, May 2, 1987. Copyright © Nancy Julia Chodorow, 1989

elaborate clinically upon the theoretical contributions of psychoanalytic
feminism, focusing not only on the deficiencies in psychoanalytic theory
but also on the role and treatment of women in society.[2] In spite of these
overlaps, it seems to me that different discussions are going on, among
different sets of people.

Briefly, psychoanalytic feminists begin, somewhat in the manner of
the Freud of "Studies on Hysteria," "Three Essays on Sexuality," and
" 'Civilized' Sexual Morality and Modern Nervousness," from a critical
and evaluative theoretical position. We take gender and sexuality as we
typically know these to be socially, culturally, and psychologically
problematic, and wish to understand how gender and sexuality develop
and are reproduced in the individual and thereby in society. Psychoanalysts begin, somewhat in the manner of the Freud who asks "how [a
woman] comes into being" (1933, p. 116), from a query about how
gender and sexuality develop and are played out in life, and how, in
individual cases, these do not follow the route prescribed or described as
normal. Their evaluative stance tends to assume a bifurcation of
masculinity and femininity in more or less traditional cultural terms and
a heterosexuality with partners in complementary but different roles and
sexual stances.

We are compellingly reminded of the professional and intellectual
separation of worlds. For the most part, psychoanalysts do not seem to be
aware of or to care much about the enormous exciting ferment in
psychoanalytic feminist theory that is in the forefront of a number of
academic disciplines. Psychoanalysts work more as scientists, for whom
empirical reality has definite primacy, if not exclusive claim to document
truth. They are more likely to think that science can be value-free and
have tended to see feminism as a political or politicized practice rather
than as a theory that is relevant to their own theory or practice. (For
further discussion of these issues see Chodorow, 1987.)

Reciprocally, psychoanalytic feminists often seem to go about their
business paying little attention to the claims of those who by profession,
as clinicians and researchers, would seem to have the best right to decide
among psychoanalytic claims. Psychoanalytic feminist literary critics,
philosophers, and epistemologists work more exclusively from a text,

---

[2]Jessica Benjamin, Jane Flax, and I among object-relations feminists and Jean Baker
Miller and her colleagues among interpersonal feminists are clinicians. Prominent
feminist psychoanalysts include Carol Nadelson and Malkah Notman, whom I would
place in terms of my discussion below closest to the feminist interpersonal school, as they
have collaborated frequently with Jean Baker Miller, and Ethel Person, whom I would
locate more as an object-relations feminist psychoanalyst (for further discusson of
feminist psychoanalysts see note 3 below).

"story," or theoretical argument, so that evidential claims don't as much affect their assessments about persuasive arguments.

To me, this separation is problematic. My discomfort here could be taken to rest on individual biography and identity: I am a social scientist who writes in the field of object-relations feminism and is in psychoanalytic training. Questions about the varieties of psychoanalytic theories of gender seem particularly problematic for social scientists, who privilege both empirical "reality" and theory, who draw upon a variety of interpretive and explanatory strategies, and who tend to grant that there is no such thing as value-free science. However, I would argue that it is generally necessary for psychoanalytic feminists, who claim to draw upon psychoanalysis, to come to terms with what psychoanalysts *say* gender is about, even if and as we want to say something different. By complement, since psychoanalysis is a cultural discourse and not just a therapeutic practice, psychoanalysts would probably do well to know something of the debates and claims of psychoanalytic feminism.

Psychoanalytic Theories of Women and Gender

All modern developments, both psychoanalytic and feminist, are in dialogue with the traditional Freudian theory of the development of femininity. Three features of this view are relevant here. First, sex difference doesn't matter until the phallic phase, around age four, at which stage "the little girl is a little man" with a masculine sexuality (Freud, 1933, p. 118). Second, for both sexes sexual knowledge until puberty is monistic: sexual difference is presence or absence of the penis, and the vagina (for classical psychoanalysts, *the* female sexual organ) is unknown, both consciously and unconsciously. Third, the developments of heterosexuality and maternality in the girl are a secondary product of her sense of failed masculinity.

The classical view, followed by some modern theorists, speaks not so much of gender as of sex and sexuality. Freud and his colleagues were concerned with the nature and meaning of erotic experience as this is mediated through body zones and organs, and with sexual object choice. Insofar as we can infer from this account, conceptions of gender identity (how we cognize and what we make of our own gender; our sense of feminine or masculine self) and gender personality (males' and females' character, psychic structure, and psychological processes) are in the first instance tied to apprehension of genital constitution: Does a boy give up his mother (or his father, in case he is tempted into a passive sexual position vis-à-vis this father) in exchange for his penis? Does a girl accept her "castration" or protest against it? Does she go through life seeking a penis? The creation of sexual orientation, the desire for parenthood, masculine and feminine identifications with the same sex parent, all result from what the child does with her or his sense of genital difference.

There was, of course, a major dissident position on female sexuality from almost as early as Freud discussed it, but active debate about the nature of femininity nevertheless disappeared for some time. The topic was kept alive indirectly through clinical case discussion, but rarely in ways that maintained or constructed any fundamental challenge to the theory. In the last fifteen years or so, however, theoretical, clinical, and empirical discussion has emerged into active reformulation and debate. As I read the literature, contemporary psychoanalytic debate centers on three issues, two developmental and one clinical.[3]

First, attention has been focused especially on the question of genital awareness, when and how it develops, and what its impact is on gender identity, gender personality, and the sense of self. Specifically, psycho-analysts now claim, against Freud's view that sex difference doesn't matter until the phallic phase, that genital awareness develops in the second year, in what would have formerly been called the *pre*genital period.

There are two positions within this view. Roiphe and Galenson (1981 and elsewhere) follow Freud, in that they understand early genital awareness as an awareness of sexual *difference,* and difference in the

----

[3]I do not consider here those whom I call feminist psychoanalysts, who do have the potential to bridge the psychoanalytic and psychoanalytic feminist approaches that I discuss. I am not yet clear how to characterize theirs as an autonomous theoretical contribution, as their writings seem rather to substantiate and clinically specify and elaborate dominant psychoanalytic feminist positions. Perhaps as a result of their explicit feminism, they are rarely published in the mainstream orthodox journals. At the same time, their writing, like that of most psychoanalysts, does not seem to be much read by the academic psychoanalytic feminists whom I discuss. Both classical analysts who write about femininity and psychoanalytic feminists tend to write more from a developmental perspective, whereas Nadelson, Notman, Person, and their collaborators write more from a clinical perspective about adult women's issues.

Nadelson and Notman have written on, among other topics, aggression, rape, and the female life cycle. See, e.g., Miller, Nadelson, Notman, and Zilbach (1981); Nadelson, Notman, Miller, and Zilbach (1982); Nadelson, Notman, and Carmen (1986); Nadelson and Notman (1979, 1985); and several articles on marriage, work, motherhood, reproduction, and menopause, in Nadelson and Notman (1982).

Person has written on, among other topics, gender identity, sexuality, women and work, romantic love, and bias in psychoanalytic theory and theories of the psychoanalytic process (see. e.g., 1980, 1982, 1983, 1985, 1986, 1988; and Person and Ovesey, 1983).

These feminist psychoanalysts have been joined in recent years by a series of writers published in such anthologies as Bernay and Cantor (1986); Alpert (1986); Kirkpatrick (1980, 1981). The tendency in these writings as well is toward a clinical rather than a developmental perspective and toward a focus on adult women's issues.

traditional sense: presence or absence of the penis is what matters. They claim that the one-year-old girl's response to her discovered castration is *the* organizing influence, both inhibiting and enhancing, from this time onward, not just on psychosexual development, sexuality, and the girl's turn to her father, but on ego and object-relational development as well.

Other recent psychoanalytic accounts agree with Roiphe and Galenson's claim for early genital schematization, but they provide different views of what this schematization is and its role in the formation of gender identity and gender personality. In one way or another, these formulations all challenge Freud's view that the little girl is a little man with a "phallic" (active, clitoral) sexuality who doesn't know her own feminine organs consciously or unconsciously. They rely on a notion of primary femininity, arguing that in both boys and girls a primary genital *awareness,* involving a primary cathexis of their own genital organs, precedes the observation or schematization of genital *difference.* Such awareness proceeds directly out of body experience, though for different writers it can be more or less affected by parental labeling and treatment.

I include several people in this group. Chasseguet-Smirgel (1976) argues along with Horney that sexual monism in either sex does not result from lack of knowledge but from repression or a splitting of the ego and that the Freudian picture of the woman who lacks vagina, penis, an adequate erotic object, or any intrinsic feminine qualities she could enjoy is *"exactly the opposite of the primal maternal imago* as it is revealed in the clinical material of both sexes" (p. 281), Kestenberg (e.g., 1968, 1980a, 1980b) not only argues for knowledge of the vagina but also develops a positive conception of its role, or the role of inner-genital experience and an inner-genital phase preceding the phallic phase (which Kestenberg might prefer to call the outer- or external-genital phase) in the libidinal development of both sexes. Her conception paves the way for what we might call a libidinally based feminine developmental line, drawing us from a conception of femininity solely in terms of passive vaginal heterosexuality in relation to men to one that stresses maternality as well. Kleeman (1976), Lerner (1976), and others point to the role of vague and inaccurate parental labeling of the external female genitalia — vulva and clitoris, often generically called vagina — in hindering schematization of that part of her genital which a girl can most directly see and touch.[4]

---

[4]Some analysts might argue that labeling was really not relevant, that the issue of genital schematization was an internal issue and not an external one, and that internal factors detemine how a child of a particular age can and will understand his or her body (see, for instance, Freud's arguments about cloacal theory and theory of anal birth). Both Kestenberg and Bell (1965) make the point that parents (and psychoanalysts) don't do well

Mayer (1985) suggests that the mental representations defining a sense of femaleness for a girl begin not with vaginal awareness but with conceptions of the vulva, leading girls to experience their genitals as having an opening and potential inside space. Women's valuation of this genital openness may be observed in derivative symbolic form, as they value emotional openness, access to inner feelings, empathetic capacities, and receptivity. Castration anxiety in this context involves the fear of being closed over both genitally and emotionally. Women's characterizations of men as emotionally closed and unable to be receptive or aware of inner feeling are a symbolic reflection of a more basic genital fear.

A second strand of recent psychoanalytic theories of feminine (and masculine) development focuses not so much on genital awareness as on gender identity, following the argument developed by Money and Ehrhardt, Kohlberg, and others that cognitive labeling of gender, or core gender identity—the sense of femaleness and maleness—develops in the first few years of life. As with the issue of genital awareness, we can find two positions on the question of gender identity. The first and dominant position, like Freud's implicit view that gender identity is a matter of sexual orientation and genital constitution, hinges gender identity, even if it is cognitively developed and not necessarily based on invidious comparison of the girl's with the boy's genitals, on genital awareness (see, e.g., Mayer, 1985, Chehrazi, 1986, and Tyson, 1982). Tyson (1982), for instance, claims that the boy's first task in the establishment of his core gender identity is the discovery of his penis and its integration into his body image and that his first step in gender *role* assumption is upright urination in identification with his father. She discusses body experience and body representation as central to the establishment of the girl's core feminine gender identity as well.

An alternate account of the development of gender identity is found in the work of Kleeman and Stoller, who hinge gender identity on cognitive and interpersonal factors and make genital experience distinctly derivative. Kleeman (1976) argues that although genital experience and self-stimulation occur in the young child, such behavior is no more important than object relations, self development, cognitive development, and other aspects of behavior. Against Freud's early claims, Stoller (1964, 1965, 1968, 1975, and elsewhere) argues that the sense of femaleness is more easily attained than the sense of maleness, and that male gender-identity development runs a continual risk of being under-

---

with the male genitalia either, in this case letting the more external, phallic term—penis—stand for parts of the genital function that seem to have more inner functions and aspects (we might also point to the psychoanalytic phallicization of castration, which in fact means removal of the testes, not the penis).

mined by a primary feminine identification that emerges from a close tie to the mother. Thus, against the psychoanalytic mainstream, these theorists accord much more weight to interpersonal psychodynamics in gender development than to genital awareness and genital difference. For them, core gender identity is a composite result of biological forces, sex assignment, and parental labeling at birth and in the early years, parental attitudes about that sex, family psychodynamics, and the infant's interpretation of these experiences. The Stoller-Kleeman position has been influential in establishing gender identity as a feature of cognitive self-concept that is not the same as sexual orientation and in stressing the importance of labeling and object relations in the creation of gender identity and genital experience.[5]

To review, with the exception of the Stoller-Kleeman account, modern psychoanalytic developmental interest in female psychology has centered on female sexuality, defined as what girls make of their own genitals and genital difference. In a sense, this modern attempt to deal with the empirically incorrect (as well as sexist) early Freudian theory of primary masculinity turns further toward an essentialist view of gender identity and gender role. Whereas classical psychoanalytic theory begins from a more generically conceived sexuality and mobile unconscious drives that in turn create genital experience (and character), in contemporary theories of gender, direct genital awareness and experience become primary determinants, and sexuality (as well as object relations and character) becomes more derivative.

In addition to discussion concerning the developmental theory of gender, the third central area of contemporary psychoanalytic debate concerns cross-gender transference. Much of the early discussion of psychoanalytic technique and process derived from cases of women hysterics treated by male analysts, and Freud (1931) pointed out that women analysts had made fundamental discoveries about the psychology of women as a result of the specific transferences they experienced from women patients. Recently, psychoanalysts have become concerned with the nature of the transference that *men* patients develop toward women analysts, and some have argued that men do not develop an erotic or paternal transference to their female analysts (see, e.g., Lester, 1985, Goldberger and Evans, 1985, Karme, 1979, and Tyson, 1980).[6] More

---

[5]For another example that stresses the role of object relations, see Clower (1976).

[6]I distinguish debate here from an extensive resurgence in clinical writing on many women's issues — aggression, work inhibitions, later life-cycle transitions (see references in note 3 as well as Applegarth [1976]). I focus on cross-gender transference because the issue has been cast so much as a debate and because of the profound importance for psychoanalytic theory and practice of any implicit or explicit claim that women cannot fully analyze men.

over, they have not seen this "finding" as difference. Rather, they claim that an analysis is not complete without an erotic transference.

Responses to these claims have taken several forms (forms that incidentally move us toward psychoanalytic feminism). The simplest challenge is empirical, simply providing clinical evidence of male patients who have developed such transferences (Tyson, 1986). A more sophisticated version of the empirical claim holds that analysts of either gender are more likely to recognize certain transferences than others because they are more culturally and psychologically syntonic, and that we must recognize and analyze latent as well as manifest transferences in different gendered pairs (Mayer, 1986). Thus, men may be less likely to recognize a maternal transference whereas they easily recognize an erotic transference from a younger woman, and women may not as easily recognize an erotic transference from a younger man. A different kind of argument takes issue with the evaluative schema itself (Person, 1985). The issue is not whether we can find some men who develop a manifest or latent erotic transference to their women analysts, but why many men, or most men—men who, according to psychoanalytic views, act out sexually more than women, are more likely to engage in various perversions, and so forth—can't become, or must deny becoming, erotically attracted to women in the analytic situation.

Psychoanalytic Feminism

As with psychoanalytic writings on gender and women, any division of psychoanalytic feminism is partly arbitrary. Three self-identified approaches stand out, and I think we can see large commonalities between the first two in comparison to the third. Here, I distinguish an object-relations and interpersonal psychoanalytic feminism from a Lacanian psychoanalytic feminism.[7]

Following for the most part the British object-relations school, object-relations feminists put self-other relations and the development of a self (whether whole or fragmented, agentic or reactive) as it is constituted through its consciously and unconsciously experienced relations in the center of development. The object-relations school has itself hardly dealt

---

[7]Lacanians sometimes call object-relations theorists Anglo-American theorists, in contrast to French theorists, and both approaches in the first group would fall under the gynecentric theoretical rubric that Miriam Johnson distinguishes from phallocentric theory (see Johnson, 1987, 1988).

with gender difference or the development of gender, but we argue that their approach can be drawn upon in such a venture.[8]

The outlines of the object-relations perspective on feminine development and personality can be summarized from my own writing (Chodorow, 1974, 1978, 1980). I have argued that, as a result of being parented primarily by a woman, men and women develop differently constructed selves and different experiences of their gender and gender identity: "feminine personality comes to define itself in relation and connection to other people more than masculine personality" (1974, p. 44); "the basic feminine sense of self is connected to the world" (1978, p. 169). Through their early relationship with their mother, women develop a sense of self continuous with others and a richly constructed, bisexual, oedipal-oscillating-with-preoedipal inner self-object world that continuously engages unconscious and conscious activity. This psychic structure and self-other process in turn help to reproduce mothering: "Because women themselves are mothered by women, they grow up with the relational capacities and needs, and psychological definition of self-in-relationship, which commits them to mothering" (1978, p. 209). This relational self can be both a strength or a pitfall in feminine psychic life, as it enables empathy, nurturance, and intimacy but can also threaten lack of autonomy and dissolution of self into others. Women's mothering itself shares this ambivalent position, as it often generates pleasure and fulfillment and at the same time is fundamentally related to women's secondary position in society.

Men develop by contrast a self based more on denial of relation and connection and on a more fixed and firmly split and repressed inner self-object world: "the basic masculine sense of self is separate" (Chodorow, 1978, p. 169). The object-relations view argues that as a result of being parented primarily by a woman, masculinity develops a more reactive and defensive quality than femininity in women: "For boys and men, both individuation and dependency issues become tied up with the sense of masculinity. . . . For girls and women, by contrast, issues of femininity, or feminine identity, are not problematic in the same way" (1974, p. 44). Dinnerstein (1976) and I point to the mother blame, misogyny, and fear of women and femininity that develop in both sexes, but especially in men, in reaction to the powerfully experienced mother (and internal mother-image), and we suggest that this fuels male

---

[8]Galenson makes a related point about the relative lack of attention to the integration of ego-psychoanalytic concepts about nonconflictual and autonomous spheres into psychoanalytic understandings of feminine development (Panel, 1976).

dominance in culture and society and creates systematic tensions and conflicts in heterosexual relationships.[9]

Writers like Keller (1985), Flax (1978b, 1983, 1986), and Benjamin (1977, 1978, 1988) have described how this arelational masculinity, based on a need to dominate and deny women, the feminine, and human and natural interconnectedness has become institutionalized in notions of scientific objectivity, technical rationality, and individualistic, hierarchical political and social theory and in practices of erotic, scientific, and technical domination. There is also a school of feminist literary criticism that draws from an object-relations perspective to investigate woman's voice, the mother-image, inner worlds, and qualities of relatedness in women writers, and male writers' unconscious attitudes to mothers and feminine power (see, e.g., Abel, 1980, 1981, 1982, and 1989; Abel, Hirsch, and Langland, 1983; Kahn, 1985; Adelman, 1987).

Thus the object-relations perspective takes the construction of masculinity and femininity to be interconnected and constitutes a critique of masculinity as well as a reformulation of our understanding of the female self. Feminist object-relations theorists have also argued strongly for theoretical and developmental treatment of the mother as a *subject*, against psychoanalytic (including object-relational) tendencies to treat her as an object whose role is evaluated in terms of the presumed needs and fantasies of the child alone.[10] This in turns entails an emphasis on intersubjectivity and the mutual recognition of the other and the self as fundamental to satisfactory development.

The interpersonal group, all practicing clinicians, has created an account of female psychology for our purposes similar to the object-relations perspective. Miller, a Sullivanian analyst, enunciated the main features of the cultural psychoanalytic perspective (1976), and the group also draws on the theories of Gilligan (1982; see also Surrey, 1985; Jordan, 1984; and Miller, 1983, 1984).[11] The interpersonal view argues for a revalorization of women's qualities—qualities of affiliativeness, relatedness, empathy, and nurturance—which are distorted in a male dominant culture that also represses and denies women's just anger. Much of the writing of this group is based on clinical cases, and in these

---

[9]I stress differences in the way reactions to the mother are constituted in men and women more than Dinnerstein does, but such distinctions are not necessary for our purposes here.

[10]On the subjectivity of the mother, see Benjamin (1977), Chodorow and Contratto (1981), Chodorow (1978, 1980, 1985), and Keller (1985).

[11]The critical political stance and general critique of social inequality found in Miller's book and later writings are not emphasized by her Stone Center colleagues, who stick more closely to psychological issues.

case descriptions, women's problems are seen to inhere mainly in the denial and devaluation of affiliative qualities both by others and by themselves. Cure consists in women's recognizing and accepting these qualities, in being caring and empathetic toward themselves. Miller's original work attributed the developmental origins of the feminine qualities she described in a general way to cultural learning. In the recent work of the interpersonal group the implicit and articulated view seems to follow the object-relations perspective, emphasizing the influence of the mother-daughter relationship on the development of what they also now call the "self-in-relation." (Jordan and Surrey, 1986, e.g., follow Chodorow, 1978, quite closely.)

This general feminist perspective is definitely bifurcated. As psychoanalytic theorists, object-relations feminists pay more attention to the complexities of the inner object world, to internalizations, to unconscious defenses and conflicts, to the unconscious structuring of self. Interpersonal theorists tend not to emphasize unconscious dynamics as much but to pay more attention to cultural and personal evaluation of different qualities and capacities. As feminists, object-relations theorists focus more on the problems that along with strengths inhere in women's psychological qualities, and we are more likely to focus on male development as a problem. Although we also may valorize women's qualities, both our social analysis and our greater attention to unconscious conflict lead object-relations theorists to hold a more tempered and critical view of these qualities (in addition to Chodorow, 1978, see Flax, 1978b, 1987).

But these views have several features in common. Although we (especially the object-relations group) focus, like contemporary psychoanalysts, on the early infantile and preoedipal period as crucial to gender development and therefore on the crucial importance of the relation to the mother, we emphatically and by definition do *not* understand genital apperception and genital difference to be causal and central in gender identity and gender personality. We focus on the experience of *self with other* and how that comes to be organized and appropriated. When feminine development is seen as problematic, such problems are seen to inhere centrally and originally in relational and self issues — conflict in the mother, devaluation by the father, experiences of lack of fit, inadequately resolved narcissistic development, and development of agency and wholeness — or in problems of cultural valuation. These are *not* built upon a more primary conflicted genital schematization or problematic genital awareness (though they may be played out partly around such issues).

The object–relations-interpersonal perspective separates gender identity and gender personality. Qualities of self or self in relation (and denial of relation is equally important here) become more important than unconsciously or consciously experienced gender identity and cognition and assessment of gender difference. It is not *because* she knows she is female that a girl or woman experiences her self in relationship (though by contrast, a boy's or man's denial of relationality may very well be a product of his sense of appropriate masculinity). Her self in relation is a developmental product, tied to her mother's sense of self, but not only to gender identity or gender role learning. The object–relations-cultural perspective does not ignore conscious gender identity and the construction of gender or unconscious meanings of these, but it claims that this is not all there is to gender, and it embeds these in object-relations or cultural sense of self. Because of this focus on qualities of self, the object-relations perspective in particular moves radically away from essentialist views of gender toward a view that constructs feminine and masculine personality in a contingent, relationally constructed context.

Lacanian feminism, the second branch of psychoanalytic feminism, like the first, reacts to the original psychoanalytic theory, but it also reacts to the object-relations, though not to the interpersonal, position. Mitchell, now a psychoanalyst, engages directly with other psychoanalysts. Her first book (1974), a founding Lacanian feminist statement, tried, via a somewhat Lacanian reading, to rescue Freud from his feminist detractors, his psychoanalytic critics and supporters, and in some sense from himself. Her recent writing (1982, 1984) sticks more closely to Lacan, and her critical polemic is directed less toward other feminists (except as they use psychoanalytic theories she doesn't like) and more toward primary femininity, Kleinian, and object-relations theories — theories that argue, against the Lacanian and Freudian stress on the oedipal father, for the importance of preoedipal mother-child experience. The more literary proponents of Lacanian theory tend to engage with Lacan and Freud among psychoanalysts, with postmodernist French critics like Derrida, and otherwise with object-relations psychoanalytic feminists. For the most part, they do not engage with post-Freudian psychoanalytic writings.[12]

Lacanian feminists argue that Freud's account of how we become sexed shows how our very sexualization is asymmetrical and unequal. In the Lacanian view, the unconscious (as opposed to the ego or internalized object relations) is the fundament of psychic life, and this linguistically

---

[12]For paradigmatic Lacanian feminist statements in addition to Mitchell (1974, 1984), see Mitchell and Rose, in Lacan (1982), and Gallop (1982). Lacanian feminist literary criticism can be found in Garner, Kahane, and Sprengnether (1985), and in an extensive literature by Gallop, Shoshana Felman, Toril Moi, Naomi Schor, and others.

constructed and structured unconscious *is* our sexuality: subjectivity emerges out of unconscious sexual drives. This sexualization and subjectivity are by definition constituted in terms of the difference, or opposition, between the sexes, an opposition that is structured linguistically and not biologically. We are also born into this sexual/linguistic setting; it precedes us and makes inevitable our developmental situation.

A person takes his or her place in the world as a subject only through entry into the "symbolic," into language and culture. This acquisition of subjectivity takes place through the intervention of a third person, or term, into the "imaginary" mother-child dyad, which is conceived to lie conceptually and emotionally outside of language and culture. The father, symbolized by his phallus (which in turn symbolizes the prohibition of desire for the mother and the threat of castration) institutes and constitutes this symbolic intervention. The phallus thus stands for entrance into the symbolic. In this view, then, subjectivity *is* sexuality, and sexuality is defined exclusively in terms of sexual difference, in terms of the presence or absence of the phallus. Sexuality and subjectivity, rooted in the unconscious, are precarious for both sexes, as they hinge on resolution of the castration complex.

In contrast to recent psychoanalytic views, in the Lacanian view there can be no primary genital awareness that is not tied to the awareness and cognizing of genital difference, which, in turn, is located and mediated in language. Nor can there be preoedipal knowledge of genital difference, since such knowledge is by definition tied to the oedipal transition and the castration complex. In contrast to object-relations feminism, there can be no subjectivity apart from schematized sexual identity: gender difference is all there is when it comes to our selfhood or subjectivity, and gender difference is experienced and cognized (through our placement in language) in terms of sexuality and genital schematization. Subjectivity and sexuality are interdependent; neither can develop without the other.

One reading of Lacan holds that the resolution of the castration complex differs for men and women and thereby institutes (and documents) sexual difference. Sexual constitution and subjectivity are different for he who possesses the phallus and she who does not. As the phallus comes to stand for itself in the theory of desire, and not even to stand in relation to the mother's desire, the woman becomes not a subject in her own right—even one who can never have the phallus—but simply a symbol or a symptom in the masculine psyche.

Another reading, and some Lacanian feminists argue that the sexually critical and liberatory potential of Lacan lies here, is that although one sex has an anatomical penis, neither sex, finally, can possess the phallus. Sexuality is incomplete and fractured for both sexes. Moreover, as men and women must line themselves up on one or another side of the linguistic/sexual divide, they need not do so on the side isomorphic with their anatomy.

Lacanian feminism makes strong feminist and psychoanalytic claims. It argues that there are no aspects to gender division, identity, or personality other than sexuality and symbolized genital difference and that there is no subjectivity outside of sexuality: any speaking being must locate him or herself in relation to the phallus. Such a theory locates every action firmly in an unequal sexual world and never loses sight of our developmentally inevitable placement in a phallocentric culture. It speaks to woman's lack of self and sense of being the Other, to her fundamental alienation from and objectification in culture.

Against a reading of Lacan which singles out woman as the lack, or the Other, we find a French feminist anti-Lacanian revolt (see Eisenstein and Jardine, 1980, and Marks and de Courtivron, 1981). In another version of the argument for primary femininity and for a genital awareness that does not hinge on perception and acceptance of unequal genital difference, Luce Irigaray, Hélène Cixous, and others reject male discourse and argue for women's reappropriation of their own unconscious, their body, and their genital configuration, for women's being in themselves rather than being a lack in the male psyche. This being in themselves expresses the self-enclosed female genitalia, the "two lips speaking together" in which a woman secures herself to herself or in relation to other like-constructed women. This argument is both about body experience and about alternate forms of linguistic construction in women — about "women's language" and "writing the body," and it pays less attention to female development than to an elaborate working out of female experience. It is, arguably, gynecentric and valorizes feminine qualities, but it pays less attention to the centrality of relations among women and the mother-daughter relationship than the object-relations account. Indeed, accounts of the mother-daughter relationship tend to retain Lacanian and traditional psychoanalytic views that mothers and mother-attachment are traps, depicting mothers who constrain, compete, and destroy. In this view, it is not from her mother that a girl attains her femininity or selfhood, but seemingly from herself, insofar as she rejects her mother.

Lacanians bring up against object-relations feminists and primary femininity theorists that, in focusing on the mother-daughter relationship, or on femininity defined not only in relation to masculinity, we fail to acknowledge the totality and all-encompassing nature of our phallocentric and unequal gendered and sexual world. They criticize views that idealize women's qualities or ignore women's situation in a male-dominant culture and language, arguing that there can be neither wholeness nor positive qualities for women or men in such a culture. There can be no experiences not generated by male dominance nor can there be a femininity defined in itself.[13]

The Lacanian critique of sexual difference combines with Lacan's anti-humanistic account of the fragmented, necessarily alienated, subject. Hence, another ground for the Lacanian critique of object-relations feminists and of post-Freudian analysts is that these accounts all speak of the self or identity (including gender identity) as if these can exist in any kind of wholeness or potential wholeness. The Lacanian subject, by contrast, can never be whole, can never have the humanistic fiction called self. The causes and future of such fragmentation can be interpreted in two ways. For some Lacanian psychoanalytic feminists it is a product of a phallocentric culture that can be transformed. For those whose reading of Lacan comes more via postmodernism and Derrida, for whom language dissolves identity and fixed difference, it is an inevitable product of culture itself.

What are the relations among these theories? Lacanians and French anti-Lacanians *seem* to have fundamental assumptions in common with the dominant psychoanalytic mainstream, locating gender difference is genital difference, but this is an accidental commonality. It encompasses the scope neither of psychoanalysis, with its complex developmental account of the emotional meanings of the genitals, nor of Lacanian theory, with its specifically linguistic account of the relationship of sexuality and subjectivity. For most classical analysts (as for object-relations feminists) there is a distinction between sexuality and subjectivity, and it makes a difference whether we have primarily a speaking subject, in which location language predominates, or a sexual subject, in which sexual difference and the phallus predominate. It is not clear that anything genital or sexual as psychoanalysts think of this (or relational as object-relations theorists think of this) matters to Lacanians.

---

[13]Johnson (1987, 1988) makes this point more concretely, arguing that the gynecentric perspective obscures the father's critical role in emphasizing and constituting gender difference and gender domination in the family. The mother, she claims, represents and institutes a common humanity in both sexes, and her own empirical research suggests that the father, by his actual behavior and not simply as a symbol of culture and the phallus, creates sexuality and gender-typed behavior in both son and daughter. The father installs male dominance, a male dominance that inheres not in the mother-child relationship but in that of husband and wife. Johnson points out that the traditional view, arguing that the boy doesn't have to change object and the girl does, obscures one important factor: the boy must make a generational transformation as radical as the girl's gender transformation. The boy's postedipal object choice must be one in which he is in the dominant, and not the subordinate position as he is in relation to his mother. The Oedipus complex and oedipal transition thereby institute male dominance and sexism.

More important, the Lacanian argument is a logical argument about
the structure of language and us as its speakers: as developing beings, we
must break out of the dyadic mother-child relationship that does not
understand itself to be constituted by an order beyond. There *must* be a
third term to institute this break, and the father, symbolized by his
phallus, *is* this third term. Evidence cannot oppose this logic, since it is a
logic, and Lacanians even have a language for dismissing evidence:
anything pre-given, natural, or "real" is repudiated by definition on the
symbolic level. We can linguistically describe or experience nothing
outside of the symbolic, which places us in that very phallic order against
which we might want to find evidence.

In this context, claims for primary femininity are by definition
inadequate, as are conceptions of gender that are not constituted as
sexual difference. Evidential claims about a genital phase in the second
year or about the early mother-child relationship cannot have impact on
the account. Cognitive and developmental psychological research about
language development cannot impinge on the Lacanian claim that
language only reacts to loss and that symbolization occurs only in the
absence of an object. Against queries about what difference the actual
presence or absence of the father makes for this theory, Mitchell claims
that the father is a symbol, definitionally present in language; his actual
presence is irrelevant.

Such views diametrically oppose those of most practicing analysts,
certainly in this country and probably in many other countries as well.
Psychoanalysts see their work as scientific, as a product of the steady
development of clinical and observational evidence. "Discoveries" are
made and "evidence" comes to light; theory is "confirmed" by clinical and
research "findings." Psychoanalytic debates, certainly in the area of gender
psychology, concern the nature and interpretation of evidence; they are
rarely cast in the language of theoretical logic. (I cannot engage here in
a sociology of psychoanalytic epistemology, but, briefly, I would suspect
that many non-Lacanian French psychoanalysts would also be more comfortable with anti-empiricist claims, as would Latin Americans influenced by Lacanian ideas. In general, European analysts, even if they are
critical of Lacanian theory and practice, are not as likely as Americans to
identify themselves as medically trained scientists, or even to be medically trained. They are thus probably more comfortable with theory in
itself, where clinical experience *illustrates,* but does not have to *confirm,* or
prove, scientific claims.) Thus, the psychoanalytic position, though apparently congruent with the Lacanian, fundamentally contrasts with it.

A different contrast holds between object-relations and interpersonal
psychoanalytic feminism and psychoanalytic gender theory. Contempo-

rary psychoanalysts certainly take object relations and the self seriously, but they have not applied these concerns to their approaches to gender, which still tend to be based in drive theory and genital experience (I have mentioned Stoller, Kleeman, and Clower as exceptions here).[14] Object-relations feminists make the development, structure, and experience of self and self-other relations into a *primary* phenomenon in our consideration of gender and not a secondary reaction to drive development or genital experience. They do not hinge gender personality on genital apperception or cognition, or even necessarily on gender identity. Here, the closing off of debate is substantively theoretical rather than epistemological.

Overlap and commonality between object-relations feminism and psychoanalysis, as in the Lacanian case, are often accidental and not intentional. For instance, Kestenberg developed a theory of libidinal-phase development that leads to maternality and the potential for nurturance in both sexes, just as object-relations theorists have developed a relational account of the same outcome. Both object-relations feminists and psychoanalysts have developed a version of a theory of primary femininity, but the former is rooted in mother-daughter identification and shared selfhood, and the latter is rooted in primary genital awareness. The object-relations developmental account concerning the role of fear of women, especially powerful women, in the development of masculinity seems to explain clinical findings about erotic transference in male patients of female analysts at least as well as and perhaps better than classic accounts about primary genital awareness or castration anxiety, but against "research" on genital awareness object-relations feminists can only claim that other things are psychologically more important.

Such a situation can lead to radically different interpretations of the same situation by people who both hold that clinical "evidence" matters. For instance, consider a woman who has enormous performance anxiety and does much worse than she could in school and in testing situations.[15]

---

[14]Stoller (1975), for example, claims: "As a description of human childhood development, Freud's observations on zonal phases have been confirmed and can be so any time with biologically normal children. However no studies have been published that confirm the implications drawn from the observations. It has not yet been shown that any class of neurosis, including perversion, or psychosis is caused by a disruption of the sensual experiences of the mouth, defecatory or urinary systems, or phallus. . . . (There is, however, much evidence that disturbed object relations during these phases cause psychopathology" [pp. 32–33]).

[15]This example is inspired by talks given back to back at "Women and Psychoanalysis: Today and Yesterday," a symposium celebrating the 50th Anniversary of the Boston Psychoanalytic Society, February 1984, one by Eleanor Galenson and the other by Jean Baker Miller, Carol Nadelson, Malkah Notman, and Joan Zilbach.

A classical analyst might say that she unconsciously experiences success as gaining a penis, that this reminds her of the early narcissistic injury when she learned that she could never have one, and that she therefore develops inhibitions. Alternately, this fantasy of gaining (stealing) a penis induces oedipal guilt and fear of punishment. An interpersonal psychoanalytic feminist might understand this same woman to symbolize success unconsciously as a denial of connection to other students and friends, in which case her refusal to succeed becomes an affirmation of her self in relationship and her desires for affiliation and connection to other women.

There is a double division between the two feminist positions. First, substantive disagreements exist concerning whether we should conceptualize psychological development in terms of object-relational and self experience or of linguistic placement in culture; whether we should conceptualize gender and male dominance in terms of consciously and unconsciously cognized sexual *difference* per se — in which case the genders can only exist and have meaning in relation one to the other — or in terms of qualities we can attribute to or feel as people of different genders; whether we should see sexuality as a product of relational development and its unconscious sequelae or as a linguistic location. Second, equally fundamental epistemological and evidential differences pose a Lacanian-feminist analysis of language and logical argument against object-relations and interpersonal feminist claims for empirical and clinical reality. At the same time, both positions unite in opposition to what they perceive as overly biological psychoanalytic interpretations and to psychoanalytic claims to a value-free "scientific" study of gender and gender difference that notices only by happenstance in the occasional case that there is something problematic in the construction and organization of gender.

The various discourses, then, have different truth criteria and different definitional realities. Logic is relevant to Lacanians: sex difference inheres definitionally in a sexuality that is cognized, oedipal, and defined vis-à-vis the phallus. Object-relations and interpersonal feminists criticize traditional psychoanalysts for focusing in an atomized way on genital possession rather than on relations of gender, self-other relations, and the establishment of self but appeal to clinical and research evidence for their own theoretical claims against both psychoanalysts and Lacanians. Psychoanalysts, by virtue of the professional separation of spheres not bound into the feminist debates, simply do their work, arguing only among themselves: because the discourse that I am discussing is, after all, psychoanalytic, and they are psychoanalysts, they needn't care so much what the feminists think (except when they find them on the couch). But in terms of the larger culture and even of the broad range of modern psychotherapies, both of which currently challenge psychoanalytic dominance, psychoanalysts who ignore or pass over feminist debate run the risk, as in their theory and practice in general, of themselves in turn being bypassed and ignored.

Clearly, this paper is a call for dialogue. On one side, psychoanalysis confronts a psychoanalytic feminism that has by and large only considered the psychoanalytic theory of women developed in the early years of psychoanalysis. Our problem as psychoanalytic feminists is the nature of our claim to appropriate psychoanalytic theory and findings and the grounds by which we choose what to accept and reject, both as theory and as clinical or empirical claim. Relying as we do on what we claim to be psychoanalysis, we cannot dismiss or ignore modern psychoanalytic work. Such a challenge is more problematic for object-relations and interpersonal feminists who are social scientists and practicing clinicians, because we are more concerned, however interpretively, with how things empirically "are" and must thus engage more directly with psychoanalytic evidence. Literary or philosophical critics, including most Lacanian feminists as well as some object-relations feminists, take psychoanalysis, in whatever variety, as a text or story and worry less about evidence.

The potential contribution of contemporary psychoanalysis to object-relations and interpersonal psychoanalytic feminism is great. Like the schools they draw upon, these theories are insightful about questions of self, other, and emotional orientation (both hetero- and homoemotional), but they have downplayed sexuality. A reconsideration of recent psychoanalytic views of primary femininity and genital awareness—if we can situate these socially and interactively, and not as essentialist, automatic dichotomies—might help to reincorporate such a focus.

On the other side, psychoanalytic feminism makes important demands upon psychoanalysis and points to areas of potential expansion and revision. The gender of the analyst is a useful place to begin. As Person and Mayer make clear, findings about male analysands and female analysts can only be understood in a socially and culturally, as well as psychologically, gendered context. In a setting where they are passive and dependent upon a women or mother figure in a position of power or authority, men's sexuality freezes or is denied. Both psychoanalytic and feminist object-relations developmental accounts have shown how male development involves denying and avoiding attachment to and dependence upon strong women, but psychoanalytic feminism in particular has stressed that the very definition of heterosexuality involves dominance and inequality. As Johnson and the Lacanian feminists suggest, the oedipal transition for the boy involves a reversal of relative power as absolute as the girl's gendered change of object.

Object-relations and interpersonal psychoanalytic feminism also constitutes a basic challenge to and revision of classical psychoanalytic (and Lacanian feminist) developmental theory and theories of gender identity, as this feminism removes the centering of the gendered psyche from the body and drives toward a recentering in the self and self with other. In questioning the extent to which female development is embedded in sexual difference and genital evaluation, this view argues against the centrality of genital apprehension in comparison to other areas of experience like object relations and the development of sense of self. Psychoanalysts, of course, focus on object relations clinically, but this focus has not been central to theory in the case of gender. Such a refocusing is suggested by some of those who have written on perversion[16] but not at all by those interested in normal sexual and gender development. In fact, the Freudian theory of the development of sexual orientation was not very persuasive, even if the Horney-Jones postulate of innate heterosexuality was also inadequate. And whereas psychoanalysts have done interesting work explaining the development of particular sexualities—those that are neither statistically nor culturally dominant—they have not systematically revised or done research toward understanding sexual development in general, and the development of "normal" heterosexuality in particular. My impression is that, in spite of Freud, most psychoanalytic accounts assume that there is some biological force that predisposes most people, in interaction with early family experience, toward heterosexuality.[17]

Lacanian feminism makes another kind of challenge to both psychoanalytic theories of gender and to object-relations feminism. It provides a persuasive argument that heterosexual desire is rooted in unequal relations and meanings of gender, and it stresses the problematic and

---

[16]Stolorow and Lachmann (1980) argue that there is a relationship between sexual fantasies and the structuralization of self and object representations and that perversions are compensations for faulty self-other boundaries, and Jucovy (1979) relates transvestism to disorders of self and identity and to separation anxiety as much as castration anxiety. See also Stoller (1985a, 1985b) and Socarides (1979).

[17]Tyson (1982) hinges the girl's turn to the father on her identification with her mother, which seems not to speak to the independence and insistence of sexual desire that psychoanalysis also describes. I think that many psychoanalysts who have been reflecting on female psychology would also not hold to Freud's penis-baby equation as the dominant motivation for motherhood in women. They would hold to unspecified biological assumptions about maternal instinct, to psychosexual claims of the sort that we find in Kestenberg's inner-genital phase or in Klein's intensive focus on internal objects and their meanings, and to theories about the girl's identification with her mother.

conflictual nature of *all* sexual identity and desire. This is an interpretation taken directly from Freud, but psychoanalysis has tended in the meantime to make problematic deviant and conflictual sexualities while seeming to assume that normal heterosexuality is relatively conflict and problem free. Such a normative theory, supplemented by a theory of perversion, cannot account for major features of heterosexuality, for instance, the pervasive intertwining of sexuality and aggression in men and of radical asymmetries in violent sexual behavior. Such an account needs a firmly psychoanalytic understanding of the dynamics of sexuality, but it needs this in a strongly feminist context that does not lose sight of dominance as a normative feature of masculinity.

In a challenge to primary femininity theories of both libidinal and object-relations varieties and to gender and self theories, Lacanian feminism, as a structuralist theory, also demands that we examine assumptions that gender need not be thought of in terms of gender relation. Can masculinity have meaning apart from femininity? How can the genitals of either sex have meaning in themselves, and not in the context of a structure of related meanings of the genitals of both?

I am stressing here relative and not absolute difference between psychoanalytic theory and psychoanalytic feminism. Many psychoanalysts think that women have been severely misunderstood by their theory, and they want to claim value for women's traditional role and genital and reproductive physiology. Occasionally, they criticize male blindness and male power in the creation of theory, and some discuss the just role of anger in feminine emotional life. But by and large in the revisions of theory, one does not hear much challenge to the division of gender and parental roles, to normative notions of sexuality, to normal masculinity and femininity. Femininity may be resuscitated and revalorized, but there is little sense that masculinity is problematic. Psychoanalytic *theory* tends toward normatively generated, essentialist, and absolutist views of gender and sexuality, and it does not incorporate or allow for the incorporation of a critical stance. Psychoanalytic feminism challenges psychoanalysis in all these arenas.[18]

Paradoxically, that psychoanalytic approach that seems closest to at least one branch of psychoanalytic feminism particularly exemplifies these problems. Following Freud, traditional psychoanalysts continue to stress the internal, endogenous components of infantile sexuality. In the

---

[18]At the same time, as psychoanalytic feminism has become so fashionable that it warrants treatment in a *New Yorker* article (see Malcolm, 1987), one begins to think that perhaps an individual psychoanalyst working with troubled patients may be doing more to change gendered lives than the psychoanalytic feminist and her elegant interpretation of texts.

case of rape and incest, psychoanalysts have found it hard to give up the view that unconscious desires on the part of the female victim were involved (see Nadelson and Notman, 1979, and Herman, 1981). By contrast, in the case of males, Stoller tends to see the *actual behavior* of the mother as directly causal of psychopathology and not to pay attention to the reciprocal role of the boy or of his internal unconscious processes in creating gender-identity problems and perversion (in this mother blame, Stoller should not be distinguished from object-relations theorists like Winnicott and self psychologists like Kohut who do not focus on gender). Like other analysts, Stoller also never questions the traditional view of masculinity against which he measures the males he studies, and he makes claims about unproblematic femininity as well. In a cultural context of radical questioning of traditional gender norms, one questions the meaning of the claim that "clear cut femininity is routinely seen [in girls] by a year or so of age" (1975, p. 26), Psychoanalytic feminists, by contrast, have been especially focused on demonstrating the fundamentally problematic nature of psychological masculinity, defined negatively and reactively in terms of that which is not feminine and based in heterosexual dominance of women and defensive denial of relationality.

There is a final problem with *all* the psychoanalytic theories of gender I have discussed. In other arenas in feminist theory, we have begun to look at gender salience, or prominence, in social and cultural life, and to see that we must understand gender as it relate to other identities and other situated aspects of social and cultural organization. I believe this is true psychologically as well. When, how, and why is gender or sexuality psychologically invoked, and how does it become relevant and in relation to what other aspects of psychological and emotional life? Psychoanalytic theories speak in global terms of "the girl," "the boy," "the man," "the woman." Is gender a continuing identity or feature of personality? Is it always a dominant identity or feature of personality? Are there characteristics that tend to differentiate the genders but which are not necessarily conceptualized psychologically as a part of gender identity?

Neither the psychoanalytic theorists of gender nor the feminist psychoanalytic theorists discuss gender salience, or, in fact, have much way to conceptualize it. Such a situation is definitionally true for Lacanian feminists, since sexuality is subjectivity. Interpersonal and object-relations feminists could build gender salience into their theories, but they have not. Roiphe and Galenson (1981) assert that gender, as genital apprehension and apperception, determines identity and psyche, but those psychoanalytic accounts that stress primary femininity also do not locate this femininity in a more general or varied sense of self. Gender is certainly part of what is often on people's minds, and it is part of what constructs (and constricts) their life consciously and unconsciously, but it is also certainly not all, and it is differentially salient at different times and places.[19] Even as we need to open dialogue, a next step for all psychoanalytic feminists and psychoanalysts who reflect on women and gender will be to build gender salience into our theories and practice.

In this context, clinical psychoanalysis in general has something important to teach *both* psychoanalytic feminists and psychoanalytic theorists of sex and gender. It reminds us forcefully that the symbolizations and transference meanings of relationships and body parts are manifold. Object-relations feminism has been interpreted to mean that the preoedipal mother-daughter relationship is almost all there is to female development and identity; Lacanian feminism seems to claim that the phallus is the phallus is the phallus; primary-femininity psychoanalysts imply that the developmental meaning of the female genitals is self-evident. Clinical psychoanalysis argues otherwise: it argues that any development and identity will build on multiple internal relationships and interpretations of experience, and that no person, symbol, or organ can hold a singular and unvarying place in any other person's psyche or symbolic system.

A melding of object-relations feminism and recent psychoanalysis might take us further in the right direction. Object-relations feminism, because it sees development as contingently determined by experience and what one makes of this experience and because it incorporates an understanding of gender characteristics, such as the self in relation, that are not necessarily available as gender conceptions, enables variability and fluidity in gender salience. Like clinical psychoanalysis, object-relations theory enables many developmental and psychological stories and leads to a recognition of variation, of ways that identities may or may not be invoked or experienced in different contexts and interpersonal or intrapsychic situations. At the same time, a theory of gender must include some understanding of sexuality and body experience, and the object-relations and interpersonal theorists have tended to downplay this area of experience that psychoanalysis has so intricately and intimately studied. Lacanian feminism would also reintroduce sexual difference and

---

[19]On gender salience, see Atkinson (1982). See also recent psychological work in gender-schema theory, e.g., Bem (1981). I am indebted for these points about gender salience not only to feminist theory, but also to many women of the second generation of psychoanalysts. In an interview study of these early women psychoanalysts, I was continually and forcefully reminded that gender was and was not salient in different parts of their lives and at different times, and that the importance they accorded to the psychoanalytic theory of gender varied in relation to other aspects of the theory and practice. I discuss these findings more extensively in Chodorow (1989).

sexuality, and it does remind us forcefully of the intertwining of the psychodynamics of gender, sexuality, and male dominance as a constitutive cultural force, but Lacan puts us in an absolute sexual and subjective world with no room for salience or fluidity: you can only accept or refuse previously given sexual positions that are always and invariably present.

My goal in this paper is as much to outline problems in professional communication as it is to seek a final answer concerning a psychoanalytic and feminist understanding of women and men. On the former issue, I simply suggest that we need to talk. On the latter, I have suggested that we could do worse than to develop an approach to gender that enabled understandings (1) of the selves and object-relational patterns of women and men; (2) of the senses (I deliberately use the plural here) of maleness and femaleness; (3) of sexual identities and interpretations of bodily experiences; (4) of masculinities and femininities; (5) of the fundamental interrelation of the unequal social and cultural organization of gender and its psychodynamics; and (6) of the fact that we are not always and in every instance determined by or calling upon these gendered and sexualized psychological experiences. Gender and sexuality are situated in, as they help to create, life in general.

REFERENCES

Abel, E. (ed.) (1980, 1981, 1982), *Writing and Sexual Difference*. Chicago, IL: University of Chicago Press.

_____ (1989), *Virginia Woolf and the Fictions of Psychoanalysis*. Chicago, IL: University of Chicago Press.

_____ Hirsch, M., & Langland, E. (1983), *The Voyage In: Fictions of Female Development*. Hanover, NH: University Press of New England.

Adelman, J. (1987). Born of woman: Fantasies of maternal power in MacBeth. In: *Cannibals, Witches and Divorce: Estranging the Renaissance,* Selected Papers from the English Institute, 1985, ed. M. Garber. Baltimore, MD: Johns Hopkins University Press.

Alpert, J. (1986), *Psychoanalysis and Women: Contemporary Reappraisals*. Hillsdale, NJ: The Analytic Press.

Applegarth, A. (1976), Some observations on work inhibitions in women. *J. Amer. Psychoanal. Assn.,* 24 (suppl.):251–268.

Atkinson, J. (1982), Anthropology (review essay). *Signs,* 8:236–258.

Bell, A. (1965), The significance of scrotal sac and testicles for the prepuberty male. *Psychoanal. Quart.,* 34:182–206.

Bem, S. L. (1981), Gender schema theory: A cognitive account of sex typing. *Psycholog. Rev.,* 88:354–364.

Benjamin, J. (1977), The end of internalization: Adorno's social psychology. *Telos,* 32:42–64.

_____ (1978), Authority and the family revisited, or a world without fathers? *New German Critique, 13:35–58.*

_____ (1988), *The Bonds of Love: Psychoanalysis, Feminism, and the Problem of Domination.* New York: Pantheon.

Bernay, T. & Cantor, D. (eds.) (1986), *The Psychology of Today's Woman: New Psychoanalytic Visions.* Hillsdale, NJ: The Analytic Press.

Chasseguet-Smirgel, J. (1976), The consideration of some blind spots in the exploration of the dark continent. *Internat. J. Psycho-Anal.,* 57:281–302.

Chehrazi, S. (1986), Female psychology: A review. *J. Amer. Psychoanal. Assn.,* 34:141–162.

Chodorow, N. (1974), Family structure and family personality. In: *Woman, Culture and Society,* ed. M. Z. Rosaldo & L. Lamphere. Stanford, CA: Stanford University Press, pp. 45–66.

_____ (1978), *The Reproduction of Mothering.* Berkeley: University of California Press.

_____ (1980), Difference, relation and gender in psychoanalytic perspective. In: *The Future of Difference,* ed. H. Eisenstein & A. Jardine. Boston, MA: G. K. Hall.

_____ (1985), Beyond drive theory: Object relations and the limits of radical individualism. *Theory and Society,* 14:271–319.

_____ (1987), Feminism, femininity, and Freud. In: *Advances in Psychoanalytic Sociology,* ed. J. Rabow, G. Platt & C. M. Goldman. Malabar, FL: Krieger.

_____ (1989), Seventies questions for thirties women: Gender and generation in a study of early women psychoanalysts. In: *Feminism and Psychoanalytic Theory.* New Haven, CT: Yale University Press & Cambridge: Polity Press.

_____ & Contratto, S. (1982), The fantasy of the perfect mother. In: *Rethinking the Family: Some Feminist Questions,* ed. B. Thorne with M. Yalom. New York: Longman, pp. 54–75.

Clower, V. L. (1976), Theoretical implications in current views of masturbation in latency girls. *J. Amer. Psychoanal. Assn.,* 24:109–125.

Dinnerstein, D. (1976), *The Mermaid and the Minotaur.* New York: Harper.

Eisenstein, H. & Jardine, A. (eds.) (1980), *The Future of Difference,* esp. Part I: "Differentiation and the Sexual Politics of Gender" and Part II: "Contemporary Feminist Thought in France." Boston, MA: G. K. Hall.

Flax, J. (1978a), Critical theory as a vocation. *Politics and Society,* 8:201–223.

_____ (1978b), The conflict between nurturance and autonomy in mother-daughter relationships and within feminism. *Feminist Studies,* 4:171–189.

_____ (1983), Political philosophy and the patriarchal unconscious. In: *Discovering Reality: Feminist Perspectives on Epistemology, Metaphysics, Methodology, and the Philosophy of Science,* ed. M. B. Hintikka & S. Harding. Dordrecht: Reidel, pp. 245–282.

_____ (1987), Re-membering the selves: Is the repressed gendered? In: *Women and Memory,* special issue of *Mich. Quart. Rev.,* 26:92–110.

_____ (1986), Psychoanalysis as deconstruction and myth: On gender, narcissism and modernity's discontents. In: *The Crisis of Modernity,* ed. Kurt Shell. Boulder, CO: Westview Press.

Freud, S. (1931), Female sexuality. *Standard Edition,* 21:223–243. London: Hogarth Press, 1961.

_____ (1933), New introductory lectures on psycho-analysis. *Standard Edition,* 22:3–182. London: Hogarth Press, 1964.

Gallop, J. (1982). *The Daughter's Seduction.* Ithaca, NY: Cornell University Press.

Garner, S. N., Kahane, C. & Sprengnether, M. (1985). *The [M]other Tongue: Essays in Feminist Psychoanalytic Interpretation.* Ithaca, NY: Cornell University Press.

Gilligan, C. (1982), *In a Different Voice.* Cambridge, MA: Harvard University Press.

Goldberger, M. W. & Evans, D. (1985), On transference manifestations in male patients with female analysts. *Internat. J. Psycho-Anal.,* 66:295–309.

Harding, S. & Hintikka, M. B. (eds.) (1983), *Discovering Reality: Feminist Perspectives on*

Epistemology, Metaphysics, Methodology, and the Philosophy of Science. Dordrecht: Reidel.

Herman, J. (1981), *Father-Daughter Incest.* Cambridge, MA: Harvard University Press.

Johnson, M. M. (1987), The reproduction of male dominance. In: *Advances in Psychoanalytic Sociology,* ed. J. Rabow, G. Platt & M. Goldman. Malabar, FL: Krieger, pp. 120–137.

———— (1988), *Strong Mothers, Weak Wives: The Search for Gender Equality.* Berkeley: University of California Press.

Jordan, J. V. (1984), Empathy and self boundaries. Work in Progress. Stone Center for Developmental Services and Studies, Wellesley College, Wellesley, MA.

Jucovy, M. (1979), Transvestism: With special reference to preoedipal factors. In: *On Sexuality,* ed. T. B. Karasu &. C. W. Socarides. New York: International Universities Press, pp. 223–241.

Kahn, C. (1985), The hand that rocks the cradle: Recent gender theories and their implications. In: *The [M]other Tongue: Essays in Feminist Psychoanalytic Interpretation,* ed. S. N. Garner, C. Kahane & M. Sprengnether. Ithaca, NY: Cornell University Press, pp. 72–88.

Karme, L. (1979), The analysis of a male patient by a female analyst: The problem of the negative oedipal transference. *Internat. J. Psycho-Anal.,* 60:253–261.

Keller, E. F. (1985), *Reflections on Gender and Science.* New Haven, CT: Yale University Press.

Kestenberg, J. (1968), Outside and inside, male and female. *J. Amer. Psychoanal. Assn.,* 16:457–520.

———— (1980a), The inner-genital phase. In: *Early Feminine Development: Contemporary Psychoanalytic Views,* ed. D. Mendel. New York: Spectrum.

———— (1980b), Maternity and paternity in the developmental context. *Psychiatric Clinics of North America,* 3:651–679.

Kirkpatrick, M., ed. (1980), *Women's Sexual Development: Explorations of Inner Space.* New York: Plenum.

———— (ed.) (1981), *Women's Sexual Experience: Explorations of the Dark Continent.* New York: Plenum.

Kleeman, J. (1976), Freud's views on early female sexuality in the light of direct child observation. *J. Amer. Psychoanal. Assn.,* 24:3–28.

Lerner, W. (1976), Parental mislabeling of female genitals as a determinant of penis envy and learning inhibitions in women. *J. Amer. Psychoanal. Assn.,* 24:269–284.

Lester, E. P. (1985), The female analyst and the eroticized transference. *Internat. J. Psycho-Anal.,* 66:283–293.

Malcolm, J. (1987), Reflections: J'appelle un chat un chat. *New Yorker,* April 20.

Marks, E. & de Courtivron, I. (1981), *New French Feminisms.* New York: Schocken.

Mayer, E. L. (1985), "Everybody must be just like me": Observations on female castration anxiety. *Internat. J. Psycho-Anal.,* 66:331–347.

———— (1986), Discussion of Tyson (1986).

Miller, J. B. (1976), *Toward a New Psychology of Women.* Boston, MA: Beacon Press.

———— (1983), The construction of anger in women and men. Work in Progress. Stone Center for Developmental Services and Studies, Wellesley College, Wellesley, MA.

———— (1984), The development of women's sense of self. Work in Progress. Stone Center for Developmental Services and Studies, Wellesley College, Wellesley, MA.

———— Nadelson, C. C., Notman, M. T. & Zilbach, J. (1981), Aggression in women: A reexamination. In: *Changing Concepts in Psychoanalysis,* ed. S. Klebanow. New York: Gardner Press, pp. 157–167.

Mitchell, J. (1974), *Psychoanalysis and Feminism.* New York: Pantheon.

———— (1984), *Women, the Longest Revolution.* New York: Pantheon.

———— & Rose, J. (1982). Introductions. In: J. Lacan, *Feminine Sexuality*. New York: Norton.

Nadelson, C. C. & Notman, M. T. (1979), Psychoanalytic considerations of the response to rape. *Internat. Rev. Psycho-Anal.*, 6:97–103.

———— (eds.), (1982), *The Woman Patient*. Vol. 2: *Concepts of Femininity and the Life Cycle*. New York: Plenum Press.

———— (1985), Rape. In: *Sexuality: New Perspectives*, ed. Z. Defries, A. Friedman & R. Corn. Westport, CT: Greenwood Press, pp. 33–44.

———— Notman, M. T. & Carmen, E. (1986), The rape victim and the rape experience. In: *Modern Forensic Psychiatry and Psychology*, ed. W. Curran. Philadelphia: F. A. Davis, pp. 339–362.

———— Notman, M. T., Miller, J. B. & Zilbach, J. (1982), Aggression in women: Conceptual issues and clinical implications. In: *The Woman Patient*. Vol. 3: *Aggression, Adaptations and Psychotherapy*, ed. M. T. Notman & C. C. Nadelson. New York: Plenum, pp. 29–46.

Panel (1976), Psychology of women, E. Galenson, reporter. *J. Amer. Psychoanal. Assn.*, 24:141–160.

Person, E. (1980), Sexuality as a mainstay of identity. *Signs*, 5:605–630.

———— (1982), Women working: Fears of failure, deviance, and success. *J. Amer. Acad. Psychoanal.*, 10:67–84.

———— (1983), The influence of values in psychoanalysis: The case of female psychology. In: *Psychiatry Update: The American Psychiatric Association Annual Review*. Washington, DC: American Psychiatric Press, 2:36–50.

———— (1985), The erotic transference in men and women. Differences and consequences. *J. Amer. Acad. Psychoanal.*, 13:159–180.

———— (1986), Working mothers: Impact on the self, the couple and the children. In: *The Psychology of Today's Woman*, ed. T. Bernay & D. W. Cantor. Hillsdale, NJ: The Analytic Press, pp. 121–138.

———— (1988), *Dreams of Love and Fateful Encounter: The Power of Romantic Passion*. New York: Norton.

———— & Ovesey, L. (1983), Psychoanalytic theories of gender identity. *J. Amer. Acad. Psychoanal.*, 11:203–226.

Roiphe, H. & Galenson, E. (1981), *Infantile Origins of Sexual Identity*. New York: International Universities Press.

Socarides, C. (1979), A unitary theory of sexual perversions. In: *On Sexuality*, ed. T. B. Karasu & C. W. Socarides. New York: International Universities Press, pp. 233–241.

Stoller, R. (1964), A contribution to the study of gender identity. *Internat. J. Psycho-Anal.*, 45:220–226.

———— (1965), The sense of maleness. *Psychoanal. Quart.*, 34:207–218.

———— (1968), The sense of femaleness. *Psychoanal. Quart.*, 37:42–45.

———— (1975), *Perversion: The Erotic Form of Hatred*. New York: Pantheon.

———— (1985a), *Presentations of Gender*. New Haven, CT: Yale University Press.

———— (1985b), *Observing the Erotic Imagination*. New Haven, CT: Yale University Press.

Stolorow, R. & Lachmann, F. (1980), Sexual fantasy and perverse activity. In: *Psychoanalysis of Developmental Arrests*. New York: International Universities Press, pp. 144–170.

Surrey, J. L. (1985), Self-in-relation: A theory of women's development. Work in Progress. Stone Center for Developmental Studies and Services, Wellesley College, Wellesley, MA.

Tyson, P. (1980), The gender of the analyst. *The Psychoanalytic Study of the Child*,

35:321–338. New Haven: Yale Unversity Press.

_____ (1982), A developmental line of gender identity, gender role, and choice of love object. *J. Amer. Psychoanal. Assn.*, 30:61–86.

_____ (1986), The female analyst and the male analysand. Paper presented to the San Francisco Psychoanalytic Institute, February.

June 1987

Discussions

Dr. Rocah:

I am pleased to have the opportunity to read and discuss Dr. Chodorow's work. From the dual perspectives of sociology and psychoanalysis, she discusses the issues connected with influences on men and women pertaining to their gender identity, sexuality, and normative development. Although the paper is an overview of her own, Lacanian, and some recent psychoanalytic challenges to Freud's ideas on these matters, I will confine my remarks to Dr. Chodorow's (1978) theoretical ideas, viewed from a clinical perspective.

Freud's (1931) views concerning women stressed three points. First, he asserted that sexual difference did not matter until the phallic phase. Second, he assumed a preoedipal phallic monism in children of both sexes until they became aware of gender differences through the perception of the girl's penisless state. Third, femininity was understood as a secondary development following the girl's renunciation of phallic negative oedipal aims toward her mother. As a result of this renunciation, the girl turned to heterosexual interests that Freud termed the positive oedipal configuration. Within this configuration she began a lifelong search for substitute gratifications for her missing penis in the form of babies and marriage. Absence of a penis defined a woman's sexual orientation, participation in the sexual act, desire for parenting, and character, including gender roles.

Like Freud (1931), Dr. Chodorow focuses on the preoedipal relationship with the mother as crucial to gender development in both sexes. She differs from Freud insofar as she does not understand perception of genital differences to be causal and central to the formation of gender identity and personality. Rather, she focuses on the experience of self in relationship with mother, on how the self becomes organized, and on social norms regarding women's gender roles which are perpetuated through identificatory processes.

Although I am in agreement with her view that gender development cannot be understood in isolation from self development, she moves away more radically than I do from the significance of apperceptions of gender. Freud (1925) was correct in his understanding that a child's awareness of his or her own genitals and those of other people is an affectively laden perception. His (Freud, 1925) assumption, however, that both sexes believe themselves to be phallic is hardly a demonstration of a universal theory generated by children to explain the significance of sexual differences. Rather, it is an example of erroneous conclusions that some children come to, and retain in adulthood, which are the products of the child's assimilative processes at work on cognitive issues too complex for the child to understand. Young children tend to reason finalistically and predeterministically about matters of gender that result in fantasies and beliefs about their own body and their origins. I wish to emphasize that the significance of these fantasies lies in their motivational potential within the child to determine interactions with others.

Dr. Chodorow places less emphasis than I do on the inherent factors in children that shape their view of themselves. She reasons that both the feminine and the masculine personalities evolve from specific features of the mother/child dyad. In her view, boys and girls are initially matricentered. Boys disidentify with their mothers because of developmental pressures toward autonomy, separateness, and masculinity. This results in a character structure in which emotions are repressed, women are disparaged, and rigid moralistic attitudes develop, which Freud identified as superego strengths in men that protect them from regressive temptations to return to a matricentered universe. This masculinity is defined by Dr. Chodorow as the outcome of a defensive struggle to break emotional ties to the preoedipal mother. This path is seen by her as obligatory due to the asymmetrical gender-role assignment of the woman as the significant functional parent of early childhood. In contrast to boys' normative development, girls remain identified with their preoedipal and oedipal mother in a seamless web. In Dr. Chodorow's view, this identification shapes a girl's character more significantly than awareness of her own and her mother's castrated state. The complex endopsychic world that is the outcome of this seamless identification with the mother perpetuates mother-child bonds intrapsychically and fosters the formation of new displaced bonds outside the family. Insofar as the girl remains enmeshed with her mother she experiences difficulty in achieving separateness.

Girls often envy boys insofar as they believe that a penis is required to negotiate a separate existence from mother. Is this a reality fact, arising from social norms, or an organizing fantasy? I (Rocah, 1984) have reported on a woman I analyzed who dreamed of having a third leg to stand on. This associatively turned out to be a phallic prop that described her use of men as tools for her pleasure and autonomy modeled on her mother's behavior with men. I understood her unconscious wish for a third leg to reflect attempts to relieve her anxiety within the transference that threatened to remobilize her symbiotic attachment to her mother. I do not consider these wishes to be universal for all women as they struggle with the complexities of their relationship with their mothers.

Dr. Chodorow's sociopsychological formulations are asserted as inevitable outcomes of family structures where women mother. Although she rejects Freud's (1931, 1933) phallocentric views to account for the development of femininity, she defines masculinity as secondary to a boy's attempt to disidentify with his mother and defend himself against the regressive pull of a matricentered universe through searches for idealizable men as models from whom he can learn and identify. In both Freud's and her theories one gender emerges as a secondary, defensive construction against a primary sex. Freud's combination of psychology and biology or Chodorow's combination of sociology and object-relations psychoanalysis demonstrates the interpretive biases of each discipline. Each system suggests bedrock outcomes. How, then, can we assess these complex issues?

In a recent paper (Rocah, 1987) I proposed that within psychoanalysis itself a pluralistic approach to these matters is necessary, utilizing new conceptual developmental interactive models, knowledge of cognitive development and learning, as well as our usual interest in drives, unconscious conflicts, defense, fantasy, and identifications. Freud's (1933) approach utilized additive groupings to define maleness as phallic, masturbatory, active, aggressive, and dominant and characteristics of femaleness as castrated, nonmasturbatory, passive, and submissive. Analysis reveals that children, as well as adults, sometimes act as if these parts can be exchanged or substituted for one another. Freud himself proposed this kind of substitution when he equated a woman's motivation for motherhood with an unconscious wish for her missing penis. In my view, it is more accurate to think of gender as a gestalt rather than as an additive system, in which the parts cannot be substituted for or exchanged and the total is more than the sum of the separate elements. Cognitive development must advance significantly beyond the age when the child makes the first gender differentiations for the child to appreciate this gestalt. If Freud was a biological-evolutionary theorist and minimized interactive factors clinically, I feel Dr. Chodorow errs in the opposite direction in her sole reliance upon object-relations theory to describe these matters. In calling for a pluralistic approach, I am asserting that multiple perspectives within psychoanalytic work are required to comprehend these issues in both a clinical and a social setting.

Dr. Chodorow indicates that psychoanalysis and psychoanalytic feminism can meet in the study of the effect of gender of the analyst on male and female patients, since analysis takes place in a socially, culturally, as well as psychologically gendered context. Although the vicissitudes of cross-gender analysis are most often considered in these discussions (see Karme, 1979; Person, 1985; Tyson, 1980), I would like to present my work with a woman patient to demonstrate the complexity of transference remobilizations in that situation. I place special emphasis on this woman's bisexuality.

This young woman sought analysis because of anxiety, depression, and ineffectual work in her profession. Early in our work, she developed an intense idealizing transference that was an organizing factor on her behavior. This transference configuration enabled her to integrate some of her professional ambitions into more effective actions. In the course of our work she often reported variations on a dream theme: she saw herself in the men's bathroom or wanted the key to the men's bathroom. We understood something about these recurrent dreams and the significance of the idealizing transference from work on the following material.

One day she reported the following dream.

I was straddling my bed. I triumphantly urinated over the covers, without shame. Then I reassured myself that I could clean up the mess.

She reported thoughts about terminating her analysis. She felt strong while we worked together and grateful for what she experienced as our perfect union. She felt I was appreciative of her insight and responsive participation in the analytic work, and she, in turn, stroked my ego by admiring my wisdom. She said it was like a good screw. She saw this as a continuation of her childhood feeling that she was the favorite of both her parents. She worried that termination might jeopardize the triumphant stance represented in her dream.

The next day she reported the following dream.

I saw a cock, a male chicken, sitting in the sink producing an enormous bowel movement. An intellectual woman came over and criticized me for smoking a pipe out of the wrong hole.

Her associations reviewed her father's and younger brothers' toilet activities. Their noisy flatus filled the room with odors and the sounds penetrated the bathroom door. She recalled teasing her youngest brother by inviting him to come into the bathroom to examine her technicolor feces. She provocatively flushed the toilet as he approached. She imagined that I would be critical of her wish to terminate. I suddenly responded: "So that's what it means to get the key to the men's bathroom. You can make big bowel movements like your father and your younger brothers and overpower people so that your messes won't count. You feel you have acquired that power from your work with me and you are uncertain about sustaining it on your own." She initially felt excited by this interpretation. This was followed by embarrassment as she realized that she had totally misjudged the significance of their bathroom habits. On that basis she had unconsciously let making shit (our interpretation of her messy errors in her school and professional work) become a gratifying rebellious activity. We discovered that she was convinced that her flawless beauty would silence her superiors and distract them from errors that she made at work. In this manner, she reassured herself that her shit did not smell. By the end of the hour she felt paralyzed and depressed.

In the next hour we discussed her paralysis as a reaction to my interpretation. She told me that she had told one of her brothers the insight that I had provided for her into her neurosis and identification with the men in the family. She bragged about our work even though inwardly she felt shaken and insecure about what had been said. I said I thought she was repeating her childhood attempts to deal with feeling intimidated by her father's and brothers' flatus and penis and with my interpretation by impressing her brother with her powerful neurosis. This brought almost immediate relief.

This dream can be understood in the context of a father transference. Dr. Chodorow asserts that women do not wish to become men; they wish to detach themselves from the mother and become autonomous. Because they have to justify their rejection of their mother they project the positive side of the ambivalence onto father, thus forming the kind of idealizing transference this woman demonstrated. This formulation is a partial explanation for what I am describing. In addition, this patient transformed penis, maleness, shit, odor, intimidation, and power into a version acceptable to her view of herself as a *woman:* technicolor feces, charisma, overwhelming beauty that rendered her messes odorless. In this manner she thought she had discovered an adaptive strategy that would allow for independent functioning. This proved to be an illusion. She believed that by identification with male power to intimidate others she could, through her overpowering beauty, silence her detractors and insure personal success through a route other than acquiring the knowledge and information she needed to do her work properly. A new edition of this identification emerged in her analysis in her belief in her perfect union with me. This illusion provided her with a key to the men's bathroom. Her identification with the males in her family shielded her from disillusionment in her father. When I intruded into her illusions in the transference, she was no longer sustained by her idealization of me and felt overwhelmed. Her admiration of me was limited to my participating in her perfect union and not disillusioning her about its magical powers.

Later in her analysis we explored attitudes connected to her femininity. She wished to approach the task of motherhood with a positive attitude and confidence rather than have children because she was uncertain what to do with her life. Her mother, a refugee who had been sent with her older siblings to England to escape the Nazis, had been torn in her late adolescence between continuing her matriarchal aristocratic heritage of wealth and social position and venturing into uncharted academic realms. Her early marriage to an older, established, ambitious, corporate lawyer relieved her of her indecision. She settled for a life filled with volunteer work in charitable organizations and devotion to her daughter and three younger sons. Her life of financial ease never relieved the insecurity born of her traumatic separation from her family. Mother was adamant in encouraging her daughter to be different from her and to identify with people who were high achievers. As my patient grew up, mother criticized anyone who challenged her daughter's preeminence, and often got negative feedback reversed.

In the context of work on two dreams we learned more about these issues.

A miniaturized boy was sitting on a high chair. He looked defective.

I met you in your office. I was showing you brown and red color samples. I went to the women's washroom and there was a hot-shot woman lawyer in the stall I routinely use. She was carrying a baby who had a soft spot on his abdomen. She gave the baby to me to hold and I calmed the baby down by rubbing his soft spot.

In her associations she denigrated women who did not think well of themselves. She thought about men who sought unthreatening women. She recalled a mocking and confusing piece of advice offered by relatives who valued achievement to forgo her own intellectual interests and think about marrying a successful man. This advice seemed consistent with her mother's attitudes, which she mindlessly followed, not heeding the intellectual challenges of college. She recalled feeling hopeless, in her childhood, about ever achieving social success because she was so unappealing. She remembered getting her menarche in school and feeling embarrassed because she soiled herself. Perhaps, she thought, the brown and red samples in her dream referred to her menarche. Her confused attitudes about her messiness and her entitlement to preeminence continued to plague her. She reported an incident at work where she was severely criticized for making messy errors. Although manifestly respectful of her boss as an authority, and feeling inwardly that she deserved the criticism, she silently said "fuck you" to her boss when he reprimanded her. She recalled wooing her father as a child by bringing him uncompleted homework to finish and correct. She had grown up feeling in awe of her father. I inquired whether there was an inconsistency in her present attitudes toward authoritarian men. Was she saying "fuck you" to the very people she designated as superior?

This led to a group of associations focused on her uncertainty about her worth as an individual. She had struggled with feeling that she was a very special person, both inferior and superior simultaneously. She said, "I grew up thinking there was something terribly wrong with me that could be corrected by emulating some successful person, and I grew up thinking I was perfect and beyond criticism." While in analysis she has tried to figure out how I go about my life and has patterned herself on what she assumes is true about me. Although becoming a mini-Rocah has had beneficial aspects, it has also been a constant reminder to her that she was inferior to me, a child with defects that needed to be corrected by emulating someone else. I responded by saying that there had been many models, such as myself, in her life in accordance with her mother's prescription. The act of miniaturizing herself to superior people functioned in fantasy as a means of overcoming limitations that were associatively connected in her mind with being an insecure woman. As long as there was an endless supply of models, there was no limit on what she could become or how she could live her life. She had counted on her capacities as an actress to overcome her limitations. She quipped and said she did not want to be limited to the boys' or the girls' bathroom. All women big or small use the bathroom in the same way. If you want to do it differently you have to go into the boys' bathroom!

Thus we learned anew that she saw limitless potential in identificatory processes to overcome the restrictions of a single-gender category. Even her estimation of her beauty contained elements of her unconscious bisexuality. She felt that in some respects she had spent her life perfecting her appearance by symbolically cleaning up her menstrual blood, leaving untouched her pleasurable identification with the men who produced the symbolic messes that we had discussed earlier in her analysis. She had become a painted doll-woman that could successfully entice men to provide herself with partners she could live through vicariously, avoiding the necessity to prepare for independence. Unconsciously she elaborated a grandiose fantasy of a femme fatale. This bisexual fantasy satisfied her wishes to surpass her mother's success with men, as well as deal with her envy of phallic power. It was possible now to interpret the symbol of the baby with the soft spot as a man who had temporarily lost his magical phallic power that she could restore by her caresses. This placed her in the position of power and reversed the image of herself as the defective child.

What does this clinical vignette demonstrate about gender development as reconstructed from analytic work, and about the technical implications of clinical work with patients of the same gender as the analyst? The essential issue for analysis is what the patient makes of gender, his or her own and the analyst's, and what the analyst makes of the patient's beliefs. These beliefs, of both analyst and patient, emerge, as Chodorow suggests, in a social, cultural, as well as psychologically gendered universe. The particular fantasies that emerged in the course of this woman's analysis provided some information concerning the interface between psychologically gendered meanings and social and cultural values.

We discovered in reconstructive analytic work that her gender identity had two components. The first was derived from her view of her mother's dependency upon her husband. My patient adopted her mother's solution to deal with anxiety by attaching herself, through illusions of perfect union, to successful men who gave her symbolic keys to the men's bathroom and allowed her to overcome immaturity or limitations in her ability. It should be noted that this woman was encouraged by her mother to disidentify with her manifest personality. No doubt my patient's acceptance of herself as a painted doll-woman was socially reinforced. It was, at the same time, a psychologically motivated pattern to solve matters originating in her family context. The second component of her gender identity involved her unconscious fantasy of being a femme fatale. This unconscious fantasy formed the basis of sexual competition with her mother as well as dealing with her envy of men. It involved unconsciously viewing her whole body as an intimidating, powerful sexual tool that could alternately rob men of their phallic power and restore it. This fantasy also found some social reinforcement from her family and societal values.

Thus, if we look at the manifest behavior in my patient we see that the social object-relations theories such as Chodorow elaborates have some explanatory potential as we examine her relationships with others whom she idealized, seduced, overpowered, and triumphed over, while they seduced, deprived, overestimated, and reinforced behaviors in her. However informative these representations of interactions are in understanding this woman, her unconscious subjective organizations of experience, her unconscious motives, and her gendered meanings emerged only in the course of psychoanalytic work. Change in this woman in the direction of more realistic perceptions of herself as a woman capable of real accomplishments through personal effort rather than through identification was accomplished through intensive psychoanalytic work with the unconscious bisexual compromises that formed her personality.

Psychoanalytic reconstructions such as I have illustrated in this discussion are limited sources of knowledge about development as it is observed in childhood. Psychoanalytic reconstructions give the illusion of linearity in development rather than reflecting the changing reorganization of multiple elements. Of course, social-cultural object-relations theories are equally condensed and obscure many idiosyncratic elements into generalizations and formulaic statements. I agree with Chodorow that we need complex interdisciplinary bridges. In a recent paper (Rocah, 1987) I advocated pluralistic perspectives to comprehend self perception and perceptions of others in a gendered context.

We learn something about the interface of multiple perspectives when we look at issues connected with the gender of the analyst in psychoanalytic work with patients of the same and the opposite sex. Many patients request an analyst of a specific sex because of personal myths concerning the origin of their problems, or conscious wishes to avoid complications with the analyst of the same or the opposite sex. This patient wished to see a woman analyst to avoid the sexual complications she was certain would arise in work with a man analyst (see Person, 1985). When she had briefly seen a man psychiatrist in the past she enacted a defense against these imagined sexual complications by dressing in baggy clothes. In our work an erotic father transference emerged around her seductions of my intellectual vanity as well as her efforts to castrate me by saying "fuck you" to what she regarded as my pretensions. Perhaps the sameness of our actual gender permitted more open emergence of these issues in the transference than in her work with a man because there was no real danger of my responding phallically to her sexualized advances and put-downs. This is suggestive of one type of adolescent homosexual play between girls. In this play the girls pretend to be man and woman with each other in a relationship where equality exists without any danger of phallic penetration.

Interestingly, the mother transference was more deeply repressed and conflicted. Fragments of its erotic, competitive, and identificatory aspects have been mentioned in this discussion. I concluded from work with this patient and others that what happens in an analytic situation is not limited by the social realities of the gender of analyst and patient. That is not to say that the gender of the analyst is a neutral factor. The essential issue, as I stated previously, is what the patient and analyst make of the patient's gendered beliefs and wishes in the transference. In this instance the erotic father transference emerged in a form suitable to the analytic situation. This transference defended against a deeper maternal transference which emerged later. Both aspects of the transference needed to be analyzed before significant change in attitudes about herself as a woman took place. The reality of our both being women did not seem to interfere with the emergence and ultimate integration of her bisexuality.

I wish to thank Dr. Chodorow for her scholarship, her attempts to build significant bridges between the diverse disciplines of sociology and psychoanalysis and to integrate feminism into both of these disciplines. She stimulates multiple challenges to my work.

REFERENCES

Chodorow, N. (1978), *The Reproduction of Mothering.* Berkeley: University of California Press.

Freud, S. (1925), Psychical consequences of the anatomical distinction between the sexes. *Standard Edition,* 19:243–258. London: Hogarth Press, 1961.

_____ (1931), Female sexuality. *Standard Edition,* 21:223–245. London: Hogarth Press, 1964.

_____ (1933), Femininity. *Standard Edition,* 22:112–125. London: Hogarth Press, 1964.

Karme, L. (1979), Analysis of a male patient by a female analyst: Problem of negative oedipal transference. *Internat. J. Psycho-Anal.,* 60:253–261.

Person, E. (1985), The erotic transference in women and men; Differences and consequences. *J. Amer. Acad. Psychoanal.,* 13:159–188.

Rocah, B. (1984), Fixation in late adolescent women: In: *Late Adolescence: Interdisciplinary Studies,* ed. D. D. Brockman. New York: International Universities Press, pp. 53–92.

_____ (1987), Pluralistic concepts of gender identity. Unpublished paper presented to the American Psychoanalytic Association, May.

Tyson, P. (1980), The gender of the analyst. *The Psychoanalytic Study of the Child,* 35:321–338. New York: International Universities Press.

October, 1987

Dr. Cohler:

Nancy Chodorow is among the most eminent scholars in the study of gender and society. She has argued (Chodorow, 1974, 1978) that, while men are socialized into a plurality of adult roles, from earliest childhood, women are socialized to the role of mother. Her discussion, which expands on Komarovsky's (1950, 1956) earlier observation and anticipates Gilligan's (1982) later contributions, is also unique in the extent to which she integrates psychoanalytic and social-science formulations. Indeed, together with Parsons, Platt and Weinstein, and Smelser, Professor Chodorow is among the small number of sociologists explicitly concerned with the integration of psychoanalysis and sociology. This effort, so well demonstrated in her paper at this meeting, raises a number of important questions for study, including the relationship of social context and gender socialization, the contribution of earlier and more recent psychoanalytic perspectives in understanding this process, and integration of contributions from literature and the arts as a means for fostering increased understanding of the determinants of gender socialization.

Psychoanalysis and the Formation of Gender Identity

From the outset, it has been difficult for psychoanalysis to account for the construction of women's distinctive world-view in our society. This is in large part a result of the preeminent contribution of Freud's own self-analysis as the basis for subsequent psychoanalytic inquiry. While there has been little question regarding the adequacy of Freud's formulation of nuclear conflict and its consequences among men, problems of a quite different sort are posed in understanding the lives of women. As Parsons and Chodorow both have shown, resolution of the nuclear complex, the so-called oedipal complex, is not symmetric for boys and girls. Unique problems are posed for girls as a result of the fact that the rival is also the source of love and affection. Little boys are more fortunate in that respect, since they can take on father as a rival and still maintain diffuse ties of affection to their mother. This asymmetry leads to ambivalence so-often reported among women and their mothers, although this intergenerational conflict may modulate across the second half of life (Cohler, 1987).

Chodorow contrasts Freud's observations (1931, 1933) with those of later theorists, noting the many problems stemming from Freud's equation of gender and awareness of genital configuration (Nagera, 1975). As Chodorow, Chehrazi (1986), and others have shown, Freud may have overemphasized anatomical differences as the basis for formation of gender identity without devoting sufficient discussion to the child's understanding of the meaning of these observed differences. The unique contribution of the clinical-psychoanalytic method in developmental study is emphasis upon study of meanings and intents. In clinical presentations as diverse as observations regarding gender-identity formation in girls (Parens, Pollock, Stern, and Kramer, 1976; Galenson and Roiphe, 1976; Roiphe and Galenson, 1981) or boys (Freud, 1895; Bornstein, 1935) and symbolization of the meaning of gender development as expressed in play (Bettelheim, 1954), what is significant is the manner in which children represent to themselves attributes of each gender, and the meaning of these differences. Clearly, anatomic differences are noted; the important question is the sense that children make of these changes at particular ages.

Much of this perspective has been summarized and extended by Fast (1984) her discussion of the concept of gender differentiation. Fast emphasizes the importance of studying this subjective or meaning component. Using this perspective, Fast argues that:

> . . . an individual's personal gender constructs are established in, and structured by the processes of gender differentiation. . . . major developments in the establishment of personal gender constructs begin when children become focally aware of sex differences and continue through what is generally referred to as the oedipal period [p. 80].

Fast notes that this is the reverse of Freud's view that sex differences follow realization of sense of gender. At the outset, boys and girls are not subjectively aware of gender. Consistent with Stoller's (1968) theoretical perspective, as well as with clinical observations reported by both Parens, Pollock, Stern, and Kramer (1976) and Roiphe and Galenson (1981), Fast maintains that children become aware of gender differences in response to caretaking rather than in response to genital physical sensations. Chodorow has reviewed the many theoretical positions supporting this perspective.

It is well accepted, then, that sex ascription begins at birth; the caretaking environment treats boys and girls in ways that encourage gender-appropriate understandings. This, of course, is the basis for Chodorow's formulation of caretaking as the means by which gender-stereotyped behaviors are transmitted across generations. Indeed, as Gutmann (1975) has argued, the advent of parenthood leads to a sense of emergency that evokes particularly stereotyped gender-related behavior on the part of each parent. At no other point in the course of life are these gender distinctions so clearly drawn. The consequence for gender socialization is that little boys are early inducted into particularly restricted definitions of what it means to be masculine, and little girls into what it means to be feminine.

Based on Fast's differentiation hypothesis, supported by formulations of Chodorow and Guttman, it may be argued that both boys and girls experience body limits, including the genital anxiety known as castration complex. Children of both sexes alternate between efforts to be both male and female, as in little boys' fantasies of anal birth (Bornstein, 1935; Erikson, 1950) and, at the same time, experience these limits as losses. Girls view loss as a lack of maleness, early expressed as so-called penis envy (Freud, 1925), whereas boys view possible loss as a limitation on receptivity and a certain kind of creativity realized through bearing children.

Over time, experienced losses by each gender become integrated with early learned sex differences in the formation of gender-based identity for self as differentiated from others. Maleness is attributed to boys, and femininity to girls, with implications for understanding both anatomic differences, and the interpersonal consequences of these differences. Awareness of gender identity is clearly evident by the third year of life and is consolidated over the ensuing year or two as a consequence of the same-sex parent experienced as a part of self, including both aspirations and ideals, and differentiated from the opposite-sex parent. Just as later in adolescence (Blos, 1967), rivalry with the same-sex parent assists in the process of determining self as apart from others, while affection reflects the comforting and affirming aspects of the same-sex parent. Again, Chodorow has reviewed a number of cognitive developmental perspectives that are consistent with Fast's account of the development of this gender-identity perspective.

The differentiation concept, as formulated by Fast, has the advantage of integrating the alternative formulations of gender identity so clearly portrayed by Chodorow. The problem with the differentiation approach arises from explaining the empathy possible for each gender as a means of understanding the other. Parsons (1955) has suggested that the internalization of the earliest mother-child relationship, the building block of self, makes it possible for the little boy to understand the woman's role. The little girl also learns the mother's world in that first dyadic encounter; only as a result of subsequent family experience is it possible for the little girl to learn and take the role of father.

Psychoanalytic study of intergenerational relations has proceeded through dual developmental study and observation of transference reenactments. There has been much study of the mother-son relationship; indeed, concern with that relationship has been the cornerstone of psychoanalytic inquiry. More recently, as a result of studies by Lamb (1976) and his colleagues in developmental psychology and Cath, Gurwitt, and Ross (1982) within psychoanalysis, as well as Ross's (1977,

1979, 1984) contributions, the father-son relationship has received increased detailed study. Again, there has been much study of the origins and course of the mother-daughter relationship across childhood and adulthood (Cohler and Grunebaum, 1981; Cohler, 1989). However, there has been much less study of the father-daughter relationship. The significance of the father for the girl's psychological development requires additional study. It is clear that fathers are important in helping their little girls to affirm their own femininity.

Culturally determined taboos regarding sexual interests of fathers and daughters may be partially responsible for the lack of developmental study in this area. From the time of Freud's (1905) postscript on transference, in understanding Dora's interruption of her analysis, the implications of this relationship for the transference have been widely appreciated and studied. However, these clinical findings have had little impact on the developmental study of the tie between father and daughter. Further, in view of Chodorow's discussion of gender identity and transference enactments over the course of psychoanalysis, while there has been much developmental study of the mother-son tie, the enactment of this relationship in the clinical process has been much less well studied than the enactment of the father-daughter tie, even though there is little normative developmental study of the father-daughter relationship.

The Lives of Women, and Women's Lives as Text

In her paper Chodorow both contrasts more traditional psychoanalytic perspectives with recent reformulations, particularly the so-called object-relations tradition, and raises questions regarding humanistic contributions, particularly those influenced by Lacan and his colleagues. Chodorow correctly faults psychoanalytically informed feminist scholarship as experience distant and not relevant to understanding womens' lives. She contrasts the object-relations and the cultural or interpersonal perspective with literary perspectives, suggesting that, while the two approaches share a critique of culture, including the culture of psychoanalysis, as male dominated, the object-relations approach may be better able to understand broad issues of gender, including problems not just of womens' lives but also of the lives of men in this society. In her discussion, echoed by Malcolm's discussion in a recent *New Yorker* article, Chodorow faults the literary feminists as too removed from the reality of suffering and symptom seen in clinical psychoanalysis.

Chodorow opts for an object-relations rather than an interpersonal foundation for studying gender. She suggests that, since the interpersonal approach appears to negate the fundamental contribution of clinical-psychoanalytic approaches, the interpersonal approach makes it additionally difficult to study persons' understandings or meanings, based on interpretation of enactments over the course of the psychoanalytic interview. For this reason, the interpersonal approach is less likely than a more intrapsychologic approach to discern the nature of subjective appraisals or wishes and intents, which provides the basis of the definition of the situation (Thomas, 1928).

The problem posed by psychoanalytic study based on texts rather than study of lives is complex, and goes well beyond the topic of the Chodorow paper. However, as applied to the study of womens' lives, these two approaches may be more complementary than may at first appear. Over the past two decades, in disciplines as apparently dissimilar as anthropology, criticism, and history, there has been a reconsideration of method of approach, leading to renewed emphasis upon issues of meaning derived from present interpretations of the work. Theorists as diverse as Hirsch (1967, 1976) and Hoy (1978) in criticism, Geertz (1972) in anthropology, and Haydon White (1972–1973) in history, have suggested that it is the present construction of events, facts, or texts which must be the focus of scholarly study. Within psychoanalysis, the focus of inquiry is upon the relationship as constructed by analyst and analysand, emphasizing study of the course of transference reenactments, rather than the prior life history to which they are believed to refer. As Novey (1968) and Schafer (1981, 1983) have emphasized, the only history that can be reconstructed in psychoanalysis is the history of the analysis itself. More generally, the only life history which we are able to study is that presently told, representing an effort to integrate life as lived, as an interpretive or narrative action (Cohler, 1982).

This approach has led to renewed interest in those aspects of the human sciences which, in the terms initially posed by Dilthey (1910) represent the human sciences (Habermas, 1968, 1983). Within psychoanalysis, there has been a similar interpretive turn, expressed by Novey (1968) in his discussion of psychoanalytic reconstruction, George Klein (1976) in his focus on the self, and both Ricoeur and Schafer in their discussions of the interpretive turn. As both Kohut (1971, 1973, 1977) and Klein have separately suggested, and as already noted here, the preeminent contributions of psychoanalysis have been those based on clinical study or theory, rather than on Freud's metapsychology, emphasizing "the world behind (or beyond) consciousness," and based on the working out of Freud's prepsychoanalytic neurological program (Freud, 1898; Gill, 1976).

At the same time, the "interpretive turn," as portrayed by Rabinow and

Sullivan (1979), poses problems in moving between viewing lives as texts and texts as lives. In the first place, there is the problem, noted by Ricoeur (1970, 1971) and Hirsch (1976), that regardless of the present construal of a text, the author had a particular intent in composing a work with a particular structure. Questions of motivation or intent in the writing are less salient than portraying the author's intent through an argument that represents the reader's encounter with the text. Strict deconstructionist and psychobiographic approaches, while apparently at opposite ends of the spectrum of interpretation, have a similar effect of ignoring the author's intention in the written text, either through denying that any such intention exists outside of the present interpretation of the text, or through positing intents that stand outside of the author's own intent. Indeed, as Freeman (1985) has noted, Ricoeur sees important distinctions between written and spoken texts. Speaking, including the discourse of the clinical psychoanalytic interview, is of a nature different from the written text. The possibilities for expressing intent are greater in writing than in speech.

Also important in the interpretive perspective, and common to spoken texts, such as the psychoanalytic interview, and the study of the text, it is the act of making the interpretation, or the construction of an "intermediate space," in Winnicott's (1953) terms which is essential in understanding the meaning of the work. The focus of study in both clinical psychoanalysis and other interpretive disciplines is upon understanding the narrative presently constructed in terms of the relationship itself, rather than upon efforts to make sense of data external to this relationship. Baron and Pletsch (1986) have documented the importance of this process in their study of the relationship between biographer and person, and similar issues have been raised in the just-published volume edited by Moraitis and Pollock (1987). This relationship has some similarities to the study of transference and countertransference/counteridentification enactments in psychoanalysis.

The relationship of interpreter and text — either a cultural event such as the cockfight observed by Geertz (1972), analyst and analysand in the clinical interview, or interpreter and text, in the case of criticism — share a common focus on relationship. The basis for study in all three areas is language, the importance of which has been noted by both Wittgenstein (1966) and Lacan. Chodorow argues against the Lacanian-feminist critique that all study of lives is inherently gender based, since language itself reflects the salience of gender in our own society, and language structures reality. However, it is possible to recast Chodorow's critique of the French perspective as negating socialization, the basis for learning gender.

If all culture is a representation of language, then what is learned is not culture but language and modes of expression. Focusing on concepts such as the relationship as text in the experience-near encounter, as posed by Klein, Gill, and Kohut, the concept of "intermediate space," as proposed by Winnicott, the "proximal zone of development," as posed by Vygotsky (1934, 1978), or the there is little value in distinguishing between inside and outside, or in employing constructs such as internalization in understanding formation and maintenance of gender identity. As both Litowitz and Litowitz (1983), Litowitz (1987), and Haroutunian (1986) suggest, albeit from different perspectives on language, meaning must be studied in terms of context itself, as a socially constructed attribute. The very concept, unique to our culture, of a connection between action and intent is a function of the word "because." In the same manner, gender influences the very terms in which we speak, including that regarding anatomical differences between the sexes, which precedes gender identity and acquisition of language, reflecting a "tilt" toward the masculine, and toward inherent inequality in gender in our society.

CONCLUSION

I believe Chodorow to be correct in her assertion that the focus of our study must be on meaning, including attributions of gender forming the basis of experience of self and others. Even though there is recent work by Gilligan and others emphasizing the significance of gender differences in thought, all too often, both within and without psychoanalysis, femininity is defined merely as the absence of masculinity. We need to know much more about the origins and course of girls' experience of self in the context of our particular culture as differentiated from masculinity. Study of texts in no way substitutes for detailed inquiry into lives over time. However, approached from an interpretive perspective, study of lives as texts, and texts as lives, complements and enriches our understanding of the human dilemma.

REFERENCES

Baron, S. & Pletsch, C. (1985), *Introspection in Biography: The Biographer's Quest for Self-Awareness.* Hillsdale, NJ: The Analytic Press.
Bettelheim, S. (1954), *Symbolic Wounds.* New York: Free Press.
Blos, P. (1967), The second individuation process of adolescence. *The Psychoanalytic Study of the Child.* 23:162–186. New York: International Universities Press.
Bornstein, S. (1935), A child analysis. *Psychoanal. Quart.,* 4:190–225.
Cath, S., Gurwitt, A. & Ross, J. (eds.) (1982), *Father and Child: Developmental and Clinical Perspectives.* Boston: Little, Brown.
Chehrazi, S. (1986), Female psychology: A review. *J. Amer. Psychoanal. Assn.,* 34:141–162.

Chodorow, N. (1974), Family structure and feminine personality. In: *Women, Culture, and Society,* ed. L. Lamphere & M. Rosaldo. Stanford, CA: Stanford University Press, pp. 43–66.

——— (1978), *The Reproduction of Mothering: Psychoanalysis and the Sociology of Gender.* Berkeley: University of California Press.

——— (1987), What is the relation between the psychoanalytic psychology of women and psychoanalytic feminism? Address to conference on Contemporary Women and Psychoanalysis: Critical Questions Reconsidered. The Institute for Psychoanalysis, Chicago, May 2.

Cohler, B. (1982), Personal narrative and life-course. In: *Life Span Development and Behavior,* ed. P. Baltes & K. W. Schaie. New York: Academic Press, 4:205–241.

——— (1987), The mother-daughter relationship in the family of adulthood. *J. Geriat. Psychiat.,* 21:51–72.

——— & Grunebaum, H. (1981), *Mothers, Grandmothers and Daughters: Personality and Child-Care in Three Generation Families.* New York: Wiley.

Crapanzano, V. (1980), *Tuhami: Portrait of a Moroccan.* Chicago: University of Chicago Press.

Dilthey, W. (1910), The construction of the historical world in the human studies. In: *Selected Writings,* ed. & trans. E. Rickman.

Erikson, E. (1950), *Childhood and Society* (rev. ed.). New York: Norton.

Fast, I. (1984), *Gender Identity: A Differentiation Model.* Hillsdale, NJ: The Analytic Press.

Freeman, M. (1985). Paul Ricoeur on interpretation. *Human Devel., 28:295–312.*

Freud, S. (1895), Project for a scientific psychology. *Standard Edition,* 1:295–387. London: Hogarth Press, 1966.

——— (1898), Letter to W. Fliess of March 10. In: *The Complete Letters of Sigmund Freud to Wilhelm Fliess, 1887–1904.* Cambridge: Harvard University Press, 1985, pp.

——— (1905), Fragment of an analysis of a case of hysteria. *Standard Edition,* 7:112–123. London: Hogarth Press, 1953.

——— (1909), The analysis of a phobia in a five year old boy. *Standard Edition,* 11:5–152. London: Hogarth Press. 1955.

——— (1925), Some psychological consequences of the anatomical distinction between the sexes. *Standard Edition,* 19:241–258. London: Hogarth Press, 1961.

Galenson, F. & Roiphe, H. (1976), Some suggested revisions concerning early female development. *J. Amer. Psychoanal. Assn.,* 24 (Suppl.):29–58.

Geertz, C. (1972), Deep play: Notes on the Balinese cock-fight. *Daedalus,* 101.

Gill, M. (1976), Metapsychology is not psychology. In: *Psychology Versus Metapsychology: Psychoanalytic Essays in Memory of George Klein [Psychological Issues,* monogr. 36], ed. M. Gill & P. Holzman. New York: International Universities Press.

Gilligan, C. (1982), *In a Different Voice: Psychological Theory and Women's Development.* Cambridge, MA: Harvard University Press.

Gutmann, D. (1975), Parenthood: A key to the comparative study of the life-cycle. In: *Life-Span Developmental Psychology: Normative Crises,* ed. N. Datan & L. Ginsberg. New York: Academic Press, pp. 167–184.

Habermas, J. (1968), *Knowledge and Human Interests.* Boston: Beacon Press, 1971.

——— (1983), Interpretive social science vs. hemeneuticism. In: *Social Science as Moral Inquiry,* ed. N. Haan, R. Bellah, P. Rabinow & W. Sullivan. New York: Columbia University Press, pp. 251–270.

Haroutunian, S. (1986), A challenge to mentalistic explanations in psychology. Unpublished manuscript, University of Chicago.

Hirsch, E. D. (1967), *Validity in Interpretation.* New Haven: Yale University Press.

——— (1976), *The Aims of Interpretation.* Chicago: University of Chicago Press.

Hoy, D. (1978), *The Critical Circle: Literature and History in Contemporary Hermeneutics.* Berkeley: University of California.

Klein, G. (1976), *Psychoanalytic Theory: An Exploration of Essentials.* New York: International Universities Press.

Kohut, H. (1971), *The Analysis of the Self.* New York: International Universities Press.

—— (1973), The psychoanalyst in the community of scholars. *This Annual,* 3:508–516. New York: International Universities Press.

—— (1977), *The Restoration of the Self.* New York: International Universities Press.

Komarovsky, M. (1950), Functional analysis of sex roles. *Amer. Sociol. Rev.,* 15:508–516.

—— (1956), Continuities in family research: A case study. *Amer. J. Sociol.,* 62:466–469.

Lamb, M. (1976), *The Role of the Father in Child Development.* New York: Wiley, 1983.

Litowitz, B. (in press) Patterns of internalization. In: *Learning and Education: Psychoanalytic Perspectives,* ed. K. Field, B. Cohler & G. Wool. New York: International Universities Press.

—— & Litowitz, N. (1983), Development of verbal self-expression In: *The Future of Psychoanalysis,* ed. A. Goldberg. New York: International Universities Press, pp. 397–427.

Malcolm, J. (1987), Reflections: J'appelle un chat un chat. *New Yorker,* April 20.

Moraitis, G. & Pollock, G. (eds.) (1987), *Psychoanalytic Studies of Biography.* New York: International Universities Press.

Nagera, H. (1975), *Female Psychology and the Oedipus Complex.* New York: Aronson.

Novey, S. (1968), *The Second Look: The Reconstruction of the Personal History in Psychiatry and Psychoanalysis.* New York: International Universities Press, 1985.

Parens, H, Pollock, L., Stern, J. & Kramer, S. (1976), On the girl's entry into the Oedipus complex. *J. Amer. Psychoanal. Assn.,* 24 (Suppl.):79–108.

Parsons, T. (1955), Family structure and the socialization of the child. *In: Family, Socialization, and the Interaction Process,* ed. T. Parsons & R. Bales. New York: Free Press, pp. 35–132

Rabinow, P. & Sullivan, W. (eds.) (1979), The interpretive turn: Emergence of an approach. In: *Interpretive Social Science: A Reader.* Berkeley: University of California Press, pp. 1–244.

Roiphe, H. & Galenson, E. (1981), *Infantile Origins of Sexual Identity.* New York: International Universiities Press.

Ross, J. (1977), Toward fatherhood: The epigenesis of paternal identity during a boy's first decade. *Internat. J. Psycho-Anal.,* 58:327–347.

—— (1979), Fathering: A review of some psychoanalytic contributions on paternity. *Internat. J. Psycho-Anal.,* 60:317–327.

—— (1984), Fathers in development: An overview of recent contributions. In: *Parenthood: A Psychodynamic Perspective,* ed. R. Cohen, B. Cohler & S. Weissman. New York: Guilford Press, pp. 373–390.

Schafer, R. (1976), *A New Language for Psychoanalysis.* New Haven: Yale University Press.

—— (1901), *Narrative Actions in Psychoanalysis.* Worcester, MA: Clark University Press.

—— (1983), *The Analytic Attitude.* New York: Basic Books.

Stoller, R. (1968), *Sex and Gender.* New York: Aronson.

Thomas, W. I. (with D. S. Thomas) (1928), *The Child in America: Behavior Problems and Programs.* New York: Knopf.

Vygotsky, L. (1934), *Thought and Language,* trans & ed. A. Kozulin. Cambridge, MA: M.I.T. Press, 1986.

—— (1978), *Mind in Society: The Development of Higher Psychological Processes,* trans. & ed. M. Cole, V. John-Steiner, S. Scribner & E. Souberman. Cambridge, MA: Harvard University Press.

White, H. (1972-1973), Interpretation in history. In: *Tropics of Discourse*. Baltimore, MD: Johns Hopkins University Press. 1978, pp. 51-80.

Winnicott, D. W. (1953), Transitional objects and transitional phenomena. *In: Collected Papers: Through Paediatrics to Psychoanalysis*. New York: Basic Books, pp. 229-242.

Wittgenstein, L. (1958), *Philosophical Investigations* (rev. ed.), trans. G.E.M. Anscome & ed. G.E.M. Anscome & Rush Rhees. New York: Macmillan.

Sexual Doubles and Sexual Masquerades: The Structure of Sex Symbols

WENDY DONIGER, Ph.D. (Chicago)
with discussion by
HARRY TROSMAN, M. D. (Chicago)

There are many stories about a woman who secretly or magically replaces another woman in a man's bed—or of a man who replaces another man in this way; and there are many stories about a woman who secretly or magically gets another woman to replace her in a man's bed—or of a man who does this. These themes take on many different forms in different retellings throughout the world. I wish to explore a few of the many different variations that different cultures, particularly in India, have played upon the basic theme; and to show how the theme takes on different meanings as it moves back and forth among supernatural stories dealing with goddesses, fairytales dealing with woman who have magic powers, and realistic stories dealing with human women. I will try to take account of both the human, psychological meanings of these stories and the theological meanings, in my attempt to demonstrate a few ways in which we share with Hindus—and perhaps, though by no means necessarily, with other cultures—certain underlying assumptions about the sexual doubling of men and women.

The richest development of this theme in English literature occurs in the comedies of Shakespeare, who made use of many sources, some of them folk sources—indeed, some of them *Indian* folk sources, perhaps transmitted through Islam.[1] In *A Midsummer Night's Dream, A Comedy of*

I have treated other variants of the theme of this paper in an earlier essay, published as the University Lecture in Religion at Arizona State University, April 10, 1986.

[1] The plot of *All's Well that Ends Well,* for instance, seems to have been taken from the story of Muladeva in the Sanskrit *Kathasaritsagara,* the Ocean of Story.

Errors, Twelfth Night, Measure for Measure, and *All's Well that Ends Well,* sexual doubles proliferate at the drop of a curtain. Another genre of sexual doubles may be traced through European romantic literature, beginning with the medieval romances. In Gottfried von Strassburg's *Tristan,* the heroine, Isolde the Fair, has numerous doubles, three of them actually named Isolde: the first is her mother; the second, Isolde of the White Hands; and the third, a statue of Isolde (also named Isolde, and accompanied by a statue of Isolde's other double, Brangane), who consoles Tristan in the absence of the Ur-Isolde. Moreover, Isolde's maid Brangane substitutes for Isolde on her wedding night with King Mark, since Brangane is a virgin and Isolde has already lost her virginity to Tristan. In another branch of medieval courtly literature, the Arthurian cycle, Elaine tricks Lancelot into lying with her and giving her a child by taking the place of Guinevere in the dark.

The theme of the woman who doubles for another woman in bed endures in our contemporary mythology primarily in opera, in Mozart's *Marriage of Figaro,* in Wagner's variant of the myths of Tristan and Isolde and of Siegfried and Brunnhilde (where Siegfried takes the place of Brunnhilde's husband on their wedding night), and in Richard Strauss's *Arabella, Die Frau ohne Schatten,* and *Rosenkavalier.* In our day, the theme remains popular in films such as Greta Garbo's *Two-Faced Woman* or Joanne Woodward's *The Three Faces of Eve* or in all of those melodramatic tours de force in which Bette Davis and Joan Crawford played their own twin sisters. We may see the shadow woman, too, in science as well as art, in the raging controversy over the surrogate motherhood in the case of Baby M; there is clinical evidence (personal communication, Sudhir Kakar) that women who allow others to conceive their children for them may eventually experience serious depression. Another sort of surrogation is manifest in the techniques of certain rather shady rather than shadowy women who call themselves sexual therapists and offer to serve as sexual surrogates to allow their male clients literally to act out, in private sessions, the sexual hang-ups that they experience with the woman whom the therapist replaces on the couch.

A classical example of the theme of the sexual surrogate occurs in the Hebrew Bible, in the story of Jacob, Rachel, and Leah.

> Laban had two daughters: the name of the elder was Leah, and the name of the younger was Rachel. Leah was tender-eyed; but Rachel was beautiful and well-favored. And Jacob loved Rachel, and said, "I will serve you seven years for Rachel thy younger daughter." And Laban said, "It is better that I give her to thee, than that I should give her to another man: abide with me." And Jacob served seven years for Rachel; and they seemed unto him but a few days, for the love he had

to her. And Jacob said unto Laban, "Give me my wife, for my days are fulfilled, that I may go in unto her." And Laban gathered together all the men of the place, and made a feast. And it came to pass in the evening, that he took Leah his daughter, and brought her to him, and he went in unto her. And Laban gave unto his daughter Leah Zilpah his maid for an handmaid. And it came to pass, that in the morning, behold, it was Leah; and he said to Laban, "What is this thou hast done unto me? Did I not serve with thee for Rachel? Wherefore then hast thou beguiled me?" And Laban said, "It must not be so done in our country, to give the younger before the firstborn" [Gen. 28: 15-24].

Later, Jacob married Rachel as well. When Rachel remained barren she sent her maid to Jacob, to bear him children that Rachel regarded as her own; Leah, too, when she became barren, sent her maid to Jacob. Eventually both Rachel and Leah conceived by Jacob.[2]

This story contains both of the two basic variants, depending on whether we view it from the standpoint of Rachel or of Leah. From Leah's standpoint, the initial episode is a sexual masquerade: a woman (Leah) secretly replaces another woman in bed. But from Rachel's standpoint, this same episode is a sexual surrogation: a woman (willingly or unwillingly) allows another woman to replace her in the bed of a man whom, for one reason or another, she cannot sleep with. This second pattern is then repeated when Rachel sends her maid to Jacob when she cannot bear him children.

The plot thickens, however, when we consider the ambivalence of Rachel, who both does and does not want her sister to sleep with Jacob. Did she know what Laban was plotting? Was the great feast designed to make Jacob too drunk to know whom he was in bed with (a frequent motif in myths on this theme)? And what purpose is served on that first night by Laban's maid, newly bequeathed to Leah and fated to sleep with Jacob later in the story? The Hebrew Bible is silent.

But Rachel's ambivalence is wonderfully developed in the Midrash,[3] in a passage in which Rachel complains to God about his destruction of the Temple and of his own people: then she says,

"Jacob loved me very much [best], and served my father for seven years, for *me*. When the time came for him to marry me, my father insisted that my sister be married instead of me. This was very difficult for me. I told my husband [i.e., Jacob, her husband to be], and I made

---

[2]One day, when Leah's son had brought her mandrake roots that Rachel wanted, Leah gave the roots to Rachel and, in exchange, Rachel let Leah lie with Jacob that night, and Leah conceived again.

[3]David Shulman told me of this passage and translated it for me.

a secret sign between him and me, so that he could distinguish the two of us, in order to thwart my father's plan.

"But then I changed my mind, and I mastered my passion. And I felt pity for my sister, lest she be disgraced. In the night, they substituted my sister for me. All the secret signs that I had made with my husband, I told my sister, so that he would think she was me. Not only this: I went under the bed where he was making love with my sister. Whenever he spoke to her, she was silent, and I would answer, so that he would not recognize her voice. I did this out of my compassion and kindness to her. And I wasn't jealous of her. I would not allow her to be disgraced.

"But *you* were jealous of those idols [and therefore destroyed the Temple to punish the Jews for idolatry], though they are nothing, as you yourself know. You exiled my children, and they were slain and ill-used by strangers."

Then God was moved: his mercy rolled around, and he said, "For *your* sake I will bring the Jews back. As it is said [and here he quotes himself], 'Rachel weeps for her children and will not be comforted.' 'Stop your voice from lamenting, and your eyes from weeping, for there is a reward for your action.' Stop weeping, your children will come home" [Lamentations Rabbah 24].

Some of these themes are familiar from other myths of this genre. The "secret signs" by which one lover knows another indicate the Midrash's determination to deal realistically with the problem of deceiving a man who has known a woman well, for seven years—who knows her voice as well as her body. The problem of realistic recognition is one to which we shall return. The barrenness, which only appears *later* in this story, and for a while afflicts both Rachel and Leah, is in many Indian myths the cause of the original substitution. The sexual competition between the younger and older sisters is also a common theme (recall the tale of Cinderella, whose ugly older sisters attempt to persuade the prince that it was one of them who wore the glass slipper). And the children who are injured—here, exiled and slain—remind us of the blinded, pale, or impotent sons of surrogate parents in many myths (of which the story of Oedipus is perhaps the defining example).

But then the Jewish text takes a very different turn. The right of the older sister to be married first, and, more significant, the compassion of one sister toward another (in contrast with the usual situation of sibling rivalry in most versions of the tale) turns the plot around. Jealousy is overcome by the realization that the other woman is a true human form of oneself, related not only by family blood but also by a broader humanity, by common goals, by being part of the same people. The sexual jealousy that is overcome in this way is then analogized, in a brilliant original stroke of this text, to the divine jealousy that God feels toward *his* surrogates — toward the images of him that substitute for him in heathen temples even as false lovers substitute for one another in lustful beds. The fact that Rachel supplies the *voice* of her surrogate is particularly important in this context, since voice is the only contact with God in Jewish theology; you never *see* God, but you often hear his voice. This makes the theme of the sexual masquerade in the dark all the more appropriate as a metaphor for union with God. "I mastered my passion," says Rachel, referring to sexual passion, lust, desire. In this way she moves God to give up the passion that has blocked his mercy, that has made him, in a sense, barren — a killer of his own children — even as the two sisters had been barren. When Rachel gets back her children, God gets back his children, too.

The problem that the double women have in telling the original from the copy is vividly illustrated in a Hindu story from the *Yogavasistha*, a Sanskrit text composed in Kashmir in about A.D. 1000. This is the tale of Queen Lila, in which the two aspects of the double woman confront each other face to face. Both of them are named Lila, "play" or "art," a term used for the illusory sport of an artist, magician, or god; this word is a clue, given at the very start, that the well-known theme of the shadow woman is here going to be given a special twist (*Yogavasistha* 3.16–59; see also O'Flaherty, 1984, 101–3).

Queen Lila was the wife of King Padma. When he died, Lila prayed to the goddess, who explained to her that the king had now been reborn as King Viduratha. Since Lila had not been reborn, the king had taken a new wife, whose name just happened to be Lila. The goddess used her magic powers to transport herself and Queen Lila through the air to the palace where King Viduratha lived; invisible, they saw him in his court. When a great battle took place, they went to the battlefield; there Lila caught sight of the second Lila, who had the very same form as hers, like a reflection in a mirror. Puzzled at this, the first Lila asked the goddess how there could be another woman just like her. The Goddess replied with a long lecture on the projection of mental images from inside to outside, as in dreams. These words were overheard by the second Lila; as they began to converse, the battle commenced in earnest; and when Viduratha seemed to be winning, the second Lila said to the first Lila, "See what a lion our husband is."

But in the end, Viduratha was killed by his enemy, and when he died, the second Lila died, too, since, as the goddess pointed out to the first Lila, the second Lila was merely a delusion, a dream of Viduratha. This second Lila was then transported back to the tomb of Padma, and the goddess and Lila also returned to Padma's tomb. The goddess explained to the first Lila that her own body, which had been

lying beside the corpse of her husband for thirty days, had been taken
to be a corpse and had been burnt by the royal ministers. Now,
however, both the first Lila and the second Lila had spirit bodies. The
goddess then revived Padma, who opened his eyes and saw two Lilas
standing in front of him, alike in form and shape and manner and
speech, and alike in their joy at seeing him alive. "Who are you? And
who is this? And where did she come from?" he asked. The first Lila
said, "I am Lila, your queen from a former life. This second Lila is
your queen by my art, produced for you by me; she is just a
reflection." Then Lila embraced him, and he embraced her, and they
rejoiced. Thus King Padma won the happiness of the three worlds.
Together with the two Lilas, the king ruled for eight thousand years.

The text takes pains to distinguish the first Lila from the second, calling
them "the first" and "the second" Lila, or "the former" and "the latter"
Lila, or "Padma's Lila" and "Viduratha's Lila," or, significantly, "the
enlightened Lila" (*prabuddhalila*) and "the imaginary Lila" (*samkalpalila*). In
contrast with the single king, who is reborn, the two Lilas exist
simultaneously. Perhaps as a result of being thus anchored in both worlds
at once, the two Lilas understand the vision, while the king is unaware of
what is going on. The woman understands what the man does not,
because when she doubles herself she is aware of both doubles at once,
while when he doubles himself he knows only one form at a time.

The doctrines that the goddess uses to explain these events are
complex, and I have discussed them elsewhere (O'Flaherty, 1984). Here,
however, we may note that the Indian perception of these events is such
that the king is able to experience a happy *ménage à trois* with his two
wives, whom he receives not from two marriages (as in Noel Coward's
Blithe Spirit) but from two incarnations. The second Lila is a delusion of
the second king, a dream that he dreams as a result of the magic of the
first Lila, who apparently projects an image of herself to function as the
second wife of her erstwhile husband. The second Lila is thus in a sense
the product of the combined mental processes of Padma and his queen.

What separates Lila from her husband in this myth is not his
adulterous longings but his death. The second wife with whom Lila
competes is therefore a double that the first Lila herself creates for him;
it is herself. (This may have been suggested by the theme that we have
already encountered in the story of Rachel and Leah, of the first wife
who—usually because she is barren—herself procures the second wife or
sexual surrogate.) Since Lila *is* the other woman, she is not jealous; the
king can live with both of them happily forever. In the Midrash story of
Rachel and Leah, jealousy was overcome by the realization that the other
woman is a true *human* form of oneself. A very different solution is

offered by this ultimate Vedantic variant on the theme of the woman who masquerades as her husband's "other" woman: the realization that, once one has come to understand the nature of illusion, one *is* the other woman that one's husband is sleeping with. The philosophy of illusion, as expressed in the *Yogavasistha*, demonstrates that there is no difference at all between the two women, just as the Buddhist logicians asserted that there is no difference between the everyday world of emotional involvement (*samsara*) and the enlightenment world of release from all involvement (*moksha*). In this way, and in this way alone, the tension of the myth is resolved; the contradiction is unmasked as purely illusory, girl meets girl, and everybody lives happily ever after.

But the solution offered by the story of the two Lilas is hardly typical, for it happens only in an India where a king can rule for eight thousand years. The story of the Lilas is a myth, involving deities in magical situations; but the story of Rachel and Leah takes place on a more banal and human level, where servants or sisters often assume the role played by magical doubles in the myths. One Indian folk variant of the sexual masquerade achieves a realistic happy ending, though not without the intercession of supernatural powers. The story combines the theme of two separate human women — the wife and the whore of a single man — with the theme of a double who impersonates the husband:

> There was a newly wedded woman whose husband never slept with her; he spent every night with his mistress, a courtesan, and returned to the wife only to eat, in silence, the food that she prepared for him. She made a magic potion to win his love, but then threw it away in fear that it might kill him; a snake in the garden drank it and fell in love with her. Every night he entered the house, took the form of the husband, and made love to her, to her great happiness. Eventually she became pregnant and had a son; the serpent lover helped her to prove her chastity through an act of truth: handling a deadly cobra (her lover, of course), who raised his erect and expanded hood and wound it around her neck. Her husband began to be attentive to her, and to make love to her; the mistress was spurned by the husband; and the wife, with the help of the serpent lover, tricked the mistress into becoming her servant (carrying water for her). But finally the snake lover came in one night to see her asleep beside her husband, their son sleeping between them; overcome with jealousy, the snake hung himself in her hair. The woman buried him with the rites for a close friend.[4]

The story begins with a purely human problem; the man has two women, one to be his official woman, and to nourish him, the other to be his

---

[4]A Kannada folktale, from A. K. Ramanujan.

sexual partner. The wife wishes to be both to him and takes measures to achieve this reintegration of herself; she fails in this, however, and succeeds instead only in doubling him—or rather, in splitting him: one half of him is the phallic snake, a purely erotic partner and nothing else to her. This magical, fantasy episode is then shattered when she has a son; in the Indian context, this is the act not of an erotic woman but of a mother; or, to put it differently, the son must be the son of her husband, not the son of her lover. In order that this may be so, the fantasy lover must vanish; first he ceases to be her lover, then he dies. At midpoint, it would seem that the woman is once again reduced to one-half of the possibly integrated woman: all maternal, and not at all erotic. But the story finds its way to a happy ending within the realm of the purely realistic. The *real* mistress vanishes, not magically, like the snake lover, but socially; and both the wife and the husband are integrated at last. But the happy ending is made possible only through the continuous intervention of a magical helper. And for that helper, the story ends in tragedy.

It may well be, as A. K. Ramanujan has suggested, that the situation depicted in the middle section of this story, the episode of the snake lover, reflects an imaginative version of the true situation that prevails in most Indian marriages: custom prevents the husband from expressing any affection for his wife in public, so that he may well be one man to her by day—cold and indifferent—and another by night—warm and loving.

Mythical versions of the story of the split woman appear both in the "great tradition" texts of Sanskrit and in the vernacular folk materials, or the "little tradition"; so do the realistic versions of the story. Indeed, one of the most famous examples of this theme is told first in the Sanskrit epic, where the woman is a human woman named Renuka, and then, much later, in a Tamil oral tradition, where she is a goddess named Mariatale. This is the Tamil version (several times removed: it is my translation of an eighteenth-century Frenchman's translation from the oral Tamil):

> Mariatale was the wife of the ascetic Jamadagni and mother of Parashurama. This goddess ruled over the elements, but she could only keep this empire as long as her heart remained pure. One day she was fetching water from a pool, and, following her usual custom, was rolling it up in a ball to carry home. She happened to see on the surface of the water several male demigods (Gandharvas), who were sporting gymnastically [here one suspects a French euphemism] right under her head. She was taken by their charms, and desire entered her heart. The water that she had already collected immediately turned to liquid

and mingled back with the water of the pool. She could no longer carry it home without the help of a bowl.

This impotence revealed to her husband that his wife had ceased to be pure, and in the excess of his anger, he commanded his son to drag her off to the place set aside for executions, and to cut off her head. This order was executed; but the son was so afflicted by the loss of his mother that the husband told him to go and get her body, to join to it the head that he had cut off, and to whisper in its ear a prayer that he taught him, that would immediately revive her. The son ran in haste, but by a singular oversight he joined the head of his mother to the body of an outcaste woman who had been executed for her crimes — a monstrous assemblage, which gave to this woman the virtues of a goddess and the vices of an unfortunate wretch. The goddess, having become impure through this mix, was chased out of her house and committed all sorts of cruelties; the gods, seeing the ravages that she was making, appeased her, by giving her the power to cure smallpox and promising her that she would be supplicated for this disease . . . Only her head was placed in the inner sanctuary of the temple, to be worshiped by Indians of good caste; while her body was placed at the door of the temple, to be worshiped by Pariahs . . . Mariatale, having become impure through the mixing of her head with the body of a outcaste, and fearing that she would no longer be adored by her son Parashurama, begged the gods to grant her another child. They gave her a son, Kartavirya; the Pariahs divide their worship between his mother and him. This is the only one of all the gods to whom are offered cooked meats, salted fish, tobacco, and so forth, because he came from the body of a Pariah.[5]

In addition to explaining the relationship between certain high-caste and low-caste goddesses, this myth may be seen as a twisted variant of the theme in which a woman masquerades as another woman in order to sleep with a forbidden man. Here, Mariatale wishes to sleep with a man who is not her husband; that wish alone causes her to be split in two, but she is revived as a split woman. This woman is not the explicit sexual partner of the lusted-for demigod, but she has an integrated, ambiguous nature that the original, monolithic Mariatale lacked.

The unreasonable image of the entirely pure wife, symbolized by the impossible ability to roll water up, solid and dry, with nothing to support it, cannot be sustained; the woman's natural emotion is expressed in the vision of the water that melts back into its natural liquidity and mingles again with the waters of the pool from which it was frozen. Such a

---

[5]Pierre Sonnerat, *Vovages aux Indes orientales* (Paris, 1782), pp. 245–247; presumably based on Abraham Roger's *Offne Thür* [1663].

.

woman, a pure woman who feels passion, an ice maiden who is melted by lust, can exist only when she is physically split. Her mythical pure half, the half that can roll up water, is her upper-caste half, which is preserved in her head, the source of her sexual identity and her legal status: if she has an upper-caste head, she is an upper-caste goddess. Her impure half, the half that lusts for the demigod, is the *real* woman, the denied woman, the passionate woman, as polluting and despised as the Untouchable. This half becomes the body of the integrated Mariatale.

This mixed woman is a monster, impure and destructive; she is disease incarnate — ambivalent disease, whose Untouchable body brings the fever that is cooled by the grace of the upper-caste head. The tension within her is so great that she does not remain integrated in ritual; she is split up once again, the upper-caste head at last purified by being divorced from its polluting body, and the Pariah body put literally on to the doorstep, liminal, forever marking the pale of the Hindu society that sees woman as an upper-caste-headed and Untouchable-bodied monster.

Mariatale is schizophrenic in her motherhood, too; her first son expresses his ambivalence toward her by first beheading her and then reviving her; but when, through *his* error, she becomes impure, he rejects her. She then creates another son, entirely impure — Kartavirya. The Pariahs then further split (!) their worship between the impure body of the goddess and the son born of that *body* — that is, not born of the upper-caste part of her at all. For the son of the upper-caste head and the upper-caste body is pure, while the son of the upper-caste head and the Pariah body is impure; the son's quality is determined not by his mother's head but by her body (though it is the father's head that gives the son his social status). The tale of Renuka/Mariatale thus tells of a woman caught between two men (her legal husband and her dream lover), a woman who then becomes a synthesis of two women.

Another story of transposed heads, taken from a medieval Sanskrit text,[6] was retold by the great Indologist Heinrich Zimmer (1948); Zimmer's good friend Thomas Mann (1941) later developed the story into a novella. The Sanskrit text, in Zimmer's translation, reads as follows:

> Then there was that curious tale of the transposed heads, the tale of the two lifelong friends and a girl. The maid married one of the two, but the marriage was not particularly happy. Shortly following the wedding, the couple, together with their bachelor friend, set forth on a visit to the parents of the bride. On the way, they came to a sanctuary of the

---

[6]It is told in the "Twenty-five tales of a Vampire" (*Vetalapancavimsati*) and retold in the *Bhavisya Purana*.

bloodthirsty goddess Kali and the husband excused himself, for a moment, to go into the temple alone. There, in a sudden excess of emotion, he decided to offer himself to the image as a sacrifice, and with a keen edged sword that was there, lopped his head from his shoulders and collapsed into a pool of blood. The friend, having waited with the bride, went into the temple to see what had happened, and when he beheld the sight was inspired to follow suit. At last the bride came in, only to take flight again intent on hanging herself from the limb of a tree. The voice of the goddess commanded her to halt, however, and sent her back to restore the lives of the two young men by replacing their heads. But because of her distraction, the young woman made the interesting mistake of putting the friend's head on the husband's body, and the husband's on the friend's.

The role of the demigod in the tale of Renuka/Mariatale is here played by the husband's best friend. (In an earlier version [Tawney and Penzer, 1968], it is the woman's brother who is beheaded together with her husband, which introduces a whole other series of problems.) But in order to avoid her husband, or in order to have the best of both men, the woman splits not herself but *them* — so that there is only one of her but two of them, each *combined*. The human woman's happiness is short-lived, however; her solution is intolerable. For in India (indeed, in most of Indo-European literature) a woman cannot have two men. The tale therefore immediately poses a question: Which of the two does she belong to? And the answer, predictably, is: "The one with the husband's head."

The myths of Renuka/Mariatale present us with two transitions: the transition from woman to goddess and the transition from woman to man. The first of these transitions suggests that, while rationalization may indeed occur in mythology (myths of goddesses being translated into stories of women), the opposite process is perhaps both more common and more important. Stories of women become inextricably entangled in the toils of human sexual tragedy and take flight in the illusion provided by myth, the illusion that the Brahmin woman's head can be grafted on to the Untouchable woman's body, or that the husband's head (the intellectual's head, in Thomas Mann's version of the story) can be grafted on to the friend's body (the athlete's body, in the Mann version). Thus we might do well to see the human concerns as the logical and psychological base from which the theological versions were derived. For the myth is a bridge between actual human sexual experience and the fantasy that grows out of that experience. Some variants narrow the gap by rendering the fantasy in almost realistic terms; but the gap, however small, remains nevertheless.

As for the second transition, from split woman to split man, it is worth noting that the tale of the split woman cannot be simply transformed into a tale of split men; the woman's fantasy is not simply the inverse of the man's fantasy. For her fantasy is to be whole, with both aspects of herself valued, if not by one man, then by two; while his fantasy is to have her split into two different halves, and, perhaps, to split himself in two to enjoy her in two different ways.

Let us consider the implications of this imbalance of the two fantasies as we attempt to come to some sort of extended conclusion about the meaning of these stories. Since the mythology of sexual doubling deals with men as well as women, we can argue that it is concerned with an ambivalent attitude to sexuality in general rather than to women in particular. The plot of the narratives seems to have fascinated people of many cultures.[7] Can we generalize about the human meanings that flesh out the abstract armatures in all of these myths? We cannot, I think, make many statements of this sort that will apply to *all* the myths, but we can isolate several patterns that do seem to occur in many of them and that may represent several alternative views of human sexuality. Some very basic meanings attach themselves to the basic structure in *all* variants of the myth, while other meanings attach themselves to many variants, and still others serve rather to show how very differently any two retellings of the myth may view the point of the myth.

The one clear constant in all the myths of doubling is, *tout court,* doubling—or, more precisely, doubling in situations of pairing. That is, one thing that all the myths are about is the tension between the desire to remain whole and the desire (or necessity) to split into two. The dyad of "integrated" and "split" is itself a basic contrasting unit in mythology; that is, any split image may be used to form one half of a pair, the other half being the integrated image of which it is the dissection; the decision to split something in half is in itself a question that may be answered by yes or no. (Indo-Europeans have usually answered "yes" to this question.) On this level, the structure *is* the meaning; the medium is the message. We may seek the origins of these apparently universal dyadic structures in the rational processes of the bicameral human brain.

Or we may see these myths in psychological terms, as stories in which intolerable conflict leads to splitting and doubling. We may analyze them in terms of Otto Rank's study of the double, or in terms of Melanie Klein's concept of projective identification.

The universal sexual impulse engenders a major tension when it comes

---

[7]We encounter good and evil mothers, male and female doubles, and androgynous women in Africa and Polynesia, and among the Navajo tribes of North America, as well as in Semitic mythology, a spread that suggests that the theme may well be universal.

into conflict with the particular exigencies of human society, when nature meets culture—or, indeed, when culture meets culture, when two cultures meet or when one culture maintains two conflicting ideals. The result may be a major human contradiction: two human truths that are simultaneously true and mutually opposed. In such a situation, as Claude Lévi-Strauss has taught us, the myth arises as a mediating factor between nature and culture. In the myth, the conflict turns into a narrative that expresses a contradiction that can never be resolved. The splitting that seems to solve the original problem of conflict or ambivalence is in itself a source of new anxiety; the solution to the problem of doubling is a new integration, with new tensions. And we might expect these tensions to be approached differently by different cultures.

One set of variants tells of a woman who creates a double in order *not to be* in the bed of a man who would force her to be there; another tells of a woman who masquerades in order *to be* in the bed of a man who would not want her to be there. These may be seen as two aspects of the same myth: the woman wants not to be with one man and to be with another man. She wishes to disappear secretly from one bed in order to appear secretly in another. The two aspects collapse together when the wife wishes to masquerade as her husband's mistress (or the mistress as the wife); she wants to be with one man, but to be a *different woman* to that man. The doubles of people may occur in response to other doubles: the wife masquerades when her husband takes another woman, or doubles herself when a man other than the man she loves forces her to his bed.

It also useful to try to sort out the different conflicting views of the men and women in these stories.[8] In the relatively rare myths in which a

---

[8]It is difficult to know whose voice is speaking to us in these myths, the voice of a woman or the voice of a man. For, although the Indian myths are almost always written and recorded by men, there is good evidence within the tradition itself that women were always the source of some, if not indeed most, of the storytelling; theirs might well have been an oral contribution to the tales that were ultimately written down by men. Yet it is also good to bear in mind the likelihood that women will share the dominant mythology of their culture; they learn and assimilate the images that men have of them, and express those images in their own storytelling, even as men express images of themselves that they have learned from women. Since woman were excluded from the Sanskritic tradition that is preserved in the myths recorded in the Epics and the Puranas, we might hazard that guess that the women's contribution was stronger in the realm of the vernacular, oral folklore than in the realm of Sanskrit texts. But again it would be difficult to substantiate such a claim—especially since there is no clear demarcation between the "great" and the "little" variants of any story. In any case, if we do grant that these stories are not entirely male creations, we may view the sexual doubling in some of these myths from the standpoint of the man and in others from the standpoint of the woman, even if we cannot prove that a man expressed the former and a woman the latter. And some myths seems to express both viewpoints at once.

woman masquerades as a different woman in order to make possible a
sexual encounter, and in the many, many myths in which a man
masquerades as a different man in order to trick a woman into bed, the
man seems to be saying, "The woman whom I desire and who desires me
cannot be the same as my wife, the woman who is the mother of my
children; the child who inherits my wealth must be *my* child and the child
of a nonpromiscuous (hence nonerotic) mother." This may correspond to
the split between the images of what Freud described as the madonna and
the whore. In Indo-European culture at large, the man's fantasy of
having two different women is endorsed in a way that the woman's
fantasy of having two different men is not; he can indulge in his fantasy
without casting doubt on the parentage of his heirs, while she cannot.
The stories that were either composed or preserved by men reveal a male
fantasy that attempts to stage the sexual masquerade within a one-sided,
monogamous system that tolerates the adultery or the sexual aggression
of the man far more than the adultery or the sexual aggression of the
woman. Thus, on those relatively rare occasions when a woman does
masquerade in bed in order to sleep with a man who does not want to
sleep with her, that man is her own husband, who has been sleeping with
another woman, his concubine. The man's dominant fantasy makes him
masquerade as two different men so that he can enjoy two different
women, both his permitted woman and the forbidden woman.

But women, too, fantasize; and the woman is saying something else in
these myths. She may want to be both erotic and childbearing, or both
sexual and spiritual, to the same man, but he wants to have one woman
for each purpose, and so he splits her in his fantasy. And the woman may
not share this fantasy. Indeed, as we have seen, she is often split against
her will; but even when she willingly allows the surrogate, as Rachel
allowed Leah to lie-in for her, she may have a deep-seated resistance
against being replaced in this way.

The woman sees herself, as indeed we all see ourselves, as multiple in
a positive sense, and struggles to function, and to be perceived, as an
integrated person. Her fantasy is to remain combined; it is her husband's
intolerance of this condition that forces her to split. The woman's image
of herself remains integrated even when doubled: it is two of the *same*
woman. This wish on the part of the woman reinforces the pattern that
we have just seen from the male standpoint: on those relatively rare
occasions when she masquerades as another woman, it is in order to be
the other woman to her *own* husband.

Often the woman in our myths (like the woman with the snake lover)
experiences her own husband as two different men. But even in the
(again rare) myths in which the woman has two men (like the myth of the

transposed heads), there is still only one of her.[9] In most of the oldest variants of the tale of the shadow woman, the shadow serves to exonerate the woman herself from any possible defilement at the hands of the demonic rapist or unwanted husband. Often, when one person splits into two, one of the halves experiences the event and the other does not; one of them is "there," and the other is not. Thus the meaning of the splitting as perceived by the person who is split is not merely "I am one, but I am also two," but "This is happening to me and this is not happening to me," and "I am here and I am not here." These myths may express the woman's reaction to sexual violence; they may express a kind of personality dissociation in reaction to a rape: "This happened to some other woman, not to me." The double implies that the "real self" did not experience the event (see O'Flaherty, 1984, pp. 95–96).

The image of the split woman in these myths is a female fantasy; she does not want to sleep with the man who will merely give her children or who will merely take his pleasure from her in the dark, and so she splits away the part of herself that is being used in this way. When the unwanted partner is the legal husband, she identifies her true self with the erotic woman; when he is the demonic rapist, she identifies herself with the chaste wife. So, too, in myths where one man masquerades as another, the woman is exonerated from the defilement by a stranger: "I could not tell them apart." The stories in which a woman produces a double to avoid a man she does not want outnumber those in which a man produces such a double in part because both biology and society conspire to produce the former situation far more often than the latter; women are more often raped against than raping.

Thus our myths fall into two contrasting groups. Where there are two different women or two of the same man, we may see the man's point of view. Such myths are relatively rare in India, though common in Europe. Where there are two different men or two of the same woman, we may see the woman's point of view. And this is by far the prevalent pattern, the dominant message of the Indian myths and one that is common in Europe as well. Thus, contrary to what we might have expected from the textual tradition, we hear the woman's voice more than the man's in these myths. But if we bear in mind the incidental damage done to the children of these supernaturally divorced pairs, children who are often blinded or

---

[9]Indeed, the two prevalent forms of the story are often combined, as they represent two views of the same situation: where the woman is forced to have two different men, only one of whom she desires—either because her husband procures for her an unattractive surrogate or because she has a lover but is forced to marry a man she does not love—she produces a double of herself to sleep with the man she does not love, in order to keep her true self for the man she does love.

mutilated or abandoned, we might do well to consider the myths from the standpoint of the child, the hapless mediator between the two divided (and subdivided) parents.

Is there really any point in distinguishing the "mythical" variants of the theme from the "realistic" ones? Is it only the supernatural ring of invisibility or merely natural darkness that makes this masquerade possible? Does it happen only in myths, or in life? Is it true everywhere, or only in France, that, Dans la nuit, tous les chats sont gris? (Roughly, "In the night, all cats are white.") How could it be possible that someone could sleep with two different women, or two different men, on several occasions and never tell the difference?

One can suggest several reasons why the male objects of the sexual masquerade cannot tell the difference between the two women in bed in myths told from the standpoint of the woman who creates a double to *avoid* an unwanted liaison. Traditional concepts of marriage, or traditional marriage partners, do not value individualism as an element of eroticism as do romantic concepts of love or romantic partners; the official partner seeks not the personality but the persona (or indeed, the body) of the woman in bed. The lover, the unofficial, erotic partner, *does* know the difference; indeed, the female surrogate may be created precisely because the woman in love cannot tolerate the embrace of any man other than the man she loves—the man who knows the difference. Surrogates work only on the people who are not erotically attached, but are merely officially or physically attached, to the woman who creates the surrogate.

Many of the characters in this complex of myths are cursed to be blind. (Blindness is the human aspect of what is expressed on the magical or mythical level as invisibility.) In this impersonal context, the visual element of sexual love predominates, while other more intimate factors such as actions, words, or smells don't count. In the Freudian view, of course, the distortion of upward displacement makes blindness a metaphor for castration, an appropriate punishment for any form of sexuality that the culture defines as unacceptable—in this case, a punishment for the impersonal sexuality that is unacceptable in the romantic view.

The woman may fantasize that the man she does not love "could not tell the difference." But this is also a macho male fantasy, an antiromantic locker-room fantasy—"Put a bag over her head"—to gain power over a woman by implying that no one particular woman has power over a man. Again, this may be a biological bias: a man's active role in the sexual act produces more obvious grounds for distinction and comparison than does that of a passive woman ("Close your eyes and think of England"). This line of reasoning contributes to the preponderance, in folklore, of women rather than men replacing one another in the dark, and *not getting caught;* men, by contrast, more often seduce women in masquerades that take place *before* anyone gets into bed, and it doesn't matter if the man gets caught: by the time she notices the difference, the prize has already been won.

But there might be two other reasons to explain why the man cannot tell the difference in bed. In fact, the man (or woman) may half suspect and half not suspect that the woman (or man) who *seems* to be the wife or the husband is not really the legitimate partner; this is made quite explicit in folk variants such as the story of the snake lover: she pretends that she thinks it is her husband, in order to legitimize the episode, but she enjoys it because she knows it is not her husband. We may see this phenomenon also in the story of the return of Martin Guerre,[10] where the woman did indeed know that the surrogate was false, but preferred him to her real husband.

Or, finally, it may be that the man cannot tell his (forbidden) beloved from the (permitted) woman who impersonates her because they are in fact the same person; only the myth preserves the fantasy that accompanies the act, the fantasy that there are two separate women there. It was Freud, after all, who pointed out long ago that whenever two people make love, there are four people in bed—those present, and those fantasized. In India, there are hundreds of people in the bed.

When, each for his or her own reason, the man and the woman close their eyes to an intolerable reality, each sees in the dark the myth that makes the reality tolerable. The woman fantasizes that she is in bed with a god or that she is not there at all. The man fantasizes that he is in bed with a woman who is not his wife—or who is an Untouchable. To this degree, *all* of the tales of the sexual surrogate, even the realistic ones, are mythological in the broadest sense of the term: they imagine what cannot ever be in real life. More precisely, they imagine what might be most natural to *real* real life devoid of the constraints of human culture (a situation that can never exist for us).

The supernatural and the realistic stories are alike in some ways, different in others. They are alike in that they deal with the same sets of human problems, though they express those problems differently according to the idioms of each genre. But they differ in the solutions that they can offer to those problems. The realistic stories often end in tragedy: once the fantasy has been acted out, there is a price to pay—the masquerade is discovered, the woman is punished, the trick does not

---

[10]Both in Nathalie Ziemon Davis's analysis and in Janet Lewis's *The Wife of Martin Guerre.*

work, the dream lover vanishes. Tragedy is, in this sense, the myth of the failure of mediation. But the myth may at least imagine the ideal solution, the perfect integration. By expressing our sexual fantasies, myths transcend the paradoxical tension between illicit erotic love and legal marital love, a tension that can never be overcome in real life — except, perhaps, among the gods.

REFERENCES

Lévi-Strauss, C. (1955), The story of Asdiwal. In: *The Structural Study of Myth and Totemism,* ed. E. Leach. Bloomington: Indiana University Press, pp. 1–48.
_____ (1968), The structural study of myth. In: *Myth: A Symposium,* ed. T. Sebeok. New York: Methuen, pp. 50–56.
Mann, T. (1941), *The Transposed Heads: A Legend of India.* New York: Knopf.
O'Flaherty, W. D. (1984), *Dreams, Illusion, and Other Realities.* Chicago: University of Chicago Press.
Sonnerat, P. (1782), *Voyages aux Indes orientales.* Paris.
Tawney, C. H. & Penzer, V. M. (eds. & trans.) (1968), *The Ocean of Story.* Delhi: Banarsidasa.
Zimmer, H. (1948), *The King and the Corpse: Tales of the Soul's Conquest,* ed. J. Campbell. Princeton, NJ: Bollingen.

June 1987

Discussion

DR. TROSMAN:

There are so many interesting issues discussed in Dr. Doniger's paperthat it is difficult to know where to start. My remarks will be essentially directed by an interest in a psychoanalytic view of some of this rich material, considering it from the point of view of both the differentiation between contemporary men and women and the differentiation between Western and Eastern conceptions of psychology.

Quite clearly, the themes of sexual doubles and sexual masquerades cut across both Eastern and Western societies, and are not specific to either gender. Eastern and Western myths and stories are replete with these themes. The theme of one person taking the place of another in the sexual act clearly goes back to biblical times, and our contemporary concern with sexual surrogates clearly has a long-standing history. As we find today, even when the aspect of deceit is lacking and sexual surrogates are chosen for practical reasons, this arrangement does not always work out harmoniously. Surrogates who take the role of another, as in the process of giving birth, soon find themselves convinced that they are the rightful parent and not *in loco parentis*. Indeed, there seems to be a difficulty when one plays the role of double in accepting that this is only a temporary state and not one that is lacking authenticity. Perhaps the biological and psychological function of giving birth is too insistent an activity to be subsequently denied.

Dr. Doniger's retelling of the Hindu myths and stories raises many questions with regard to the conception of object relations in both Eastern and Western societies. Quite clearly, in the Midrash story of Rachel and Leah jealousy is overcome by the realization that the other woman is a true human form of oneself. Thus one might claim that the establishment of identity between one human and another, independent of self, is an example of a preobject identification, a conception of oneness. In the Eastern myth, the woman who masquerades as her husband's other woman is able to live out an illusion and to conceive of herself as in fact being the other woman, is capable of overcoming object differentiation, thus accepting a state of postobject relationship and once again reestablishing a sense of oneness with the world.

Dr. Doniger is sensitive to the wishes that are being expressed in these Eastern and Western myths. The woman who wishes to avoid a sexual encounter and substitutes another woman in her place and the woman who, wishing to attain a sexual object, takes the place of another woman are living out both a wish and a defense against a wish in a heterosexual matrix. One should also consider the role of homosexual interests in such fantasies and the specific relationship that is set up between two women, one of whom becomes a substitute or double for another. The women may indeed be acting out a sexual relationship in which the primary sexual interest is directed toward the other woman. Freud dealt with this particular phenomenon when he described the preoccupation of jealous men who were highly curious about the sexual activities of their deceitful heterosexual objects. They clearly derived sexual gratification from the account of the sexual encounter when related to them by their betraying partner. In addition, one must consider other aspects of the paired relationship aside from the sexual one, and it is an insightful stroke to point out that often the third party in a sexual encounter may fulfill expressive and affectionate longings that are not being fulfilled in real life.

A critical psychoanalytic contribution can be offered in considering the tales as indicative of manifestations not only of splits that occur because of the conflict between biological nature and cultural norms. In addition, they may be a result of the internal intrapsychic conflict that resides in individuals who have divided natures. Among such intrapsychic conflicts psychoanalysts have long been familiar with the tendency to split which is characteristic of bisexuality, the differentiation that takes place between sexual objects who are characterized as either madonnas or prostitutes, and the split that takes place between sexual and tender aspects as far as modes of relating to others are concerned. The differentiation between the madonna and the prostitute — and specifically in the recounted stories in this paper — is also seen in the medieval practice of the rights of the seigneur, in which the lord of the manor deflowers the young bride before the bridegroom has an opportunity to consummate the marriage. We see sufficient evidence in our clinical practice of the difficulty in establishing normal heterosexual relationships because of failures of development, residues of infantile conflict that continue into adult life, and the threat that is associated with sexuality because of the intrusion of aggression, fear of retaliation, anxiety, and guilt.

These days, we are particularly interested in the psychoanalytic conception of the relationship between part and whole. Originally, psychoanalysis began in a sense with concerns with regard to part. Conflict was seen as involving impulse and defense, and sexuality was designated as a critical etiology of neurotic conflict formation. Today, we are also concerned with the totality of human personality, and the link between the part and the whole has become critical to our theoretical understanding. Not only do we see the dichotomy between two varying aspects of the mind, such as the physical and the psychological, the aggressive and the sexual, the impulse and the defense, but currently we are also interested in the harmonious integration between the part and the totality. To some extent, the Indian myths, which find totality "in the head," reflect the view that a man for a woman is a representation of a totality, particularly when the woman feels the need to describe herself as affiliated with the man's head.

Do we detect in these myths, particularly in the Eastern myths, the conception that a woman is more interested in integration and totality, that her fantasy — as Dr. Doniger states — is to be whole and that she wishes to unite both aspects as valued? The man in fantasy is more willing to consider himself as split in two halves and to find satisfaction in the gratification of the singular halves rather than in the totality. Clearly, ambivalent attitudes toward sexuality are present in both men and women, but the activity to resolve this ambivalence is variable. The myths indeed suggest that the interest in achieving integration becomes a more predominate vector in the woman than it does in the man.

In a contemporary version of a Western myth, Margaret Atwood in *The Handmaid's Tale* points out the difficulty for a woman in achieving a synthesis between the reproductive and the sexual when she is subjugated in a society in which the reproductive activity becomes isolated, and love and sexuality become divorced from it. Atwood characterizes a repressive society in which men are able to function in this manner because they are characteristically conditioned to do so. On the other hand, women, who find themselves turned essentially into reproductive objects, become debased when they are unable to unite this reproductive activity with sexuality per se. A man may be able to maintain a dominant fantasy of enjoying two different women, a permitted woman and a forbidden woman. For women, the cost is too great.

In East and West, the myth enables us to read into the depths of the mind. The myth is a manifestation of fantasy which is not fulfilled in real life. The conception of the double, the surrogate, or the masquerader enables us to glimpse that particular aspect of unconscious fantasy which can be experienced only as an expressive illusion rather than a step toward a potential reality.

We are grateful to Dr. Doniger, who has provided us with an opportunity to rethink the underlying psychological processes to which the myths and stories are clues.

October 1987

V

PSYCHOANALYSIS AND CHILD DEVELOPMENT

A Prospective Constructionist View of Development

E. VIRGINIA DEMOS, Ed.D. (Cambridge, MA)
with discussions by
MARIAN N. TOLPIN, M.D. (Chicago)
MARJORIE C. BARNETT, M.D. (Chicago)
and BERTRAM J. COHLER, Ph.D. (Chicago)

This paper will discuss development in the first two years of life and will focus on what I and my colleagues have learned while working on a remarkable longitudinal study headed by Dr. Louis Sander. Let me begin with a brief description of the study. It was originally designed by Dr. Eleanor Pavenstedt in 1954, when she was chairman of the Department of Child Psychiatry at Boston University School of Medicine, and it was funded for the first five years by NIMH. Her goals were to provide a training resource for the child fellows who were learning to interview families, and to study the effects of different levels of maternal maturity on the developing infant. Thus thirty families, all expecting their first child, were selected to participate in the study. They were selected on the basis of an extensive prenatal assessment to represent three different levels or degrees of maternal psychological maturity.

I used the word "remarkable" earlier when referring to this study because of the richness and density of data that were collected on the children over first three years of their lives. In addition to the prenatal

This research was supported by grants from the Spencer Foundation and from the MacArthur Foundation.

assessment, which included projective testing as well as extensive interviews, the birth of each baby was observed, often by Dr. Sander, the
babies were observed in the neonatal nursery on several occasions, the
mothers were interviewed daily while in the hospital, and they were
provided with a visiting nurse for the first three weeks at home. Then
over the next three years at regular intervals the families were visited and
observed at home, were asked to come to the clinic for interviews, infant
testing, and pediatric visits, and from the middle of the second year on,
regular play sessions were added. This produced contact between the
families and the research staff at a frequency of once every two to three
weeks. By contrast, other longitudinal studies that follow subjects over
several years collect data at three- or six-month intervals. This study is
therefore unique in the frequency of contact with the families and in the
detailed data that such contact produced. Such extraordinary data have
provided the opportunity for me and my colleagues, Drs. Kaplan,
Stechler, and Halton, to look at a large number of individual cases in
considerable depth in a longitudinal context, and to develop a methodology for describing and understanding each individual life as it is lived,
day by day, in a particular family setting. In other words, these data have
provided the opportunity for us to embark on the prospective construction of the psychological organization of these individuals.

The demands of this task required us to come to terms with two
persistent, if not to say unrelenting themes, namely, complexity and the
search for lawfulness, or as Dr. Sander has phrased it, "uniqueness and
order." These themes are not entirely new, and have taken on other
names in other contexts where they are usually placed in opposition to
each other, such as the ideographic approach versus the nomothetic
approach, or individual differences versus universal norms. They have
developed methodologies either to emphasize the unique complexity of
the individual at the cost of demonstrating universality, or to control a set
a variables, as in an experimental design, in order to highlight the lawful
relationship between two particular variables, at the cost of ignoring
individual differences or treating them as a nuisance.

Yet it became increasingly clear to us that if we were going to do justice
to the richness of these lives we had to find a way to encompass both
complexity and lawfulness. We could not sacrifice either. We had to find
a way to retain the unique details of each life without becoming
overwhelmed by them, and still look for lawfulness. The longitudinal
format gave us some leverage, as it is an ideal methodology for gradually
separating the wheat from the chaff. From the mass of incidental or
coincidental occurrences one is able, over time, to see the emergence of
patterns and to test a series of hypotheses as one follows each case

through time. (In this respect, the process is not unlike the therapeutic process.) Nevertheless, there were surprises. We each began with fairly strong ideas about what a young child needed in order to develop well. But I can say, without exaggeration, that everything we thought we knew was of only limited usefulness. In other words, while some of our theories held in some cases, in other cases they were not applicable. We had to acknowledge that there was no single or simple formula that worked for every case, that there were inputs in a young child's life from many sources, and that the patterns that emerged were different for different children. Thus factors that were present and seemed determining in one case were either not present or did not have the same determining effect in another case.

What can we conclude from this? Perhaps we just haven't hit upon the right theory yet; we haven't been able to discover that all encompassing dynamic that will explain everything. While this remains a theoretical possibility, in the sense that our human capacities for understanding may be too limited to perceive some overarching lawfulness, I prefer to think that it is a fallacy to expect there to be one grand, or even two or three major dynamic forces at work. These data strongly suggest that there are many processes at work in a developing child. Therefore, when our formulations have only a limited usefulness, it does not mean they are not valid, but rather that they are valid for that particular set of circumstances, or for that particular combination of factors or variables, at that particular developmental moment. The temptation to overgeneralize a promising set of findings to try to explain the entire developmental process or to explain every case must be resisted. Our progress has been hindered too long by the adherence to grand theories and by our continued search for one. Instead we need to focus our energies on trying to specify the conditions under which any set of variables act together to produce a lawful relationship, and the conditions under which that same, particular coordination of variables will be overridden or altered by the presence of other factors, and so on.

Dr. Sander was always reminding us of the studies of the roundworm that were reported in *Science* magazine several years ago. The roundworm is an organism comprised of a small number of cells, each of which could be traced from its embryonic form, through a series of transformations until it took its place in the corpus of the mature roundworm. But it was discovered that no set of cells ever followed the same pattern of transformations. There seemed to be an infinite number of routes taken, yet the end product was always the same, a mature roundworm. If there can be such complexity and variation in the simple roundworm, with a finite number of cells, imagine the infinite number of combinations and permutations of variables operating within the human infant, developing in its familial context.

In an example closer to home similar results have been reported by Gruber (1985), who studies adult problem-solving with a finely grained examination of cognitive processes. He asked a group of professional physicists to solve an elementary mechanics problem. These individuals, acting separately and privately, produced at least sixteen different pathways to the solution, and indeed were surprised and dismayed by each other's approaches. Gruber believes that if one looks closely enough at any human activity, one will find a similar array of significant variation, and argues for a developmental theory "that would not make us all alike even for one developmental instant" (p. 138). In such a theory, individuals would take different developmental routes, but would arrive at similar places (not exactly the same place) which he calls developmental way stations or zones. These examples of the roundworm and adult cognitive processes, as well as the data from the longitudinal study, all suggest that while variability seems to be the rule, at the same time there are constraints operating to produce some commonality or regularity in arriving at a similar endpoint.

If we accept this variability, how can we begin to conceptualize the constraints that produce commonality and regularity? Before I can approach that question directly, I must describe some basic postulates about the human infant that have informed our approach to the data. For although our efforts have been directed at understanding the infant's intrapsychic development, we begin with a set of premises that differ substantially from those postulated by traditional psychoanalysis. In that earlier view it has been easy to think of psychic organization in terms of the individual alone and as developing from simple elements to later complexity and from no capacity to regulate or inhibit overwhelming instinctual urges to a gradual increase in ego controls. Thus, for example, in Mahler's theory we begin with an undifferentiated passive, helpless infant, equipped with libidinal and aggressive drives, protected against external stimulation, and defended against any awareness of separateness. As the infant slowly becomes aware of outer reality, somewhere in the fifth or sixth month of life, this engagement becomes the impetus for an increasing complexity of organization of drive, reality, conflict, and defense (Mahler, Pine, and Bergman, 1975). By contrast, and here I borrow a phrase from Dr. Sander, we have been "thinking differently" about development. This thinking draws from current biological ideas about living systems, from recent research findings on the infant's perceptual, cognitive, and affective capabilities, and from theoretical advances in affect theory and motivation as represented by the work of Silvan Tomkins.

Biologists, such as von Bertalanffy, have insisted that all living systems *begin* with highly complex organization plus something he termed "primary activity"—that is, an impetus arising endogenously, from within the organism, that governs initiation of action and function. They are equipped to regulate internal changes and exchanges with the external environment. They are, therefore, self-regulating, and seem to be governed by an overriding motivation to maintain their organization and integration. All living systems, then, operate simultaneously within a highly complex internal organizational system and an external, environmental system.

If we apply the biologist's formulation to the human infant, it fits remarkably well with research findings in the last twenty years on the infant's extraordinary perceptual, cognitive, and memory capacities. Excellent summaries of these findings appear in the work of Stern (1983), Lichtenberg (1983), and others. I will present only some of the highlights here. The infant is aware of and alert to the external environment from the beginning, and is an active seeker of stimulation; thus optimal levels of stimulation have become a research focus. The infant does *not* begin with simple, uncoordinated perceptual functions, such as a visual schema and an auditory schema, and gradually construct more complex units, such as visual-auditory schema, as Piaget has argued, but rather begins with a highly complex perceptual system that operates across modalities in an abstract way. With experience and time the infant fills in the details of specific characteristics of objects, but is aware from the beginning of their three dimensionality, of their contours, speed, location, and permanence (Bower, 1977). The infant is also well adapted to live in a human environment, is biased toward human stimulation in general, and rapidly learns to discriminate the specific people in his or her environment. Infants, even neonates, are able to discriminate between stimuli emanating from the inside and stimuli coming from an external source, are aware of the effects of their actions on the external world, and are affectively engaged in their actions. Thus, for example, in a study reported by DeCasper and Carstens (1981), neonates quickly learned to lengthen the pauses between each burst of sucking in order to turn on the sound of a female voice singing. These infants became upset the following day when they were placed in the same experimental situation, this learned behavior did not produce the same result. The fact that infants reacted affectively to this change in the experiment raises the issue of the neonates' affective capacities.

Traditionally, infants have been described as having only two global emotions, namely, quiescence and distress. I have argued elsewhere (Demos, 1988) that infants are born with a full array of affective responses and the capacity to make connections between the antecedents and consequences of these states. My arguments were based on my own videotaped records of infant expressions, on descriptions of infant expressions in the literature, and on Silvan Tomkins's theory of affect. Tomkins conceptualizes affects as biologically inherited programs controlling facial-muscle, autonomic, bloodflow, respiratory, and vocal responses. Each discrete affect program is designed to amplify a particular pattern of stimulation impinging on the organism, and to produce through these facial, autonomic, and respiratory responses an inherently punishing or rewarding experience. Thus "affect either makes good things better or bad things worse" (Tomkins, 1978, p. 203). Affect, then, creates an urgency that is experienced as motivating and that primes the organism to act. Tomkins argues that affect is the primary motivating system, acting as a general amplifer for drives, cognition, perception, and action.

This model of affect, when combined with the available evidence on infant affect expressions, allows us to take neonatal affect seriously, not as a derivative of drives, but as a central, organizing system in its own right. Not only is the neonate capable of experiencing the full range of primary affects, but I would argue that this experience is also real and meaningful, in the sense that the discrete affective quality of each negative affect will be experienced as uniquely punishing, the distinctive qualities of each positive affect will be experienced as uniquely rewarding, and each of these states will prime the infant to respond in a corresponding manner. For example, the interested baby will focus its eyes intently on a stimulus, holding its limbs relatively quiet, and will tend to scan the stimulus for novelty (Wolff, 1965, Stechler and Carpenter, (1974). The joyful baby will smile and tend to produce relaxed, relatively smooth movements of its limbs, savoring the familiar, (Tomkins, 1962; Brazelton, Koslowski, and Main, 1974). The angry baby will square its mouth, lower and pull its brows together, cry intensely, holding the cry for a long time, then pause for a long inspiration, and will tend to kick and thrash its limbs forcefully, or arch its back (Tomkins, 1962; Demos, 1986). By contrast, a distressed infant will produce a more rhythmical cry, with the corners of the mouth pulled down and the inner corners of the brows drawn up, and will tend to move its limbs and head around restlessly (Tomkins, 1962; Wolff, 1969). Thus the discrete characteristics of each affect are important aspects of the infant's early experience because they create discrete motivational dispositions in the infant and therefore become occasions for learning and for organizing experience.

When taken altogether, these findings demonstrate that the infant of the 1980s, as opposed to Freud's, Mahler's, Klein's, Winnicott's, or Piaget's infant, possesses a number of highly organized and coordinated systems that remain more or less constant throughout life in their essentials, but are capable, through learning, of incorporating substantial amounts of specific information. It should be noted at this point in the discussion that this view of development also differs from the view proposed by attachment theory as represented in the works of Bowlby (1969), Ainsworth et al. (1978), Sroufe and Waters (1977), and others. Attachment theory argues that there is a preorganized behavioral, emotional, perceptual system specialized for attachment which has been inherited from our primate ancestors and is designed to decrease the physical distance between the infant and the caregiver in time of danger. By contrast, the view presented here speaks of highly organized and coordinated systems that the infant has inherited from evolutionary processes but conceptualizes these systems at a more basic and general level, e.g., the perceptual, cognitive, affective, motor, and homeostatic systems, which are designed to function equally well in the inanimate or animate world, and in safe as well as dangerous moments. They are also designed to combine and recombine in flexible and changing coassemblies in response to adaptive demands. Thus, in this view, it would make no sense to speak of predetermined "social emotions" or "attachment behaviors." The only biases for human stimuli that have been reported in the literature occur in the perceptual system, but even here they are described as functioning at a general nonspecific level. For example, because of the small size of the infant's ear, it hears high-frequency sounds better than low-frequency sounds; thus, for example, female voices are heard more easily than male voices, but so are all high-frequency noises. Also the visual perceptual preferences of the infant, such as contrast, contours, and movement, are all contained in the human face, but are not exclusively found there. Any object with these characteristics will attract the infant's attention.

How, then, does the infant become bonded to the caregiver? When the infant smiles or gazes with intense interest at the wallpaper, or cries, the wallpaper cannot smile back, or move, make sounds, and provide variations on a theme that will prolong the infant's interest and enjoyment, or comfort the infant the way a human caregiver can. The infant's interactions with people, then, become more sustained and rewarding than interactions with inanimate objects. Thus the multifaceted and growing engagement between infant and caregiver is based not on feeding, as postulated in traditional psychoanalytic theory (A. Freud, 1946), or on such a narrow basis as a preorganized attachment system designed to protect the organism from danger, but rather develops from the broad-based responsiveness of the caregiver to the infant's various affective experiences and cues (Schaffer and Emerson, 1964). If the caregiver is not responsive, then bonding between the infant and that particular caregiver is unlikely to occur.

I would like to return now to our discussion of the infant of the 1980s. Development, in this view, does not go from the global, disorganized, undifferentiated, or simple to the individuated, organized, and complex. Nor does it begin with a specialized, preorganized system for attachment. But, rather the infant begins with complex systems organized at a general abstract level and, capable of flexible intercoordination with each other, and actively acquires specific information relevant to its particular environment. But that is not all. In addition to these continuous capacities, the infant also possesses a maturational timetable that will, at certain developmental moments, introduce new capacities into this ongoing complex organization. And these new capacities, such as crawling, walking, and speaking, to mention only some of the most dramatic changes, must become integrated into the more continuous functions. Thus the human infant is simultaneously experiencing and organizing internally both change and continuity over time, and while all this is going on, the infant is also participating actively in and integrating an interpersonal environment.

Louis Sander has described a series of issues that must get negotiated between infant and caregivers in the first two years of life. These issues incorporate maturational changes in the infant that bring about new possibilities for interpersonal exchanges and patterns of interacting, so that certain capabilities and foci seem to emerge in a particular sequence and in a particular time frame. Thus, for example, in the first month or two of life mother and infant seem primarily, although not exclusively, focused on regulating cycles of waking and sleeping, eating and eliminating. Sander's studies of infants who experienced a change in caregiver after the first ten days of life demonstrate conclusively how much the regulation of these biological functions is a product of the mutual negotiating process between the infant and the caregiver (Sander, et al., 1979). By the third and fourth months of life, infant and caregiver are focused on playful social exchanges. These face-to-face exchanges have received much attention from several investigators using microanalytic techniques who describe complex patterns of behaviors that are mutually regulated by both infant and mother (Fogel, 1977; Stern, 1974; Tronick, Als, and Brazelton, 1980), Sander has called this phase "reciprocal interchanges" and has argued that each infant-mother pair must negotiate how, to what degree, and in what form these interchanges take place. We saw many variations within our sample of cases, all the way from one mother placing the infant outside in a carriage so she would not be tempted to play with him, lest he control her life; to other mothers who could become playfully engaged when the mood suited them, but otherwise seemed unaware of the infant's readiness for play; to mothers who thoroughly enjoyed playing with their infants. I do not have the space here to describe the complete sequence of issues that Sander articulates, but should mention that they provided one of the major frameworks that helped us organize the longitudinal data. (See Sander, 1962, for a fuller description of these issues.) These brief illustrations are meant to suggest the complexity of the young infant's world intrapsychically and interpersonally and to focus our attention on how the young infant manages all of this. How does the infant organize these multiple levels and ongoing processes?

Again I must turn to the work of Louis Sander. He has made fundamental and groundbreaking contributions to our thinking about the organization of the psychological systems of the infant and the infant-mother system. These insights are represented in a few central hypotheses. First,

> The infant's initial inner experience consolidates around the experience of his own recurrent states. A capacity for inner experience exists at the outset of postnatal life — as an initial level in the organization of consciousness. This initial root of the sense of self does not await the organization of a body image or depend on production effects, or on visual or tactile experience, . . . The ego begins as a "state" ego, rather than a body ego [Sander, 1982, p. 20].

Sander's assertion that the capacity for inner experience exists from the beginning of life and represents an initial level in the organization of consciousness, which he has termed "state," provides an important conceptual framework for understanding the infant's efforts to organize experience. State then becomes the organismic context within which events are registered and can be operated upon. Sander has argued that "state has a very specific empirically valid definition as a descriptor of the complexity yet the unity of a living system. It is defined as that configuration of the values of a set of variables that characterize the functioning of the system as a whole, a configuration that recurs, and can be recognized whenever that same configuration recurs again." He gives the example in the newborn of the range of states on the sleep-awake continuum. And I have argued and presented evidence elsewhere that the waking states, as described in the literature, are affect states (Demos, 1988). Affects are discrete, observable states, central to regulation, adaptation, and communication. The concept of state, then, provides us with operational and observational access to the infant's inner world.

Sander goes on to say in his second hypothesis that "the infant's own states, where coherent, recurrent, desired, or essential to key regulatory coordinations that become established with the caregiver, become the primary target or *goals* for behavior." If we can accept for the moment that these initial states, as described in the literature are affect states, then Sander's second hypothesis fits well with Tomkins's (1981) statements regarding affect dynamics.

> In the case of the human being, the fact that he is innately endowed with positive and negative affects which are inherently rewarding or punishing, and the fact that he is innately endowed with a mechanism which automatically registers all his conscious experience in memory, and the fact that he is innately endowed with receptor, motor, and analyzer mechanisms organized as a feedback circuit, together make it all but inevitable that he will develop the following General Images (1) Positive affect should be maximized; (2) Negative affect should be minimized; (3) Affect inhibition should be minimized; (4) Power to maximize positive affect, to minimize negative affect, to minimize affect inhibition should be maximized. [p. 328].

Thus the goal to reexperience positive affect, or to re-create the situations associated with the experience of positive affect, while minimizing or avoiding negative affect, can motivate and shape the young child's behavior from birth onward. The Papouseks and their associate come to a similar conclusion based on their experimental work with young infants. "Infants appear to be just as attracted to the expectation of a pleasurable outcome that accompanies success as they are motivated to avoid the negative affect experienced with too much incongruency, dissonance, or the inability to discover the contingencies and adjust their own behavior accordingly" (Papousek, Papousek, and Koester, 1986, p. 99). Dr. Kaplan and I have reported in a recent issue of *Psychoanalysis and Contemporary Thought* (Demos and Kaplan, 1986) a description of two infant girls. When alone, on separate occasions, at roughly five and a half weeks of age, they were each observed to regulate their gazing in order to overcome mild fussiness. The sequence was as follows. As fussy vocalizations began and as arms and legs began to cycle, each baby began to move her head from side to side and started to scan the environment. They each found an object, visually focused on it, became motorically and vocally quiet, and continued to gaze for several minutes. Then they would look away, the fussiness would begin to build up again, and they would return their gaze to the object, once again becoming focused and quiet. This cycle was repeated several times before the mothers returned and intervened. We are assuming that, although the initial scanning may have been unmotivated and part of the fussy movements and thus the first encounter with the object may have been accidental, the subsequent refocusing on the same object looked like an active attempt by each infant to repeat a successful organizing experience. In other words, the infants were motivated to recapture the affective experience of interest with its organizing potential, which felt more rewarding than the unfocused, fussy state.

The goal of reexperiencing positive affect and avoiding or escaping from negative affect, then, is one kind of lawful dynamic that seems to be operating in development. It represents one of the places we can look for lawful relationships among variables, such as the relative balance between positive and negative affect experienced by the child, the specific people, situations, and affects involved, and at what intensities. The details of this learning will vary from child to child and produce different patterns, but these variations will nevertheless be governed to some extent by the child's efforts to enhance positive affect and to minimize, avoid, and/or escape from negative affect. The variety and complexity of these patterns can be illustrated by several of the children in the longitudinal study, each of whom was faced with an uncontainable and insoluable problem which required each gradually to impose idiosyncratic constrictions and solutions. Three families, and I will refer to them by number — numbers 6, 14, and 15 — showed a marked ambivalence toward the child, which in each case involved a major interactional issue, and thus cut across a wide range of situations and activities. Each of these parents seemed stuck, and could only act repeatedly on both sides of their ambivalence, at every opportunity. Having failed to resolve these major issues themselves, they were in no position to help their children resolve them.

In family 6 the issue involved an ambivalence about closeness. The mother could allow closeness for only so long and then would withdraw, but would become angry if the child turned to another adult for comfort or interaction. The father was mostly absent and unsupportive. This child gradually became defiant, turned away from help offered by others, and preferred and insisted on doing things alone. In family 14 the ambivalent issue involved enjoyment of life. The mother would encourage or permit the child's participation in an activity, but in the middle of the child's excitement and enjoyment, she would suddenly interfere and prohibit the activity — a veritable killjoy. The father was more positive and responsive, but was frequently absent. This child gradually became oversensitive to intrusions, narrowed his interests, and defended them with stubborn persistence. In family 15, the mother's ambivalence centered around how much support and help to give her child, and yet still help her child to be tough and strong. Thus she would usually begin by providing help, but would then start to tease and frustrate the child until the child dissolved in tears, at which point the mother would once again become comforting and supportive. The father was benign but uninvolved. This child gradually took on the mother's teasing, aggressive style and developed an insistent need to be in active control of interactions and a grim tenseness in pursuing plans.

Two other families produced a different kind of uncontainable problem, namely, a minimal investment in the child. In family 2, although the mother hovered anxiously over the child's physical functions, her more characteristic stance was to feel overwhelmed and to experience her child's active initiatives as exasperating or bad. Thus she offered no support, protection, or facilitation, and often tried, unsuccessfully, to curtail the child's activities by yelling at or hitting the child. The father, at times, could facilitate the child's efforts, but he was also harsh and impatient with the child's expressions of distress or fear. This child learned to fear and comply with the father, and to defy and oppose the mother, thereby existing always in a win-or-lose situation, and never experiencing the middle ground of negotiation, compromise, cooperation, etc. Without support for a wide range of initiatives or protection from danger, this child also began to constrict his activities and skills. In family 20, the parents were very young and the mother felt trapped and depressed by parental responsibilities. She developed a breezy, inattentive, almost negligent style of parenting. Father was somewhat more attentive, but both expected the child to be independent and to work things out on his own. As this child struggled to master a variety of situations without parental help, he manifested a defensive or precocious independence, his plans became more limited, less ambitious, and he focused on learning new skills, turning away from people and relationships.

In all of these cases involving an uncontainable problem, the child was faced with a pervasive, insoluble difficulty. Thus each family had failed to keep the level of challenges within the child's capacities to resolve, and in each case the child responded by constricting its scope in some way. It looked as if each child did so in order to maximize the possibilities for mastery and success and to minimize defeat, or in other words, in order to cut the challenge down to a more manageable size. Thus these children preferred to do the doable, and to avoid or escape from the undoable, even though that choice resulted in a constriction of their focus and their repertoire of strategies and skills. The preservation of an area of positive successful functioning and the avoidance of failure therefore seemed to be paramount.

But there are other factors operating in the solutions just described which involve the importance of the child's experience of him/herself as an active agent in determining events. In order to discuss this factor I must return to Sander's hypotheses and his third proposition.

> . . . infant competence in initiating and organizing self-regulatory behaviors to achieve desired states as goals represents a systems competence, i.e., dependent on facilitation of goal realization as well as providing conditions for the infant's initiation of goal-organized behavior. Such systems competence insures a sense of agency in the infant. The emergence of infant-as-agent must be granted by the system because it means a reorganization of the system to admit the newcomer. If the system is such that it can permit the entrance of a new agent within it, it provides the conditions which establish not only the capacity for self-awareness, but conditions which insure the use of such inner awareness by the infant as a frame of reference in organizing his own adaptive behavior, i.e., being in a position that permits him to appreciate what behaviors lead to what states. The valence of this inner experience under these conditions of self-initiated goal realization will be felt as the infant's "own" [Sander, 1982, p. 17].

In this proposition Sander is not only stressing the importance of experiencing the self as an active agent but is also emphasizing that the capacity to use one's inner awareness as a frame of reference in organizing one's own adaptive behavior is directly related to the family's capacity to allow and foster the growth of a new agent within its midst. His fourth proposition states that "each infant-caregiver system constructs its own unique configuration of regulatory constraint on the infant's initiative to organize self-regulatory behavior, which configurations then become enduring coordinations or adaptive strategies between the interacting participants" (p. 17). Here, then, is another place to look for lawful relationships among variables. There are an infinite number of ways in which infants and families can construct configurations of regulatory constraint on initiative. In the remaining pages I would like to describe some of the configurations we observed by focusing on how this dynamic interacts with the affective dynamic described earlier. In particular I would like to focus on the importance of affective sequences in the construction of these configurations.

Earlier I spoke of the relative balance of positive and negative affect in the infant's experience, and described how the infant seeks to enhance positive affect and to avoid or minimize the effects of negative affect. Here I would like to discuss how the motivational impact of these goals is increased when positive and negative affects occur in particular sequences. A number of sequences are possible, but I will be focusing on positive-negative-positive affective sequences and positive-negative-negative sequences.

When positive affect is frequently embedded in a sequence of positive affect, followed by negative affect, followed by positive affect, its motivational force is augmented because the child learns that positive affect can be reliably reestablished, that negative affect can be reliably endured or managed, or gotten over, and that the child him/herself can be an active agent in causing these things to happen. Such a sequence can be experienced at the micro level, which would involve momentary shifts in affect. For example, a child experiences interest and enjoyment as she plays, then encounters an obstacle, and expresses distress and anger. This expression brings the mother, who helps the child resolve the difficulty, and the child reexperiences interest and enjoyment. The child's experience of herself as an active agent occurs because of the contingency between her expression of distress and the mother's appearance. When this contingency has been reliable from the beginning, the child learns by the third month of life to signal for help intentionally, and fully expects the caregiver to respond. Once the caregiver becomes involved, the degree of agency the child continues to experience is a function of the skill of the parent in offering help while still allowing the child some scope to participate in the solution. This can be done in a number of ways such as simplifying the task for the child which allows the child to proceed without further help, or offering verbal encouragement, etc.

This positive-negative-positive affective sequence can also be experienced at the macro level, which involves a more prolonged struggle that eventually ends in mastery. And it can involve any combination of positive and negative affects. When it becomes a characteristic family sequence, and therefore occurs in many settings and across many issues, it gradually creates in the child a strong expectation that things will work out, and that difficulties can be mastered. Translated into motivational terms, the young child experiences one or more of the following: I can do things, I can solve problems, I can endure frustration and discouragement because I know things will get better, bad things don't last long, etc. When such a motivational stance is firmly established, the child approaches each new situation with confidence and optimism, and can persist, in spite of difficulties.

The four families in our longitudinal sample that produced the most well-functioning, resilient children all shared two characteristics that were either not present or were present to a more limited degree in the other families. They maximized opportunities for the shared experience of positive affects, and they were quick to reestablish shared positive affect whenever there was a break, e.g., an angry scolding, or an experience of negative affect by the child. Thus they were frequently engaged in creating positive-negative-positive affective sequences. Mothers 7 and 10, for example, although they maximized opportunities for the shared experience of positive affect on many occasions, were both also capable of sudden, harsh prohibitions, thereby inducing distress or even fear in their children. But they would both quickly make up afterward by hugging and kissing their child. Thus, however intense or distressing and frightening these moments may have been for each child, they were characteristically brief and were reliably followed by an affectionate coming back together. They rarely left their child in an intense negative state and seemed to be committed to reestablishing positive communication. Neither child showed evidence of a generalized fearfulness as a result of these sudden, intense barrages. By contrast, mothers 1 and 16 were not harsh disciplinarians, and therefore did not create such dramatic extremes for their children, but consistently fostered positive exchanges with them. All four mothers also found ways to help their respective children whenever they experienced distress, anger, fear, or shame in the ordinary course of events. For example, mother 10 would jolly-up or distract her child following a frustration or disappointment, whereas mother 1 was more likely to come up with a creative compromise and thereby create a positive, cooperative experience. And mother 16 bent over backward to try to facilitate her child's wishes, thereby avoiding or quickly remedying negative experiences for her child.

As can be seen from these few examples, there are many subtle differences in the way these sequences occurred. These details are important in shaping the child's unique psychic organization and in creating the specific strategies the child will have available for use in coping with negative affect or in reestablishing positive affect. Ideally, in order for the positive-negative-positive affective sequence to be most effective, the parent has to acknowledge or respond directly to the negative affect, as well as help the child reestablish a positive state. For example, if a child becomes frustrated while trying to build with blocks, the mother might say something like, "Oh, those blocks just won't do what you want them to," in a sympathetic voice, thereby verbalizing the child's frustration, and then either offer instrumental help with the blocks or emotional support, e.g., "try again, maybe it will work this time." Each subtle variation will create its own unique configuration of strategies. Mother 10, for example, reestablished positive affect by distracting or jollying-up her child after a frustration or a scolding. At such times, she seemed to be teaching her child to forget about what just happened and to move on to something else more positive. This capacity can be very useful in certain situations, but it does not help the child cope directly with the negative affect, and thus does not provide the child with experiences of enduring such states when they cannot be quickly forgotten or escaped. This child was remarkably adaptive and resilient, but she was also vulnerable to feeling overwhelmed by intense negative affect, in certain situations.

I would like to shift our attention now to positive-negative-negative affective sequences. These generally occur in some mixture with positive-negative-positive sequences. In two families manifesting this mixed pattern, numbers 3 and 5, the parents only encouraged behaviors that gratified them and actively discouraged or ignored all other behaviors. In these family contexts the children gradually gave up attending to and pursuing their own initiatives and focused on their parents as the sources of important cues. Winnicott has described this process as the beginning of "the false self," but here I would like to emphasize the affective dynamics involved. I have suggested elsewhere (Demos, 1982) that every affective moment involves three components occurring simultaneously: a trigger or stimulus, the affect per se, which involves facial, vocal, and autonomic patterns of expression and experience, and the response, which includes plans, behaviors, and fantasies, as well as memories of similar events in the past. A parental response, therefore, affects all three components of an experience, regardless of the parent's particular focus or intent. When parents focus on their child's behavior, as did these parents, the affective-motivational component of the child's experience is not acknowledged, validated, or shared. Thus opportunities for maximizing the child's interests and enjoyments, invested in many of the child's plans and behaviors, or for minimizing and mastering the child's distresses, angers, shames, or fears evoked by ordinary events, are lost.

When these children engaged in behaviors that interested or pleased their parents, positive-negative-positive affective sequences occurred, but the positive affective components of the experience were not acknowledged and therefore not maximized. And at all other times when these children engaged in behaviors that displeased or did not interest their parents, there was no effort or commitment by their parents to help the children overcome difficulties or to reestablish positive communications after a scolding. Thus there were many occasions when positive-negative-negative affective sequences were experienced by these children. For example, the child would manifest interest in an activity, encounter a frustrating or distressing difficulty, try to engage the parent, and the parent would ignore, scold, or discourage the child, thereby compounding the child's original distress and/or anger. In these sequences, the child's positive affects were minimized, the negative affects were compounded and intensified, and the child was then left alone to cope with the consequences. In motivational terms, these children were learning that their affective states and the plans, ideas, and fantasies related to them did not seem to be very important or valuable. Thus the inclination to use their inner awareness of these states and plans as a frame of reference for organizing adaptive behavior was not supported. In terms of agency they were learning that by themselves they are unable to develop skills and to solve problems, unable to endure or master negative affect states, and unable to reestablish positive affect states. At such times, they experienced themselves as devalued, ineffective, and helpless. In such a state the need for parents is heightened, and these children focused all their efforts on obtaining and sustaining their parents' involvement. In this shift away from using an awareness of inner states as a useful frame of reference for guiding behavior, these two children began to develop skills as readers of parental states and availability, began to overvalue the parents, and to develop those abilities and behaviors that pleased the parents. Thus the range and depth of their own unique developmental potentialities were considerably narrowed.

Positive-negative-negative affective sequences can occur with many subtle variations, including the relative intensities of the positive and negative elements, the particular negative affects involved, the frequency of occurrence, and in many different mixtures with positive-negative-positive sequences. Thus one parent can be committed to maximizing positive affect while the other can be more focused on controlling the child's behaviors and create many positive-negative-negative experiences for the child. Or a parent can be invested in the child's initiatives and promote positive experiences at one point in development, but become much more punitive and controlling at another point. Thus, for example, in families 9 and 18, when each child became more assertive and more invested in his or her own plans at around sixteen to eighteen months of age, these mothers became more focused on molding their children into obedient, docile, conformists than on maximizing positive affects, and their increased frequency of prohibitions produced an increase in positive-negative-negative sequences for these children. I described earlier three families who were caught in ambivalent stances toward their children and thus they constantly created and then spoiled positive experiences for their children. This is a particularly insidious form of a positive-negative-negative sequence, because the positive element is shared and maximized up to a point and is then spoiled; thus the child's hopes are raised and then dashed repeatedly. The child must find a way to protect against this "seduction into disappointment" and, as described earlier, each one seemed to develop a unique configuration of constrictions and strategies that preserved a positive area of functioning, protected from parental intrusion, while avoiding negative consequences.

Six families in the longitudinal sample, numbers 2, 4, 8, 12, 13, and 19, produced few occasions for the sharing of positive affect and manifested predominately positive-negative-negative affective sequences. They consistently interfered with or failed to support their children's interests and enjoyments, and compounded and intensified their children's negative states with shaming, punishment, abandonment, or lack of support. Thus, for all six of these children, experiences of positive affect that occurred in interactions with parents almost always led to negative consequences. Depending on the balance of forces, these children tended to become either defiant or compliant, but in either case their sense of agency was severely constricted. For example, in family 4, the mother had early on experienced the child's initiatives as a threat to her control and, as was described earlier, had put the child outside in a carriage so as not to be tempted to play with him. As soon as this child began to display initiative in a persistent manner, somewhere in the middle of the first year, the parents perceived life as a battle and stated unequivocally "he will fight, but we will win!" They presented this child with a trio of insurmountable forces: (1) a united front, (2) hypervigilance, which included a relentless interference with the child's plans, and (3) the use of shaming and humiliation to obtain compliance. Following an illness at around fifteen months, the child finally gave up an active struggle and became listless, wan, and an irregular sleeper and eater. Family 19 was also relatively inflexible and adopted negative techniques to obtain compliance, namely, spankings, angry commands, isolation, and threats of abandonment and banishment, allowing the child only two choices — surrender or defiance. But unlike child 4, whose initiatives were relentlessly interfered with by hypervigilant parents, child 19 was left alone for long periods of time and was able, when alone, to carry out her own plans and to act out defiant fantasies and conflicts around obedience.

As can be seen even from the fragmentary examples of affective sequences I have presented, there are many variations in time, place, density of affect, direction of change of affect, people, and actions involved in each episode. Tomkins calls such episodes "scenes," which are the most basic elements in life as it is lived; in other words, the scene is the basic unit of analysis. The simplest scene includes at least one affect and at least one object of that affect, which may be the perceived activator or the response to the activator or to the affect. It is a happening with a perceived beginning and end. Because the human infant is capable of perceiving the connections between its own states, actions, and effects on others or on the environment, it is assumed that the infant quickly begins to relate one scene to another. Perhaps the simplest and most powerful principle for relating one event to another is on the basis of similarity. But, as Tomkins has argued, similarity is not merely repetition, since exact repetition leads to habituation and boredom, but similarity also with a difference — variations on a theme. Any of the elements mentioned above, e.g., time, place, people, actions, or affects, can vary or stay the same, in combination or singly. Similarity can also be perceived at a higher level of abstraction by perceiving analogies between scenes.

When the infant connects one affect-laden scene with another affect-laden scene, what Tomkins has called "psychological magnification" occurs. In psychological magnification, the meaning of a scene is magnified by its perceived similarity to earlier scenes. According to Tomkins two propositions follow from this. First, "the effect of any set of scenes is indeterminate until the future happens and either further magnifies or attenuates such experience," and second, "the consequence of any experience is not singular but plural . . . there are *many* effects which change in time" (Tomkins, 1978, p. 219). "Any gratuity must be built upon to reward in the long run; any threat must be elaborated by further action to become traumatic" (Tomkins, 1985, p. 20). Thus development cannot be adequately described by a unilinear model of progression and regression; perhaps an image of an irregularly branching tree comes closer to representing the psychological phenomena described here. Through psychological magnification families of scenes are created with varying degrees of connectedness. As this process occurs, the individual begins to construct scripts to deal with sets of scenes.

In Tomkins's formulation, scripts are sets of ordering rules for the production, evaluation, interpretation, prediction, and control of a magnified set of scenes. They are selective in the number and types of scenes they order; they are incomplete rules and vary in their accuracy, and are therefore continually reordered and changing. In the early stages of magnification the set of scenes determine the script, but as magnification increases, the script increasingly determines the scenes. Scripts also have the property of modularity, whereby the modular components of a script can be combined, recombined, and decomposed. Some of the major components of any script involve specification of quantities, ratios, and directionality of positive and negative affects in general, e.g., how much positive and negative affect is anticipated and enacted? in what ratio? and of specific affects, e.g., is excitement greater than anger? does interest lead to distress? They also specify different strategies of relating risks, costs, and benefits so that one can strive for the greatest benefits and least costs at least risks; or strive for optimal benefits and costs at a moderate level of risk; or strive for modest benefits with modest costs and modest risks.

Tomkins argues that varying quantities and ratios of positive and negative affects will lead to the formation of four major types of scripts, with a number of subtypes for each depending on other components. The four major types are: (1) affluent scripts which govern predominantly positive affect, (2) limitation-remediation scripts which attempt to transform negative into positive affect scenes with varying degrees of success, (3) contamination scripts which govern ambivalent and plurivalent scenes that resist complete and enduring contamination, and (4) antitoxic scripts which govern purely negative affect scenes with limited success. Everyone will enjoy some positive scenes via scripts of affluence, remedy some negative scenes, be plagued with enduring ambivalent scenes, and be threatened with some toxic scenes. But individuals will differ in the degree to which any type of script dominates their psychological space, either at any given moment, or during a lifetime. The domination of any type of script and interscript relationships will be affected by the density of the ratio of positive to negative affect. When this density reaches a critical level, it can become a relatively stable equilibrium, both self-validating and self-fulfilling. At that point the possibility of radical change, though always present, becomes a diminishing probability, requiring even more densely magnified countervailing forces of positive and negative affect.

This has been an incomplete and somewhat sketchy description of Tomkins's script theory. But I hope it has been sufficient to convey the way in which it conceptualizes the lawfulness of psychological experiences, without sacrificing complexity. Earlier, I described affective sequences that were being formed and were discernible in the first two years of life. With the aid of this formulation, we were able to see how these sequences were leading to the formation of early scripts. The fate of these early scripts is yet to be determined. This is work in progress, and there is much data yet to be analyzed. There are extensive data on the third year of life; data at age six, when these children entered the first grade, include observations of the children in school, testing, and interviews with teachers and parents; and recently a follow-up study of these individuals who are in their late twenties was completed. These data, collected under the direction of Dr. Sander, include projective, cognitive, and neurological testing as well as interview material collected over several visits with the subjects, and in separate interviews, with their parents.

What I have presented here represents our current state of thinking and the formulations that helped us make sense of the first two years of life, and I have tried to illustrate at least some of these ideas with clinical examples. I have focused on the conceptual framework because I believe it is a new way to think about development, and because we are now facing a major conceptual challenge as we try to understand the developments over the longer life span. Many things happen between the ages of two and twenty-five. For example, fathers, who are not much in evidence during the first two years, begin to play a far more meaningful role, as do peers and other adults. And of course, there are the monumental psychological and maturational changes that occur in adolescence. We will undoubtedly need to develop new concepts and to integrate them with what we have found useful thus far.

REFERENCES

Ainsworth, M., Blehar, M., Waters, E. & Wall, S. (1978), *Patterns of Attachment: Observations in the Strange Situation and at Home.* Hillsdale, NJ: Lawrence Erlbaum Associates.
Bower, T.G.R. (1977), *The Perceptual World of the Child.* Cambridge, MA: Harvard University Press.
Bowlby, J. (1969), *Attachment.* Vol. 1: *Attachment and Loss.* New York: Basic Books.
Brazelton, T. B., Koslowski, B. & Main, M. (1974), The origins of reciprocity: The early mother-infant interaction. In: *The Effect of the Infant on the Caregiver,* ed. M. Lewis & L. Rosenblum. New York: Wiley, pp. 49–76.
DeCasper, A. J. & Carstens, A. A. (1981), Contingencies of stimulation: Effects on learning and emotion in neonates. *Infant Behav. & Devel.,* 4:19–35.
Demos, E. V. (1982), Affect in early infancy: Physiology or psychology? *Psychoanal. Inq.,* 1:553–574.
——— (1986), Crying in early infancy: An illustration of the motivational function of affect. In: *Affective Development in Early Infancy.* Norwood, NJ: Ablex, pp. 39–73.
——— (1988), Affect and the development of the self. A new frontier. In: *Frontiers in Self Psychology: Progress in Self Psychology, Vol. 3,* ed. A. Goldberg. Hillsdale, NJ: The Analytic Press, 27–53.
——— & Kaplan, S. (1986), Motivation and affect reconsidered: Affect biographies of two infants. *Psychoanal. & Contemp. Thought,* 9:147–221.
Fogel, A. (1977), Temporal organization in mother-infant, face to face interactions. In: *Studies in Mother-Infant Interaction,* ed. R Schaffer. London: Academic Press, pp. 119–151.
Freud, A. (1977), The psychoanalytic study of infantile feeding disturbances. *The Psychoanalytic Study of the Child,* 2:119–132. New York: International Universities Press.
Gruber, H. (1985), Divergence in evolution and individuality in development. In: *Evolution and Developmental Psychology,* ed. G. Butterworth, J. Rutkowska & M. Scaife. New York: St. Martin's Press, pp. 133–147.
Lichtenberg, J. (1983), *Psychoanalysis and Infant Research.* Hillsdale, NJ: The Analytic Press.
Mahler, M., Pine, F. & Bergman, A. (1975), *The Psychological Birth of the Human Infant.* New York: Basic Books.
Papousek, H., Papousek, M. & Koester, L. S. (1986), Sharing emotionality and sharing

knowledge: A microanalytic approach to parent-infant communication. In: *Measuring Emotions in Infants and Children,* ed. C. Izard & P. Read. Cambridge: Cambridge University Press, 2:93–123.

Sander, L. (1962), Issues in early mother-child interaction. *J. Amer. Acad. Child Psychiat.,* 1:141–166.

———— (1982), Toward a logic of organization in psychobiologic development. Paper presented at the 13th Margaret S. Mahler Symposium in Philadelphia.

———— Stechler, G. Burns, P. & Lee, A. (1979), Change in infant and caregiver variables over the first two months of life: Integration of action in early development. In: *Origins of the Infant's Social Responsiveness,* ed. E. Thomas. Hillsdale, NJ: Lawrence Erlbaum Associates, pp. 809–836.

Schaffer, H. R. & Emerson, P. (1964), *The Development of Social Attachments in Infancy.* Monogr. no. 94, Society for Research in Child Development, vol. 29, no. 3.

Sroufe, A., & Waters, E. (1977), Attachment as an organizational construct. *Child Devel.,* 48:1184–1199.

Stechler, G. & Carpenter, G. (1974), A viewpoint on early affective development. In: *The Exceptional Infant.* Vol. 1: *The Normal Infant.* Seattle, WA: Special Child Publications, pp. 163–189.

Stern, D. (1974), Mother and infant at play: The dyadic interaction involving facial, vocal and gaze behaviors. In: *The Effect of the Infant on Its Caregiver,* ed. M. Lewis & L. Rosenblum. New York: Wiley, pp. 187–213.

———— (1983), The early development of schemas of self, other snd "self with other." In: *Reflections on Self Psychology,* ed. J. Lichtenberg & S. Kaplan. Hillsdale, NJ: The Analytic Press, pp. 49–84.

Tomkins, S. S. (1962), *Affect, Imagery, Consciousness.* Vol. 1: *The Positive Affects.* New York: Springer.

———— (1978), Script theory: Differential magnification of affects. *Nebraska Symposium on Motivation,* 26:201–236. Lincoln: University of Nebraska Press.

———— (1981), The quest for primary motives: Biography and autobiography of an idea. *J. Person. & Soc. Psychol.,* 41:306–329.

Tronick, F., Als, H. & Brazelton, T. B. (1980), Monadic phases: A structural descriptive analysis of infant-mother, face-to-face interaction. *Merrill-Palmer Quart.,* 26:3–24.

Winnicott, D. W. (1971), *Playing and Reality.* London: Tavistock.

Wolff, P. (1965), The development of attention in young infants. *Annals N.Y. Acad, Sci.,* 118:815–830.

———— (1969), The natural history of crying and other vocalizations in early infancy. In: *Determinants of Infant Behavior,* 2:81–109. London: Methuen.

January 1988

Discussions

DR. TOLPIN:

It is a privilege to discuss this impressive sample of the larger developmental study Dr. Demos carried out with Dr. Louis Sander. I have been asked to discuss the implications of their findings and formulations for psychoanalytic theory, and to approach this task from the standpoint of self psychology. To anticipate, it seems to me that Dr. Demos's two fold emphasis — on the regulation of self esteem by the joint work parents and children do together, and on the effect of this work on confidence, assertiveness, continuing initiative, and capacities to recover from failures — is identical with that of self psychology.

A Separate Psychological Organization from Birth On: A Point of Departure for Psychoanalysis

Despite the fact that their paternity is different and that they originate in different methods of conception, "Sander's Baby" and "Kohut's Baby" bear a striking resemblance to one another. That is to say, the psychological organization of the healthy baby and young child each describes is very similar, and it differs in essential respects from that of the baby posited by traditional psychoanalysis, modern ego psychology, and object-relations theories. To consider Sander's and Kohut's formulations and their implications for psychoanalytic theory it is first necessary to ask how the ideas underlying their respective contributions are alike. I shall mention three critical developmental ideas that are essential to the thinking of each. All three are a major point of departure for psychoanalytic theory.

1. The healthy baby is born with complexly functioning, designed-in equipment that makes for being a separate psychic entity, an independent center of initiative, impressions, and experience. Put differently, normal inborn equipment constitutes a differentiated (self) organization that exists in a phase-appropriate form from birth on. Naturally, in order to work right, the inborn equipment that constitutes an organized self requires expectable parental care. (In Kohut's words, there is never a time of a nonself, provided that the baby is part of the usual empathic world constituted by parents.)

2. Even the youngest babies have phase-specific, proto-social tendencies — they are so constituted as to want to connect up with the human and inanimate world "out there." Moreover, even the youngest babies have the capacities needed to participate actively in making the connections

---

Read at the 25th Anniversary Celebration of the Child and Adolescent Psychotherapy Program, Institute for Psychoanalysis of Chicago, October 17, 1987.

they avidly seek (these capacities are an integral part of the inborn equipment and interdigitating parental care).

Put differently, infants come equipped to need, seek out, and derive pleasure from a whole spectrum of affectively meaningful experiences with their human partners, provided these partners cooperate. Thus, they experience important others as fascinating, enlivening, and reassuring; they experience self-enhancing pleasure from their own initiative, competency, and effectualness with others, as well as from the sensual experiences that are usually stressed; and they experience pleasure from their success in eliciting the different kinds of parental participation with them that they need when their body-mind self is right. (The importance of the child's pleasure in playing an active part in his or her own recovery is largely overlooked in traditional psychoanalytic theory.) For example, infants derive a very important form of pleasure from eliciting the kinds of responses they need to recover their equilibrium after they have fallen apart (cf. Tolpin, 1971), or to allay their fears and regain a disrupted feeling of safety. This very early form of pleasure from being effectual in obtaining what is needed to regain psychological integrity continues. Later, small children like those Dr. Demos describes derive pleasure from eliciting responses that restore their shaken confidence, lost enthusiasm, and jolted expectations of mastery after they have failed. (I shall return to this point.)

When the child's complex, phase-appropriate equipment interdigitates with normal parental responsiveness this psychoanalytic baby experiences pleasure from a broad range of possibilities and does not have to be coaxed into reality from quasi-pathological psychic positions acting as magnets for later regression. For example, the infant and young child do not have to "progress" from primary narcissism, objectlessness, or hallucinatory wish fulfillment — from the start of life the human child is connected to, and actively seeks, the reality "out there" as a supreme source of inner pleasure and comfort.

3. The infant and young child, as well as the parents who care for them, are bound to go through repeated cycles of pleasure and the frustration of unpleasure — (this is part of Dr. Demos's cycle of positive/ negative affective experiences, and self psychology's cycle of cohesion/ minifragmentations). This amounts to saying that the psychology of everyday life is not all purified pleasure. Distress and frustration are inevitable, and parental assists that help the child to recover from inevitable disruptions are part of the immunization needed to make distress tolerable. Children bit-by-bit write their "scripts" from their experiences of pleasure, as well as from their experiences of distress and disruptions, and from the parental assists that help restore capacities for

pleasure. From all of these they gradually take over (internalize) capacities for pleasure in themselves, and these capacities are built into capacities to recover on their own. These internalized capacities gradually build up their confidence in the reliability of their own self-maintaining, pleasure-providing mental workings. More often than not children are responded to with pleasure—for example, from early on babies' gurgling with delight, chortling with laughter, pleasure in "conversing" are infectious—and they are also assisted to recover from disruptions and thereby return to a "positive" state. That is to say, parents who are reasonably together themselves enjoy their children, and they also respond to the signs and signals of disrupted cohesion and minifragmentation with needed psychological glue.

When parents are suffering from the self disorders that make them, for example, absent, harsh, and irritable, indifferent, and negligent, hypochondriacally absorbed with the child's body, needy of confirmation and acknowledgment for themselves (cf. Demos's descriptions) on balance, the "scripts" are negative—recovery-promoting parental responses are faulty, and hence the child's psychic structure is ultimately deficient or faulty—and the silent process of transmuting internalization (writing positive scripts) is off to a bad start. Then children who consistently experience faulty parenting more and more doubt their own capacities because they cannot rely on themselves, and a primary source of pleasure from internalized self esteem and expectations of mastery is unavailable.

There is no time here for an inventory of all the other ways Sander's and Kohut's respective brainchildren resemble each other. In fact, however, the complex, differentiated self of the "baby watchers," including Sander and others like Stern (1985) and Emde (1980), and the cohesive self and its selfobjects (Tolpin, 1971), are two sides of the same coin. The pictures of the child *constructed* from longitudinal observation and the child *reconstructed* from selfobject transferences are not identical, nor should they be—each bears the authentic stamp of its origins in different methods of observation that rely on different data. The data of self-selfobject theory derive mainly from the "psychological insides" inferred from analytic patients' transferences, dreams, and free associations. For example, these data lead to the emphasis on the normal child's inner feeling of pride and expansiveness, of flying high, of standing tall in response to the gleam in the parent's eye. Conversely, the data from Dr. Demos's Developmental studies lead to placing emphasis on the *observable manifestations* of feelings of injury, deflation, and rage when normal childhood pride is persistently punctured by a parent who is a killjoy, who turns on and off, who does not spontaneously participate or assist with injuries and the restoration of pride. That is, Demos's and

Sander's emphasis is more on the psychological insides that can be empathically inferred from the child's immediately observable behaviors — e.g., the mood changes, defiance, retreats, etc. — i.e., the beginnings of the extraordinarily important defensive organizations that are heir to the impact of erratic, intrusive, hypochondriacal, self-centered parenting.

Whatever their differences, the confluence of the findings and formulations from these two different methods leads to "a different psychoanalytic baby" (Tolpin, 1986). By "a different baby" I mean a different conception of the normality and pathology of childhood psychological development. Differing somewhat from Emde, I think this different conception shakes the developmental foundation of psychoanalysis. Beyond that I think the changed developmental conception calls for significant revisions in psychoanalytic theory and practice. Specifically, a number of id- and ego-psychology and object-relations assumptions about normal development that bear directly on treatment require rethinking and rearrangement.

I shall mention a few of these assumptions: the idea that a self and other are constituted by taming drives and separating out from a primary state of fusion and undifferentiation; the idea that there is an antithesis between the pleasure principle and the reality principle, between primary narcissism and object love; the various ideas of entitlement, normal and pathological pride, the repetition compulsion, etc. In any case, the essence of the revisions called for revolve around two fundamental implications of the work of Sander and of self psychology: (1) the state of the self organization is always uppermost in considerations of normality and pathology — its relative security (cohesion), capacities for self regulation, pride and pleasure, self-esteem, etc.; and (2) the state of the self and the multiple parental functions necessary for intactness and pleasure are inextricably intertwined in every stage and phase of childhood.

In the rest of my discussion I shall elaborate further on the convergence of Sander's and Kohut's ideas, and close with some thoughts on The Different Psychoanalytic Baby.

Child Observation and Reconstructions of Childhood — Both Roads Lead to the Centrality of the Self and Parental Functions

Kohut reconstructed the normal workings of the child's mind by reaching back into childhood via the royal road of patients' transferences. Via this route he discovered that originally normal childhood *needs* (distinguished from wishes) that were persistently thwarted return in novel transferences. These transferences take the form of patients' intensified needs for the gleam in the therapist's eye, for his or her calming presence, firmness, judgment, and strengths, for his or her basic alikeness. The patient's persisting childhood needs are for parents' "selfobject functions" — functions with enduring intrapsychic impact because they are part of the child's self organization. In normal development parents' selfobject functions are first experienced as part of the normal workings of the child's own mind. The accessibility of the parents and their needed functions is thus the precondition for the normal workings of the self and the precondition for these functions to be "transmuted" (transformed and preserved) as part of psychic structure (memory organization), i.e., as part of the child's own self organization. This structure, built up over the whole course of childhood and adolescence, is the source of adults' own equilibrium-maintaining and self-regulating capacities; of their feelings of pride and pleasure in themselves, their feelings of togetherness, strength, and power; of their capacities to recover from hurt pride and all of the other injuries and miseries that are invariably part of everyday life; and of their capacities for initiative, assertion, affection, and for love, play, and work.

Sander's prospective constructions were made by taking the road of longitudinal observations of the interplay of children and parents. On this road, before our very eyes, as it were, his studies also document the telling impact of parental functions on precisely the same developmental issues Kohut singled out. In the examples she chose for this presentation Demos shows the development-derailing impact of specific kinds of faulty, distorted, and insufficient parental functions — those of fathers as well as mothers — over which the child has insufficient, phase-expectable control. She shows the impact of parents' emotional inaccessibility, erratic closeness and distancing, disregard and inability to validate the child; and the impact of their inhibiting, constricting, and otherwise disruptive effects on the child's pleasure, self-assertion and independent initiative, goals and ambitions, feelings of pride, mastery, and self-confidence, tension states, and aggression. Conversely, she shows the kinds of parental functions (such as encouragement, backing, judgment in fractionating a task to make it manageable for the child, etc.) that interdigitate with the child's basic developmental needs and foster the confidence necessary for perseverence, pride, and eventual mastery.

It is as though the child studies of Sander and his colleagues and the clinical studies of Kohut independently turn a high-power microscope on, and illuminate, the very same areas of normal and pathological development. They both bring into focus specific childhood needs and specific kinds of parental responses — those that facilitate transmuting internalization by appropriately acknowledging legitimate needs, and those that persistently thwart basic needs, thereby interfering with transmuting internalization and the acquisition of inner capacities needed to feel pride, to persevere, and to work to obtain satisfaction. Further, they both bring into focus the fact that childrens' own efforts to preserve their injured pride and to protect themselves from being overwhelmed and from being faced with their inability to be effectual are what instigate defensive organizations (self-protective measures)—withdrawal, giving up, hostile negativism. These latter further insure against success, mastery, and self esteem.

Different Premises—A Different Psychoanalytic Baby

The reason that Kohut's and Sander's conceptions of normal and derailed development are so much alike is they are anchored in changed assumptions. These assumptions—both implicit and explicit—are a radical departure for psychoanalysis. Therefore they are worth spelling out. Until now all of the psychoanalytic theories about the child's mind and its normal workings have been "pathomorphic" theories—theories modeled from pathology. That means that analytic theories of normal infantile mental life rested on the erroneous assumption that infants and small children perceive, think, and feel much like adults who suffer from severe psychopathology (such as extreme feelings of helplessness, powerlessness, anxiety, and depression; extremes of rage, revenge, jealousy, envy, and guilt; extremes of voraciousness, sexual drivenness, and sexual perversion). The erroneous assumption that childhood normality resembles the pathology of adulthood leads to another erroneous assumption, namely, that normality is achieved by getting over ubiquitous disease or by outgrowing infantile phases dominated by a ubiquitous disease-engendering psychic position (such as drivenness and insatiability, hallucinatory wish fulfillment, and resistance to facing reality, objectlessness, delusional oneness, destructive rage, depression, and guilt, etc.)

The brand-new assumption of both Sander and Kohut is that normal development cannot be thought of as a case of minipathology that has to be outgrown. Instead, it has its own rhymes and reasons. I have already mentioned the most important of these reasons: the normal morphology of development starts with the fact that the baby comes equipped with highly complex, designed-in givens—perceptual, cognitive, affective equipment—and with the ability to actively elicit and make use of parental care (selfobject functions) to alleviate major depression, rage, etc. What a difference it makes for psychoanalytic theory and practice when we add *normal care* to our picture of the mind of the baby, the young child, the older child, and the adolescent. With normal care added to theory, the primary developmental task in each different phase and stage concerns maintenance and restoration of self-integrity (cohesion)—which especially falters at times of transition from one phase to another and at times of reorganization. When we leave normal care out of our theory we have the baby, child, and adolescent pictured by traditional psychoanalytic theories, and we have the skewed picture that treatment works by providing belated means to overcome the phase-specific diseases that were not mastered in childhood.

Conclusion

Speaking of child-observation studies and psychoanalytic investigations Freud (1905) wrote, ". . . by cooperation the two methods can attain a satisfactory degree of certainty in their findings" (p. 201), I think that is precisely what we have here: Freud's pathomorphic assumptions accepted by other analysts led to a satisfactory degree of certainty that drives and drive objects (objects of libidinal and aggressive drives) are at the center of infantile psychic life and the workings of the child's mind; with Sander's and Kohut's changed assumptions we have attained a satisfactory degree of certainty that the designed-in self and parental selfobject functions occupy the center of psychic reality, that the normal workings of the mind are an enduring memory organization of the affective, perceptual, cognitive givens as they have intermeshed with parental functions.

Clearly, the felicitous match between Kohut's and Sander's findings and conclusions leads to a different psychoanalytic baby—a changed view of development. This changed view has gained considerable acceptance and has been embraced widely in some quarters; it is still met with hostility and suspicion in others; and in still others it is neglected and ignored. In any case, I think we need to foster the further growth of this different psychoanalytic baby and discover its faults, failings, and shortcomings, as well as continue to test the strengths and successes it brings to psychoanalysis and its allied disciplines.

REFERENCES

Emde, R. N. (1980), Toward a psychoanalytic theory of affect. II. Emerging models of emotional development in infancy. In: *The Course of Life.* I: *Infancy and Early Childhood,* ed. S. I. Greenspan & G. H. Pollock. Washington, DC: Govt. Printing Office.

———— (1981), Changing models of infancy and the nature of early development:

Remodeling the foundation. *J. Amer. Psychoanal. Assn.*, 29:179–219.

Freud, S. (1905), Three essays on the theory of sexuality. *Standard Edition*, 7:130–243. London: Hogarth Press, 1953.

Stern, D. N. (1985), *The Interpersonal World of the Infant*. New York: Basic Books.

Tolpin, M. (1971), On the beginnings of a cohesive self. *The Psychoanalytic Study of the Child*, 26:316–352. New York: International Universities Press.

———— (1978), Self-objects and oedipal objects. *The Psychoanalytic Study of the Child*, 33:167–184. New York: International Universities Press.

———— (1986), The self and its selfobjects—A different baby. In: *Progress in Self Psychology*, Vol. 2, ed. A. Goldberg. New York: Guilford Press, pp. 115–128.

DR. BARNETT:

Through the ages there have been many casual observations of infants and a myriad of hypotheses about their nature. One that struck me appears in a letter Einstein wrote to his wife in 1902. He had just received notice from her father announcing the birth of their child, and he wrote, "Is she healthy? Does she already cry properly? What kind of little eyes does she have? Will she soon be able to turn her eyes towards something? Now you can make observations. I would like once to produce a child myself. It must be so interesting. She certainly can cry already, but to laugh she'll learn much later. Therein lies a profound truth" (Bernstein, 1987, p. 80).

The nature, development, classification, and theory of affect have confounded some of the best psychoanalytic minds over the last ninety years. Research by any and every method can only lead to our goal of discovering something new.

The field of infant observation, through its extensive and varied investigations into the behavior and interactions of babies, has frequently provided information in regard to what goes on in the observable world and gives an increased basis for theorizing about what goes on in the unobservable world. However, I think the psychoanalytic questions raised at a panel on affects in 1980 are still relevant for us today. "Are affects discharge or tension phenomena, or both? Should they be conceptualized as ego phenomena, signals for defense action and adaptation? Are they experiences of the self or functions of the ego? Are motives and appetites affective processes, affective derivatives, or parallel to the affect functions of the ego? What is the role of conflict, of cognition, of object relations? Should the psychoanalytic theory of affect concern itself more with content, meaning, and communication than with energy, drives, and functions?" (Panel, 1980).

Let me begin my discussion of Dr. Demos's contributions to infant research on affect and its implications for psychoanalytic theory by highlighting some of the directions her work has taken since her research and conclusions began to appear in the literature in the 1980s. Demos deals with affect in its communicative role, as the primary regulation of transactions between the infant and caretaker before the advent of language, and, in what she terms a motivational role, as regulating approach and avoidance behavior. She bases much of her theoretical work on Tomkins's conceptualizations of personality, which he defines as five interrelated subsystems—homeostatic, drive, affect, cognitive, and motor. To the homeostatic and drive systems he ascribes motivational properties under emergency situations, but under normal conditions drives do not have power enough to motivate behavior and must be amplified by affect. In fact, Tomkins and Demos state that affects are the primary motivational system of the personality, amplifying a wide range of events; physical, cognitive, and drive states.

An additional aspect of Tomkins's work that finds its way into Demos's theories is his elaboration of the nine basic inborn facial expressions of affect. Demos agrees with Tomkins that affective experiences do not require cognitive judgment. The affect mechanism is autonomous, but his theory allows for affective amplification of cognitive processes.

From the data of direct observation and videotapes, Demos speculates on, and draws conclusions about, the way in which affective events coalesce into more complex, learned, affective behavior, the emergence of the psychological self, modification of affect in view of the response of the environment, and the development of character types. Overriding these separate issues, Demos emphasizes the variety of transformations these issues undergo during the course of childhood. She writes: "New capacities are always emerging that can modify, reverse, or continue trends established in the first year." She believes that long-term longitudinal studies will clarify the reliability and validity of the data that she and others have collected during the first two years (Demos, 1982, 1983, 1984, 1985a, 1985b, in press).

It is with this background in mind that we approach the paper Dr. Demos has presented for us. In it, she elaborates the source of her longitudinal data, namely, the study started by Eleanor Pavenstedt in 1954 with thirty families. Dr. Sander was involved in the assessment of these families initially and throughout the study. The amount of detailed data collected is unique and includes projective, cognitive, and neurological testing, as well as interview material, play sessions, and follow-up interviews done some twenty-odd years later. She, as well as other investigators, have tried to find law and order in the mass of information collected on each unique child and family. Dr. Demos states: "From the mass of incidental or coincidental occurrences, one is able, over time, to see the emergence of patterns and test a series of hypotheses as one follows each case." She acknowledges that from this information there were no predictable bases for behavior. Factors that were present and seemed determining in one case were not present or did not have the same determining effect in another case. She suggests that there are so many processes at work in the development of a child that her formulations may be valid only for a particular set of circumstances or a particular combination of factors or variables at a particular developmental moment.

Her presentation of the infant of the eighties is a model of clarity and brevity, and one that encompasses many substantiating findings of the field of infant observation over the last twenty-five years. Infants have a highly complex internal organizational system with which to deal with an external environmental system. From birth there is a cross-modal perceptual system from which the infant makes abstractions. Infants can distinguish between internal and external stimuli and show a range of affective behaviors. She notes: "In addition to these continuous capacities, the infant also possesses a maturational timetable that will, at certain developmental moments, introduce new capacities into this ongoing, complex organization." This clearly contrasts with the early psychoanalytic notions of infancy, still held by some, that the infant is flooded with internal and external stimuli, by which it feels helplessly overwhelmed, and from which it is protected only by the stimulus barrier.

Dr. Demos draws on Sander's elaboration of the negotiations between infant and caretaker in the first two years of life, using his framework to help organize the longitudinal data of her own research. She tries to demonstrate how the infant seeks to enhance positive affect and minimize negative affect, such efforts being increased when the affects occur in particular sequences. In her description of several of the children in the longitudinal study, she focuses on two patterns of sequential interaction: positive-negative-positive and positive-negative-negative. Her assessment of these data includes evaluations of microcosms of interaction as well as global assertions about the nature, causes, and meanings of infant and caregiver behaviors.

Dr. Demos concludes her presentation of these affective sequences by referring to Tomkins's new work on such episodes, which he calls "scenes." Such scenes, he feels, undergo psychological magnification when connected with other affect-laden scenes. Eventually, the scenes are elaborated into scripts, which coalesce into four major types, to which he assigns the names affluent, limitation-remediation, contamination, and antitoxic. "Individuals will differ in the degree to which any type of script dominates their psychological space, either at a given moment or during a lifetime." Dr. Demos expresses the hope that her summary of Tomkins's script theory is sufficient to convey the way in which it conceptualizes the lawfulness of psychological experiences without sacrificing complexity. She feels that his formulations help to organize observations made beyond the first two years of life and that this conceptual framework is a new way to think about development.

Dr. Demos's work is imaginative, thoughtful, and very complex. She has attempted to integrate the ideas and results of other relevant investigators. She has also noted some loopholes in her own data as well as the possibility of arriving at alternative conclusions. In addition, she cites criticism of her work for relying so heavily on Tomkins's theories. I agree with her description of the baby of the eighties possessing a number of highly organized and coordinated systems that she delineates. Yet I have some nagging doubts and difficulties with the interpersonal direction in which her affect theories lead, and with their relevance for grappling with psychoanalytic questions regarding affect.

In explicating Tomkins's conceptualization of personality as a complex organization of five interrelated systems, both Tomkins and Demos express the idea that though drive systems have motivational properties they are important only in emergencies. They feel that under normal conditions drives do not have sufficient power to motivate behavior and must be amplified by affect. It seems to me that what we have here is another way of stating that unconscious drives make a demand on the mind, and when this demand becomes conscious it does so in the form of an affect or an idea. Tomkins and Demos offer no greater clarification of the issue of the substratum of drives when they try to substitute affects and their independence from physiological needs and their freedom to amplify a wide range of events. Affects, as described by Demos and Tomkins, seem to be the MSG of human development — that is, sprinkled on everything else they enhance and intensify the experience of drive, thought, and so forth. To take as the prime mover of human thought, behavior, and action something that may only enhance and intensify other aspects of the human mind would be like cooking with the MSG and leaving out the food altogether.

Ideas and thoughts also have the same enhancing and validating power as affect. When one has the experience of "putting two and two together" it provides a mental fit that is equally as powerful as an affective experience, even without the onrush of feeling that may follow it. The ability to specify and qualify an affect state, or capture the idea or memory that was involved with the affect, gives as great a sense of enhancement and intensification as the other way around.

Another difficulty I find with Dr. Demos's work is her use of affect and not drives as the primary motivator. Otto Kernberg, in his paper, "The Place of Affect in the Clinical Situation and in Psychoanalytic Theory" (Panel, 1980), seems to provide a bridge between some data of infant observation and psychoanalytic theorizing. He attempts, through an elegant set of arguments, to synthesize the role of inborn affective behavioral patterns and the relations among affect, drive, object relations, and unconscious fantasies. Very briefly, he concludes that "it is the drives, whose building blocks are the primitive affect states, that function as the hierarchically supraordinate motivational system, and are manifest in each concrete, drive-determined experience and interaction, as a particular affect state that characterizes the internalized object relation in which the drive is embedded" (p. 202). Unconscious fantasy, he feels, condenses the organization of drives and of internalized object relations in the form of concrete desires or wishes, the oedipal constellation being the most important intrapsychic organizer of drives.

I find that Dr. Demos's use of the word internal is ambiguous, if not misleading. She makes mention of the internal life of the infant, but then neglects it in her theorizing. She interprets the meaning of a situation for the child by systematically observing the child's reactions as manifested in facial expressions, verbal and vocal utterances, and other physical actions. These may be the only observable reactions, but these externals may not indicate what is going on inside. They may indeed be more valid than situational definitions, but they may not reflect the actual state of affairs inside the infant's mind. Psychoanalysts are interested in both the internal and the external events in the child's life, and these are convincingly captured in the psychoanalytic setting, from regressions in the transference, and reconstructions of primitive mental states.

Dr. Demos reiterates in several places her belief that the child is motivated to reexperience positive affect and re-create situations associated with the experience of positive affect, while minimizing or avoiding negative affect. Even casual and frustrating experiences with babies and children, in and outside of therapy, make it clear that this is often not so. At some point in every infant's life — and I think this point comes earlier rather than later — the evidence for internal unconscious mental conflict overriding any available external reward is apparent, eventuating in the universal appearance of the infantile neurosis. The argument that Dr.

Demos offers points in the direction of the behavioristic notion that people act as they do only because of rewards and punishments — positive and negative reinforcements — they have received. In B. F. Skinner's way of looking at things, the mind, and such things as memory and perception, cannot be directly observed and so are unworthy of scientific study. Such narrow behavioristic thinking leads Skinner to say, "I think cognitive psychology is a great hoax and a fraud, and that goes for humanistic psychology and brain science too" (quoted in Goleman, 1987).

Dr. Demos delineates affect as having three components: a triggering event, the affective experience per se, and the organism's responses. She also postulates that each component may consist of internal physiologic sensations, thoughts, and memories. However, the form of her observations, and her theoretical conclusions, are always couched in the motoric behaviors that are observable. Where is the elaboration of the internal events along with the external to arrive at conclusions?

What might be going on during the 80 percent of the time the newborn infant is not attending to the environment? Affect is experienced during this time without the adaptive, communicative mode; to what ends? Given the fact that 80 percent of the infant's time is spent in a state of sleep or drowsiness and only 20 percent in activity or alert inactivity, I speculate that there is much more time spent in a reworking of the interpersonal and sensorimotor events that took place during alertness. The fact that we can mentally rearrange and condense events to our own satisfaction without the use of language or symbolization in language seems to me to be a function that is available to infants early on. Whether it is Edelman's theories of selection and categorization, or Mishkin's ideas on the multiple connections among neural structures, current neuroscience would seem to indicate that memories of discrete events, and learning from those discrete events, are laid down in neuronal structure from birth, if not before. Mental representations and symbolic processes, from visual, auditory, kinesthetic, and affectively charged experiences, may have a separate course of development from symbolization in language. One way that I can conceptualize events being laid down without benefit of words is in terms of visual, auditory, and other sensory or motor mental templates. We all know that when we hear music, or witness or tactilely experience an event, we may voluntarily or involuntarily experience instant or delayed replay. We can replay it as it happened, condense it, insert new elements, delete some, or invent a new version altogether. I imagine that this is not substantially different from the later, more complex, symbolic representation in language, and it calls into question the oft-repeated assertion of Piaget's that the conceptualization of a sense of self, self-reflection, and awareness of feeling states occurs only much later, at eighteen months.

Is it Dr. Demos's hope that we extrapolate from the data of the observed population to the population at large to direct parents how to respond to children in a way that will enable them to head off potentially tragic scripts? If so, it is a laudable goal, but I do not believe it is possible. Parents have already entered the state that Tomkins calls "stable equilibrium," and would be hard-put to alter the pattern of their affective responses to their infants solely by virtue of directing their actions. Shakespeare did say, "The play's the thing," but I don't believe that script theory will help us catch the conscience of the king.

Does substituting affect sequences as the sine qua non of development enhance our ability to organize data about infancy? Affect interchanges between infant and caregiver help us highlight some of the normal and pathological outcomes over time. But do they have greater explanatory power than the concepts of epigenesis, unconscious drives, conflicts, and fantasies? At least for this observer, even noting the likelihood of being enmeshed in positive affect sequences and affluent scripts with traditional psychoanalytic theory, they do not.

We do write the scripts of our lives, but, as Dr. Demos admits, the themes are often not visible simply from the interchanges observable in the arena between infant and caregiver. It is my belief that the stamp of our individuality has its origins in our interior from amalgams and reamalgams of the unconscious fantasies, wishes, and conflicts, leavened with the rewards and punishments from the outside world.

How much of the totality of development is based on the affective scenes and scripts acted out on the interpersonal stage? Perhaps not even time will tell, as there are fads and fashions in psychology and psychoanalysis, as with everything else. Charles Brenner, in recapping the events in psychoanalysis of the last fifty years, discusses avenues of inquiry that looked "promising at first yet turned out to be less important than realized at the time" (Brenner, 1987, p. 542).

I believe that infant observation on affect is an exciting field of inquiry, gathering the visible evidence of the nature and extent of the ties that bind infants and caregivers, an adjunct to probing into the intrapsychic realm. With respect to the residual unanswered psychoanalytic questions regarding affect, I feel, along with Brenner (1987), that "the most fruitful method of research in human psychology has been psychoanalysis. The psychoanalytic method applied in the clinical psychoanalytic situation has been a research tool that has yielded, and will continue to yield, more important information about the development and functioning of the human mind than anyone could have dreamed of when it was being developed ninety years ago" (p. 554).

REFERENCES

Benjamin, J. (1969), Some developmental observations relating to the theory of anxiety. *J. Amer. Psychoanal. Assn.*, 9:652–668.

Bernstein, J. (1987), Einstein when young. *New Yorker*, July 6.

Brenner, C. (1987), Notes on psychoanalysis by a participant observer: A personal chronicle. *J. Amer. Psychoanal. Assn.*, 35:539–556.

Brierly, E. (1939), Affects in theory and practice. In: *Trends in Psychoanalysis*, ed. M. Flowers & E. Brierly. London: Hogarth Press, 1951.

Brody, S. (1981), The concept of attachment and bonding. *J. Amer. Psychoanal. Assn.*, 29:815–829.

Call, J. (1980), Some prelinguistic aspects of language development. *J. Amer. Psychoanal. Assn.*, 28:259–289.

Demos, V. (1981), Early infancy: Physiology or psychology? *Psychoanal. Inq.*, 1:533–574.

——— (1983), A perspective from infant research on affect and self-esteem. In: *The Development and Sustaining of Self-Esteem in Childhood*, ed. J. Mack & S. Ablon. New York: International Universities Press, 45–78.

——— (1984), Empathy and affect: Reflections on infant experience. In: *Empathy*, ed. J. Lichtenberg, M. Bornstein & D. Silver. Hillsdale, NJ: The Analytic Press, pp. 9–34.

——— (1985), The elusive infant. *Psychoanal. Inq.*, 5:553–568.

——— (1986), Crying in early infancy—an illustration of the motivational function of affect. In: *Affective Development in Infancy*, ed. T. Brazelton & M. Yogman. Norwood, NJ: Ablex, pp. 39–74.

——— (in press), Resiliency in infancy. In: *Resiliency*, ed. R. Coles & T. Duggin.

Emde, R. (1981), Changing models of infancy and the nature of early development: Remodeling the foundation. *J. Amer. Psychoanal. Assn.*, 29:179–219.

Freedman, D. (1981), The effect of sensory and other deficits in children on their experience of people. *J. Amer. Psychoanal. Assn.*, 29:831–867.

Goleman, D. (1987), Embattled giant of psychology speaks his mind. *New York Times*, Aug. 25.

Kaplan, L. (1987), Discussion of *The Interpersonal World of the Infant. Contemp. Psychoanal.*, 23:27–44.

Leithauser, B. (1987), The space of one breath (on artificial intelligence and self consciousness). *New Yorker*, March 9.

Levin, F. (1987), Psychological development and the organization of the central nervous system. Presented to the Chicago Psychoanalytic Society, May.

Mahler, M. & McDevitt, J. (1982), Thoughts on the emergence of the sense of self. *J. Amer. Psychoanal. Assn.*, 30:827–848.

McDonald, M. (1970), Transitional tunes in musical development. *The Psychoanalytic Study of the Child*, 25:503. New York: International Universities Press.

Mishkin, M. & Appenzeller, T. (1987), The anatomy of memory. *Sci. Amer.*, June.

Panel (1980), New knowledge about the infant from current research: Implications for psychoanalysis, L. Sander, reporter. *J. Amer. Psychoanal.*, 28:181–198.

——— (1982), New directions in affect theory, E. Lester reporter. *J. Amer. Psychoanal.*

Assn., 30:197–211.

Peterfreund, E. (1978), Some critical comments on psychoanalytic conceptualizations of infancy. *Internat. J. Psycho-Anal.*, 59:427–449.

Provence, S. (1978), A clinician's view of affect development in infancy. In: *The Development of Affect,* ed. M. Lewis & L. Rosenblum. New York: Plenum.

Rosenfeld, I. (1986), A new approach to memory and perception [with reference to G. Edelman]. *New York Review of Books,* October 9.

Stern, D. (1985), *The Interpersonal World of the Infant.* New York: Basic Books.

Terhune, C. (1979), The role of hearing in early ego organization. *The Psychoanalytic Study of the Child,* 34:371–383. New Haven: Yale University Press.

Weil, A. (1970), The basic core. *The Psychoanalytic Study of the Child,* 25:442–460. New York: International Universities Press.

Wetzler, S. & Sweeney, J. (1986), Childhood amnesia in cognitive psychological terms. *J. Amer. Psychoanal. Assn.*, 34:663–685.

DR. COHLER:

We have been treated to a rich array of developmental and clinical findings. Virginia Demos has reviewed developmental findings showing the extent of sociability, responsiveness, and intentionality among infants and toddlers. Clinical studies have portrayed instances in which this capacity for intentionality and joy in living may be replaced by lowered mood, feelings of lack of self worth, and an emotional flatness which hardly does justice to the effective richness inherent in the human experience. This presentation is also characteristic of a major paradox confronting our field. On the one hand, there is a large literature in the realm of observational and empirical study of infancy and early child-hood and, indeed, of the course of life as a whole. On the other hand, there is a large clinical literature reporting on the study and treatment of persons experiencing a sense of personal dislocation and crisis in their lives. We understand these crises in terms of past experiences.

Genetic and Developmental Approaches in Psychoanalytic Study

Since Haeckel's (1868) formulation of the fundamental biogenetic law, proposing that ontogeny repeats phylogeny, or that the present is a repetition of the past, and so important both in Freud's early laboratory studies and in his later formulation of the genetic point of view in psychoanalysis, the assumption of present personal distress has been understood in terms of past misfortune, whether this misfortune is that of

Little Hans, the guilty man, or Mr. Z., the tragic man. Regardless of whether one endorses a conflict or a deficit model of the origins of psychopathology, we have come to think of the "causes" of this psychopathology in terms of past experience. In support of this approach, we rely primarily on clinical case reports, supporting our conclusions by reference to the literature in developmental psychology.

Indeed, just as Freud had attempted to base his metapsychology on the positive experimental science of his time, we attempt to ground our developmental model of psychopathology in terms of "known" research findings. In the process, we continually feel that the experience-near clinical data are lost in the abstractions of developmental theory and findings. The problem is equally serious from the perspective of developmental psychologists, who too often dismiss these clinical observations regarding the origins of psychopathology as too subjective and "biased" to provide useful support for their developmental data. I would like to review this paradox, attempting to pose some first steps toward increased resolution of clinical and developmental perspectives on the origins and course of personal experience.

This problem as well recognized by Freud (1905a) who observed that

> The direct observation of children has the disadvantage of working upon data which are easily misunderstood; psychoanalysis is made difficult by the fact that it can only reach its data, as well as its conclusion, after long detours. But by cooperation the two methods can attain a degree of certainty in their findings [p. 201].

Freud's delight in being able to observe the forward course of development in the case of Little Hans (Freud, 1909) is obvious, as is his acuity in the empathic observation reported in "Beyond the Pleasure Principle" (Freud, 1920), where he describes something like the demonstration of object permanence in a boy aged one and a half. However, as Sadow and colleagues have noted (1968), the important developmental discovery of psychoanalysis, the nuclear or oedipal conflict, was a result of Freud's own self-analysis rather than the result of prospective developmental research.

I would like to pose three problems in the relationship between infant and child observation and the presumed validation of theories regarding the origins and course of personal distress. The first relates to culturally constructed suppositions regarding the course of development itself, the second to what is actually known regarding the connection of earlier and later events, and the third, and most problematic, to the manner in which developmental findings are used by psychoanalysis. Regarding the first of these problems, it should be noted at the outset that the very concept of the present contained implicitly in the past, the basis of the genetic or epigenetic point of view, is a distinctly Western view of the organization of lives. Indeed, we are unique among all the world's cultures in our linear or epigenetic account of lives. Ricoeur (1977) has attributed this perspective to the Western epic, beginning with classical civilization, and culminating in the novel as developed in the eighteenth century.

The Western concept of story is one in which there is a beginning, a middle, and an end, and in which there is some sensible connection between start and end. Lives, like stories, have a startling point in infancy, culminating in adult achievement of personality stability. Contrast this linear view with that portrayed by Geertz (1966) among his informants in Java who view texts and lives as circular, with endings coming full round to beginnings in a cyclical manner, and the distinctive Western view of the organization of both texts and lives becomes idiosyncratic.

The second problem posed in the use of developmental findings in an effort to understand the origins of psychological distress concerns what is actually known about lives over time. This is well illustrated by Dr. Demos's comments. It may be questioned whether such ordered, predictable development really exists—as Emde has reminded us. Following Waddington's theory of water trickling downhill, finding a variety of routes to form a stream—there are a variety of such routes—it may be that the *questions* we ask are incorrect and that the important issues in development concern change not continuity.

Not only is development less continuous and linear than has often been supposed, but in addition, the course of life may be much more subject to chance than is often acknowledged (Cohler, 1982; Gergen, 1977, 1982; Gergen and Gergen, 1983). Chance events are woven into stories or narratives that provide a sense of the meaning of life (Kris, 1956; Cohler, 1982). Psychological symptoms become apparent when the personal narrative loses its coherence, resulting in feelings of fragmentation and disintegration (Kohut, 1971, 1977). Reconstructing the patient's personal narrative is a major goal of treatment and is realized through a collaborative process of coming to understand the particular past presently experienced by the patient. Some elements of the narrative first become clear as a consequence of events recalled in psychotherapy, while others become apparent through particular enactments in the therapeutic relationship empathically apprehended by the therapist as important to a developing narrative, in which the story of the treatment becomes a parallel to the story of the patient's experienced life to date. To the extent that treatment is successful, therapist and patient collaboratively succeed in reconstructing and modifying the patient's personal narrative on the basis of transference and transferencelike enactments, as well as past memories.

From this perspective, retrospective efforts at understanding the past may enhance the capacity to reintegrate the past as a part of a coherent narrative of the course of life, including past and present experiences, and hopes and fears for the future. The adequacy of this narrative, reconstructed in collaboration between therapist and patient, is tested in terms of a shared sense of conviction that it is an adequate and coherent account, just as Freud had posed in his paper on constructions in analysis (1937). Depending on the relationship between particular patients and therapists, somewhat different narratives, with somewhat different foci, will emerge from psychotherapy. However, there are a finite number of foci relevant to narratives of a life, and those judged as most successful are those which most completely account for the presently recounted events and experiences over the course of life and which, jointly evaluated by patient and therapist, provide the greatest sense of conviction in terms of the clarity and simplicity of the narrative. I want to return to this issue when discussing the field of so-called infant psychiatry.

Developmental Study and Psychoanalytic Theory

The third and most complex of the problems posed in the use of developmental findings in psychoanalysis pertains to the very nature of the enterprise itself. As George Klein (1976) has noted, psychoanalysis makes reference to two theories, one based on psychoanalysis as an experience-distant positive science with so-called testable hypotheses based on a presumed neuroscience model, and one an experience-relevant portrayal of personal struggle and distress, including the variety of wishes and intents in our lives, and the means used to protect against awareness or realization of these wishes. It is an irony that, while the later, or clinical theory, has had the greatest impact upon both healing and arts and letters, it is the former theory that is most often associated with psychoanalytic inquiry. While Freud maintained that Chapter VII of "The Interpretation of Dreams" (1900) and the metapsychology papers of 1912–1920 were his most significant contribution to scholarship, it is the case studies, the clinical papers, and the writing on psychoanalysis and culture which have had the most profound influence on contemporary scholarly study, as can be seen in Malcolm's (1987) portrayal of the "industry" of humanistic scholarship surrounding the Dora case.

Much of the history of psychoanalysis has been preoccupied with this former mode of inquiry, and with efforts to prove that psychoanalysis is a valid, positive science able to contribute to the study of brain and behavior. From Freud's (1895) first efforts to gain the respect of neurologists in his "Project for a Scientific Psychology," through the formulation and revision of the metapsychological points of view, to efforts by Hartmann, Kris and Lowenstein, and Rapaport to square the accounts of psychoanalysis with the emerging experimental psychology in contemporary American psychology, to the most recent efforts by Kandel (1983), Reiser (1984), Cooper (1985), and others to show that psychoanalysis is a respectable brain science and truly a part of medicine, the history of psychoanalysis has been marked by efforts to gain the respect of the natural sciences.

As Klein (1976) has argued, metapsychology is more a reflection of Freud's scientific world-view than a portrayal of the origins and course of wishes and intents. Indeed, ironically, in his effort to show that mechanistic processes could not account for that experience which is distinctively human, Freud committed himself to a new mechanistic psychology. Bettelheim (1983) has argued that Freud's concern was the soul and not the psyche, and that it is primarily the translation that has posed problems for understanding psychoanalysis. However, as Hartmann's (1950) essay on the ego clearly shows, understood as a natural science, there is no room in the metapsychology for those experience-near concepts such as the soul or the self which is widely recognized as the major psychoanalytic contribution.

The problem with psychoanalysis has been the continuing confusion of metapsychology and clinical theory, including the effort to use the latter as a means of providing validation for the former. In particular, although Freud was concerned with study of wishes and intents, the subjective or experiential realm, too often the focus of the metapsychology has been on explaining behavior, particularly psychological symptoms and their origins. Nowhere has this been more apparent than in the concern with developmental processes and the origins of psychopathology. Indeed, in his essay on the claims of psychoanalysis to scientific interest, Freud (1913) equates psychoanalysis with this concern for origins, "tracing back one psychical structure to another which preceded it in time, and out of which it developed (p. 183)." The very manner in which Freud phrases this statement of development reflects Haeckel's (1868) biogenetic law, that ontogeny recapitulates ontogeny, important in guiding Freud's prepsychoanalytic neuroanatomic investigation of the evolution of the acoustic nerve as it enters the old brain.

This "analysis of composite phenomena into simpler ones" (Freud, 1913, p. 182), the essence of the genetic point of view in metapsychology, should be contrasted with the developmental or prospective approach, concerned with the forward study of developmental processes most characteristic of contemporary research in child development. As Hartmann and Kris (1945) note, genetic propositions show the relationship between present solutions of psychological conflicts and past determinants, and why some are favored over others. However, as Rapaport and Gill (1959) suggest, this genetic point of view does not appear to have the same order of abstraction as the dynamic, economic, or structural point of view. The genetic approach seeks to discover possible connections between psychological states and modes of experiencing only maturational processes which, at certain critical periods, particularly in the first years of life, are believed to have been formative in shaping such later outcomes as the capacity for warm, caring relations with others, or for self-soothing of potentially disruptive feelings of tension (Hartmann and Kris, 1945; Rapaport and Gill, 1959; Rapaport, 1960; Kohut, 1971; Mahler, Pine, and Bergman, 1975; Kernberg, 1976; Giovacchini, 1979; Solnit, 1982; Lichtenberg, 1982).

In contrast with this genetic point of view, the developmental perspective is concerned with the process of ordered change across the life cycle and is based on assumptions of the increasing differentiation and complexity of psychological functions. While the genetic point of view is based on reconstruction in the analytic setting, the developmental perspective relies principally upon observation rather than interpretation, including the verbal reports obtained in the psychoanalytic interview. As Settlage (1976) has emphasized, in any discussion of developmental issues in psychoanalysis it is important to differentiate between the contributions of developmental perspectives and the genetic point of view as a metapsychological assumption.

Discussions of the genetic approach by Hartmann and Kris (1945) and Rapaport (1960) attempt to provide support for Freud's metapsychology on the basis of empirical literature in developmental psychology in the period immediately following World War II, just as Freud had earlier relied on the empirical literature of his time in the initial formulation of genetic psychology. It is significant that in neither instance was support for this approach based on systematic clinical observation. Further, it may be questioned whether the genetic approach is as relevant to the life history as has been maintained or whether, as compared to the method of empathic, experience-near observation, it may not be more relevant to metapsychology than to clinical theory.

As a psychology beyond the realm of consciousness (Freud, 1898, p. 246), metapsychological propositions may not be amendable to empirical test (Gill, 1976; Klein, 1976; Abrams, 1977; Ricoeur, 1977). It may be questioned whether empirical observational studies of the course of child development could ever provide support for a mechanistic formulation of mental life based not on observation but on efforts to find a parallel with late-nineteenth-century concepts of brain functions—an attempt important for Freud in his effort to convince his colleagues of the scientific status of the emerging discipline of psychoanalysis (Zetzel and Meissner, 1973; Gill, 1976; Klein, 1976; Sulloway, 1979).

Klein (1976) has suggested that motivation rather than metapsychology constituted Freud's primary discovery; metapsychology merely expressed his philosophy of science. As Klein notes,

> Freud's metapsychology is not distinctively psychoanalytic. Moreover, it reduces human behavior to a conceptual domain which requires a kind of observational datum different from that available in the analytic situation . . . metapsychology throws overboard the fundamental intent of the psychoanalytic enterprise—that of unlocking meanings [p. 49].

From this perspective, continuing efforts at modifying metapsychology on the basis of such recent findings in experimental and developmental psychology and the brain sciences as Piaget's cognitive epistemology (Basch, 1977, 1982; Lichtenberg, 1981, 1982) or information processing (Peterfreund, 1978) perpetuate the functional, mechanistic psychology that Freud had sought to change.

Much of the use made of the emerging tradition of developmental study known as *infant psychiatry,* based primarily on the effort to integrate child psychiatry and child psychoanalysis, is an effort to provide support for the assumptions of the genetic point of view. This area of inquiry, first formulated by Rexford, Sander, and Shapiro (1976) as "Infant Psychiatry," has shown dramatic growth over the past few years. While the methods of observation are similar to those of traditional developmental inquiry, although more often employing the empathic method, as in a study of the course of the mother-child relationship (Sander, 1975; Stern, 1977), the goal of such inquiry is to be more explicitly concerned with the impact of earlier experiences, such as problems in the development of a satisfying tie to the mother, upon later differences in mental-health outcomes (Lichtenberg, 1982).

Significant in much of this research is a return both to concern with the biology of development, starting from Freud's own formulation (1905a, p. 239–240) of the "complemental series," and with continuing effort at linking metapsychology with infant and child observation (Lichtenberg, 1982, 1983). While much of this research provides important observational data regarding the course of development, there is often a discrepancy between the observational data which are reported and conclusions made on the basis of this data (Roiphe and Galenson, 1981). For the same reason that metapsychology is largely unable to inform clinical theory, there is sometimes difficulty in determining how studies of infant and child behavior can inform a nineteenth-century statement of the philosophy of science.

The problems posed by the emerging area of infant psychiatry, with emphasis upon normative developmental processes, potential for present and subsequent psychopathology, and efforts at remediation, are dealt with in the *Infant Mental Health Journal* and *Psychoanalytic Inquiry* (Mayman, 1982), as well as edited volumes such as Call, Galenson, and Tyson (1983). Consistent with earlier work by Caplan (1961, Caplan and Grunebaum, 1967), infant psychiatry seeks to intervene in the parent-child relationship early in life, in order both to prevent later adult psychopathology, as well as to enhance present adjustment. Much of this work assumes both a direct, linear, causal relationship between effects taking place at "critical periods" in early life (Lorenz, 1957) and later outcome, and also the idea that the earlier an intervention can be targeted among infants and young children identified as "at risk" for psychopathology, the more likely will such primary intervention reduce the potential for later psychopathology (Fraiberg, 1980; Fraiberg, Shapiro, and Cherniss, 1983). However, recent reports of research and reviews of previous research have questioned these assumptions (Clarke and Clarke, 1976, 1981; Kagan, Kearsley, and Zelazo, 1978; Emde, 1981; Lewis, 1981; Colombo, 1982; Solnit, 1982).

While some association has been reported between problems in the early mother-child relationship and such later problems as children's responses to peers in nursery-school play (Sroufe, 1979, 1982), it is less clear that a parallel can be made between critical periods in other organisms and human psychosocial development over periods of several decades. So-called sleeper effects (Kagan and Moss, 1962; Peskin and Livson, 1981), in which early factors show relationships with longer-term outcomes at one point but not at another, may represent little more than unreliability of measures in longitudinal research carried out over several decades. While intervention in the parent-child relationship may be significant as a means of improving the lives of children, it is less clear that such intervention contributes to improved mental health later in adolescence or adulthood.

Consistent with recent analysis of the course of life—discussed earlier—I would like to suggest that if there is little reason to assume that events of early childhood will directly affect adult adjustment, then it may be necessary to question at least some of the assumptions of infant psychiatry. While it is useful to understand child development as part of the life cycle, such study can be less easily justified as necessary in order to understand the origins of adult disorders viewed as directly continuous with childhood states, as suggested by such metaphorical terms as infantile or psychologically primitive mental states (Kestenberg and Buelte, 1977a, 1977b, 1983; Giovacchini, 1979). It is largely on the basis of this assumption of direct continuity between childhood states, including continued reliance upon presymbolic mental processes, that a number of analysts experienced in work with both children and adults have recommended training in child psychiatry for psychiatrists intending to work primarily with adult patients (A. Freud, 1966b; Panel, 1976; Settlage, 1977, Shane, 1977; Anthony, 1982; Kestenberg and Buelte, 1977a, 1977b). However, Cameron (1944) and Abrams (1977) both note that adulthood is more than a simple replay of early childhood and warn against reductionist uses of developmental models for the study of adult psychopathology.

Empathic Child Observation: The Developmental Approach

Except as an interesting chapter in the study of nineteenth-century approaches to psychiatry and the brain sciences, the genetic approach may be less relevant to psychoanalytically oriented psychiatric education than systematic presentation of an observational-developmental approach. Such an approach would be concerned with the prospective study of lives over time, providing increased understandings of the transformations of wishes and intentions throughout the life cycle.

It is an irony that, although psychoanalysis is most often equated with the genetic metapsychological point of view, including conflicts reflecting fixation and regression, it is actually Freud's pioneering use of empathic observation, beginning with the "discovery" of the concept of free association, which is really the hallmark of the psychoanalytic approach just as in the clinical theory. Early in his psychoanalytic career, Freud recognized the significance of an observational method for the study of development. Although Freud provides only a few instances of this method in his work, he clearly recognized the significance of observation of development for the study of lives. Indeed, in a letter to his colleague Fliess, Freud (1897, p. 192) laments that his busy schedule does not permit him the time necessary to confirm his speculations through observation of young children. When writing about the universal validity of the part played by physical impulses similar to those portrayed in the story of Oedipus in the etiology of the individual neurosis, he noted that "occasional observations on normal children" (1900, p. 261) would provide confirmation of this legend in the origins of feelings of love and hatred toward parents.

The value Freud placed on such observational study shows itself in at least two places in his work. In the case of Little Hans, Freud (1909b) reports on a five-year-old boy's recovery from a neurotic illness, as described to him by the boy's father. A second observation, in the form of a vignette, concerns a phenomenon which, in present-day developmental psychology, might be termed object-person permanence (Hartmann, 1952, 1953; Winnicott, 1953; Decarie, 1965; Mahler, Pine, and Bergman, 1975; Jackson, Campos, and Fischer, 1978; Lax, Bach, and Burland, 1984). First in a footnote to the 1919 revision of "The Interpretation of Dreams" (1900, p. 461) and then in "Beyond the Pleasure Principle" (1920a, pp. 14–17), two observations are reported on Freud's grandson Ernst (whose mother, Freud's daughter Sophie, died in 1920) at the age of twenty-seven. As an illustration of the lack of distortion of affects in dreams, Freud tells of Ernst's dream, at the age of eighteen months, in which he called out for his father, who the next day was to leave for the front (this occurred during World War I). Freud notes that the boy already played "all gone" with his toys, suggesting that he understood the concept of "gone." This incident with the toys is described again in "Beyond the Pleasure Principle" (1920a). Freud relates the manner in which the child would throw a reel, to which a string was attached, out of his bed, showing visible pleasure upon making the reel reappear from beneath the crib, and suggesting that he knew the reel still existed even when out of sight.

This tradition of observation of child development, relying upon the empathic observational method unique to the clinical theory, was continued in Europe by a group of psychoanalytically informed educators, including Bernfeld (1925), Isaacs (1932), and, most notably, Anna Freud (1927, 1966a, 1972). This tradition was later continued in the United States, particularly at the Yale Child Study Center, under the direction of Ernst Kris, and at Denver's Child Development Council, under the direction of René Spitz, as well as at the Menninger Foundation (Escalona and Heider, 1959; Murphy, 1973).

While much earlier work was normative, concerned with the maturation across infancy, toddlerhood, and the preschool years, more recent studies, influenced by increased awareness of the facilitating environment, as represented by caretaking (Bowlby, 1969, 1973, 1980 Greenacre, 1960; Winnicott, 1960; Ainsworth, 1982) has led to increased study of the early mother-child relationship, particularly the reciprocal influence of child and caretaker as a factor shaping the course of the child's development across the first years of life (Sander, 1962, 1975, 1983; Als, 1979; Fafouti-Milenkovic and Uzgiris, 1979).

Study of the caretaker-child relationship has become the developmental issue of greatest concern within psychoanalysis, and represents one of the most significant issues for the future of the field. It is also the most complex area of study, and reflects all the problems that have already been noted. Concern with this perspective is actually quite recent; Freud was content to discuss the "infantile years." Although Freud's intellectual dilemma regarding the seduction theory has been widely discussed in the past few years, much of his concern was with the resolution associated with the family romance.

In our effort to extend the psychoanalytic situation (Stone, 1961) to make sense of psychological problems concerning loss of personal identity or coherence, known by analogy as the deficit disorders or primitive mental states, there has been markedly increased interest in the child-caretaker bond. Many of the problems seen more generally in the use of child observation and in the study of psychoanalysis have been replayed in the study of the caretaker-child tie. For example, much of the use made of the separation-individuation paradigm of Mahler and her associates (1975) has been to validate genetic propositions regarding the development of autonomous ego functions. As Kohut (1971) has so cogently noted, experience-distant modes, removed from the empathic observational method of the clinical theory, have been employed in this area of inquiry. Similar problems have been posed by the studies of separation and loss initiated by Bowlby's formulation, and realized in the systematic study of Ainsworth, Waters, Sroufe, Main, and their associates (Ainsworth, Blehar, Waters, and Wall, 1978; Bretherton and Waters, 1985). As more generally in the infant-psychiatry tradition, conclusions are in the experience-distant domain outside the empathic, experience-near realm of inquiry.

This experience-distant approach may be more relevant to infant psychiatry and efforts to validate the genetic point of view than to the premises of the new developmental psychopathology, concerned with the origins of lack of sense of meaning and persona integration, founded in the realm of experience, rather than behavior. As already noted, the significant contributions of psychoanalysis have concerned the study of subjectivity rather than action. Focus on subjectivity requires an experience-near rather than an experience-distant perspective. As a discipline, psychoanalysis and allied fields have much to say about the study of the subjective realm, and very little to say about actions, the determination of which depend both on individual experience and social context. The difference here is the difference between the work of Mahler and her colleagues, and the work of Winnicott and his associates, such as Khan (1974) and Little (1986), the French psychoanalyst Andre Green (1978) and the work of Kohut and his associates.

Much of this tradition has been brought together and clarified in the pioneering volume of Stern (1985), actually mistitled *The Interpersonal World of the Infant,* since the focus of the volume is on the origins of the intrapsychologic or intersubjective world. Stern poses the question of the means by which the child comes to view caretaking as "good enough." Implicitly endorsing the view of Winnicott and, particularly, Kohut that personal integration is founded upon the experience of caretaking, Stern suggests that this experienced capacity for personal integration is founded on "living with" the caretaker (generally the mother), over long periods of months and years. If, for whatever reasons, the caretaker is conceived of as not "good enough," over very long periods of time, the child schematizes a Representation of Interactions or "RIG" in a process similar to the concept of Scripts constructed out of schemas as portrayed by Tomkins (1978), as an "evoked other," in the terms of Stechler and Kaplan (1980), as an experienced companion, or, in the terms of self psychology, as a selfobject, who fails in a critical respect. Note the difference between this way of studying developmental processes and that more characteristic of social-psychological study, as represented either by the work of Mahler's group or by that of Ainsworth and colleagues.

What is distinctive of developmental study relevant to the clinical theory in psychoanalysis is this use of the empathic method focused on the manner in which others are experienced over long periods of time. Intrapsychologic study comes to replace that founded on social psychology. Finally, consider work from an area in which I have been very much involved, that of the study of the development of children whose parents have been recurrently hospitalized for psychiatric disturbance. Surprisingly, with the exception of the lovely clinical data provided by my colleague, James Anthony, virtually all study of these offspring has focused on present behavior and categorization of symptoms rather than on the offspring's experience of caretaking.

In his report on the life of Piaget, based on Piaget's autobiography, Anthony (1976) has suggested that at least a part of Piaget's preoccupation with reality, and with the development of the sense of reality, stems from Piaget's experience of the chaos of being raised by a troubled and emotionally unavailable mother. My own work, in collaboration with Musick et al. (1987), has suggested that the child's sense of maternal emotional availability is vital in determining the child's experience of caretaking. Based on prospective developmental observation, this work has suggested that children have a particularly difficult time living with mothers who are depressed or emotionally withdrawn during the first years of the child's life. The child's construction of the experience of caretaking is not independent of the mother's personality and caretaking.

Again, consistent with Winnicott's concept of the intermediate space, the interesting question is the meaning that the child makes of this experience of living with a mother who is inconsistently present or in the terms of Emde and Source (1983) emotionally unavailable. If the caretaker is psychologically absent or, in Winnicott's terms, shows primary preoccupation or emotional unavailability, the child finds it particularly difficult to experience caretaking as good enough, providing the basis for the later capacity for solace.

Little is known about the manner in which the child deals with this deficit in the capacity for soothing; most clinical reports to date are based on the retrospective constructions of adult lives, rather than on the prospective, empathically informed clinical study of the origins and course of the use of evoked others. It is clear that experience-distant observation, such as is reflected in the work of Mahler and her colleagues (1975) studying separation-individuation, will not provide us with the information we need. Indeed, Kohut's critique of the separation-individuation literature is particularly cogent. We hope that our successive follow-through studies of the children of troubled mothers will provide findings useful in understanding changes over time in the use of evoked others as a source of solace.

Conclusion

I have argued that, as a result of continuing confusion within psychoanalysis between two theories — one representing Freud's philosophy of science, focused on explanations of behaviors, and one concerned with wishes, meanings, and intents, founded on study of the intrapsychologic or intersubjective realm — there has been a confusion in the possible mutual contributions of developmental and clinical study. To the extent that developmental study can contribute to our understanding of the intersubjective realm, such study must be founded on the same experience-near, empathic mode of observation as other aspects of the clinical theory. The distinctive contribution of psychoanalysis to developmental study is the focus on experience rather than action, and on evidence regarding such experience as realized through empathic observation in the consulting room, the nursery, the classroom, and other contexts in which persons lead their lives.

As long as psychoanalysis is identified with the mechanistic, world-view of the metapsychology rather than with the clinical theory, which is truly distinctive of psychoanalytic inquiry, and as long as psychoanalysis relies upon experience-distant modes of observation of developmental processes, such as those of academic developmental psychology, as a means of "validating" premises derived from metapsychology, it will be difficult for either discipline to appreciate the contribution of the other, or to collaborate on the creation of a truly psychoanalytically informed life-course social science. However, particularly in a more recent study of the origins of meanings, including Sander's, Stechler's and Stern's contributions regarding the origins of the sense of self, there is a hope that we may yet realize such a psychoanalytic social science of development.

REFERENCES

Abrams, S. (1977), The genetic point of view: Antecedents and transformations. *J. Amer. Psychoanal. Assn.*, 25:417–425.
Ainsworth, M. (1982), Attachment: Retrospect and prospect. In: *The Place of Attachment in Human Behavior*, ed. C. M. Parkes & J. Stevenson-Hinde. New York: Basic Books, pp. 3–31.
_____ Blehar, M., Waters, E. & Wall, S. (1978), *The Strange Situation: Patterns of Attachment: A Psychological Study of the Strange Situation.* Hillsdale, NJ: Lawrence Erlbaum Associates.
Als, H. (1979), Social interaction: Dynamic matric for developing behavioral organization. In: *Social Interaction and Communication during Infancy.* ed. I. Vzgiris. San Francisco: Jossey-Bass, pp. 21–40.
Anthony, E. J. (1976), How children cope in families with a psychotic parent. In: *Infant Psychiatry: A New Synthesis.* New Haven, CT: Yale University Press, pp. 239–247.
_____ (1982), The comparable experience of a child and an adult analyst. *The Psychoanalytic Study of the Child,* 37:339–366. New Haven, CT: Yale University Press.
Basch, M. (1977), Developmental psychology and explanatory theory in psychoanalysis. *This Annual,* 5:229–263. New York: International Universities Press.
_____ (1982), The significance of infant development studies for psychoanalytic theory. In: *Infant Research: The Dawn of Awareness*, ed. M. Mayman. New York: International Universities Press, pp. 731–738.
Bernfeld, S, (1925), *Sisyphus or the Limits of Education.* Berkeley: University of California Press.
Bettelheim, B. (1983), *Freud and Man's Soul.* New York: Knopf.
Bowlby, J. (1951), *Maternal Care and Mental Health.* New York: Columbia University Press.
_____ (1958), The nature of the child's tie to its mother. *Internat. J. Psycho-Anal.,* 39:350–373.
_____ (1969), *Attachment and Loss.* Vol. 1: *Attachment.* New York: Basic Books.
_____ (1973), *Attachment and Loss.* Vol. 2: *Separation, Anxiety, and Anger.* New York: Basic Books.
_____ (1980), *Attachment and Loss.* Vol. 3: *Sadness and Depression.* New York: Basic Books.
Cameron, N. (1944), Experimental analysis of schizophrenic thinking. In: *Language and*

Thought in Schizophrenia. New York: Norton, pp. 50–64.

Caplan, G. (1961), *An Approach to Community Mental Health.* New York: Grune & Stratton.

_____ & Grunebaum, H. (1967), Perspectives on primary prevention. *Archives Gen. Psychiat.,* 17:331–346.

Clarke, A.D.B. & Clarke, A. M. (1981), "Sleeper effects" in development: Fact or artifact? *Devel. Rev.,* 1:344–360.

Clarke, A. M. & Clarke, A.D.B. (1976), *Early Experience: Myth and Evidence.* New York: Free Press.

Cohler, B. (1982), Personal narrative and life course. In: *Life Span Development and Behavior,* ed. P. Baltes & O. G. Brim, Jr. New York: Academic Press, 4:206–243.

Colombo, J. (1982), The critical period concept: Research, methodology and theoretical issues. *Psycholog. Bull.,* 91:260–275.

Cooper, A. (1985), Will neurobiology influence psychoanalysis? *Amer. J. Psychiat.,* 142:1395–1402.

Decarie, T. G. (1965), *Intelligence and Affectivity in Early Childhood.* New York: International Universities Press.

Emde, R. (1981), Changing the models of infancy and the nature of early development: Remodeling the foundation. *J. Amer. Psychoanal. Assn.,* 29:179–219.

_____ (1983), Pre-representational self and its affective cure. *The Psychoanslytic Study of the Child,* 38:165–192. New Haven: Yale University Press.

_____ & Harmon, R. (1984), Entering a new era in the search for developmental continuities. In: *Continuities and Discontinuities in Development.* New York: Plenum, pp. 1–11.

_____ & Source, J. (1983), The rewards of infancy. Emotional availability and maternal referencing: In: *Frontiers of Infant Psychiatry,* Vol. 1, ed. J. Call, E. Galenson & R. Tyson. New York: Basic Books, pp. 17–30.

Escalona, S. & Heider, G. (1959), *Prediction and Outcome.* New York: Basic Books.

Fafouti-Milenkovic, I. & Uzgiris, I. (1979), The mother-infant communication system. In: *Social Interaction and Communication during Infancy.* San Francisco: Jossey-Bass, pp. 41–56.

Ferenczi, S. (1913), Stages in the development of a sense of reality. In: *First Contributions to Psychoanalysis.* New York: Brunner/Mazel, pp. 213–239.

Freud, A. (1927), Four lectures on child analysis. In: *The Writings of Anna Freud.* New York: International Universities Press, 1:3–69.

_____ (1951), Observations on child development. *The Psychoanalytic Study of the Child,* 6:18–30. New York: International Universities Press.

_____ (1958), Child observation and prediction of development: A memorial lecture in honor of Ernst Kris. *The Psychoanalytic Study of the Child,* 13:92–116. New York: International Universities Press.

_____ (1965), *Normality and Pathology in Childhood: Assessments of Development.* New York: International Universities Press.

_____ (1966a), A short history of child analysis. *The Psychoanalytic Study of the Child,* 21:7–14. New York: International Universities Press.

_____ (1966b), Some thoughts about the place of psychoanalytic theory in the training of psychiatrists. *Bull. Menninger Clin.,* 30:225–234.

_____ (1972), The widening scope of psychoanalytic child psychology, normal and abnormal. In: *The Writings of Anna Freud,* Vol. 8. New York: International Universities Press, 1981, pp. 8–33.

Freud, S. (1895), Project for a scientific psychology. *Standard Edition,* 1:295–387. London: Hogarth Press, 1966.

_____ (1897), Letter of February 8, 1897. *The Complete Letters of Sigmund Freud to Wilhelm*

Fliess, 1887-1904. Cambridge: Harvard University Press, 1985, pp. 229-232.

——— (1898), Letter of March 10, 1898. In: *The Complete Letters of Sigmund Freud to Wilhelm Fliess, 1887-1904.* Cambridge: Harvard University Press, 1985, pp. 301-302.

——— (1900), The interpretation of dreams. *Standard Edition,* 4 & 5. London: Hogarth Press, 19-58.

——— (1905a), Three essays on the theory of sexuality. *Standard Edition,* 7:130-243. London: Hogarth Press, 1953.

——— (1905b), Fragment of an analysis of a case of hysteria. *Standard Edition,* 7:1-122. London: Hogarth Press, 1955.

——— (1909), Analysis of a phobia in a five year old boy. *Standard Edition,* 10:5-152. London: Hogarth Press, 1955.

——— (1920), Beyond the pleasure principle. *Standard Edition,* 18:7-66. London: Hogarth Press, 1955.

——— (1937), Constructions in analysis. *Standard Edition,* 23:255-270. London: Hogarth Press, 1964.

Gergen, K. (1977), Stability, change, and chance in understanding human development. In: *Life-Span Developmental Psychology: Dialectical Perspectives on Experimental Research.* New York: Academic Press, pp. 32-65.

——— (1982), *Toward Transformation in Social Knowledge.* New York: Springer.

——— & Gergen, M. (1983), Narratives of the self. In: *Studies in Social Identity,* ed. T. Sarbin & K. E. Scheibe. New York: Praeger, pp. 254-273.

Geertz, C. (1966), Person, time, and conduct in Bali. In: *The Interpretation of Cultures.* New York: Basic Books, pp. 340-411.

Gill, M. (1976), Metapsychology is not psychology. In: *Psychology Versus Metapsychology: Essays in Memory of George Klein.* New York: International Universities Press, pp. 71-105.

Giovacchini, P. (1979), *Primitive Mental States.* New York: Aronson.

Green, A. (1975), The analyst, symbolization and absence in the analytic setting. In: *On Private Madness.* London: Hogarth Press, pp. 30-59.

——— (1978), Potential space in psychoanalysis. In: *On Private Madness.* London: Hogarth Press, pp. 277-296.

Greenacre, P. (1960), Considerations regarding the parent-infant relationship. *Internat. J. Psycho-Anal.,* 41:571-584.

Haeckel, E. (1868), *Natural History of Creation (Naturaliche Schopfungsgeschichte).* Berlin: George Reimer, 1968.

Hartmann, H. (1950), Comments on the psychoanalytic theory of the ego. In: *Essays on Ego Psychology.* New York: International Universities Press, pp. 113-141.

——— (1952), The mutual influences in the development of the ego and the id. In: *Essays in Ego Psychology.* New York: International Universities Press, pp. 155-182.

——— (1953), Contribution to the metapsychology of schizophrenia. In: *Essays on Ego Psychology.* New York: International Universities Press, pp. 241-267.

——— & Kris, E. (1945), The genetic approach in psychoanalysis. *The Psychoanalytic Study of the Child,* 1:11-30. New York: International Universities Press.

——— , Kris, E. & Lowenstein, R. (1946), Comments on the formation of psychic structure. In: *Papers on Psychoanalytic Psychology [Psychological Issues,* Monogr. 14]. New York: International Universities Press, 1964, pp. 27-55.

Isaacs, S. (1932), *The Nursery Years* (rev. ed.) London: Routledge & Kegan Paul.

Jackson, E., Campos, J. & Fischer, K. (1978), The question of decalage between object permanence and person permanence. *Devel. Psychol.,* 14:1-10.

Kagan, J. (1980), Perspectives on continuity. In: *Constance and Change in Human*

Development, ed. O. G. Brim, Jr. & J. Kagan. Cambridge: Harvard University Press, pp. 26–74.

———— & Moss, H. (1962), *From Birth to Maturity.* New York: Wiley.

————, Kearsley, R. & Zelazo, P. (1978), *Infancy: Its Place in Human Development.* Cambridge, MA: Harvard University Press.

Kandel, E. (1983), From metapsychology to molecular biology: Explorations into the nature of anxiety. *Amer. J. Psychiat.,* 140:1277–1293.

Kernberg, O. (1976), *Object Relations Theory and Clinical Psychoanalysis.* New York: Aronson.

Kestenberg, J. & Buelte, A. (1977a), Prevention, infant therapy, and the treatment of adults. I: Toward understanding mutuality. *Internat. J. Psychoanal. Psychother.,* 6:339–367.

———— & Buelte, A. (1977b), Prevention, infant therapy, and the treatment of adults. II: Mutual hold and holding oneself up. *Internat. J. Psychoanal. Psychother.,* 6:369–396.

Khan, M. (1974), *The Privacy of the Self.* New York: International Universities Press.

Klein, G. (1976), *Psychoanalytic Theory: An Exploration of Essentials.* New York: International Universities Press.

Kohon, G. (1986), *The British School of Psychoanalysis.* New Haven: Yale University Press.

Kohut, H. (1971), *The Analysis of the Self.* New York: International Universities Press.

———— (1977), *The Restoration of the Self.* New York: International Universities Press.

Kris, E. (1956), The personal myth: A problem in psychoanalytic technique. In: *The Selected Papers of Ernest Kris.* New Haven, CT: Yale University Press, pp. 272–299.

Lax, R., Bach, A. & Burland, J. (eds.) (1984), *The Emergence and Development of Self and Object Constancy: Clinical and Theoretical Perspectives.* New York: Guilford.

Lewis, M. (1981), Child development research and child analysis. *J. Amer. Acad. Child Psychiat.,* 20:189–199.

Lichtenberg, J. (1981), Implications for psychoanalytic theory of research on the neonate. *Internat. Rev. Psycho-Anal.,* 8:35–52.

———— (1982), Reflections on the first year of life. *Psychoanal. Inq.,* 1:695–730.

Little, M. (1981), *Transference Neurosis and Transference Psychosis: Toward Basic Unity.* New York: Jason Aronson.

Lorenz, K. (1957), The nature of instinct. In: *Instinctive Behavior.* New York: International Universities Press, pp. 129–175.

Mahler, M., Pine, F., & Bergman, A. (1975), *The Psychological Birth of the Human Infant.* New York: Basic Books.

Malcolm, J. (1987), Reflections: J'appelle un chat un chat. *New Yorker,* April 20.

Mayman, M. (ed.) (1982), *Psychoanal. Ing.* 1(4).

Murphy, L. (1973), Some mutual contributions of psychoanalysis and child development. *Psychoanal. & Contemp. Sci.,* 2:99–123.

Musick, J., Stott, F., Spencer, K., Goldman, J. & Cohler, B. (1987), Maternal factors related to vulnerability and resiliency in young children at risk. In: *The Invulnerable Risk,* ed. E. J. Anthony & B. J. Cohler. New York: Guilford, pp. 229–252.

Panel (1976), The implications of recent advances in the knowledge of child development on the treatment of adults, J. Thiel & N. Treurniet, reporters. *Internat. J. Psycho-Anal.,* 57:429–43.

Peskin, H. & Livson, N. (1981), Uses of the past in adult psychological health. In: *Present and Past in Middle Life,* ed. D. Eichorn, J. Clausen, N. Haan, M. Honzik & P. Mussen. New York: Academic Press, pp. 154–183.

Peterfreund, E. (19788), Some critical comments on psychoanalytic conceptualizations of infancy. *Internat. J. Psycho-Anal.,* 59:427–441.

Rapaport, D. (1960), Psychoanalysis as a developmental psychology. In: *Perspectives in Psychological Theory: Essays in Honor of Heinz Werner.* New York: International Universities Press, pp. 209–255.

_____ & Gill, M. (1959), The points of view and assumptions of metapsychology. In: *The Collected Papers of David Rapaport,* ed. M. Gill. New York: Basic Books, pp. 795–811.

Reiser, M. (1984), *Mind, Brain, and Body: Toward a Convergence of Psychoanalysis and Neuroscience.* New York: Basic Books.

Rexford, E., Sander, L. & Shapiro, T. (1976), *Infant Psychiatry: A New Synthesis.* New Haven, CT: Yale University Press.

Ricoeur, P. (1977), The question of proof in Freud's psychoanalytic writings. *J. Amer. Psychoanal. Assn.,* 25:835–872.

Roiphe, H. & Galenson, E. (1981), *Infantile Origins of Sexual Identity.* New York: International Universities Press.

Sadow, L., Gedo, J., Miller, J., Pollock, G., Sabshin, M. & Schlessinger, N. (1968), The process of hypothesis change in three early psychoanalytic concepts. In: *Freud: The Fusion of Science and Humanism — The Intellectual History of Psychoanalysis [Psychological Issues,* Monogrs. 34 & 35]. New York: International Universities Press, pp. 257–285.

Sander, L. (1962), Issues in early mother-child interaction. *J. Amer. Acad. Child Psychiat.,* 2:141–166.

_____ (1964), Adaptive relationships in early mother-child interaction. *J. Amer. Acad. Child Psychiat.,* 3:221–263.

_____ (1975), Infant and caretaking environment: Investigation and conceptualization of adaptive behavior in a system of increasing complexity. In: *Explorations in Child Psychiatry,* ed. E. J. Anthony. New York: Plenum, pp. 129–166.

_____ (1983), To begin with — reflections on ontogeny. In: *Reflections on Self Psychology,* ed. J. Lichtenberg & S. Kaplan. Hillsdale, NJ: The Analytic Press, pp. 85–104.

Settlage, C. (1976), A commentary on the 6th pre-congress on training. *Internat. J. Psycho-Anal.,* 57:205–210.

Shane, M. (1977), A rationale for teaching analytic technique based on a developmental orientation and approach. *Internat. J. Psycho-Anal.,* 58:95–108.

Solnit, A. (1982), Early psychic development as reflected in the psychoanalytic process. *Internat. J. Psycho-Anal.,* 63:23–28.

Sroufe, A. (1979), The coherence of individual development: Early care, attachment, and subsequent developmental issues. *Amer. Psychol.,* 34:834–841.

_____ (1982), The organization of emotional development. *Psychoanal. Ing.,* 1:575–599.

Stern, D. (1977), *The First Relationship of Infant and Mother.* Cambridge, MA: Harvard University Press.

_____ (1983), The early development of schemas of self, other, and "self with other." In: *Reflections on Self Psychology* ed. J. Lichtenberg & S. Kaplan. Hillsdale, NJ: The Analytic Press, pp. 49–84.

_____ (1985), *The Interpersonal World of the Infant.* New York: Basic Books.

Stone, L. (1961), *The Psychoanalytic Situation.* New York: International Universities Press.

Sulloway, F. (1979), *Freud: Biologist of the Mind.* New York: Basic Books.

Winnicott, D. W. (1945), Primitive emotional development. In: *Collected Papers: Through Pediatrics to Psychoanalysis.* New York: Basic Books.

_____ (1953), Transitional objects and transitional phenomena. In: *Collected Papers: Through Pediatrics to Psychoanalysis.* New York: Basic Books, pp. 229–242.

_____ (1960), The theory of the parent-infant relationship. *Internat. J. Psycho-Anal.,* 41:585–595.

Wolf, K. (1954), Observation of individual tendencies in the second year of life. In:

Proceedings of Conference on Infancy and Early Childhood: Transactions of the Josiah Macy Foundation. New York: Macy Foundation, pp. 121–134.

Zetzel, E. & Meissner, W. (1973), *Basic Concepts of Psychoanalytic Psychiatry.* New York: Basic Books.

INDEX

A

Abel, E., 224, *238*
Abel and Cain, story of, 205
Abraham and Isaac, story of. *See* Akedah
Abrams, S., 329, 332, *336*
Acculturation, 149
Adaptation, 63–64
  mourning-liberation process and, 150, 152
Adelman, J., 224, *238*
Adolescents, homosexual play among, 250
Aesthetic value, 159
Affect
  components of, 321
  nature of, 316–17
Affective sequences, motivational impact of,
    299–304, 322
  positive-negative-negative sequence, 302–4,
    318
  positive-negative-positive sequence, 299–302,
    318
Affect model of child development, 292–93,
    296–97, 317, 319–23
Affect states, 296–97
Affluent scripts, 306
Agee, James, 161
Agazarian, Y. M., 199, 200
Agency, sense of, 285–86
  in infant, 299
Age of analyst, "typecasting" of, 9
Aggression as disintegration product, 192
Aggressiveness, superego, 48
Aging, developmental and, 147
Ainsworth, M., 293, *307,* 333, 334, 335, *336*
Akedah, 203–12
  fatherhood and, 208–9
    psychology of, 209–10

infanticide and, 204–5
preference for second or younger son and,
    205–7
primogeniture laws and, 207–8
Alpert, J., 218, *238*
Alpha and Omega (Munch), 113
Als, H., 294, *308,* 334, *336*
Alternation of self and object representations,
    137–39
Amram, D., 175, *177*
Anal experience of music, 172
Analysis
  blaming the parent and interference with,
    194–95, 199
  common-sense factors in, 51
  inter-subjectivity of, 39
Analyst(s)
  age of, "typecasting" of, 9
  neutrality of, 8, 46–47
  sex of, 7–9, 233, 250
  shared language with analysand, 10–11
  sociocultural background of, 9–10
Angel, E., 17, *68*
Anger, blaming the parents and, 191–94
Animal behavior, 32
Anthony, E. J., 332, 335, *336*
Antitoxic scripts, 306
Anxiety
  castration, 220, 254
  depressive, working through of, 193
  separation, of artist over work, 162–63
  signal, 55–58
Anxiety—1894 (Munch), 96
Applegarth, A., 221, *238*
Archaic transferences, 4–5
Arlow, J. A., 162, 176, *178*
Artist's relationship to work, 162–63

343

Atkinson, J., 237, *238*
Attachment theory, 293
At the Death Bed — 1896 (Munch), 98
Atwood, G., 17, 39, 44, 53, *65*
Atwood, Margaret, 283
Aubert, Andreas, 93
Awareness, genital, 218-20

B

Bach, A., 333, *340*
Bailey, C., 31, *65*
Bailey, Percival, 148
Balint, M., 190, *200*
Balter, L., 135, *142*
Bang, H. E., 95, 115, 116, 117, *127*
Bardi, Bardo (fictional character), 130, 136
Baron, S., 257, *258*
Bartlett, F., 33, *65*
Basch, M. F., 189, 192, 194, 196, *200, 330,*
    336
Bathing Man — 1918 (Munch), 122, 123
Becker, E., 44, *65*
Beebe, B., 187, 197, *200*
Behavior(s), 18-19
    animal, 32
    overdetermination of, 31, 42
Bell, A., 219, *238*
Bem, S. L., 237, *238*
Benedek, T., 210, *212*
Benjamin, J., 216, 224, *238, 323*
Benvenuto, B., 64, *65*
Berezin, M. A., 172, *178*
Bergman, A., 290, *307,* 329, 333, 334, *336,*
    340
Bergreen, L., 161, *178*
Bernay, T., 218, *239*
Bernfeld, S., 333, *336*
Bernstein, J., 316, *323*
Bettelheim, B., 59, *65,* 328, *336*
Bettelheim, S., 253, *258*
Between the Clock and the Bed — 1942 (Munch),
    124-26
Beyond Interpretation (Gedo), 13
Biogenetic causation, 20-23
Blatt, S., 59, *65*
Blehar, M., 293, *307,* 334, *336*
Blindness, sexual doubling and, 278-79
Bloch, D., 199, *200*
Blos, P., 254, *258*

Boheme, Christiania, 88
Bonding, caregiver-child, 293-94
Bonhoeffer, D., 209, *212*
Bonnat, Leon, 94
Borderline psychotic transference, 6, 12, 15
Bornstein, M., 169, *178*
Bornstein, S., 253, 254, *258*
Boss, M., 17, 52, *65*
Bower, T. G. R., 291, *307*
Bowlby, J., 293, *307, 333, 336*
Brazelton, T. B., 292, 294, *307, 308*
Brenna, A., 79, 88, 89, 93, 102, *127*
Brenner, C., 43, 50, 56, *65,* 74, *127,* 135,
    142, 172, 178, 322, *323*
Breuer, J., 3, *13,* 22, *65*
Brierly, E., *323*
Brigida, Monna (fictional character), 131
Brody, S., *323*
Buelte, A., 332, *340*
Bunge, M., 34, *65*
Burland, J., 333, *340*
Burns, P., 294, *308*
Bychowski, G., 172, *178*

C

Cain and Abel, story of, 205
Cambor, G. C., 166, *178*
Cameron, N., 332, *336*
Campos, J., 333, *339*
Cantor, D., 218, *239*
Caplan, G., 331, *338*
Caregiver-infant negotiations, 294-5
Carmen, E., 218, *241*
Carpenter, G., 292, *308*
Carstens, A. A., 291, *307*
Castration anxiety, 220, 254
    resolution of, 227
    Wolf Man's, 20
Cath, S. H., 210, *212,* 254, *258*
Causation, 34-44
    apprehension of, 41-42
    biogenetic and instinctual, 20-23
    in clinical enterprise, 41
    directions of, 28-31
    double-aspect-single-aspect, 30
    exceptionless psychical, 23
    function and, 43-44
    genetic vs. dynamic, 49-50, 52-53
    historical determinism and, 44-48

interactive, 47, 48
intersectional, 37–40, 48–49
   meaning and, 34–35
   mediate, 47, 48
   motivation and, 34
   overdetermination of behaviors and, 42
Chamber of Death, The — 1892 (Munch), 98, 99
Character structure, multiple factors
   producing, 42–43
Charismatic relationship, 129–43
   alternation and/or merger of self and object
      representations, 137–39
   crisis of induced passivity and, 135
   disillusionment with, 140–41
   idealization and, 141
   modes of internalization and, 139–40
   resolution of, 140–42
   self-initiated repetition of passivity and,
      136–37
   unconscious fantasy and, 135–36
   See also Romola (Eliot character)
Chasseguet-Smirgel, J., 219, *239*
Chehrazi, S., 220, *239,* 252, *258*
Chen, M., 31, *65*
Chess, S., 38, 48, 60, *65, 69*
Childhood experiences
   adult's ability to capture reality of, 197–99
   memories of, 195–97
Child-parent interaction, 45–46
   See also Parent(s)
Children, matricenteredness of, 243–44
   See also Parent(s)
Chodorow, N., 216, 223, 224, 225, 237, *239,*
      242, 245, *251,* 252, 255, 256, 257, *259*
Chomsky, N., 36, *65*
Chrzanowski, G., 150, *157*
Clarke, A. D. B., 331, *338*
Clarke, A. M., 331, *338*
Clement, C., 64, *65*
Clinical enterprise, causation in, 41
Clinical theory, confusion of metapsychology
      and, 328–29
Clinical vs. natural-science languages debate,
      18
Clower, V. L., 231, *239*
Cognitive processes, adult, 290
Cohen, R. E., 149, *156*
Cohler, B., 252, 255, 256, *259,* 326, 335, *338,*
      340
Colombo, J., 331, *338*

Coltrera, J. T., 160, 170, 173, *178*
Common-sense factors in analysis, 51
Composers
   biographical information on, 165–67
   studies dealing with psychoanalytic treat-
      ment of, 167–69
Compromise formation, 55–58
Compulsion repetition, 5, 137, 186
Conflict(s)
   atavistic modes of coping with, 45–46
   creative act and, 162, 170–71
   intrapsychic, 55–58
      external influence vs., 187–88
      Munch on, 73
      nondrive perspective on, 190
      sexual doubling as expression of, 274,
         281–82
   in psychical organizations, 24
   in unconscious motives, 24
Conscious mentation, causal efficacy of, 28
Consciousness
   of motivation, 34
   self-reflective, 32
   source of, 27–28
Constancy principle, 21
Constructionist view of development, 287–341
   affect model of, 292–93, 296–97, 317,
      319–23
   attachment theory, 293
   drives and, 319, 320
   infant
      internal life of, 318, 320
      regulatory constraints on initiatives of,
         299
      sense of agency in, 299
   infant-caregiver relationship
      bonding, 293–94
      negotiations, 294–95
   methodological issues, 288–89
   motivational impact of affective sequences,
      299–304, 322
   positive-negative-negative sequence,
      302–4, 318
   positive-negative-positive sequence,
      299–302, 318
   organization of psychological systems, 295
   postulates, 290–93
   Sander longitudinal study, 287
   scenes and, 304–6, 318–19
   script theory, 305–6, 319, 322

Constructionist views of development
(*continued*)
self psychology and, 309–16
assumptions of, 314–15
developmental basis of psychoanalysis
and, 312, 314–15
shared ideas between, 309–12
transferences and operations of child's
mind, 312–13
self-regulation and, 291
state concept and, 295–96
theoretical issues, 289
uncontainable parent-child problems and,
297–99
Consul Christian Sanberg — 1901 (Munch), 109
Contamination scripts, 306
Contratto, S., 224, *239*
Cooke, D., 173, *178*
Cooper, A., 328, *338*
Coping with conflict, atavistic modes of, 45–46
Copland, A., 175, *178*
Coriat, I. H., 171, *178*
Cott, J., 175, *178*
Creative act, 160–61
conflict and, 162, 170–71
during periods of disorganization, 161
psychological dislocation during, 78
as quest for narcissistic closure, 161
rage and, 170–71
unconscious factors in, 78
See also Music
Creative imagination, loss and, 155
Creativity, defined, 126
Cross-gender analysis, 245
Cross-gender transference, 221–22, 245
Crucifixion fantasies, 137–39
Cultural value, 159
Culture shock, 149–50, 152

D

Dance of Life, The — 1899/1900 (Munch),
100–101, 102, 121
Darwin, C., 32, *65*
Data gathering, observer-subject transaction
and, 7–8
Daughter-father relationship, 255
Day After, The — 1886 (Munch), 84, 87, 95
Dead Mother and Child — 1901 (Munch), 96–98

Death, 44
Death Chamber, The — 1896 (Munch), 98, 104
Death in the Sick Room — 1893 (Munch), 98
Death of Marat, The — 1907 (Munch), 102, 104,
106, 109
Decarie, T. G., 333, *338*
DeCasper, A. J., 291, *307*
de Courtivron, I., 228, *240*
Dedichen, J., *127*
Defense mechanism, 55–58
of Munch, 104–5, 106, 114
Demos, E. V., 292, 302, *307,* 311, 317–20,
322, *323*
Depression, signal, 56
Depressive anxiety, working through of, 193
Determinism, historical, 23, 44–48
defined, 44–45, 48
interactive, 47, 48
mediate, 47, 48
Development
aging and, 147
of artist's work, 163
epigenetic view of, 326–27
of femininity, Freudian theory of, 217
Developmental approach, 324–27
empathic child observation, 332–36
to inspiration, 175
psychoanalytic theory and, 327–32
See also Constructionist view of development
Differentiation, gender, 253–54
Digby, G. W., 74, *127*
Dilthey, W., 256, *259*
Dinnerstein, D., 223, *239*
Disillusionment
with charismatic leader, 140–141
optimal, 193
Dittman, R., 93, 114, *127*
Dr Daniel Jacobson — 1908/1909 (Munch),
111–13
Dreams, "causes" and "meaning" of, 22
Drives, 20, 319
Dual-aspect activities, 26–34
Dualism, linguistic, 25
Dynamic causation, 49–50, 52–53

E

Eagle, M., 50, *65*
Eastman, P., 150, *156*

Eccles, J., 30, *68*
Edelheit, H., 138, *142*
Eggum, A., 73, 76, 113, 120, *127*
Ego, 58
  "state," 295–96
Ego functions of music, 172
Ego-psychological analysis of music, 175–76
Ehrenzweig, A., 173, *178*
Eisenstein, H., 228, *239*
Eissler, K., 159, 170, 176, *178*
Eliot, G., 129, *142*
Ellenberger, H., 17, *68*
Emde, R. N., 311, 312, *315, 323,* 331, 336,
  338
Emerson, P., 294, *308*
Emotion(s)
  James-Lange theory of, 27
  logic of, 50
  music as language of, 173
Empathic child observation, 332–36
Empathy, 6
  role of, 63
Environment, Freud on role of, 21
Envy, penis, 243–44
Epigenetic view of development, 326–27
Epstein, S. G., 106, *127*
Erikson, E., 38, 46, *65,* 254, *259*
Erotic transference, 221–22
Escalona, S., 333, *338*
Esman, A. H., 166, *178*
Evans, D., 221, *239*
Evening on Karl Johan Street — 1893/1894
  (Munch), 96
"Existential" issues, 44
Expressionism, 77
External influence, intrapsychic conflict vs.,
  187–88

F

Fafouti-Milenkovic, I., 334, *338*
Fairbairn, W. R. D., 17, 33, *66,* 188, 194–95,
  200
False self, 302
Fantasy(ies)
  crucifixion, 137–39
  nostalgia vs., 154
  of perfect parent, 190–91
  sexual doubling and, 276–78

unconscious, charismatic appeal and, 135–36
Farnsworth, P. R., *178*
Fast, I., 253, *259*
Father
  development of identity of, 210–11
  relationship with daughter, 255
  transference, 246–47
  See also (Akedah; Parent(s)
Fatherhood, 208–9
  psychology of, 209–10
Fear, atavistic persistence of, 55–56
Feder, S., 153, *156,* 160, 164–67, 170, 173,
  178
Feiner, A. H., 150, *157*
Female Nude, Anna — 1920 (Munch), 117, 118
Feminism, psychoanalytic, 251–61
ontemporary psychoanalytic theory and,
  233–36
  gender salience and, 236
  interpersonal, 224–26, 230–32, 234, 237,
    255–56
  Lacanian, 226–30, 234–35, 237–38
  object-relations school of, 222–26, 230–32,
    234, 237, 255, 256
  problematic nature of masculinity and, 236
  psychoanalytic theories of women and gen-
    der, 217–22
    cross-gender transference and, 221–22,
      245
    Freudian, 217, 242
    gender identity, 220–21
    genital awareness, 218–20
    theoretical position of, 216–17
    women's lives as text, 255–58
Ferenczi, S., 4, *14, 338*
Ferrono, C., 129, 135, *143*
Feynman, R., 177, *178*
Film, sexual doubling in, 264
Fischer, K., 333, *339*
Flax, J., 216, 224, 225, *239*
Flew, A., 159, *178*
Fogel, A., 294, *307*
Foucault, M., 63, *66*
Foy, J. L., 210, *212*
Frazer, J. G., 204, *212*
Free association, 35, 54
Freedman, A., 153, *156*
Freeman, M., 257, *259*
Frenchman, The — 1901 (Munch), 109
Freud, A., 4, *14,* 294, *307,* 332, 333, *338*

Freud, S., 3–6, *13, 14,* 18–23, 28, 34, 37, 38,
43, 45, 48, 49, *65, 66, 67,* 79, 135,
138, *142,* 150, 160, 171, *178,* 187, *200,*
203, 204, *212,* 216, 217, 218, 221, *239,*
242, 243, 244, *251,* 252–56, *259,* 315,
316, 325, 3277n30, 332, 333, 334, *338,*
339
Freize of Life. The (Munch), 103
Function
  causality and, 43–44
  Freud's concept of, 43

G

Galenson, E., 218, 231, 236, *241,* 253, *260,*
331, *341*
Galenson, F., 253, *259*
Gallop, J., 226, *239, 240*
Galloping Horse—1910 (Munch), 122
Gardner, R., 7, *14*
Garner, S. N., 226, *239*
Garza-Guerrero, A. C., 149, 152, *156*
Gedo, J. E., 3, 4, 5, 7, 9–13, *14,* 137, *143,*
159, 160, 163, 175, *178,* 198, *200,* 325,
341
Geertz, C., 256, 257, *259,* 326, *339*
Gender
  of analyst, 7–9, 233, 250
  apperceptions of, 243
  differentiation, 253–54
  identity, 220–21
    formation of, 252–55
  salience, 236–37
  See also Feminism, psychoanalytic
Genetic approach
  in metapsychology, 328–29
  in psychoanalytic study, 324–27
Genetic causation, 49–50, 52–53
Genital awareness, 218–20
Genital schematication, 219
Gergen, K., 326, *339*
Gergen, M., 326, *339*
Gierloff, C., 116, *127*
Gill, M., 17, 18, 49, *67,* 256, *259,* 329, 330,
339, 341
Gilligan, C., 224, *239,* 252, *259*
Gillman, R., 113, *127*
Giovacchini, P., 329, *339*
Glenn, J., 187, *200*
Goldberg, A., 5, 13, *14,* 198, *200*

Goldberger, M. W., 221, *239*
Goldin, J., 207, *212*
Goldman, J., 335, *340*
Goldstein, Emanuel, 110
Goleman, D., 321, *323*
Goodall, J., 32, *67*
Gray, P., 78, *128*
Green, A., 335, *339*
Greenacre, P., 161, 170, 175, 176, *178, 179,*
333, *339*
Greenberg, J., 188, *200*
Greenman, D., 12, *14*
Greenson, R., 50, *67*
Grinberg, L., 150, *156*
Grinberg, R., 150, *156*
Gruber, H., 290, *307*
Gr;umunbaum, A., 35, 49, 50, 52, *67*
Grunebaum, H., 255 *259,* 331, *338*
Guenther, P. W., 73, *128*
Guntrip, H., 17, *67*
Gurwitt, A. R., 210, 211, *212,* 254, *258*
Gustav Schiefler—1905 (Munch), 109
Gutmann, D., 253, *259*

H

Habermas, J., 256, *259*
Habit, 36–37
Haeckel, E., 324, 328, *339*
Hagglund, T. B., 126, *128*
Hall, E. T., 32, *67*
Hamsun, K., 89, *128*
Handmaid's Tale, The (Atwood), 283
Hanson, H., 175, *179*
Haroutunian, S., 258, *259*
Hartmann, H., 4, *14,* 17, 45, 49, 52, 63, *67,*
162, *179,* 328, 329, 333, *339*
Heider, G., 333, *338*
Heller, R., 73, 102, *128*
Herman, J., 236, *240*
Hindemith, P., 173, 175, *179*
Hirsch, E. D., 256, 257, *259*
Hirsch, M., 224, *238*
  defined, 44–45, 48
  interactive, 47, 48
  mediate, 47, 48
History, 44–55
  Freud on role of, 21
  individual, 195–96
  transference and, 49–50

Holt, R., 17, 20, 23, 33, *67*
Holzman, P., 18, *67*
Home, H., 17, *67*
Homeless, 155
Homesickness, 153–54
Homosexuality, sexual doubling and, 281
Homosexual play, adolescent, 250
Horowitz, J., 175, *179*
Hoy, D., 256, *260*
Hulda — 1886 (Munch), 91–93, 102
Humphrey, M., 12, *14*
Hunter, R. R., 165, *179*
Husserl, E., 19, *67*

I

Id, 58
Idealization in charismatic bond, 141
Identification
    end products of, 140
    as mediate and interactive determinism, 48
Identity
    culture shock and vicissitudes of, 152
    of father, development of, 210–11
    gender, 220–21
        formation of, 252–55
Id functions of music, 172
Ignatieff, M., 154, 155, *156*
Imagination, creative, 155
Incorporation, 140
Indian folk tales and myths, sexual doubling
    in, 269–73
Individual history, concept of, 195–96
Individuation, 149
Infant(s)
    infant-caregiver relationship, 47–48
        bonding, 293–94
        negotiations, 294–95
    internal life of, 318, 320
    psychopathology theories based on observa-
        tions of, 325–32
    regulatory constraints on initiatives of, 299
    sense of agency in, 299
    See also Parent(s)
Infanticide, 204–5
Infantile neurosis, 320
Infantile sexuality, 235–36
Infantile trauma, 38
Infant psychiatry, 330–32
Inspiration, developmental perspective on, 175

Instincts, 20
Instinctual causation, 20–23
Interactionism, monistic dual-aspect, 24–32
Interactions, characteristics of, 28
Interchanges, reciprocal, 294–95
Internalization, modes of, 139–40
Interpersonal school of psychoanalytic femi-
    nism, 224–26, 230–32, 234, 237,
    255–56
Interpersonal World of the Infant, The (Stern), 335
Interpretive turn, 256–57
Intersectional causation, 37–40, 48–49
Intersubjectivity of analytic enterprise, 39
Intrapsychic conflict, 55–58
    external influence vs., 187–88
    nondrive perspective on, 190
    sexual doubling as expression of, 274,
        281–282
Introjection, 140
Isaacs, S., 333, *339*

J

Jackson, E., 333, *339*
Jacob, biblical story of, 264–67
Jacobs, J., 207, *212*
Jacobson, Daniel, 110, 111–113
Jacques, E., 126, *128*
Jaeger, H., 102, *128*
Jaeger, Hans, 88–96, 98–101, 105, 107
James, P., 163, *179*
James, W., 36, *67*, 111, *128*
Jardine, A., 228, *239*
Jealousy, sexual, 266–67
Jealousy — 1896 (Munch), 99–100, 101, 117
Jessner, L., 210, *212*
Jobe, T., 129, 135, *143*
Johnson, M. M., 222, 229, *240*
Jones, E., 135, *143*
Jordan, J. V., 224, 225, *240*
Jucovy, M., 234, *240*
Juna, J., 174, *179*
Junova, H., 174, *179*

K

K;umachele, H., 60, *69*
Kagan, J., 331, *339, 340*
Kahane, C., 226, *239*

Kahn, C., 224, *240*
Kandel, E., 328, *340*
Kandel, R., 31, *67*
Kantrowitz, J., 12, *14*
Kaplan, K. J., 204, *212*
Kaplan, S., 296, *307*
Kardiner, A., 33, *67*
Karme, L., 221, *240*, 245, *251*
Katz, A., 12, *14*
Kearsley, R., 331, *340*
Keller, E. F., 224, *240*
Kennedy, R., 64, *65*
Kernberg, O. F., 48, 59, *67*, 136, *143*, 199,
     200, 320, 329, *340*
Kestenberg, J., 219, *240*, 332, *340*
Key therapeutic metaphor, 198
Khan, M., 335, *340*
Kinetic-syntactic signification in music, 174
Kirkpatrick, M., 218, *240*
Kleeman, J., 219, 220, 221, 231, *240*
Klein, G. S., 17, *67*, 137, *143*, 162, *179*, 186,
     190, 199, *200*, 256, *260*, 327-30, *340*
Klein, M., 4, *14*, 33, 192, *200*
Kleiner, J., 153, *156*
Kleinman, A., 40, *67*
Kline, P., 56, 58, *67*
Klyman, C. M., 168, *179*
Kneeling Female Nude Crying—1919
     (Munch), 117, 119
Knoibloch, F., 174, *179*
Koester, L. S., 196, *307*
Kohon, G., *340*
Kohut, H., 4, 5, 6, 12, *14*, 17, 38, 40, 59, 61,
     62, *67*, 141, *143*, 172, *179*, 188,
     192-95, *200*, 203, *212*, 236, 256, *260*,
     309, 312, 313, 314, 326, 329, 334, 335,
     340
Komarovsky, M., 252, *260*
Koslowski, B., 292, *307*
Koutsky, Z., 174, *179*
Kramer, S., 253, *260*
Kris, E., 4, *14*, 45, 49, *67*, 115, 121, *128*,
     162, 171, 173, *179*, 326, 329, *339*, *340*
Krohg, Christian, 79, 84, 91, 107
Kubie, L., 74, *128*

L

Lacan, J., 64, *68*, 226, 255, 257
Lacanianism, 64

psychoanalytic feminism based on, 226-30,
     234-35, 237-38
Lachmann, F. M., 187, 190, 192, 197, *200*,
     201, 234, *241*
Lamb, M., 254, *260*
Langaard, J. H., 119, 121, *128*
Langer, S. K., 160, 165, 173, *179*
Langland, E., 224, *238*
Language, 257-58
     object-relations theory and, 58-60
     shared, between analyst and analysand,
          10-11
     symbolization in, 321-22
Larson, Tulla, 106
Lax, R., 333, *340*
Leader, charismatic, 135
     disillusionment with, 140-41
Leah, biblical story of, 264-67
Lee, A., 294, *308*
Lee, H. B., 170, 171, *179*
Lerner, H., 59, *65*
Lerner, W., 219, *240*
Lester, E. P., 221, *240*
Levarie, S., 172, *179*
Levin, F., 11, *14*
Levinson, D., 46, *67*
Lévi-Strauss, C., 36, *68*
Lewis, M., 164, *179*, 331, *340*
Liberation-mourning process, 146
     nostalgia and, 153-56
     type of loss and, 152-53
Lichtenberg, J. D., 60, *68*, 291, *307*, 329,
     330, *340*
Liebert, R. S., 163, 167, *179*
Lifton, R., 33, 44, *68*
Limitation-remediation scripts, 306
Linde, Max, 106-9
Lindtke, G., 108, *128*
Linguistic dualism, 25
Lisowitz, G. M., 166, *178*
Literature, sexual doubling in, 264
Lithman, Y., 31, *68*
Litowitz, B., 258, *260*
Litowitz, N., 258, *260*
Little, M., 335, *340*
Livson, N., 331, *340*
Loewald, H., 140, *143*, 164-65, *179*
Loewenstein, R., 4, *14*
Logic of human emotional response, 50
Lonely Ones, The—1895 (Munch), 104

Lonely Ones, The—1899 (Munch), 104
Lorenz, K., 331, *340*
Loss, creative imagination and, 155
Lowenfeld, H., 161, *179*
Luborsky, L., 41, 50, *68*

M

MacAlpine, I., 165, *179*
McDonald, M., 173, 175, *179, 323*
McDougall, J., 137, *143*
Madonna—1894-1895 (Munch), 92, 102, 117
Madonna and whore, images of, 276
  differentiation between, 282
Magnification, psychological, 305
Mahler, M., 175, *179*, 290, *307, 323,* 329,
    333, 334, 336, *340*
Main, M., 292, *307*
Malcolm, J., 235, *240, 260,* 327, *340*
Mandelbaum, M., 35, 36, *68*
Man in the Cabbage Field, The—1916 (Munch),
    122, 123, 124
Mann, T., 272, *280*
Mariatale/Renuka myths, 270-72, 273
Marks, E., 228, *240*
Martin, A. R., 153, *156*
Martin, P. A., 160, 164, 169, *179*
Masquerades, sexual, 269-70, 275-76
Masson, J., 40, *68*
May, R., 17, *68*
Mayer, E. L., 219, 220, 222, 233, *240*
Mayman, M., 331, *340*
Meaning, 27
  causation and, 34-35
Meissner, W. W., 139-40, *143,* 330, *342*
Melema, Tito (fictional character), 129-34
Men Bathing—1907 (Munch), 109, 110
Mental representations, 321-22
Mentation
  conscious, 28
  unconscious, 18-19, 23-24
Merger of self and object representations,
    137-39
Messer, T. M., 73, 102, *128*
Metaphor, key therapeutic, 198
Metapsychology, 328-30
  music analysis and, 169-74
  psychology vs., 18
Meyer, A., 37, *68*
Meyer, L., 174, *180*

Michel, A., 170, 172, *180*
Migration, 145-58
  forced, 147-48, 151-52, 154
  leaving vs. arriving, 150-51
  mourning-liberation process and, 146
    adaption and, 150, 152
    culture shock and, 149-50, 152
    line of development, 147
    outcomes of, 147
    separation/individuation and, 149
  nostalgia and, 153-56
  voluntary, 148-49, 51
Military Band on Karl Johann Street—1884
    (Munch), 93
Miller, A., 40, *68*
Miller, J., 325, *341*
Miller, J. B., 216, 218, 224, *240*
Miller, M. D., 166, 172, *178, 180*
Miller, M. L., 153, *156*
Mind, "faces" of, 25-26
Mind-body problem, 24-32
Mitchell, J., 226, *240*
Mitchell, S., 188, *200*
Modell, A., 12, *14*
Money, 220
Monistic dual-aspect interactionism, 24-32
Montani, A., 170, 171, *180*
Mooney, W. E., 166, 170, *180*
Moraitis, G., 257, *260*
Morning Girl at Bedside (Munch), 81
Moss, H., 47, 331, *340*
Mother-child relationship, 254, 255
  adult psychopathology and, 331
  preoedipal, 242-43
  psychiatrically disturbed mother and,
    335-36
Motherhood, surrogate, 264
Mother transference, 250-51
Motivation, 330
  causation and, 34
  consciousness of, 34
  Humean model of, 35-36
  instinctivist theories of, 20-23
  in phenomenological psychoanalysis, 32-34
  tension-release concept of, 33
  unconscious, 23-24, 34
Mourning-liberation process, 146
  adaptation and, 150, 152
  culture shock and, 149-50, 152
  line of development, 147

Mourning-liberation process (*continued*)
  nostalgia and, 153–56
  outcomes of, 147
  separation/individuation and, 149
  type of loss and, 152–53
Munch, Edvard, 73–128
  adolescence, 88–89
  alcohol abuse by, 105, 106, 108, 110
  on art and psychic conflict, 73
  artistic periods, 73
    homelife during, 76–77
    late, 113–14
    middle, 77–78, 114
    parallels between early and late, 76
  attempts to disengage from family, 79–82,
      89–90
  background information, 75–76
  defenses of, 104–5, 106, 114
  diagnoses of illness, 74–75
  focus on colors, 120–24
  hospitalization, 110–11
  intemperate behaviors, 105
  Jacobson and, 110, 111–13
  Jaeger and, 88–94, 100–101, 105, 956
  Krohg and, 79, 84, 91
    father's death and, 94–95
  Larson and, 106
  Linde and, 106–9
  portrayals of women
    conflicted sexuality in, 101–2
    in late period, 117
  public respect and appreciation, 114–16
  Thaulow and, 82, 84
  Warnemunde stay, 109–10
Munch's Father Crucified—1890 (Munch), 95
Murphy, L., 333, *340*
Music
  analysis of, 159–81
    conceptualizing function and, 167
    developmental perspective, 173
    ego-psychological, 175–76
    future directions in, 174–77
    metapsychological approach, 169–74
    methodological errors in, 159–60, 174,
        177
  "interpersonal" qualities of, 174
  as language of emotions, 173
  positions on signification in, 174
  psychosexual understanding of, 172
Musicians

  separation issues and, 175–76
  studies dealing with psychoanalytic treat-
      ment of, 167–69
Musick, J., 335, *340*

N

Nadelson, C. C., 216, 218, 232, 236, 240, 241
Nagera, H., 252, *260*
Narcissistic transferences, 5
Narcissistic vs. oedipal problems, distinguish-
    ing between, 12
Narrative point of origin of pathology, 198
Nass, M. L., 160, 163, 164, 166, 170, 173,
    175, 176, *180*
Natural-science vs. clinical languages debate,
    18
Neuroses, 45
  infantile, 320
Neutrality, analytic, 8, 46–47
Neutral monism, 25
Neve, C., 73, 74, *128*
Niederland, W. G., 113, *128,* 173, 175, *180*
Nielson, Jappe, 115
Nissim-Sabat, M., 53, 61, *68*
Nostalgia, 153–56
Notman, M. T., 216, 218, 232, 236, *240,*
    241
Novey, S., 47, *68,* 256, *260*
Noy, P., 170, 174, *180*

O

Object-relations theory
  blaming the parents and, 189–90
  Eastern and Western conception of, 281
  language and, 58–60
  of psychoanalytic feminism, 222–24, 226,
      230–32, 234, 237, 255–56
Object representations, 46
  alternation and/or merger of self and,
      137–39
Observable actions (behaviors), 18–19
Odysseus myth, 203
Oedipal vs. narcissistic problems, distinguish-
    ing between 12
Oedipus complex, 229, 234, 242, 252, 325
Oedipus myth, 203
O'Flaherty, W. D., 267, 268, 277, *280*
Old Man Praying—1902 (Munch), 95

Opera, sexual doubling in, 264
Optimal disillusionment, 193
Oral experience of music, 172
Oremland, J. D., 168, *180*
Ornstein, A., 190, *200*
Overdetermination of behaviors, 31, 42
Ovesey, L., 218, *241*

P

Paolitto, F., 12, *14*
Papousek, H., 296, *307*
Papousek, M., 296, *307*
Parapraxes, 22
Parens, H., 253, *260*
Parent(s)
    blaming the, 185–201
        anger and, 191–94
        as attitude, 199
        history of development of psychoanalytic
            theory and, 187–88
        individual history and, 195–96
        interaction of intrapsychic and interper-
            sonal experiences and, 197
        interference with analytic work, 194–95,
            199
        language of psychoanalysis and, 186–87,
            190
        object relations theory and, 189–90
        self psychology and, 189–90
        sense of personal agency and, 185–86
    fantasy of perfect, 190–91
    internalized, 188
    selfobject functions of, 313
    See also Akedah
Parent-child interaction, 45–48
    uncontainable problems in, 297–99
Parsons, T., 252, 254, *260*
Part-whole relationship, sexual doubling and,
    274, 276–77, 282–83
Passivity
    induced, charismatic relationship and, 135
    self-initiated repetition of, 136–37
Pavenstedt, E., 317
Penfield, W., 28, *68*
Penis envy, 243–44
Person, E., 216, 218, 222, 233, *241,* 245, 250,
    251
Personal agency, sense of, 185–86
Personal integration, 335

Personality, Tomkins's conceptualization of,
    319
Perversions, 234*n*
Peskin, H., 331, *340*
Peterfreund, E., 52, *68, 324,* 330, *340*
Pfeifer, S., 171, *180*
Phallic experience of music, 172
Phenomenological psychoanalysis, 17–69
    adaptation, 63–64
    causation, 34–44
        biogenetic and "instinctual," 20–23
    defined, 19
    history, transference, phenomenology, and
        unconsciousness, 44–55
    id, ego, superego, 58
    intrapsychic conflict, signal anxiety, defense,
        compromise function, 55–58
    Lacanianism, 64
    language and "object"-relations theory,
        58–60
    monistic dual-aspect interactionism, 24–32
    motivation, 32–34
    self psychology, 61–63
Phenomenological reduction, 19–20
Phenomenology, 18, 27–28, 44–55
    genetic-dynamic causal hypotheses through,
        52–53
Photographs, sense of loss and, 155
Piaget, J., 36, *68,* 175, *180*
Piers, G., 149, *156*
Piers, M., 149, *156*
Pine, F., 198, *200,* 290, *307,* 329, 333, 334,
    336, *340*
Play, homosexual, 250
Pleasure principle, 21, 33
Pletsch, C., 257, *258*
Polányi, M., 8, *14*
Pollock, G. H., 149, 153, *156, 157,* 165, 166,
    167, 170, *180,* 253, 257, *260,* 325, *341*
Popper, K., 17, 30, 45, 57, *68*
Post, J. M., 135, *143*
Posthypnotic suggestion, 54–55
Postolka, M., 174, *179*
Post-traumatic stress disorder (PTSD), 40
Prestoe, B., 89, *128*
Primal-scene schema, 138
Primary activity, 291
Primogeniture, laws of, 207–8
Prison and Despair (Jaeger), 96
"Project, The" (Freud), 20–21

Prostitute and madonna, images of, 276
differentiation between, 282
Przybyzewski, Stanislaus, 107
Psychiatry, infant, 330–32
Psychical causation, exceptionless, 23
Psychical organizations, conflicting, 24
Psychoanalytic feminists. *See* Feminism, psychoanalytic
Psychoanalytic theory
blaming the parent and history of, 187–88
developmental basis of, 312, 314–15
genetic approach, 324–27
integration with social science, 40–41
psychoanalytic feminism and, 233–36
Psychoanalytic theory, developmental study and, 327–32
Psychological magnification, 305
Psychology vs. metapsychology debate, 18
Psychopathology
infant/child observations and theories of, 325–32
models of origins of, 325
narrative point of origin of, 198
Psychosexual understanding of music, 172
Puberty — 1885/1886 (Munch), 84, 86, 95

R

Rabinow, P., 256–57, *260*
Rachel, biblical story of, 264–67
Racker, H., 168, 171, *180*
Rage, creative act and, 170–71
Ragland-Sullivan, E., 64, *68*
Ramana, C. V., 168, *180*
Ramanujan, A. K., 270
Rapaport, D., 36, *68*, 162, 169, *180*, 329, *341*
Rasmussen, T., *68*, 122
Rat Man, 6
Reciprocal interchanges, 294–95
Reclining Nude — 1896 (Munch), 117
Reduction, phenomenological, 19–20
Referential signification in music, 174
Refugees, stress-strain in, 150
Reiser, M., 31, *68*, 328, *341*
Renuka/Mariatale myths, 270–72, 273
Repetition compulsion, 5, 137, 186
Repetition of passivity, self-initiated, 136–37
Representation of Interactions (RIG), 335
Repression, 56
Resistance, 56

Revold, R., 119, 121, *128*
Rexford, E., 330, *341*
Ricoeur, P., 17, 18, 33, *68*, 256, 257, 326, 329, *341*
RIG, 335
Riviere, J., 199, *200*
Rocah, B., 243, 244, 250, *251*
Rogers, C., 62
Roiphe, H., 218, 236, *241*, 253, *259, 260*, 331, *341*
Romola (Eliot character)
brother's death and, 131, 136–37
imprisonment of, 130
independence of, 141–42
marriage to Melema, 131–32, 136
Savonarola and, 131–35, 140–41
See also Charismatic relationship
Rose, J., 160, 175, 226, *241*
Rosen, G., 154, *157*
Rosen, V. H., 171, *180*
Rosenblatt, B., 17, *68*, 140, *143*
Ross, J. M., 210, *212*, 254–55, *258, 260*
Rothenberg, A., 160, 173, 175, *180*
Roundworm, 289–90
Russian Revolution, forced migration resulting from, 154

S

Sabbeth, D., 173, *180*
Sabshin, M., 325, *341*
Sadow, L., 325, *341*
Safirstein, S. L., 168, *180*
Salience, gender, 236–37
Sampson, H., 50, *69*
Sand, B., 82, *128*
Sander, L., 294, 295, 299, *308*, 313, 314, 330, 334, *341*
Sandler, A. M., 194, *200*
Sandler, J., 17, *68*, 140, *143*
Sandler, J. S., 194, *200*
Sashin, J., 12, *14*
Savonarola, Girolamo, 129, 131
at Church of San Marco, 132, 137–38
crucifixion fantasies of, 137–38
Scenes, 304–6
Schachtel, E., 60, 173, *180*
Schafer, R., 17, 19, 22, 33, 39, *68*, 139, *143*, 185, 186, 190, 194–98, *200*, 256, *260*
Schaffer, H. R., 294, *308*

Schematization, genital, 219
Schilder, P., 175, *181*
Schjeldahl, P., 73, *128*
Schlessinger, N., 325, *341*
Schneiderman, S., 64, *68*
Schreiner, K. E., 73, 116, *128*
Schwartz, D. W., 165, 166, *181*
Scream, The—1893 (Munch), 96–98
Scream—1895 (Munch), 104
Scripts, 304–6, 319, 322
Searles, H., 5–6, *14,* 41, *69*
Seated Model—1906 (Munch), 117
Segal, H., 170, *181*
Selection, sexual, 63–64
Self
  alternation and/or merger of object repre-
    sentations and, 137–39
  false, 302
  traditional concepts of, 62
Self-initiated repetition of passivity, 136–37
Selfobject functions of parents, 313
Selfobject transferences, 6–7
Self Portrait (Munch), 80
Self Portrait on the Beach—1907 (Munch), 109,
  110
Self psychology, 6, 61–63
  blaming the parents and, 189–90
  constructionist view of development and,
    309–16
    assumptions of, 314–15
    developmental basis of psychoanalysis
      and, 312, 314–15
    shared ideas between, 309–12
    transferences and operations of child's
      mind, 312–13
Self-reflective consciousness, 32
Separation anxiety of artist over work, 162–63
Separation-individuation, 149, 334
Separation issue, musicians and, 175–76
Sessions, R., 167, 173, 175, *181*
Settlage, C., 329, 332, *341*
Sex of analyst, 7–9, 233, 250
Sexual doubling, 263–83
  blindness and, 278–79
  Eastern and Western conceptions of psychol-
    ogy and, 280–81
  in European romantic literature, 264
  as expression of contradiction or conflict,
    274, 281–82
  in film, 264

homosexual interests in, 281
  in Indian fold tales and myths, 269–73
  "integrated"-"split" dyad (part-whole relation-
    ship), 274, 276–77, 282–83
  in Jacob, Rachel, and Leah story, 264–67
  male vs. female fantasies, 276–78
  in opera, 264
  Renuka/Mariatale myths, 270–72, 273
  sexual jealousy and, 266–67
  sexual masquerades, 269–70, 275–76
  in Shakespeare's comedies, 263–64
  surrogates, 264–65, 281
  transposed-heads tales, 270–74
  in *Yogavasistha,* 267–69
Sexuality
  infantile, 235–36
  in Munch's portrayals of women, 101–2
  subjectivity and, 227
Sexual jealousy, 266–67
Sexual selection, 63–64
Sexual surrogates, 264–66, 281
Sexual therapists, 264
Shane, M., 332, *341*
Shapiro, T., 330, 331, *341*
Shulman, D., 265
Sick Child, The—1885/1886 (Munch), 83–84,
  91, 95
Sick Child—1880/1881 (Krohg), 84, 85
Signal anxiety, 55–58
Signal depression, 56
Signification in music, 174
Silverman, L., 56, *69*
Sin, The—1901 (Munch), 106
Single-aspect processes, 26–34
Skinner, B. F., 321
Sleeper effects, 331
Smith, J., 64, *69*
Socarides, C., 234, *241*
Social science, integration with psychoanalysis,
  40–41
Soldiers, forced-migration phenomenon
  among, 152
Solnit, A., 329, 331, *341*
Solomon, L., 12, *14*
Sonnerat, P., 271, *280*
Source, J., 336, *338*
Spence, D., 19, 49, 50, *69,* 187, 195, 197–98,
  200
Spencer, K., 335, *340*
Spiegel, R., 150, *157*

Spitz, R., 38, *69,* 175, *181*
Sprengnether, M., 226, *239*
Srnec, J., 174, *179*
Sroufe, A., 293, *308,* 331, *341*
Stabell, D., 82, *128*
Standing Nude—1900 (Munch), 117
Standing Nude—1920 (Munch), 117
Stang, R., 73, 90, 108, 119, *128*
Starry Night—1923/1924 (Munch), 122
State(s)
  affect, 296-97
  concept of, 295-96
"State" ego, 295-96
Stechler, G., 292, 294, *308,* 335
Stein, H. F., 149, *157*
Steinberg, S., 74, 75, *128*
Sterba, E., 153, *158,* 165, 166, *181*
Sterba, R., 165-68, 173, *181*
Stern, D. N., 5, *14,* 47, 60, *69,* 185-86, 187,
  195, 197, *200,* 291, 294, *308,* 311, *316,*
  324, 330, 335, *341*
Stoller, R., 220, 221, 231, 234, *241,* 253, *260*
Stolorow, R., 17, 39, 44, 53, *65,* 185, 188,
  190, 192, *200, 201,* 234, *241*
Stone, L., 334, *341*
Story, western concept of, 326
Stott, F., 335, *340*
Stravinsky, I., 175, *181*
Stress-strain in refugees, 150
Strindberg, August, 107
Structural theory, Kohut on, 61
Structures, cognitive, 36
Study of the Death Chamber—1892 (Munch), 98
Subjectivity, sexuality and, 227
Sullivan, H. S., 39, 63, *69*
Sullivan, W., 188, 256-57, *260*
Sulloway, F., 330, *341*
Summer in the Park—1903/1904 (Munch), 122
Summer Night—1903 (Munch), 109, 122
Sun, The—1909/1914 (Munch), 119, 120
Superego, 58
Superego aggressiveness, 48
Superego functions of music, 172
Surrey, J. L., 224, 225, *241*
Surrogate(s), 264-65, 281
  mothers, 264
  sexual, 264-66, 281
Symbolization, 321-22
Symptoms, multiple factors producing, 42-43

T

Tension-release concept of motivation, 33
Thaulow, Milly, 82, 84
Therapeutic modalities, hierarchy of, 13
Thoma, H., 60, *69*
Thomas, A., 38, 48, 60, *65, 69*
Thomas, W. I., 256, *260*
Three Stages of Woman, The—1894 (Munch),
  117
Ticho, G. R., 152, *158*
Tolpin, M., 310, 312, *316*
Tomkins, S. S., 292, 296, 305, *308*
Transference(s), 3-15, 44-45
  analyst's age and, 9
  analyst's sex and, 7-8
  analyst's sociocultural background and, 9-10
  archaic, 4-5
  borderline psychotic, 6, 12, 15
  cross-gender, 221-22, 245
  defined, 13
  erotic, 221-22
  as experimental method, 46
  father, 246-47
  history and, 49-50
  mother, 250-51
  narcissistic, 5
  nonoccurrence of, 3-4
  selfobject, 6-7
  shared language between participants and,
    10-11
  transition from one type to another, 12-13
  workings of child's mind and, 312-13
Transitional object, 153
Traumata
  infantile, 38
  nature and timing of early, 45
Tronick, F., 294, *308*
Tucker, R. C., 135, *143*
Turkle, S., 64, *69*
Tyson, P., 220, 221, 222, 234, *241, 242,* 245,
  251

U

Unconscious, 44-55
  creative act and, 78
Unconscious fantasy, charismatic appeal and,
  135-36

Unconscious mentation, 19
  motivation and, 23–24, 34
Unconscious motives, conflicting, 24
"Ur-motive," 44
Uzgiris, I., 334, *338*

V

Value, aesthetic or cultural, 159
Vampire, The—1893 (Munch), 98–99, 100
Vampire—1894 (Munch), 104
van der Chijs, A., 171, *181*
Violet Book, The (Munch), 95
Voice, The—1893 (Munch), 101, 103
Vygotsky, L., 258, *260*

W

Waelder, R., 194, *201*
Wall, S., 293, *307,* 334, *336*
Wallace, E., 18, 19, 20, 22, 24, 25, 27, 28,
  33, 34, 35, 37, 39, 41, 44, 49–52, 54,
  55, 57, *69*
Wallerstein, R., 198, *201*
Walter, Bruno, 167–68
Waters, E., 293, *307, 308,* 334, *336*
Wave, The—1921 (Munch), 122, 124
Waves beating Against the Rocks—1916 (Munch),
  122
Weigert, E., 210, *212*
Weiner, H., 28, *69*
Weiss, J., 50, *69,* 74, 75, *128*
Weissman, P., 78, 126, *128,* 160, 173, *181*
Werman, D. S., 154, *158*
Western concept of story, 326
White, H., 256, *261*
Whore and madonna, images of, 276
  differentiation between, 282

Willner, A. R., 135, *143*
Winer, J. A., 129, 135, *143*
Winnicott, D. W., 4, *15,* 154, *158,* 175, *181,*
  189, 193, *201,* 236, 257, *261, 308,* 333,
  341
Winter in Kragero—1912 (Munch), 122
Wisdom, J. D., 54, *69*
  Freud's definition of, 49
Wittenberg, R., 168, *181*
Wittgenstein, L., 257, *261*
Wolff, P., 292, *308*
Wolf Man, 20, 38
Women
  lives as text, 255–58
  Munch's portrayals of
    conflicted sexuality in, 101–2
    in late period, 117
  psychoanalytic theories of, 217–22
    cross-gender transference and, 221–22,
      245
    Freudian, 217, 242
    gender identity, 220–21
    genital awareness, 218–20
Women on the Beach—1898 (Munch), 104
Wylie, H., 74, 75, 96, 113, *128*
Wylie, M., 74, 75, 96, 113, *128*

Y

Yogavasistha, 267–69

Z

Zelaxo, P., 331, *340*
Zetzel, E., 12, *15,* 50, *69,* 330, *342*
Zilbach, J., 218, 232, *240, 241*
Zimmer, H., 272, *280*